Called unto Holiness
Volume 2

The Second Twenty-five Years, 1933-58

CALLED UNTO HOLINESS

VOLUME 2

The Second Twenty-five Years, 1933-58

W. T. PURKISER, Ph.D., D.D.

Nazarene Publishing House
Kansas City, Missouri

ISBN 083-410-8682

9 780834 108684

10 9 8 7 6 5 4

Contents

Preface   7

1. The Early Years   17
   The Beginnings. Establishing a Denominational Life.
   Leadership. Headquarters. Summary.

2. Nazarene Self-image in 1933   55
   A Holiness Church. An Evangelistic Church. Interchurch
   Relationships. Social Awareness. Summary.

3. The Lean Years   79
   Depression and the New Deal. The Silver Anniversary
   Observance. Financial Pressures. The Challenge of Foreign
   Missions. Home Missions and Ministerial Relief. The *Herald of
   Holiness* and the Publishing House. Crisis in the Colleges.
   Amending the Constitution. The Crusade for Souls. Summary.

4. The Gathering Clouds of War   109
   The Ninth General Assembly. C. Warren Jones and Foreign
   Missions. Leadership Losses. Fleming and the NMBA. Other
   Changes. Nazarene Colleges to the Eve of World War II.
   Summary.

5. The Church in a World Aflame   131
   The Church Looks Ahead. War and the General Church.
   Missions in a World at War. A Publication Landmark.
   Education in War Years. The Passing of Pioneers. Crisis in
   Leadership. Summary.

6. Entering the Postwar World   158
   Facing a New Age. The Changing Leadership. The Generals
   Become a Board. New General Officers. Expansion in Kansas
   City. Expansion Overseas. In the Continental United States.
   Educational Expansion. "Showers of Blessing." Summary.

7. Mid-Century Crusade for Souls   218
   Laying the Groundwork. New Hands at the Helm. Two
   Generals Die in Office. Launching the Mid-Century Crusade.
   Financial Crisis and the Ten Percent Program. The
   Quadrennium in Education. Publishing House Developments.
   Missions Marches On. Summary.

8. The Struggle over Standards   256
   Gains in the British Isles. A Middle Course on Standards.
   Headquarters and the Publishing House. Education in the
   Middle Fifties. Foreign Mission Developments. Overseas
   Home Missions. Summary.

9. Back to Pilot Point   287
    Planning Ahead. Gospel Workers Church of Canada. The
    Church Abroad. Education to the Golden Anniversary.
    Church Schools. The Golden Anniversary. Pilgrimage to Pilot
    Point. Evaluating Results. Summary.

Epilogue   307

Appendix A. General Superintendents, 1933-58   315

Appendix B. General Church Officers, 1933-58   315

Appendix C. General Board Members, 1933-58   315

Appendix D. General Officers, Auxiliaries, 1933-58   317

Appendix E. Executive Secretaries of the Departments   318

Appendix F. Presidents, Institutions of Higher
                Education, 1933-58   319

Appendix G. District Superintendents, 1933-58   320

Appendix H. Missionaries in Service, 1933-58   327

Bibliography   339

Index   349

Preface

This volume is intended to be a sequel to Dr. Timothy L. Smith's outstanding book, *Called unto Holiness: The Story of the Nazarenes: The Formative Years.*[1] It is an attempt to tell the story of the Church of the Nazarene during its second 25 years.

The record of this period lacks much of the drama and excitement of the formative era. By 1933, the main directions had been established and the major moves made. Church structures had been worked out, as were patterns of administration and organization. Routines had been set up and even some traditions had developed. There would always be adjustments to make in the face of changing conditions and new leadership. But that is what they would be—adjustments in structures already established. Yet the story of the second quarter century, for all its more pedestrian character, has a meaning of its own. It was a shaking and a testing time, and the work of the founders stood the test well.

The history of a church is different in at least one important way from the histories of other human institutions. The church lives in two realms. It has its existence among men with its feet on earth. Yet its essential life is from above. The course of the church on earth is part of the overall history of mankind. But it cannot be fully understood apart from its theological dimension. Each particular denomination owes its shape to two conditioning factors: its place in the stream of history, and its participation in the life of the universal Church.

It is the theological dimension that makes any church part of *the* Church and distinguishes it from all other institutions or agencies. When the church is the Church, it is more than the individuals who make up its membership. That "more" is the presence of the risen Lord in the congregation, breathing His life into His people by His Spirit through His Word. The Church has always viewed itself as the *ecclesia,* the company of the called-out ones. Its most radically distinguishing feature is the presence of God in the midst

---

1. Kansas City: Nazarene Publishing House, 1962.

of the believing congregation and the sense of His continued presence when they are dispersed.

Church history is the record of the life of the pilgrim people of God on earth, lived in the dust and heat of the common lot of man. Yet as has often been suggested, just as its Lord has both a divine and a human nature, so has His Church. The divine nature is evident in biblical descriptions of the Church as the Body of Christ—a metaphor, as John Knox says, that is more than a metaphor, an analogy that is more than an analogy.[2]

For these, among other reasons, church history is not easy to record. When one has told the story of what has happened and has explored whatever reasons therefore that may be open to investigation, he is still conscious of an elusive element in it all that defies historical analysis and sociological evaluation.

Thus there is an element of paradox in telling the story of the Nazarenes, as in telling the story of any segment of the people of God on earth. It is a story that in one dimension is subject to the canons of historical investigation and analysis. But it is also, in the vision of its adherents, part of "His story"—the walk and work of a portion of the people of God living under the Lordship of the risen Christ in the communion of His Spirit.

This is not to suggest that the human dimension of the story is not important. Someone has commented that one of the problems of this generation is that it has not read the minutes of the last meeting! We do not understand ourselves because we do not know from whence we are. We do not know our own age because we have not made the ages our own. "To vilify our past is stupidity; to deify it is idolatry; to clarify it—and so to learn from it—is maturity."[3]

Even the historical dimension presents difficulties of its own. Dr. Smith closed his account of the formative years at the beginning of the 1930s. Writing 30 years later and referring to the time that had elapsed from the 1930s to the 1960s, he said,

> The story of the last thirty years would . . . be a tempting one for us to try to tell. But the time is not yet ripe for it. To appraise accurately the significance of the deeds of men still

2. John Knox, *Life in Christ Jesus* (Greenwich, Conn.: Seabury Press, 1961), p. 46.

3. Paul S. Rees, "The Positive Power of Negative Thinking," *World Vision Magazine*, vol. 14, no. 2 (Feb., 1970), 32.

living and to evaluate the programs and the controversies in which they have taken part would be far more difficult than writing the narrative of the earlier decades, and much less appropriate in a volume being published by the denomination itself.[4]

We are still perilously close to the second 25 years. Many of those whose names appear here are still living, and their sons and daughters are carrying on their work. Historians of the future will no doubt see much in a different light from that in which it is possible to view it now.

Add to this the fact that the second 25 years in the story of the Nazarenes covers a period in history marked by more significant changes worldwide than had characterized the preceding 250 years. The accelerated industrialization and urbanization of society, the most severe economic crisis in history, the most devastating war in the life of mankind, the increasing mobility of the people, the dawn of the atomic age with its ever-present threat of nuclear holocaust, and much, much more—all are packed into one brief quarter century.

The Church of the Nazarene itself went through a complete change in its top leadership. Of the general superintendents, general church officers, and department heads in office in 1933, only H. Orton Wiley, D. Shelby Corlett, and M. Lunn were still alive in 1958—and only the durable Lunn was still in office. The growth rate and turnover in church membership was such that fewer than 10 percent of those who were ministers and members of the church in 1958 had been Nazarenes 25 years before.

It is not possible to tell the story of the Nazarenes without constant reference to "holiness," the "holiness movement," and a "holiness church." Holiness, as its adherents in Wesleyan circles understand it, is the quality of life and spirit that comes from entire sanctification in the twofold sense of total consecration and complete deliverance from sin, when sin is understood as rebellion in act or attitude against the known will of God. This entire sanctification comes not in the initial commitment of life to Christ in conversion, but as the gift of divine grace in a second epoch in the

---

4. *Called unto Holiness*, p. 350.

spiritual life. In its broadest sense, holiness is life under the Lordship of Christ in the fullness of His Spirit.

The Church of the Nazarene saw its reason for being in the special advocacy of holiness of heart and life. There is no indication at the end of the second 25 years of any real change of direction or purpose in the church. If anything, there seems to have been an even greater consciousness of the importance of holding to that course. The Church of the Nazarene on its Golden Anniversary was still very much a holiness church and still very much concerned with taking the whole gospel to the whole world.

This is a finding at variance with the widely publicized judgment of Elmer T. Clark in his 1937 book, *The Small Sects in America.* Clark operates on the thesis that all denominations begin as sects, originating mainly among the religiously neglected poor. They tend, he says, to elevate the necessities of their class—frugality, humility, and industry—into moral virtues. They are pietistic in the sense of locating morality almost solely in the realm of personal conduct. They give free rein to the emotions.

In the second generation, says Clark, the sect begins to lose its character. Its members prosper. The spiritual needs and economic forces which drew the sect out of the church turn about to transform the sect into a church. Of his own family of Methodist churches, Clark said, "The last century witnessed the completion of this process. The Church of the Nazarene is now [1937] in the period of transformation."[5]

"There are signs that vital perfectionism is already on the decline in the Church of the Nazarene," Clark claimed. Part of the reason, he believed, is the tendency "to ape The Methodist Church in polity, superintendence, centralization of authority, complexity of organization, attention to statistics, striving for bigness, and similar details." The result is loss of "the freedom, spontaneity, and democracy so essential to the perfectionist spirit."

Clark put heavy weight on the changed names of Nazarene colleges as indicating that they were "embarrassed by the holiness label."[6] What should be noted is that Texas Holiness University, Illinois Holiness University, Pentecostal Collegiate Institute, and Oklahoma Holiness College all changed their names in the process

---

5. Rev. ed. (New York: Abingdon Press, 1949), pp. 16-17. First published in 1937.
6. Ibid., p. 75.

of becoming identified with the Church of the Nazarene and not with any evidence of reticence about their holiness commitment.

A WORD ABOUT METHOD

No denomination exists in a vacuum. All churches live and work in a broader context than their own individual histories. The Church of the Nazarene identifies itself as an evangelical church totally committed to the final authority of Scripture and to the preaching of the saving gospel to all people everywhere. P. F. Bresee, founder of the western section of the church, typically proclaimed himself brother to every "Blood bought and Blood-washed" soul in the universe. What happened in the Church of the Nazarene was closely related to what happened in other evangelical groups living in the same society through the same years—although Nazarenes have not always sensed that fact.

One who attempts to tell the story of any complex organization through a limited period of time immediately faces a difficult choice. The story may be told topically, each segment or function of the whole traced in succession through the entire period. Or the story may be told chronologically in an attempt to see the development of the organization as a whole. For example, one may consider each of the varied ministries of the group in turn and follow each through the period under consideration: changes in administrative structures, evangelism at home, missions overseas, education, publication, discipling programs, etc. Or one may attempt to deal with the development of a more or less integrated whole. Each procedure has its advantages and each its liabilities.

The following pages seek to tell the story of the Nazarenes through their second 25 years in chronological sequence. What tips the scale in favor of a time framework is the Nazarene attempt to maintain an integrated program. The thematic approach is particularly appropriate for denominations in which the varied interests of the church are directed by semiautonomous boards such as boards of evangelism, missions, education, social work, or stewardship, where each ministry develops a certain measure of independence. The Nazarenes experimented with such a structure early on. They soon dropped it, however, in favor of a "general board" approach in which each interest becomes a "department" of the whole. That the several departments tend to go their own ways cannot be denied. A restructuring undertaken by the Nazarenes in the early 1980s was in part an attempt to restore a greater degree of integration to multiplying departments.

The account that follows may be faulted for its concern with general church structures. The Nazarenes have chosen to follow the pattern of church government developed in American Methodism. Supreme legislative and elective power is vested in a delegated gathering held usually every four years. All accountability is ultimately vested in the General Assembly. It reviews the past, elects officers, projects goals, lays plans, and gives general direction to the work of the denomination.

It is quite true that the dynamics of church leadership do not necessarily reside in such large public gatherings as General Assemblies have become. The dynamics of leadership are more often at work in the commissions and boards that patiently labor out of the public view. But these dynamics more often than not surface in the large public gatherings which then become springboards for direction and motivation. Part of the result of this quadrennial structure is a unique rhythm in the life of the church that seems to affect even its rate of growth.[7]

Yet the essential work of the church goes on week after week in the thousands of groups of gathered believers that constitute the "local churches." There the gospel is preached, the sacraments are administered, and Christians are discipled. The cooperative activities of the members of these local churches in teaching Sunday School classes, participating in services of worship and evangelism, caring for the sick and needy, contributing their means in tithes and offerings, and functioning as parts of a living organism, all feed into the life of the whole denomination. Conversely, denominational plans and emphases find expression, when they do, in the daily activities of pastors and lay people around the world.

---

7. When annual percentages of growth in church membership are considered in each of the four-year intervals marked off by General Assemblies, in 10 out of the 12 quadrenniums from 1932 to 1980 the high point was reached in the second or third years, and in 10 out of the 12 the low point was either the year of the General Assembly or the year immediately following. The differences between high and low are generally not large but still statistically significant. The raw data are given in the *Journal of the Twentieth General Assembly of the Church of the Nazarene,* pp. 302-3. (References to the *Journals* hereafter are abbreviated GAJ followed by the year of the assembly and the page reference.)

A PERSONAL WORD

This has been the most difficult assignment I have ever been given; yet there has been a peculiar joy in living through this segment of our denominational past—a joy tempered by awe at the measure of sacrifice and devotion unveiled. I have attempted to be objective in the only sense in which a member of a group can be objective. I have tried to paint the picture as I have been able to see it, "warts and all." I have been humbled again and again by the degree of commitment and breadth of vision I have sensed through these difficult years.

In one particular, I have deliberately departed from the canons of historical objectivity. I have used the terminology of Christian experience as understood among the Nazarenes in reporting such events as "he or she was converted" or "was sanctified" or "came into the experience of entire sanctification" rather than the more cautious form preferred by professional historians, "He or she *professed* conversion or *testified to* entire sanctification."

I have also used the "in house" terminology current during the period under consideration. That is, the missionary society has been identified as the Women's Foreign Missionary Society (WFMS) during most of the second quarter century. Nazarene Youth International was the Nazarene Young People's Society (NYPS). "World missions" were "foreign missions."

Any merit these pages have is due in large part to the many who have given willing help. General Secretary B. Edgar Johnson, and the denomination's archivist, Stephen D. Cooley, have been particularly helpful. Cooley, a professionally trained archivist, has given hours to tracking down elusive data and documents. Mrs. Esther Schandorff, director of learning services and archivist of the Rohr collection in Point Loma College's Ryan Library, has been untiring in her helpfulness. Dr. Mary Scott spent days of her own time compiling a list of missionaries in service during the interval from 1933 to 1958.

Nazarene Publishing House Manager M. A. (Bud) Lunn and Betty Fuhrman, publishing/editorial coordinator, have put the resources of the publishing house at my disposal.

Dr. Samuel Young, whose service in the general church covered most of this period, has helped immeasurably at critical points with his keen insight into the workings of the church and his comprehensive grasp of its mission and thought. Other members of the history commission—Dr. Charles Strickland representing the Board of General Superintendents, Dr. Donald Metz, and Dr. Ted Martin—and the other members of the Board of General Superintendents have lent their interest to the project and have reviewed the manuscript.

I am greatly indebted to Dr. Timothy L. Smith who read an early draft of the manuscript and made many helpful suggestions. While he is in no way responsible for errors of fact or judgment, these pages would be much less than they are without his help.

In addition to those listed in notes and bibliography as giving personal interviews, there are many in various levels of church life who have been of substantial help in shaping my understanding of the period.

Above all, I have appreciated the patience of my wife, Billie, with her supposedly retired husband's involvement in the most demanding special assignment of his career.

There are substantial gaps in the records and not all of the statistics are internally consistent, particularly the foreign missions data of the early 1950s. Where discrepancies have been observed, I have given preference to the published records of the general secretary's office. Four years of the minutes of meetings of the Board of General Superintendents during the middle 1930s are missing, as are large portions of the correspondence files of general officers.

The task of putting together this material has involved countless hours of going through papers, correspondence, reading journals, minutes, and materials both published and unpublished. I am sure there are gaps in the story that better trained minds than mine will see and hopefully later fill.

I have written with the awareness that practically everything reported here will be better known to some who will read these lines. I can only ask their patience and hope they will contribute their more complete information and better understanding to the archives at International Headquarters of the Church of the Nazarene.

For this is of necessity an unfinished task. We are so close to the events that large portions of the story must be in the nature of a chronicle, not history *per se.* As Kenneth Scott Latourette has suggested, time lends perspective impossible to proximity so that "in each generation there must be those who will undertake to review for their fellows the scroll as it has thus far been unrolled."[8] The final evaluation must await another time and another place. "Now we see but a poor reflection; then we shall see face to face. Now I know in part; then I shall know fully, even as I am fully known" (1 Cor. 13:12, NIV).

W. T. PURKISER

Abbreviations

GAJ	*Journal of the . . . General Assembly of the Church of the Nazarene.* Kansas City: Nazarene Publishing House. (Date indicates year of the General Assembly and of publication of the *Journal.*)
HH	*Herald of Holiness.* Official organ of the Church of the Nazarene. Kansas City: Nazarene Publishing House. Published weekly 1912 to 1971; biweekly or semimonthly thereafter.
OS	The *Other Sheep.* "A Monthly Journal Devoted to the Missionary Interests of the Church of the Nazarene." Published by the General Board of the Church of the Nazarene, printed by the Nazarene Publishing House.
PGB	*Proceedings of the General Board of the Church of the Nazarene and Its Departments.* Kansas City: Nazarene Publishing House. (Date indicates year of the General Board meeting and of publication of the *Proceedings.*)
Archives	Nazarene Archives, located at International Headquarters, Church of the Nazarene, 6401 The Paseo, Kansas City, MO 64131, U.S.A.
Manual	*Manual/Church of the Nazarene.* Kansas City: Nazarene Publishing House, published (revised) after each General Assembly. (Date indicates year of the General Assembly and publication of the *Manual.*)

---

8. *A History of Christianity,* rev. ed. (New York: Harper and Row, 1975), 2:xiii.

1

The Early Years

The Church of the Nazarene grew out of the holiness movement in America during the last half of the 19th century and the first part of the 20th. It developed in the midst of some of the most profound changes in western civilization—the transformation of a generally rural, agricultural, and religious social order into an urban, industrial, mechanized, and increasingly secular society.

I. THE BEGINNINGS

The holiness movement itself came from the blending of two closely related yet distinct streams of religious emphasis: a concern for the "higher Christian life" that cut across many denominations, and the distinctive Wesleyan emphasis that Methodism had inherited from its founder.

A. Interdenominational Holiness

The interdenominational revival of concern for Christian holiness had its initial impulse in the widespread religious revival in America at the beginning of the 19th century known as the Second Great Awakening. The revivalists of this period, says Winthrop Hudson, "demanded an immediate confrontation with God . . . [and] placed increasing stress upon the possibility of perfect sanctification, thus arousing a hunger for holiness and a life free from sin."[1]

Sydney Ahlstrom reports a "great surge of perfectionism that swept almost every denomination after 1835 and figured promi-

---

1. Winthrop S. Hudson, *Religion in America,* 2nd ed. (New York: Charles Scribner's Sons, 1973), p. 182. The significance of this broader advocacy of "perfection" is brilliantly detailed by Timothy L. Smith, *Revivalism and Social Reform* (Baltimore: Johns Hopkins University Press, 1980), with a 12-page afterword by the author.

nently in the great revival of 1858."[2] Edwin Scott Gaustad writes that the holiness emphasis "cut a wide swath in nineteenth-century American religion." The utopianism of the period was largely a social ideal; the holiness ideal was largely a personal one. "The Christian justified by the grace of God was not to rest therein; rather he should press on toward sanctification, toward full obedience to the divine command 'Be ye therefore perfect, even as your Father in heaven is perfect.'" This teaching, Gaustad went on to say,

> stimulated great moral earnestness and striving in America. Joining a Christian society was the beginning of a redeemed life, not the end. The convert proceeded to reform first himself and then society—to overthrow slavery, to stamp out political corruption, to promote temperance, to eliminate poverty, war, disease and hunger. One minister [Britain's William Arthur in *The Tongue of Fire*, 1880 ed., p. 145] wrote in 1854: "Nothing short of a general renewal of society ought to satisfy any soldier of Christ." Those pursuing holiness were as leaven in the whole loaf of American culture. By this leavening, might not America itself be made holy?[3]

The holiness phase of the Great Awakening flowered in the ministry of Presbyterian-turned-Congregationalist, Charles G. Finney (1792-1875) and his younger colleague at Oberlin College in Ohio, Asa Mahan (1800-1889), a Congregationalist who later became a Wesleyan Methodist. It involved an outstanding coterie of preachers and writers including: Presbyterians William E. Boardman (1810-86) who wrote *The Higher Christian Life* (1858), R. Pearsall Smith whose Quaker wife Hannah Whitall Smith (1832-1911) penned *The Christian's Secret of a Happy Life*, and A. T. Pierson (1837-1911), who later became convinced of the necessity of baptism by immersion and joined a Baptist church; Congregationalist Thomas C. Upham (1799-1872), who authored *Principles of the Interior or Hidden Life* and was one of the early lights of modern psychology; Baptists A. B. Earle, A. J. Gordon (1836-95), and Deacon George Morse; Salvationists William Booth (1829-1912) and Samuel Logan Brengle (1860-1936); and a score of others. What has been called "The Great Prayer Meeting Revival" of 1857-58 (or by some, "The Third Great Awakening") was in fact

---

2. Sydney E. Ahlstrom, *A Religious History of the American People*, 2 vols. (Garden City, N.Y.: Doubleday and Co., 1975), 2:289.

3. Edwin Scott Gaustad, *A Religious History of America* (New York: Harper and Row, Publishers, 1974), p. 149.

largely a holiness revival and touched a wide range of denominational groups.[4]

In the United States, the rallying point for the interdenominational holiness men as well as their Methodist counterparts was a series of sectional camp meetings held during the summer of each year. Later the National Association for the Promotion of Holiness—or more briefly, the National Holiness Association—was founded in 1867, two years after the close of the American Civil War. Although largely under Methodist auspices, the NHA and its various local affiliates provided a holiness fellowship for many whose church membership was outside Wesleyan circles.

In England, a similar role was played by the famous Keswick summer conferences for "promoting practical holiness." The Keswick conferences began in 1875 largely through the influence of Americans Asa Mahan, William Boardman, and Hannah Whitall Smith. Manned chiefly by Calvinistic and Anglican ministers, the emphasis at Keswick shifted slowly toward the idea that the baptism with the Holy Spirit is given for power in service rather than for purity of heart. This emphasis came back to America in the teaching of Dwight L. Moody (1837-99), Reuben A. Torrey (1856-1928), J. Wilbur Chapman (1859-1918), the Northfield schools, and Chicago's Moody Bible Institute.

The influence on later developments from the interdenominational stream in the holiness movement is seen in the fact that among the founders of the groups that came together to form the Church of the Nazarene were such men as Baptists William Hoople and C. Howard Davis, Presbyterian Edward F. Walker, Cumberland Presbyterian J. O. McClurkan, Congregationalists Aaron M. Hills and George Sharpe of Scotland, Quakers Edgar P. Ellyson and Seth C. Rees, and Advent Christian John W. Goodwin.[5]

B. Holiness in the Methodist Church

Parallel with the interdenominational roots of the holiness movement was the strong "perfectionist" or sanctification emphasis of

---

4. Cf. William G. McLoughlin, *Revivals, Awakenings, and Reform,* Chicago History of American Religion, edited by Martin E. Marty (Chicago: University of Chicago Press, 1978). McLoughlin prefers to reserve the title Third Great Awakening for the period from 1890 to 1920, a period which would cover the formation of the Church of the Nazarene.

5. Timothy L. Smith, *Called unto Holiness,* p. 21.

Methodism during the middle and late 19th century. In partial eclipse because of the stern necessities of frontier evangelism in the early part of the century, the holiness motif (at first *pro* and later *con*) became the dominant concern of the last half. Even after American Methodism split north and south over the slavery issue in 1845, both segments of the church stressed the doctrine of Christian perfection.

Founder John Wesley (1703-91) had held an ideal of holiness long before his evangelical conversion at Aldersgate Street in 1738. Wesley professed to have been shaped in his ideals by the reading of Bishop Jeremy Taylor's (1613-67) *The Rule and Experience of Holy Living* and *The Rule and Experience of Holy Dying,* Thomas á Kempis' (1380-1471) *Imitation of Christ,* and William Law's (1686-1761) *Serious Call to a Devout and Holy Life* and *On Christian Perfection* — as well as by his determination at the age of 26 "not only to read, but to study, the Bible as the one, the only standard of truth, and the only model of pure religion."[6] "Hence I saw," Wesley continues,

> in a clearer and clearer light, the indispensable necessity of having "the mind which was in Christ," and of "walking as Christ also walked"; even of having, not some part only, but all the mind which was in Him; and of walking as He walked, not only in many or in most respects, but in all things. And this was the light, wherein at this time I generally considered religion, as a uniform following of Christ, and entire inward and outward conformity to our Master.[7]

A voluminous writer, never a rigidly systematic theologian, and always growing in his observation, understanding, and experience, Wesley left some gaps and ambiguities over which his followers have long debated. He also held in creative synthesis two elements in sanctification that have tended to pull apart—instantaneous or critical sanctification, and sanctification as progressive.

There is little doubt, however, that his *Plain Account of Christian Perfection,* first published in 1766 and last revised 11 years later when Wesley was 74 years of age, represents a normative statement of his views on entire sanctification. Wesley's writings

---

6. John Wesley, *A Plain Account of Christian Perfection* as believed and taught by the Reverend Mr. John Wesley from the year 1725 to the year 1777, reprinted from the complete original text as authorized by the Wesleyan Conference Office in London, England, in 1872 (Kansas City: Beacon Hill Press of Kansas City, 1966), p. 11.

7. Ibid.

and those of his colleagues and immediate successors were highly influential in American Methodism. The *Plain Account* was part of the American Methodist *Discipline* until 1797 when it was taken out to save space and published separately thereafter.

John Fletcher (1729-85) was Wesley's highly prized supporter and chosen heir apparent, although, as it turned out, Fletcher died six years before Wesley. Fletcher wrote his famous *Checks to Antinomianism,* the last of which dealt specifically with Christian perfection. *Checks* was published in a first American edition in 1791, with two more editions out by 1820.

Richard Watson's (1781-1833) *Theological Institutes* clearly articulated the doctrine of perfect love as Wesley understood it, and the book was widely read by American Methodist circuit riders. The 1860 *Discipline* of the Methodist Episcopal church listed in the first year of the Course of Study for ministers the first part of Watson's *Institutes* and Wesley's *Plain Account* along with Fletcher's *Appeal* and Clarke's *Mental Discipline.*[8]

Influential in the holiness emphasis in Methodism were laypersons, Dr. Walter C. Palmer (1804-83), a prominent New York physician, and his even more illustrious wife, Phoebe (1807-74).[9] Mrs. Palmer began the "Tuesday Meeting for the Promotion of Holiness" in 1835, and Timothy Smith reports that hundreds of Methodist preachers, including five who then or later held the office of bishop, were sanctified through Mrs. Palmer's influence.[10]

Methodist Timothy Merritt began publishing the *Guide to Christian Perfection,* later known as the *Guide to Holiness,* in 1838, and the magazine reached a peak circulation of over 40,000 subscribers by 1873. Randolph S. Foster, later elected bishop, wrote *The Nature and Blessedness of Christian Purity* in 1851.

In post-Civil War Methodism, the emphasis became even stronger to the degree that Winthrop Hudson can state that "Methodism as a whole continued to be preoccupied with the quest for holiness throughout the latter half of the nineteenth century."[11]

---

8. Frederick A. Norwood, *The Story of American Methodism* (Nashville: Abingdon Press, 1974), pp. 293, 306. See the full account of the holiness teaching in American Methodism in Smith, *Revivalism and Social Reform,* pp. 114-34.

9. Hudson, *Religion in America,* p. 343.

10. *Called unto Holiness,* p. 12.

11. *Religion in America,* p. 343.

The celebration of American Methodism's centenary in 1866 sparked a distinct holiness revival. Methodists were from the beginning at the front in leadership in the National Holiness Association. John S. Inskip, chairman of the New York Methodist Preachers' Meeting, was the first president of the association.[12]

The first president of Drew Theological Seminary in 1867, J. C. McClintock, was a believer in holiness. He chose Foster to be the first professor of systematic theology. Methodist layman Washington C. DePauw, a wealthy Indiana glass manufacturer and patron of the university that still bears his name, was head of the National Publishing Association for the Promotion of Holiness.

The first "General Holiness Assembly" met in the Park Avenue Methodist Church in Chicago in 1885. Many bishops of both northern and southern branches of Methodism were committed to and actively involved in promoting scriptural holiness. By 1888 there were 206 full-time holiness evangelists in the field, and four years later the list had grown to 304. Most of them were Methodists but lacked regular assignments from church superiors.[13]

Despite Hudson's legitimate generalization that Methodism as a whole was preoccupied with the quest for holiness, the course of Christian perfection within the church ran far from smooth. Theological questions began to be raised. A growing laxity in matters of personal piety as Methodists gained numbers, wealth, and social status tended to make holiness preaching unpalatable particularly in large city parishes.

What had been deemed the obvious interpretations of Wesley's teachings were questioned. The Wesleyan Methodist Connection had severed itself from its parent church in 1843 over the slavery issue. The Free Methodists withdrew in 1860 over the issue of worldliness. In both cases, commitment to clear, second-blessing holiness was an underlying factor.

In the 1880s more and more voices of dissent against definite holiness teaching began to be heard in Methodist circles. Some objections were theological; more were in reaction to what was felt to be the separatist tendencies developing in the associations and

---

12. Norwood, *Story of American Methodism,* pp. 292-94, 298.
13. Ibid., pp. 298-99; cf. Ahlstrom, *Religious History of the American People,* 2:289; John L. Peters, *Christian Perfection and American Methodism* (New York: Abingdon Press, 1956), pp. 90-180.

missions spawned in liberal numbers by holiness people. Ahlstrom suggests that

> the most basic aspect of the antagonism, however, was the gradual drift of Methodist church practice away from the old Wesleyan landmarks and toward the sedate forms of middle-class Protestantism. The climax came in 1893 and 1894, when the trust between the Methodist churches and the Holiness associations ended. Secessions and expulsions became common during the turn-of-the-century decades.[14]

"Come-outers" vied with "push-outers." The result was the formation of a number of independent congregations and groups of congregations

C. The Question of Church Relationships

Meanwhile, a cleavage appeared within holiness ranks. Many who were influential in the National Holiness Association were Methodist denominational loyalists. Their emphasis was on the importance of remaining in their present denominational homes and "leavening the lumps" from within. Others, some frankly "come-outers" but many describing themselves as "put-outers" or "shoved-outers," became by intention or in fact separatists.

What the separatists would do with respect to church membership was a crucial issue. They could join one of the existing holiness churches: the Wesleyan or the Free Methodist, or the Church of God (Anderson, Ind.) founded in 1881 as an avowedly separatist organization. But these denominations were small and concentrated geographically in western New York, Michigan, Illinois, and Indiana. Another alternative was the establishment of independent local congregations.

The latter alternative proved to be the one most frequently chosen. Many had tried the option of a local "association" which permitted continued membership in a parent church. The associations proclaimed entire sanctification and cultivated the holy life in meetings held at times other than those regularly set aside for church services.

The option was a stopgap at best and failed to provide the well-rounded church life needed for individual growth and collective action. Association meetings were also largely defenseless

---

14. *Religious History of the American People,* 2:289.

against outbreaks of fanaticism that tended to give the cause of holiness a bad name.

As opposition to holiness stiffened in both interdenominational and Methodist circles, local independent holiness missions and churches began to appear. The opposition was not entirely doctrinal and ethical, particularly in the Methodist churches north and south. Much of it was distrust of burgeoning associations, missions, periodicals, schools, evangelistic parties, and ventures into social service that could not handily be brought under the control of existing church structures. It was out of these missions and churches and the groups they formed that the Church of the Nazarene took shape.

D. The Association of Pentecostal Churches

The earliest independent group later to become Nazarene was the People's Evangelical Church, organized in South Providence, R.I., July 21, 1887. Its membership was composed chiefly of persons who withdrew from Saint Paul's Methodist Church when their leader, Fred A. Hillery, was expelled from the church. The new congregation numbered almost 75.

Other missions and churches were organized in the area shortly after, chiefly in Massachusetts. These joined the South Providence group in 1890 in the formation of the Central Evangelical Holiness Association.

The association held annual meetings until 1897, by which time most of its member congregations had merged with the New York-based Association of Pentecostal Churches of America. This group of congregations grew up around work founded in Brooklyn by William Howard Hoople, a Congregationalist turned Baptist, and Charles BeVier, a Methodist.[15] By 1897, the association numbered 15 congregations.

---

15. "Pentecostal" at this period had no connotation of glossolalia or "unknown tongues" such as it acquired later. The modern Pentecostal movement, emphasizing speaking in unknown tongues as the evidence of the baptism with the Holy Spirit, originated in 1901 and received its major impetus from the Azusa Street revival in Los Angeles in 1906-8. See Vinson Synan, *The Holiness-Pentecostal Movement in the United States* (Grand Rapids: William B. Eerdmans Publishing Co., 1971). None of the groups which became a part of the Church of the Nazarene accepted glossolalia as a genuine spiritual gift, and the adjective "Pentecostal" in the name of the denomination became so confusing that it was officially dropped by the General Assembly of 1919.

The association made rapid strides during its early years. Under the leadership of Hiram F. Reynolds (1854-1938), a Vermont Methodist minister who joined Hoople and the association in 1895, foreign missionary work was begun in India when five missionaries were sent to the field in 1898. John J. Diaz was sent back as a missionary to his native Cape Verde Islands in 1900. The Pentecostal Collegiate Institute was established in Saratoga Springs, N.Y., in 1890, with a college preparatory course and a "Biblical seminary." The school was reorganized at North Scituate, R.I., in 1902 where it became Eastern Nazarene College in 1918 and moved to Wollaston, on Boston's south shore, in 1919.

At the time of its 1907 merger with the Los Angeles-based Church of the Nazarene, the Association of Pentecostal Churches had 47 congregations scattered from Maine to Iowa with a membership of 2,371 and property values totalling $175,640. Eighty-four students were registered in the Pentecostal Collegiate Institute. Three mission stations had been established in India and one in the Cape Verde Islands, with Reynolds serving as executive missionary secretary and superintendent of Foreign Missions.[16]

E. The Church of the Nazarene

With background and early development differing in many ways from the Association of Pentecostal Churches, the Church of the Nazarene had its birth and early development in Los Angeles beginning in October, 1895. The association owed more to the interdenominational holiness movement than did the Church of the Nazarene, which was more closely tied in origin and polity to the Methodist Episcopal church. Several strong and equally well established leaders pioneered the Eastern work, whereas the figure of Phineas F. Bresee (1838-1915) clearly dominated the West.

Bresee had served as a Methodist minister for 37 years in Iowa and in southern California. In California he had pastored the First Methodist churches of Los Angeles and of Pasadena and had been presiding elder (district superintendent). When in 1894 he sought to associate himself with the work of the Peniel Mission in Los Angeles while retaining his membership in the Methodist church,

---

16. Smith, *Called unto Holiness,* pp. 54-90; cf. M. E. Redford, *The Rise of the Church of the Nazarene* (Kansas City: Nazarene Publishing House, 1948), pp. 82-118, 146.

his request was turned down by the conference, and Bresee was "located," that is, not given a conference ministerial assignment.

Differences soon developed with T. P. and Manie Payne Ferguson, directors of the mission, and Bresee was asked to withdraw. So it was in the fall of 1895 that Dr. J. P. Widney, until the year before president of the University of Southern California and a wealthy and highly respected Los Angeles physician, joined forces with Bresee in renting the Red Men's Hall in downtown Los Angeles. Services were announced for Sunday, October 6. Two weeks later, the Church of the Nazarene was organized, its name chosen by Dr. Widney. Before the charter was closed, 135 members had joined. Within a year, membership had grown to 350, and the congregation was housed in its own wooden tabernacle in downtown Los Angeles.

The Los Angeles congregation soon began to branch out. Within 10 years a total of 26 organized congregations made up an infant denomination. Four were located in Los Angeles and 6 elsewhere in southern California; 3 were in northern California, 5 in Washington and Idaho, 3 across the plains states, and—an important fact for later developments—5 in Illinois.

In 1902, Pacific Bible College was founded under Nazarene control—the parent school from which Pasadena College (later named Point Loma College) emerged. By 1907, there were 52 Churches of the Nazarene with 3,827 members and property valued at $224,284. A foreign missionary program was receiving $4,000 per year in contributions; a publishing house had been established with a weekly *Nazarene Messenger* reaching out across the nation; and the Bible college had just relocated with a gift of $30,000 and a new name—Deets Pacific Bible College—honoring its donor.

F. Union in Chicago

Contacts between individuals representing the Association of Pentecostal Churches in the East and the Church of the Nazarene in the West went back to within a year of the beginnings. By 1906, correspondence regarding a possible union was under way. The association voted to send a committee to the fall General Assembly of the Church of the Nazarene in Los Angeles. A return visit of westerners to the association meeting in the spring of 1907 resulted in the working out of a plan for union, and an assembly was called to meet in Chicago in October to put the finishing touches on the wedding. At that time, P. F. Bresee and H. F. Reynolds were elected general superintendents, and a national holiness church was on the way to reality.

The name chosen for the new denomination was the Pentecostal Church of the Nazarene, a combining of elements of both names. The use of the word "Pentecostal" in the church name became confusing as the growing "unknown tongues" movement preempted the title "Pentecostal," at least in the public mind. The adjective was dropped in 1919 for this reason, returning the church to Widney's choice of name, the Church of the Nazarene.

G. The Holiness Church of Christ

Meanwhile, the cause of holiness flourished in the South. As early as 1894, a year before Bresee's Los Angeles venture, Robert Lee Harris, a Methodist evangelist who had previously been in independent mission work in Africa, launched the New Testament Church of Christ in Milan, Tenn., about 95 miles out of Memphis. The group soon established congregations throughout Tennessee and into west Texas, each congregationally governed and related to the others only in doctrine and by sentiment.

In the meantime, near Greenville and Commerce, Tex., 50 or so miles northeast of Dallas, E. C. DeJernett, a Southern Methodist evangelist, bought land and established a camp meeting and a small community he called Peniel. Here in 1899, Texas Holiness University was founded, and A. M. Hills (1848-1935), a Congregational evangelist and teacher at Asbury College in Wilmore, Ky., was called to be the president. The college and community became a center for the Holiness Association of Texas, and here was formed the Independent Holiness church with C. B. Jernigan (1863-1930) as president and young evangelist James B. Chapman (1884-1947) as secretary.

Another center of holiness work developed at Pilot Point, Tex., 65 miles to the west, where the New Testament Church of Christ and the Independent Holiness church joined in 1905 to become the Holiness Church of Christ. Within three years, the young denomination added 150 new congregations to the 75 included in the original union; engaged in extensive educational and publication work and foreign mission ventures in Mexico, India, Africa, and China; and developed a congregational form of polity with a limited superintendency. There were approximately 90 churches extending from Boulder, Colo., to Cape Sable, Fla., and from Kentucky south to the Mexican border. Some 300 preachers, evangelists, and other workers, and 3,500 members constituted the personnel of the denomination.[17]

H. Pilot Point, October, 1908

Representatives of the Holiness Church of Christ were invited and had been present at the Chicago union of the Association of Pentecostal Churches and the Church of the Nazarene for the purpose of initiating steps to bring all three sectional groups together. To accomplish this, a Second General Assembly of the Pentecostal Church of the Nazarene was called to meet in connection with the Fourth General Council of the Holiness Church of Christ in Pilot Point, Tex., October 8, 1908. Here, tensions were resolved and compromises effected, and amid great rejoicing at 10:40 a.m., October 13, 1908, a motion to unite the Holiness Church of Christ and the Pentecostal Church of the Nazarene was carried by a rising unanimous vote.

Before the assembly adjourned, Bresee, Reynolds, and Edgar P. Ellyson (1869-1954) were elected general superintendents. Ellyson had been a Quaker minister and educator who joined the Pentecostal Church of the Nazarene when the Peniel group came into the church in April, 1908.

The denomination resulting from the 1908 merger reported 228 churches, 10,414 members, and total church property valued at $559,953. The Sunday Schools enrolled 7,780 and youth societies 523. The church officially owned three schools—in Los Angeles, in North Scituate, R.I., and in Pilot Point. Two other colleges were closely related, one at Peniel, Tex., and the other at Vilonia, Ark. There were three periodicals, and missionary work was being conducted in Mexico, India, China, Africa, and the Cape Verde Islands.

The story of the early period is not complete until other important accessions are noted. Part of the rapid growth of the first seven years resulted from bringing into the church a number of substantial local independent holiness congregations that had not been affiliated with any of the three uniting groups.

---

17. Redford, *Rise of Church of the Nazarene*, p. 149.

One block of 15 churches was the eastern conference of the Holiness Christian Association in Pennsylvania. This was the group from which Bresee's early assistant pastor at Los Angeles, C. W. Ruth (1865-1941), had come. The churches joined as a group in September, 1908, and their leader, W. G. Trumbauer, became the Nazarene district superintendent of a new Pennsylvania District. The result of this and other lesser accessions was that within three years of the Pilot Point union, the denomination doubled its membership and nearly tripled its Sunday School enrollment.

I. The Pentecostal Mission

Three years after the formation of the Association of Pentecostal Churches in the East and the Church of the Nazarene in the West, J. O. McClurkan (1861-1914), a sanctified evangelist of the Cumberland Presbyterian church, established the Pentecostal Alliance (later, the Pentecostal Mission) in Nashville. By 1903, the work had expanded to embrace a total of 28 missions, most of them in Tennessee; missionary work in Cuba, Guatemala, and India; a flourishing paper, *Zion's Outlook*; and the beginnings of a Bible institute that was the parent institution of Trevecca College.

McClurkan's vision, as the original name of his organization indicates, was, from the beginning, interdenominational or, perhaps better, undenominational. However, personal friendships and the exchange of evangelistic efforts had put the mission leaders in touch with the developing holiness churches farther west. When the Pentecostal Church of the Nazarene was formed in 1907 and 1908, McClurkan and his associates followed the developments with great interest.

Negotiations between McClurkan and the Nazarene leaders seemed to promise an early union. But a number of obstacles arose, not the least of which was McClurkan's own reluctance. A Third Nazarene General Assembly was convened in Nashville in 1911 chiefly to facilitate the union. But it was not until shortly after McClurkan's death three years later that the union was consummated on February 13, 1915, in Nashville. During the extended negotiations, both individuals and missions of the Nashville group had one by one joined the Pentecostal Church of the Nazarene, so the actual numbers involved in the 1915 union were smaller than they would have been otherwise.

J. The Pentecostal Church of Scotland

The year 1915 also witnessed another group accession, this time overseas. George Sharpe (1865-1948) was born in Scotland but came to the United States as a management trainee in a manufacturing plant in New York State. There he joined the Methodist church and began to preach. While pastoring the Methodist congregation at Chateaugay, N.Y., in 1898, Sharpe and his wife entered the experience of entire sanctification.

A visit to his native Scotland in 1901 persuaded Sharpe that he should return to his own country to preach holiness. After six years as pastor of Congregational churches first at Ardrossan and then at Parkhead in Glasgow, Sharpe was forced out by opponents of his holiness ministry, and the Parkhead Pentecostal church was founded in October of 1906.

Soon holiness congregations emerged nearby, and in 1909 the Pentecostal Church of Scotland was organized. The new denomination adopted as its statement on holiness, church membership, "general rules," and "special advices," the paragraphs dealing with these matters in the *Manual* of the Pentecostal Church of the Nazarene, a copy of which had been sent to Sharpe by a friend in America.[18]

As early as the Nashville Nazarene General Assembly in 1911, steps were taken to bring the Scottish group into the Pentecostal Church of the Nazarene. The union was finally consummated in November of 1915. While the number of churches and members was not large—eight congregations in all with 635 constituents and property valued at $45,350—this accession was a first step in constituting the Church of the Nazarene an international organization.

K. The Laymen's Holiness Association

Another surge in geographical expansion and membership increase occurred in 1922 and 1923 when J. G. Morrison (1871-1939) led the Dakota-based Laymen's Holiness Association into the Church of the Nazarene. The association was chiefly a Methodist

---

18. Jack Ford, *In the Steps of John Wesley: The Church of the Nazarene in Britain* (Kansas City: Nazarene Publishing House, 1968), p. 48. Cf. Ford's account of Sharpe and the beginnings of the Pentecostal Church of Scotland, pp. 35-63. Cf. also T. Crichton Mitchell, *To Serve the Present Age: The Church of the Nazarene in the British Isles* (Kansas City: Nazarene Publishing House, 1980), pp. 7-22.

group and had long felt the pressure of denominational leaders opposed to emphasis on the second blessing. Matters came to a head when the movement was threatened by an invasion of fanaticism. Morrison acted quickly. He joined the Church of the Nazarene himself and urged his associates to do the same. A large number followed, and the Nazarenes increased their number of churches from 1,145 with 43,708 members at the close of 1921 to 1,304 and 50,631 at the end of 1923.

Both geographical and numerical growth continued through the teens and twenties. Geographical penetration, indicated by the number of local churches, was particularly striking with the 228 congregations in 1908 growing to 2,030 by the end of the first 25 years. Membership grew from 10,414 to 111,905 during the same period. The average size of local congregations increased from 46 in 1908 to 55 in 1933.[19]

II. ESTABLISHING A DENOMINATIONAL LIFE

Even more significant than geographical spread and growth in numbers during the first quarter of a century was what Timothy L. Smith described as "Achieving the Inner Reality of Union."[20] The major issues were, as Dr. Smith points out, working out a polity relating to general administration and bringing a semblance of order into the combined programs established previously by the uniting sectional groups in the fields of foreign missions, publication, and education.

Added to this was the rounding out of the denomination's programs in Christian education at the local level, youth work, and the women's missionary organization. And underlying it all was the development of attitudes of churchliness that would enable the Church of the Nazarene to take its place in the family of Protestant denominations as a vital and viable part of "the Church of Jesus Christ in advancing God's kingdom among men."[21]

---

19. Statistics throughout have been abstracted from the official General Assembly *Journals* published by the Nazarene Publishing House. Complete sets of the *Journals* are available in the archives at International Headquarters in Kansas City, and in most of the reference libraries of the colleges and seminary of the church.

20. *Called unto Holiness*, chapter title, pp. 243-71.

21. *Manual of the Church of the Nazarene*, each edition since 1928, preface to the Constitution. All editions of the *Manual* since 1915 are published by the Nazarene Publishing House. Hereafter cited as *Manual* with year of publication.

A. Polity

By 1933, these objectives had been fairly well achieved. The polity of the denomination as a whole had been shaped up in the early years of the first quarter century. The central organization achieved greater unity in 1923 with the establishment of the General Board which replaced a multiplicity of uncoordinated "general boards" competing for support of specific denominational interests.

The present constitution of the church was adopted in 1928, placing in more permanent constitutional form the Articles of Faith, the General Rules, and the major outline of polity. The often conflicting claims of congregationalism and superintendency were brought into balance, while the supreme elective and legislative powers were vested in the General Assembly.

Development of the polity was no small achievement in itself. The East and the South had been fiercely congregational. They had been moving slowly but steadily, however, toward a superintendency in their years of separate existence—largely through the practical need for cooperation in home and foreign missions. The West, on the other hand, began with a modified superintendency with P. F. Bresee functioning as "general" superintendent.

The Chicago union that brought East and West together had made a concession of some magnitude to the congregationalism of the East by providing that "any church of the Association [of Pentecostal Churches of America] going into this organization which may feel it imperative with them to continue to hold their property in like manner as at present [that is, with title fully vested in the local group] shall be at liberty to do so."[22]

But when the three-way union of 1908 was consummated, it was Bresee's form of superintendency that prevailed.

B. District Organization

Following the pattern already established in the West, the new denomination was divided into geographical districts each with its own superintendent. The 25th anniversary found the church di-

---

22. *Manual of the Pentecostal Church of the Nazarene,* published by authority of the General Assembly held at Chicago, Illinois, 1907 (Los Angeles: Nazarene Publishing Co., 1907), p. 17.

vided into 29 districts in the United States with 2 additional ones in Canada and 1 in the British Isles.

In many cases in the United States, district boundaries followed state lines: Arizona, Arkansas, Colorado, Iowa, Louisiana, Nebraska, North Dakota, and Tennessee.

Four states were divided into more than one district: Texas into Abilene, Dallas, and San Antonio districts; Oklahoma into Eastern and Western Oklahoma districts; Indiana into Indianapolis and Northern Indiana districts; and California into Southern and Northern California districts.

Other states included portions of more than one district. A number of districts included part or all of two or more states. The Alberta District included the province by that name in Canada with the portion of British Columbia east of the Rocky Mountains, while the portion of British Columbia west of the Rockies was part of the North Pacific District. The Manitoba-Saskatchewan District included the two provinces by that name. Ontario was included in the Michigan District, and the Maritime Provinces were made part of the New England District.

District assemblies were, as now, held annually. The membership of the assembly is composed of all ordained and licensed ministers holding membership in churches on the district; Sunday School superintendents, presidents of local women's missionary societies and young people's societies; and lay delegates elected in proportion to the membership of the local churches. The assembly elects its district superintendent, a District Advisory Board of equal ministerial and lay membership, and other district boards.

C. The General Assembly

Each district also elects an equal number of ministerial and lay delegates to the General Assembly and elects (or nominates with the force of election) the members of the boards of control of the zone educational institutions.

General Assemblies have been numbered from the Chicago meeting of 1907, with the Second General Assembly meeting at Pilot Point in 1908. The third meeting was held in Nashville in 1911. Thereafter, every four years until 1923, sessions were held in Kansas City. A five-year interval elapsed before the Seventh General Assembly in Columbus, Ohio, in 1928. After 1928, the assemblies were held every four years until 1980, when another five-year interval was adopted.

The General Assembly is the supreme legislative and elective body of the church. It is empowered "to legislate for the Church of the Nazarene, and to make rules and regulations for all the departments related to or associated with it in any respect," provided only that such actions do not conflict with provisions of the constitution of the church.[23]

The General Assembly decides how many general superintendents shall be elected. Ordained ministers between the ages of 35 and 68 are eligible for election. Election is by an open ballot in which each member of the assembly lists his choices up to the number to be elected. Election requires a two-thirds vote of the number of delegates present and voting. Eligible incumbents are now elected by a yes or no ballot.

D. The General Board

The development of the General Board mentioned earlier is an illustration of the process by which details of polity were hammered out on the anvil of experience. The first general board was established in 1907 as the General Missionary Board with oversight of both home and foreign missions. For the next four years, general administration was in the hands of the general superintendents and the missionary board.

The 1911 General Assembly created a General Board of Education, specifically to deal with the surplus of Nazarene schools resulting from the unions; a General Board of Publication to direct formation of a central publishing house; a Rescue Commission to gather information and advise districts on local rescue and mission work; and a General Board of Church Extension to assist local churches with their building programs. In 1915, the Rescue Commission was broadened to a General Board of Rescue Work, and a General Orphanage Board was also created.

The 1919 Assembly added a General Colportage Board to organize and direct tract distribution; a General Board of Mutual Benefit; and a General Board of Ministerial Relief—bringing the total to 10. Nor was this the apparent end, for General Assembly

---

23. *Manual,* each edition since 1928, Constitution.

committees on youth societies and deaconess work were moving toward general board status.

Most of these general boards had been given power to incorporate, to establish budgets, and to raise money. This put the most active boards into direct competition in promoting their programs. Board employees were given little supervision with resulting huge deficits and sometimes careless keeping of the legal and financial records involved.

The 1919 Assembly made an attempt at coordination by man dating a joint annual meeting in a "Correlated Board," but without much tangible result. Two efforts to draw up a common budget failed, as did attempts to organize an executive committee. In fact, the result was that steps were taken to organize the Nazarene Young People's Society whose General Council would become, in effect, another general board.

By 1923, the accumulating deficits of the publishing house forced another attempt at unification. Several plans were considered, and it was finally agreed to consolidate the work of the general boards of foreign missions, church extension, ministerial relief, and publication as departments of one General Board with a common budget and actions subject to approval by the general superintendents.

The move achieved some success but obviously did not go far enough. The final step was taken by the General Assembly of 1928. It dissolved the General Colportage Board and the General Board of Mutual Benefit. It combined the General Board of Rescue Work (by that time known as the General Board of Social Welfare) with the General Orphanage Board for the purpose of closing down their respective projects and disposing of their properties. A restructured General Board of Education became a new department of the General Board, as did a new Department of Church Schools. Two already existing departments were organized into one Department of Home Missions and Church Extension, later Home Missions and Evangelism.

The result was a General Board with six departments: Foreign Missions, Church Schools, Home Missions and Evangelism, Publication, Ministerial Relief, and Education. The board set up a Finance Committee with representatives of the several departments to have responsibility for the General Budget which had been initiated in 1923. The action came none too soon, for the church was facing the economic slide that began in 1929 and bottomed out in 1933, with a very gradual climb back during the balance of the '30s.[24]

The concept of a unified budget for all general work seemed particularly difficult to establish. Although a General Board and a General Budget had been set up in 1923, as late as 1932 the general superintendents were lamenting the fact that department heads were still raising money for their specific interests without reference to the unified General Budget. "Theoretically we have operated a General Budget," they said, "but actually we have not done so."

Two options were outlined: either a General Budget with all departments of the church participating "fully and freely and each one supporting all the items of the budget, or second, we must have a separate budget for missions altogether."[25] The 1932 General Assembly opted for the General Budget, but the problem did not go away.

E. The Women's Missionary Society

The women's missionary auxiliary had its earliest beginnings in the East, where the influence of Mrs. Susan N. Fitkin was a determinative factor. It was not until 1915, however, that the Nazarene Women's Missionary Society was authorized with Mrs. Fitkin, Mrs. Ada F. Bresee of Los Angeles, and Mrs. John T. Benson of Nashville as the committee to write the first constitution.

The society quickly found a significant place for itself in the denominational structure, with a General Council meeting annually and a General Convention held immediately prior to each General Assembly. By 1932, the society had district organizations active on each district and nine foreign fields and reported a membership of 29,000 with offerings for missions approaching one-half million dollars during the preceding four years.

F. The Youth Organization

From the earliest days, many of the larger congregations of the church had organized youth work. A prototype had been the

---

24. Cf. study paper prepared by General Secretary B. Edgar Johnson titled "A Review of the General Board's Organizational Development," n.d.; and Robert E. Harding, "A History of the General Board of the Church of the Nazarene," B.D. thesis, Nazarene Theological Seminary, Kansas City, 1948.

25. GAJ, 1932, p. 187.

Brotherhood of Saint Stephen for young men, and Company E for young women in Los Angeles First Church.

The number of young people in local organizations multiplied rapidly until in 1923 the General Nazarene Young People's Society was formed. Donnell J. Smith (1893-1936) was elected president and D. Shelby Corlett executive secretary—a post Corlett filled for the following 13 years. By 1932, the General NYPS reported 1,122 societies in local churches with an aggregate membership of 48,500—this out of a total church membership of 117,947.

G. Sunday Schools

The story of Nazarene Sunday Schools parallels that of the women's missionary work and youth work. Local churches as a matter of course held Sunday Schools, but the denomination was 15 years into its first quarter century before E. P. Ellyson was elected chief editor of Sunday School publications. Dr. Ellyson performed yeoman service in developing materials for use in local church schools, a task already begun by C. J. Kinne who had been Bresee's publishing agent and the first manager of the Nazarene Publishing House in Kansas City. Ellyson led the way in perfecting local, district, and general organizations to aid the work of Christian education in the local church, constitutions for which were adopted in 1928. By 1932, church schools enrolled a total of 239,341, more than twice the church membership, and reported an average weekly attendance of 141,111.

H. Foreign Missions

An evangelical denomination is almost by definition a missionary church. Winthrop Hudson notes that "the missionary thrust of a religion is one of the most sensitive indices of its vitality."[26] The history of foreign missions (as this phase of the work was called until well into the 1960s) is a dramatic story.

Though each of the uniting groups brought some foreign missionary activity into the young denomination, much of the early denominational interest in foreign missions came from the zeal of the eastern association, led by H. F. Reynolds. H. Orton Wiley, associated with Bresee's Church of the Nazarene from its earliest years and present as one of the Nazarene representatives at Chi-

---

26. *Religion in America,* p. 372.

cago in 1907, confessed, "It was an enlarged vision of the mission field that was brought to us in the West when, at Chicago in 1907, the Eastern and Western divisions of the holiness churches merged their work into a single denomination—the Church of the Nazarene."[27]

As early as 1897, the Association of Pentecostal Churches in the East had sent a party of five missionaries to India. They were followed in 1903 by representatives of the Nashville Pentecostal Mission and in 1906 by missionaries from the Los Angeles-based Church of the Nazarene. In 1933, in the depths of economic depression, India reported five Nazarene missionaries, 39 national workers, and 123 members with 33 probationers in two mission stations and 16 outstations.

The numbers scarcely represent the scope of the work being done. In fact, India was on the eve of a spiritual breakthrough, tokened by an outstanding revival in the Buldana church in 1932. The revival carried through into the first of an innovative series of "jungle camps" begun that summer. Numerical growth was more rapid from that point than it had been before.

The association also pioneered work in the Cape Verde Islands beginning in 1900. The mission was started and served by John J. Diaz and his wife who labored there alone for 35 years winning their way slowly through severe persecution.

Diaz was the son of a Cape Verdian seaman and shipper from the island of Brava. He had been brought to the United States at the age of 16 by his father, where he was converted and sanctified in a mission at New Bedford, Mass., a work later affiliated with the Association of Pentecostal Churches and thus with the Church of the Nazarene. By the time of the Nazarene Silver Jubilee, Diaz had one national helper and two organized churches with a total of 75 members.

In 1901, the Pentecostal Mission sent workers to Guatemala. The mission had made substantial progress when the parent body joined the Church of the Nazarene in 1915. Additional missionaries were sent, and the work extended into British Honduras (now Belize). By 1933, the field had seven missionaries, 17 national workers, two mission stations, and 17 outstations with 500 full

---

27. Foreword to Olive G. Tracy, *Tracy Sahib of India* (Kansas City: Beacon Hill Press, 1954), p. 7.

members and 300 probationers in nine organized churches. A Bible training school enrolled 19 students.

The Independent Holiness church of Texas began work in Mexico in 1903, although Spanish work was begun by May McReynolds from Los Angeles First Church soon after the church was organized in 1895. Mexico was closed to missionaries by the revolution in 1910; but by 1933, 14 national workers pastored 17 churches and 22 preaching points with 912 full members and 96 probationers. At the same time, among the Spanish-speaking people along the U.S. border, and thus under the supervision of the Foreign Missions Department, there were four missionaries and 17 national workers supervising 13 churches and five outstations with a total membership of 571 plus 116 probationers.

Japan became a Nazarene mission field in 1905 when the Holiness Church of Christ began work first in Tokyo and later in Kyoto. In 1933, two missionaries and 24 national pastors supervised 25 organized churches with 1,299 members.

Africa, the largest and most rewarding mission field in which the church has worked, was penetrated by Harmon Schmelzenbach in 1907. Schmelzenbach belonged to the independent holiness church at Peniel, Tex., which became a Nazarene congregation in April, 1908. By 1933, some 26 Nazarene missionaries and 153 national workers served in Africa with seven mission stations, 125 outstations and preaching points, and 1,471 full members plus 1,701 probationers. There were five Bible training schools with almost 200 enrolled. Raleigh Fitkin Memorial Hospital, established in 1925 by Dr. and Mrs. David Hynd near Bremersdorp (now Manzini), Swaziland, gave outstanding support to the missionary program. A strong nursing school was in operation as early as 1930.

After the union of Pilot Point, what later became the Nazarene mission in Argentina was begun as an independent endeavor of Rev. and Mrs. Frank Ferguson who were affiliated with the Pentecostal Mission in Nashville. The Argentine field was without missionary supervision for two years, 1933-34, but strong national leadership served five organized churches and eight outstations with 160 members and 82 probationers.

China was entered in 1913 when Peter and Anna Kiehn and Miss Glennie Sims began work there. Twenty years later, in terms of missionary personnel, it had become the second largest missionary field. A 100-bed hospital had been completed in 1930, although by 1933 it was without a missionary doctor. There were 11 missionaries and 55 national workers serving 10 mission stations and 38 outstations. A total of 1,121 members belonged to the Church of the Nazarene in China in 1933.

The handwriting was already on the wall as far as the prospects for Christian missions in China were concerned. Reporting as Foreign Missions secretary in 1932, J. G. Morrison lamented the revolutionary turmoil and political chaos in China and with rare prescience warned that "such is the turbulent condition of that sorely beset empire as to make the abandonment of our field there very imminent, and fairly probable."[28]

As was the case in Argentina, so in Peru, what became the Nazarene mission was started by independent missionaries in 1914 when Rev. Roger Winans and Mrs. Mary Hunt Winans began work there. In 1917, the Winanses were commissioned as missionaries of the Church of the Nazarene. By 1933, six missionaries and 30 national workers labored in three mission stations and 29 outstations. There were 370 full members and 378 probationers.

In 1919, Carlotta Graham, a native of Barbados in the British West Indies who had been converted and joined the Church of the Nazarene in New York, was sent to her home island as a missionary by a group of fellow Barbadian Christians. In 1926, the mission was extended to Trinidad. By 1933, two missionaries and 20 national pastors served 20 organized churches with 893 full and 139 probationary members in the British West Indies.

Syria was added to the list of Nazarene missions in 1920. In 1933, it still had only one missionary and one organized church with 50 members. Work was begun in Jerusalem the year following the opening of the Syrian mission, and it also had one missionary and one organized church with 46 members by the time of the Silver Jubilee.

The summary report of the Department of Foreign Missions for the 25th anniversary year listed 66 missionaries working on 12 fields assisted by a total of 378 national workers. A total of 109

---

28. *Proceedings of the General Board of the Church of the Nazarene and Its Departments,* January, 1932, p. 106. Hereafter, annual proceedings will be cited as PGB and the date. The *Other Sheep,* vol. 19, no. 5 (November, 1931), p. 2, reported that Bresee Hospital in Tamingfu had suffered heavy damage from gunfire in August as government troops battled approximately 1,000 insurrectionists. The *Other Sheep* is hereafter cited as OS.

organized churches had been established, and the gospel was being preached at an additional 261 outstations. Full membership in foreign mission churches stood at 7,568 with an additional 2,885 probationers.

The church was operating 84 day schools on its mission fields, most of them in Africa, with 1,990 pupils enrolled. Ministerial training was being provided in 92 Bible training schools enrolling approximately 250 students. Medical facilities included two hospitals, one in Africa and one in China, and 14 dispensaries staffed with a total of eight physicians and 24 nurses. In 1933, a total of 29,359 patients were treated.[29]

The numbers themselves, though not large, represented the major general interest of the denomination, and their support was its primary general obligation. There were agonizing years ahead, and the real surge in foreign missionary activity for the Church of the Nazarene would have to wait until the late 1940s.

I. Publishing

The passion for evangelism and missions was primary for all the groups that merged to form the Church of the Nazarene. A close second, and viewed as a necessary means to that end, came education and publishing. Each of the merging groups brought to the union at least one periodical and a budding publishing concern.

The General Assembly of 1911 took steps to combine the periodicals. It authorized the establishment of a Nazarene Publishing House in Kansas City, with C. J. Kinne as the manager. The official denominational magazine to be published weekly would be known as the *Herald of Holiness.* Sunday School helps were to be prepared and published, and a monthly missionary journal, the *Other Sheep,* was started.

For a decade, the publishing house floundered on the verge of bankruptcy. Inadequate equipment, lack of working capital, and an unending series of annual deficits threatened the very existence of the young concern. The continuing crisis required repeated financial drives through the church with receipts never sufficient to cover the need. By 1921, the accumulated indebtedness totalled

---

29. Cf. Russell V. DeLong and Mendell L. Taylor, *Fifty Years of Nazarene Missions,* 3 vols. (Kansas City: Beacon Hill Press, 1955), 2:273-76; and GAJ, 1936, pp. 373-92.

$104,000, a staggering sum in terms of 1921 dollars and membership.

The turning point came in 1922 when the Board of General Superintendents persuaded Mervel S. Lunn, a young layman accountant who had been employed by the house since 1913, to become general manager. A church-wide campaign was launched to raise $100,000 to "save the publishing house." A total of $72,000 was received over a period of two years.

But the real turnaround was internal. Lunn reorganized the entire business end of the enterprise and began to operate it with a balance of income over expense. By 1933, at the depth of the depression, the house was able to contribute $40,000 to the denomination from its surplus and reported a net worth of well over a third of a million dollars. It was completely out of debt. The last of the bonds outstanding on construction of the building at 2923 Troost Avenue were redeemed on December 31, 1933.[30]

J. Education

One of the most pressing problems growing out of the merging of three denominational entities was dealing with a multiplicity of schools and colleges. By 1933, consolidations and closures had reduced the number of liberal arts colleges to six, with one additional junior college, plus a Bible college operating in Western Canada. The church was divided into "educational zones," groupings of districts for the financial support and student recruitment for the colleges.

Four of the colleges had been started by the groups later merging to form the Church of the Nazarene. In 1899, a group of holiness people in Peniel, Tex., established Texas Holiness University with 27 students. A. M. Hills was chosen as president. The school became successively Peniel University and Peniel College, and merged in 1920 with Oklahoma Holiness College at Bethany, a suburb of Oklahoma City, to become Bethany-Peniel College.

---

30. Smith, *Called unto Holiness*, pp. 337-38; GAJ, 1936, p. 336; PGB, 1934, pp. 63, 99-100. For the early history of the publishing work of the church see Smith, *Called unto Holiness*, pp. 263-66; Billy J. Lakey, "The Contribution of the Nazarene Publishing House to the Church of the Nazarene" (B.D. thesis, Nazarene Theological Seminary, Kansas City, 1954); and Elden E. Rawlings, "A History of the Nazarene Publishing House" (Master's thesis, University of Oklahoma School of Journalism, Norman, Okla., 1960).

Central Nazarene University, founded at Hamlin, Tex., in 1910, joined the merged institution in 1929, followed by the 31-year-old Arkansas Holiness College at Vilonia, Ark., in 1931. A. K. Bracken had been president since 1920, with a two-year intermission from 1928 to 1930. Bethany-Peniel College drew its support from the assembly districts of Arkansas, Dallas, Abilene, San Antonio, New Mexico, Eastern and Western Oklahoma, Louisiana, Kansas, Kansas City, and Nebraska.[31]

The school that became Eastern Nazarene College in 1918 was founded in Saratoga Springs, N.Y., in 1900 as the Pentecostal Collegiate Institute. It was moved to North Scituate, R.I., two years later and in 1919 transferred to Wollaston Park, Quincy, Mass., its present campus. R. Wayne Gardner became president in 1930 and served until 1936. In 1933, the college had the dubious honor of carrying the heaviest debt in dollar terms of all the institutions, although the situation at Trevecca was actually more critical.[32] Eastern Nazarene College had as its constituency the British Isles, New England, New York, Washington-Philadelphia, and Pittsburgh districts, and Ontario, Quebec, and the Maritimes in Canada.

In 1901, J. O. McClurkan founded the Pentecostal Literary and Bible Training School in Nashville, the precursor of Trevecca College, later to be named Trevecca Nazarene College. By 1910, the school offered a four-year course leading to a baccalaureate degree. A small, independent holiness college in northeastern Tennessee, Ruskin Cave College, joined forces with Trevecca in 1917, and shortly thereafter Southeastern Nazarene College of Donalsonville, Ga., also merged. The Silver Jubilee found Trevecca in a most precarious position, occupying a temporary campus on White's Creek with its former Gallatin Road property sold for

---

31. Gordon C. Wickersham, "Bethany Nazarene College: Official College of the West Central Educational Zone," *Conquest*, vol. 16, no. 8 (May, 1962), pp. 4-7. The history and development of all the schools to 1948 is sketched by Kenneth Robinson, "Educational Development in the Church of the Nazarene" (B.D. thesis, Nazarene Theological Seminary, Kansas City, 1948), and to 1957 by L. C. Philo, "The Historical Development and Present Status of the Educational Instituions of the Church of the Nazarene" (Ph.D. diss., University of Oklahoma, Norman, Okla., 1958).

32. Donald L. Young, "Eastern Nazarene College," *Conquest*, vol. 16, no. 9 (June, 1962), pp. 12-15; James R. Cameron, *Eastern Nazarene College: The First Fifty Years, 1900-1950* (Kansas City: Nazarene Publishing House, 1968).

bankruptcy and its future bleak indeed.[33] Dr. C. E. Hardy, physician and ordained minister, was president. Trevecca's zone included the Southeast Atlantic, Georgia, Florida, Kentucky-West Virginia, Tennessee, Alabama, and Mississippi districts.

In the West, Pacific Bible College was established in 1902 by the Nazarenes in Los Angeles, where it later became Deets Pacific Bible College. It was moved to Pasadena in 1912 to become first Nazarene University, then Pasadena University, and finally in 1923 Pasadena College. H. Orton Wiley was the president in 1933, having just returned from Kansas City after a five-year stint as editor of the *Herald of Holiness*.[34] The Southwest educational zone included the Arizona, Southern California, Northern California, and Colorado districts.

In 1905, a small, independent group known as the Apostolic Holiness church in Hutchinson, Kans., under the leadership of Mrs. Mattie Hoke, began a Bible school called Kansas Holiness College. In 1909, the congregation and their school joined the Church of the Nazarene, and the college was later named Bresee College. By 1933, it was operating as an academy and junior college, sharing its support with Bethany-Peniel and Pasadena— specifically the Kansas, Kansas City, Nebraska, and Colorado districts. S. T. Ludwig, later to become General NYPS executive secretary and then general church secretary, was president.[35] The school merged with Bethany-Peniel College in 1940.

In 1909, seven members of the Eastern Illinois Holiness Association obtained a charter from the state of Illinois for Illinois Holiness University, which they established on a 14-acre campus 14 miles south of Danville. They called A. M. Hills to be the first president and enrolled 147 students studying under 14 faculty members the first year.

In 1912, the college was turned over to the Chicago Central District of the Church of the Nazarene, and E. F. Walker became the president. The name was changed to Olivet University, and the

---

33. Mildred Bangs Wynkoop, *The Trevecca Story* (Nashville: Trevecca College Press, 1976), pp. 61-157; Homer J. Adams, "Trevecca Nazarene College," *Conquest*, vol. 17, no. 3 (December, 1962), pp. 12-15.

34. James Proctor Knott, *History of Pasadena College* (Pasadena, Calif.: Pasadena College, 1960); Tom Floyd, "Pasadena College," *Conquest*, vol. 16, no. 12 (September, 1962), pp. 18-21.

35. Smith, *Called unto Holiness*, pp. 225-26; Robinson, "Educational Development," pp. 13-14.

village that grew up around the school was known as Olivet. By 1933, it had become known as Olivet College and was struggling for existence, with T. W. Willingham as president.[36] Olivet's educational zone consisted of the Chicago Central, Northern Indiana, Indianapolis, Ohio, Michigan, Missouri, and Iowa districts—some of the strongest in the church.

Northwest Nazarene College had its beginning in 1913 as a grade school and Bible school in Nampa, Ida., with layman Eugene Emerson as its main backer. The first portion of its present campus was purchased in 1915, and the school was named Idaho-Oregon Holiness College. It became Northwest Nazarene College the following year, and H. Orton Wiley was called from Pasadena to become its president. By the time he left to return to Pasadena in 1926, the school was on sound footing academically, although struggling financially. Reuben E. Gilmore was president in 1933.[37] The Northwest, Idaho-Oregon, Rocky Mountain, North Dakota, and Central Northwest districts comprised its constituency, with the addition of the North Pacific District excluding the portion of the district in British Columbia.

In 1921, the pressing need for ministerial leadership in Canada led E. S. Mathews, pastor of the Calgary, Alberta, Church of the Nazarene, to establish Calgary Bible Institute. In 1923, Charles E. Thomson assumed leadership destined to continue for 18 years. Relocated in Red Deer, Alberta, in 1927, the school was first known there as the Alberta School of Evangelism, but the name was changed to Northern Bible College when, in 1928, the four western provinces of Canada (British Columbia, Alberta, Saskatchewan, and Manitoba) were set apart as the support zone for the college. It was later to become Canadian Nazarene College and eventually move to Winnipeg, Manitoba, where it became an all-Canadian school.[38]

The economic depression had brought extreme hardship to the colleges of the church. The address of the Board of General

---

36. R. L. Lunsford, "Olivet Nazarene College," *Conquest*, vol. 16, no. 11 (August, 1962), pp. 12-15.

37. Helen G. Wilson, "Northwest Nazarene College," *Conquest*, vol. 16, no. 10 (July, 1962), pp. 12-15; Russell L. Carlson, "A Documentary Sourcebook for the History of the Church of the Nazarene" (B.D. thesis, Nazarene Theological Seminary, Kansas City, 1955), p. 185.

38. Arnold E. Airhart, "Canadian Nazarene College," *Conquest*, vol. 17, no. 1 (October, 1962), pp. 4-7.

Superintendents to the 1932 General Assembly had pointed out the extremely precarious state of the financial support for the colleges: "Our schools constitute an unsolved problem of the denomination. Scholastically and spiritually we are at ease with regard to the schools, but as yet we have found no adequate means of supporting the schools financially."[39]

The financial report to the General Assembly that year illustrated the problem clearly. Out of total denominational giving for the preceding four years of $13.5 million, only $227,021 had gone to the eight schools and colleges of the church, or 1.67 percent of the total. Total giving for general interests during the same period was 7.61 percent and district giving added up to 6.08 percent.

In addition to limited income for current operations, the colleges struggled with indebtedness which in terms of 1932 dollar values was a staggering burden. The Department of Education reported the capital debt figures as follows: Bethany-Peniel, $30,838; Eastern, $153,095; Northwest, $32,277; Olivet, $41,076; Pasadena, $64,062; Trevecca, $25,000; Bresee, $14,000; and Northern Bible (Canada), $3,800. In addition to capital indebtedness, most of the schools carried large accumulated current deficits, large enough in the case of Trevecca to force the college into bankruptcy.[40]

The colleges were all small in terms both of facilities and student enrollments, averaging slightly more than 132 students each plus those registered in the high school departments or academies some of the college maintained. It is to the credit of the sacrificial spirit of administrations and faculties that none of the schools was forced to close its doors as was the case with many other private colleges during this difficult period.

III. LEADERSHIP

The leadership of the young denomination in 1933 was in seasoned hands. The General Assembly held in Wichita, Kans., in June, 1932, had reelected three men as general superintendents and one to the newly created office of general superintendent emeritus.

---

39. GAJ, 1932, p. 187.
40. Ibid., p. 258.

A. General Superintendents

The senior general superintendents were John W. Goodwin and Roy T. Williams, both elected originally by mail vote of the district superintendents in January, 1916, after death claimed General Superintendents P. F. Bresee and W. C. Wilson within three months of their election by the General Assembly of 1915.

Goodwin had his roots in the Advent Christian church in New England. He had been active in interdenominational holiness work before becoming affiliated with the Association of Pentecostal Churches. Moving to southern California in 1905, he transferred to the Church of the Nazarene and became pastor of its Pasadena congregation. He was elected superintendent of the Southern California District in 1908. Goodwin was 47 years old when elected general superintendent and 63 at the time of his 1932 reelection.[41]

Roy Tilman Williams was a southern evangelist, pastor, and educator who had joined the Church of the Nazarene in 1908 at the General Assembly that brought together the Holiness Church of Christ and the Nazarenes. He had served on the faculty of his alma mater, Texas Holiness University, and became its president at the age of 28. In 1913, he resigned his administrative post and entered the field of evangelism. He was just a few weeks short of his 33rd birthday when chosen general superintendent.[42]

The third of the active general superintendents was James B. Chapman. Chapman had first been elected to the office in 1928, having served as associate editor and then editor of the *Herald of Holiness* since 1921. Chapman had come into the Church of the Nazarene via the Independent Holiness church and the Holiness Church of Christ. He whimsically recalled that he had joined only one church and after that let his church do the joining. He had been a highly successful pastor and evangelist and had also served as president of Texas Holiness University. He was 48 years of age

---

41. A. E. Sanner, *John W. Goodwin* (Kansas City: Nazarene Publishing House, 1945); Frank W. Watkin, "A History of the General Superintendency of the Church of the Nazarene" (B.D. thesis, Nazarene Theological Seminary, Kansas City, 1949), pp. 108-13.

42. G. B. Williamson, *Roy T. Williams: Servant of God* (Kansas City: Nazarene Publishing House, 1947); Watkin, "History of the General Superintendency," pp. 102-7.

when reelected in 1932, approximately 18 months younger than Williams.[43]

The "grand old man" of the Board of General Superintendents was Hiram F. Reynolds. Reynolds had been active in holiness circles as a Methodist pastor in New England in the 1880s. He became Foreign Missions secretary of the Association of Pentecostal Churches and represented the association at the union with the Church of the Nazarene in Chicago in 1907. With Dr. Bresee, he was elected a general superintendent of the resulting denomination as well as executive secretary of its General Missionary Board. A year later at Pilot Point, Bresee, Reynolds, and Edgar P. Ellyson were elected general superintendents, and Reynolds had served in that capacity until given emeritus status in 1932 at the age of 78.[44]

B. General Officers

Other denominational leaders were men of stature. General church secretary was E. J. Fleming, who had held that office since 1919. Fleming was also secretary of the Department of Ministerial Relief and General Stewardship secretary as well as executive director of the Nazarene Mutual Benevolent Society.

General treasurer was layman Mervel S. Lunn, who doubled as manager of the Nazarene Publishing House. He had served as treasurer since 1925.[45]

Joseph G. Morrison, who had led the Laymen's Holiness Association into the Church of the Nazarene in 1922-23, had served as Foreign Missions secretary since 1927 and would continue in that post until elected general superintendent in 1936.

The editor of the *Herald of Holiness*, elected in 1928 and again in 1932, was H. Orton Wiley, former president of Pasadena College and of Northwest Nazarene College and soon to return to Pasadena College as president.

---

43. D. Shelby Corlett, *Spirit-filled* (Kansas City: Nazarene Publishing House, 1948); Watkin, "History of the General Superintendency," pp. 113-19.

44. Amy Hinshaw, *In Labors Abundant* (Kansas City: Nazarene Publishing House, 1938); Watkin, "History of the General Superintendency," pp. 82-87.

45. For a year and a half—from the General Assembly of 1932 to the meeting of the General Board in January of 1934—J. G. Morrison was general treasurer and M. Lunn was "comptroller." This was not a happy arrangement, and Lunn was persuaded to resume the treasurer's responsibilities which he ably carried, along with his duties as manager of the Publishing House, until 1945.

Edgar P. Ellyson was editor of the church schools periodicals, a position he held from 1923 until retirement in 1938.

General secretary of the NYPS was D. Shelby Corlett. By 1933 he had served in this post for 10 years and was newly appointed managing editor of the *Herald of Holiness* as well as executive secretary of the General Board Department of Home Missions, Church Extension, and Evangelism.

Miss Emma B. Word was the recently elected treasurer of the Women's Foreign Missionary Society, a post she filled until 1950.

C. General Board

Serving on the church's General Board in 1933 were the equal number of ministers and laymen provided for by the General Assembly since 1928. The members were elected by geographical zones, roughly equivalent to the educational zones with the addition of a "British Isles-Canadian Zone."

Representing the Eastern Zone was Rev. C. Warren Jones, superintendent of the Pittsburgh District in western Pennsylvania; and Mr. E. S. Carman of Cleveland, Ohio.

Dr. C. E. Hardy, a medical doctor turned minister and then president of Trevecca College; and Mr. R. B. Mitchum, a businessman from Nashville, were the elected representatives of the Southeastern Zone.

Rev. J. W. Short and Mr. John W. Felmlee, a foreman for the General Electric Co., at Fort Wayne, Ind., had been chosen in 1932 from the Central Zone. When Short was elected superintendent of the Western Oklahoma District later that year, he was replaced by Rev. C. A. Gibson, superintendent of the Ohio District.

Dr. A. K. Bracken, president of Bethany-Peniel College, and Mr. Charles A. McConnell of Bethany, Okla., represented the Southern Zone.

From the Southwestern Zone came Rev. J. T. Little, pastor of the Alhambra, Calif., church; and Mr. E. P. Robertson of Newton, Kans., a public school administrator.

Superintendent J. E. Bates of the North Pacific District, and contractor S. W. True of Spokane, Wash., represented the Northwest Zone.

The British Isles-Canadian Zone was represented by Rev. George Sharpe of Glasgow, Scotland; and President C. E. Thomson of Northern Bible College in Red Deer, Alberta, Canada—both ministers. Because of the cost of travel, the arrangement was that they would actually alternate in meeting with the board.

The special interests were represented by Mrs. S. N. Fitkin, who by 1933 had moved to Oakland, Calif., and was still president of the Women's Missionary Society; Rev. G. B. Williamson of Cleveland, Ohio, for the Nazarene Young People's Society; Rev. C. B. Widmeyer of Pasadena for Church Schools; and Dr. Orval J. Nease, president of Pasadena College, for education.

D. General Auxiliaries

A large (23-member) Women's General Missionary Council was headed by Mrs. S. N. Fitkin, president; Mrs. Paul Bresee of Los Angeles, executive vice-president; Mrs. Florence Davis of Colorado Springs, first vice-president; Miss Mary E. Cove of Wollaston, Mass., second vice-president; Mrs. Roy G. Codding of Kansas City, secretary; Miss Emma B. Word, also of Kansas City, treasurer. Mrs. Olive M. Gould of Wollaston was superintendent of study, and Mrs. T. D. Aughey of Madison, Tenn., was superintendent of publicity.

Seven young ministers composed the General NYPS Executive Council: G. B. Williamson, general president; D. Shelby Corlett, general secretary; L. A. Reed, pastor of Kansas City First Church; Jarrette E. Aycock, an evangelist headquartered in Bethany, Okla.; Weaver W. Hess, pastor of Pasadena First Church; Milton Smith, pastor of the church in Norman, Okla.; and Donnell J. Smith, pastor of Portland, Ore., First Church. It would not be until the 1950s that lay people would be elected to the NYPS General Council, although many served with distinction in district offices.

E. District Superintendents

The 1933 roster of district superintendents included many experienced churchmen, and a number just beginning long and outstanding tenures. Almost without exception, the district superintendents had made their mark as pastors or evangelists before appointment or election. The earliest concept of the district superintendent as a district evangelist, concerned chiefly to dig out new churches on his district, was beginning to change as districts grew and administrative responsibilities multiplied.

Included in the superintendents' list were such names as V. B.

Atteberry of Abilene, E. S. Mathews of Alberta, Oscar Hudson of Arizona, J. C. Henson of Little Rock, Robert Purvis in the British Isles, B. V. Seals on the Central Northwest District, E. O. Chalfant of Chicago Central, C. W. Davis in Colorado, P. P. Belew in Georgia, N. B. Herrell on the Kansas City District, L. T. Wells in Kentucky, R. V. Starr in Michigan, John Gould in New England, Roy F. Smee in Northern California, J. W. Montgomery in Northern Indiana, Charles A. Gibson in Ohio, C. Warren Jones on the Pittsburgh District, A. E. Sanner in Southern California, L. B. Matthews in Tennessee, and J. W. Short in Western Oklahoma.

A particularly notable group of men served on the Olivet zone: E. O. Chalfant, R. V. Starr, J. W. Montgomery, C. Warren Jones, C. A. Gibson, and J. W. Short. They exercised large influence in denominational affairs, in part through their personal relationship with General Superintendent R. T. Williams. All except Short were members of the Olivet college board, and most of them were or had been members of the General Board. Known at times as an oligarchy, they were men to be consulted in any significant moves. They were all men of vision and drive and administered their respective districts with strong hands.

As a move to coordinate the church's leadership, the 1932 General Assembly authorized an annual meeting of the general and district superintendents at the time of the General Board meeting each January. The "council," as it was first called, or "conference" as it later became known, met first January 10-12, 1933. Although only about half of the district superintendents attended, R. T. Williams commented that "this gathering marks an epoch in the progress of our movement."[46] It was not until 1944, however, that the superintendents' conference became a regular feature in the church's annual calendar.[47]

Many of the superintendents would be worthy of special note. None could be presented as typical of all. All were individuals, each outstanding in his own way. Yet at least passing notice may be given to three of these men.

E. O. Chalfant was in many ways an eccentric. Yet he estab-

---

46. *Herald of Holiness*, vol. 21, no. 46 (Feb. 8, 1933), p. 5; no. 15 (July 6, 1932), p. 2; and no. 44 (Jan. 25, 1933), p. 2. Hereafter cited as HH with volume, number, date, and page(s).

47. Mendell L. Taylor, "Handbook of Historical Documents" (bound mimeographed volume, n.d.), p. 213.

lished a record in his 30 years as superintendent of the Chicago Central District that would be difficult to surpass. The district, at the beginning of Chalfant's leadership, covered the entire states of Illinois and Wisconsin. Before he retired, the area had been divided four ways, Chalfant himself remaining with the core Chicago area district.

Chalfant came to the Church of the Nazarene from the United Brethren church. Born in 1882, he was converted at the United Brethren College in his home state of Indiana at the age of 17 and sanctified three years later. Feeling that he would have greater opportunities for ministry in the younger Church of the Nazarene, he transferred his ministerial membership in 1916. After pastorates in Muncie, Ind., and Indianapolis Westside, he was elected superintendent of the Chicago Central District in 1922.

As with many of his peers, Chalfant was a man of rugged convictions. There was never any question as to where he stood when issues arose. He was an early riser, usually up by 4 a.m. for two hours of study and prayer with a well-marked Bible and a worn copy of one of Adam Clarke's six volumes of Bible commentary.

As a district superintendent, Chalfant organized some 260 churches in all and saw the membership of the churches in the area he served grow from 2,200 to 14,000. He made 1,000 pastoral arrangements and placed 300 young ministers in their first charges before retiring in 1952 at age 70. Beyond the boundaries of his district, he served 14 years in three different terms on the General Board. He was a dominant figure in the affairs of Olivet Nazarene College and played a leading role in moving the college from Olivet to Kankakee, Ill.[48]

Three years after Chalfant took up the superintendency of the Chicago Central District, Charles A. Gibson became superintendent of the Ohio District, covering the western two-thirds of the state. He had previously served for four years as superintendent on the Northern California District. Gibson, also an Indiana man, had come to the Nazarenes from the Holiness Christian church. He was an omnivorous reader, having read over 700 books in the first

---

48. Cf. Chalfant's own recollections in *Forty Years on the Firing Line* (Kansas City: Beacon Hill Press, 1951); telephone interview with Rev. Morris Chalfant, July 14, 1982.

seven years after his conversion at age 20. Ordained a Nazarene minister in 1913, Gibson served as a pastor and an evangelist until 1920 when he began a career as district superintendent that was to extend over 35 years on four districts.

Gibson was typical of the superintendent who doubled as district evangelist in holding home mission campaigns. Many of the new congregations were started in depression-emptied storefront buildings across the state. He led in the establishment of 165 new congregations in 18 years in Ohio before moving on to Michigan and later Wisconsin.[49]

Across the continent to the west, A. E. Sanner became superintendent of the Southern California District in 1933. Sanner had come to the Church of the Nazarene from the Church of God (Holiness), centered in College Mound, Mo., the fellowship that also contributed G. B. Williamson and D. I. Vanderpool to the church. Prior to his southern California ministry, Sanner had been district superintendent in Colorado and on the Idaho-Oregon District.

Sanner was superbly gifted as an administrator. His slogan, "Let's Do Something," will be remembered by all who served with him. He also organized almost 100 churches during his years in the district superintendency. He was a strong supporter of Pasadena College and led the district in constructing the Memorial Auditorium on the campus that served both as a camp meeting auditorium during the summer and as a combination chapel and gymnasium for the college during the school year. He was a member of the General Board for 20 years and closed his career as superintendent of Casa Robles, the missionary retirement home in Temple City, Calif.[50]

IV. HEADQUARTERS

The headquarters offices of the church in 1933 were in the substantial three-story reinforced concrete building at 2923 Troost Avenue in Kansas City built by the Nazarene Publishing House and

---

49. Cf. the account in C. T. Corbett, *Our Nazarene Pioneers* (Kansas City: Nazarene Publishing House, 1958), pp. 91-96.
50. Ibid., pp. 103-8; personal interview, April 3, 1981.

occupied in 1926. It housed the entire publishing operation at the time as well as offices for the administration of the church.

After enduring the much more cramped quarters at 2109 Troost Avenue for 14 years, the new facility had seemed spacious indeed. It soon filled up, however, and the growth of both the publishing house and the headquarters staff made it necessary to secure additional space for offices in 1936 in a converted apartment building at 2901 Troost.

SUMMARY

In 1933, the Nazarenes were 117,947 in number worldwide, of whom 111,905 lived in the United States, Canada, and the British Isles. They worshipped and worked in 2,019 congregations. They supported 66 missionaries and 378 national workers in other lands. They had developed a workable form of church government and were led by capable and committed churchmen. They maintained six small liberal arts colleges in the United States and one junior college, with a Bible school in Canada. They were served by a fiscally sound and rapidly growing publishing arm. Their first 25 years, as they understood it, was the prologue to bigger and better things to come.

2
Nazarene Self-image
in 1933

A church is measured not only by its leadership and organization but also by its shared concepts and convictions as to its reason for being. It is important to understand how Nazarenes saw their role in the Christian world in 1933.

The denomination had preserved in its 1928 constitution the basic statement that appeared first in Bresee's 1903 *Manual* and was adopted at both Chicago in 1907 and Pilot Point in 1908. "The Church of God," it proclaimed, "is composed of all spiritually regenerate persons, whose names are written in heaven."

The churches severally, on the other hand, "are to be composed of such regenerate persons as by providential permission, and by the leadings of the Holy Spirit, become associated together for holy fellowship and ministries."

The Church of the Nazarene, then, is composed of "those persons who have voluntarily associated themselves together according to the doctrines and polity" of the church for the purpose of "holy Christian fellowship, the conversion of sinners, the entire sanctification of believers, [and] their upbuilding in holiness." The church seeks "the simplicity and spiritual power manifest in the primitive New Testament Church," and its aim is "the preaching of the gospel to every creature."[1]

An anonymous bit of blank verse adorned the cover of the *Herald of Holiness* for June 15, 1932—published in connection with

---

1. *Manual,* 1932, pp. 31-32.

the Eighth General Assembly meeting at the time in Wichita, Kans.:

> *O Church of the Nazarene,*
> *To thee has been given a sacred trust*
> *Of holding aloft the torch of truth,*
> *That its illuminating rays may pierce*
> *The dreary night of doubt and fear*
> *And show a sin-weary world,*
> *Its way to the Cross.* [2]

General Superintendent John W. Goodwin had delivered the Quadrennial Address of the Board of General Superintendents to the Wichita assembly. He had listed seven fundamental characteristics of the Church of the Nazarene which, as Editor Wiley commented, "were never summarized in a clearer and more definite form":[3]

1. The church "stands for the whole Bible." Its people believe that the Bible not only contains the Word of God but also that it "is the Word of God" and may be preached from Genesis to Revelation "as the revealed will of God and plan of God for us, for our salvation and our activity."

2. The church places its emphasis "on vital experience, holy character and holy living." One must be saved from sin and have a clean and holy heart "that furnishes the fountain from which comes right motive, divine love and correct Christian ethics."

3. The church "stands for fundamental doctrines." It has never been concerned with nonessentials or superficial things. "We believe that we should work from the center to the circumference and not from the circumference to the center."

4. The church has "a spiritual urge" at its heart. Its heart cry is for spiritual things. The four years just past had been characterized by "the most outstanding and far-reaching revivals" ever known in the church's history.

5. The church is marked by a "deep desire to know God as a personal God" rather than as "an opinion of philosophy or a theological formula."

6. Spiritual freedom, a "simplicity of Pentecostal worship," has characterized the church from its beginnings. People are at-

---

2. HH, vol. 21, nos. 12 and 13 (June 15 and 22, 1932), p. 1.
3. HH, vol. 21, no. 14 (June 29, 1932), p. 2.

tracted and held by "joyous freedom in the ministry of the Word and the glad testimonies of saving grace" which alone can assure the permanency of the movement as a spiritual force.

7. The church has never felt itself an end within itself but always a means to the end of the salvation of a lost world. "Throughout the denomination there is a burning passion, both in the pulpit and in the pew, for lost souls."[4]

I. A HOLINESS CHURCH

The statement was frequently made that the distinguishing doctrine of the Church of the Nazarene is the concept of entire sanctification as a work of grace following regeneration or the new birth. Such a concept of Christian holiness was required to "Christianize Christianity." Few if any issues of the *Herald of Holiness* appeared without one or more articles on some phase of the doctrine, experience, or ethics of holiness.

In a front-page article in the *Herald* in the spring of 1933, General Superintendent J. B. Chapman meditated on "The Nazarene Task":

> When our church came into the field twenty-five years ago many outside observers interpreted its task as that of shepherding the scattered holiness people in such places as there seemed to be a sufficient number of them to support a local program. It may be that some who joined the ranks thought only in terms of local needs and very limited possibilities. . . .
>
> But those who read the skies aright believed and preached from the very first that the Church of the Nazarene came to spread scriptural holiness in a world parish. And these never agreed to accept a defensive attitude. They interpreted Dr. Bresee's motto of responsibility literally—"We are debtors to every man to give him the gospel in the same measure as we have received it"—and they proposed by every possible means to make payments on this debt.[5]

Two weeks before the beginning of the official observance of the Silver Anniversary in the fall of 1933, Editor Wiley published an editorial titled "Our Distinctive Tenet." That tenet Wiley defined as "this message of full salvation, . . . this precious experience of heart cleansing."

---

4. GAJ, 1932, pp. 183-84.
5. HH, vol. 22, no. 9 (May 24, 1933), p. 1.

Wiley explained that the term "entire sanctification" refers primarily to the "purification of the soul from all sin, and its full devotion to God." He noted that "perfect love" and "Christian perfection" are other terms used to describe "that state of grace in which the Christian has been cleansed from all sin and filled with perfect love." Redemption is perfect and complete only as far as the cleansing of the heart from sin is concerned. The Christian enjoying this experience may thereafter grow in grace and in the knowledge of God "without the antagonisms of sin within his being."[6]

The character of the church as a holiness body was set forth clearly in the statements on the doctrines of original sin and entire sanctification the uniting groups brought with them in 1907 and 1908 and in the formal creed finalized in 1928. It also shows up in the distinctives of the holy life expressed in "General and Special Rules." And it is to be seen in the way holiness was preached and the experience sought.

A. In Doctrine

We have already noted that the groups joining to compose the Church of the Nazarene all came out of the holiness movement of the middle and later 19th century. The local congregations first, and then groupings into incipient denominations, were formed to conserve the fruit of holiness evangelism and further its interests. The conditions under which these churches and associations were begun virtually guaranteed that all of their members would be staunch adherents to belief in second blessing holiness.

Each of the uniting groups stated its reason for being in these terms. The Association of Pentecostal Churches had adopted its constitution and summary of doctrines in December, 1895. It declared that "entire sanctification is that work of God's grace by which we are made holy, cleansed from all sin, love God with all the heart, and are baptized with the Holy Spirit." This is an instantaneous work, received by faith following conversion, to which the Holy Spirit bears witness. It is not imputed, "but inwrought in the soul of the believer."[7]

Bresee's 1898 *Manual of the Church of the Nazarene* had described the members of the organization as being "generally con-

---

6. HH, vol. 22, no. 30 (Oct. 18, 1933), p. 3.
7. Quoted by Redford, *Rise of the Church of the Nazarene*, p. 106.

vinced that God had called them unto holiness, and to preach and teach this doctrine, and to lead others into the experience." Both the Word of God and their own experiences had taught them that this is "a second definite work of grace, and is received by faith in Jesus Christ." It is "the peculiar treasure of New Testament doctrines. . . . The very heart of the religion of Jesus Christ is the baptism with the Holy Ghost and fire." "The salvation of men is to be through believers thus baptized."[8]

The statement on entire sanctification in Bresee's 1898 *Manual* was titled "Christian Perfection"—influenced by Methodist terminology—and was stated informally:

> We believe in the doctrine of Christian Perfection, or Entire Sanctification. That it is a second definite work of grace in the heart, whereby we are thoroughly cleansed from all sin. That only those who are justified and walking in the favor of God can receive this grace. That is not absolute perfection, that belongs to God alone. It does not make a man infalable [sic]. It is perfect love—the pure love of God filling a clean heart. It is capable of increase. It prepares for more rapid growth in grace. It may be lost, and we need to continually watch and pray. It is received by faith. It is accomplished by the baptism with the Holy Ghost and fire, which is the baptism of Jesus Christ, foretold by John the Baptist. It is loving the Lord our God with all the heart, soul, mind and strength, and our neighbor as ourselves—Matt. 22:37-39. It was this which the Apostles and Disciples received in the upper room at Jerusalem on the day of Pentecost, for which Jesus commanded them to wait. It is the inheritance of the Church, and with it comes preparation and anointing and power for the work to which God has called us. Our preachers are to definitely preach it, and urge it upon all believers. It is the privilege and duty of all believers to seek and obtain it. It is this to which we are called: "That we might be made partakers of His holiness" Heb. xii.10.[9]

The First General Assembly that brought east and west together adopted a Doctrinal Statement that contains material later formulated into the 15 Articles of Faith which now comprise the credo of the church. The statement on original sin said that it is "that corruption of the nature of all who are engendered as the offspring of Adam." As a result each person is "very far gone from

---

8. *The Manual of the Church of the Nazarene,* promulgated by the Assembly of 1898, held in Los Angeles (Committee of Publication, n.d.), p. 9.
9. Ibid., pp. 18-19.

original righteousness, and is inclined to evil, and that continually." The Bible calls such sin "'The Carnal Mind,' our 'Old Man,' 'The flesh,' 'Sin that dwelleth in me,' etc." It cannot be pardoned. It "continues to exist with the new life of the regenerate until eradicated and destroyed by the baptism with the Holy Spirit."

The accompanying statement on entire sanctification declared it to be "that act of God, subsequent to justification, by which regenerate believers are made free from inbred sin, and brought into the state of entire devotement to God, and the holy obedience of love made perfect." Entire sanctification is provided "through the meritorious blood of Jesus, and wrought upon the full and final consecration of the believer, and a definite act of appropriating faith." The work is accomplished "by the gracious agency of the Holy Spirit," and "to this work and state of grace the Holy Spirit bears witness."

Entire sanctification is also known by other terms that represent different phases, such as "Christian Perfection," "Perfect Love," "Heart Purity," "The baptism with the Holy Spirit," "The fullness of the blessing," "Christian Holiness," and others.[10]

In 1928, after a careful five-year review, the doctrinal statement was formulated as 15 Articles of Faith. The statement on original sin, with a slight variation in wording, became Article V; and the statement on entire sanctification, also slightly reworded, became Article X. Both have been retained virtually unmodified to the present time.[11]

The 1907 and 1928 statements on entire sanctification lack the emphasis on growth in grace that is found in Bresee's 1898 creedal statement on Christian perfection: "It [perfect love] is capable of increase. It prepares for more rapid growth in grace. It may be lost, and we need to continually watch and pray." To compensate for this lack, an item was placed in the 1928 *Manual* in the Special Rules, a collection of matters not included in the Constitution but deemed of sufficient importance to warrant special emphasis. The item was titled "Growth in Grace." Its substance had previously appeared as an explanatory note appended to Article X. It read:

> There is a marked distinction between a perfect heart and
> a perfect character. The former is obtained in an instant, the

---

10. *Manual of the Pentecostal Church of the Nazarene,* 1907, pp. 18-25.
11. *Manual,* 1932, pp. 27, 29.

result of entire sanctification, but the latter is the result of growth in grace.

Our mission to the world is not alone the spreading of scriptural holiness as a doctrine, but it is also that we be "an example of the believers, in word, in conversation, in charity, in spirit, in faith, in purity." Our people should give careful heed to the development of holiness in the fear of the Lord, and to the development of the Christian graces in the heart and of their manifestation in the daily life.[12]

The doctrinal emphasis on holiness, clear in periodical and creedal statement, was no less evident in book-length publications. In the fall of 1933, the Nazarene Publishing House carried in stock 113 books and pamphlets of its own publication. Of these, 19 were specifically on one or another phase of holiness. Included were T. M. Anderson's *After Holiness, What?* Basil Miller's *Bible Readings on Holiness;* J. A. Kring's *Conquest of Canaan;* C. B. Jernigan's *Entire Sanctification; The Establishing Grace, or Sanctification in the Book of Romans,* by A. M. Hills; Free Methodist Evangelist E. E. Shelhamer's *Helps to Holy Living;* J. W. Goodwin's *Miracle of Pentecost;* J. G. Morrison's *Our Lost Estate;* Howard W. Sweeten's *More Excellent Way;* and R. T. Williams' *Sanctification: The Experience and the Ethics.* [13]

B. In Life-style

As indicated in the statement on growth in grace, holiness was not only viewed as a doctrine to be believed and an experience to be received. It was also a distinctive life-style to be lived.

What came later to be called General Rules were found in substance in Bresee's 1898 *Manual* as part of the membership covenant. They had come down through both the 1907 and 1908 unions with only minor rewording and rearrangement. In the Church Constitution adopted in 1928, along with the Articles of Faith and a section titled "Articles of Organization and Government," the General Rules were incorporated in a section titled "The Church."

There it is said that all who hold membership in the Church of the Nazarene are required to show evidence of "salvation from their sins by a godly walk and vital piety." They are to be "or earnestly desire to be" cleansed from all indwelling sin. Members are

---

12. Ibid., pp. 45-46.
13. HH, vol. 22, no. 29 (Oct. 11, 1933), pp. 18-22.

to show evidence of their state of grace: "First. By avoiding evil of every kind. . . . Second. By doing that which is enjoined in the Word of God, which is both our rule of faith and practice. . . . [and] Third. By abiding in hearty fellowship with the church, not inveighing against its doctrines and usages, but being in full sympathy and conformity therewith."

Each of the first two general rules was spelled out in a series of specifics. Evils to be avoided included "Taking the name of God in vain"; "Profaning the Lord's Day, either by unnecessary labor, or business, or by the patronizing or reading of secular papers, or by holiday diversions"; using or "trafficking" in intoxicating liquors or "tobacco in any of its forms"; "Quarreling, returning evil for evil, gossiping, slandering, spreading surmises injurious to the good names of others"; "Dishonesty, taking advantage in buying and selling, bearing false witness, and like works of darkness"; "The indulging of pride in dress or behavior. Our people are to dress with the Christian simplicity and modesty that become holiness" (1 Tim. 2:9-10; 1 Pet. 3:3-4); "Songs, literature, and entertainments not to the glory of God; the theater, the ball room, the circus, and like places; also, lotteries and games of chance; looseness and impropriety of conduct; membership in or fellowship with oath-bound, secret orders or fraternities" (Jas. 4:4; 2 Cor. 6:14-17).

"Doing that which is enjoined in the Word of God," on the other hand, included "Being courteous to all men"; "Contributing to the support of the ministry and the church and its work, according to the ability which God giveth"; "Being helpful to those who are of the household of faith, in love forbearing one another"; "Loving God with all the heart, soul, mind, and strength"; "Attending faithfully all the ordinances of God, and the means of grace, including the public worship of God, the ministry of the Word, the Sacrament of the Lord's Supper; searching the Scriptures and meditating therein; family and private devotions"; "Seeking to do good to the bodies and souls of men; feeding the hungry, clothing the naked, visiting the sick and imprisoned, and ministering to the needy, as opportunity and ability are given"; "Pressing upon the attention of the unsaved the claims of the gospel, inviting them to the house of the Lord, and trying to compass their salvation."[14]

---

14. *Manual*, 1932, pp. 33-36. The General Rules were rearranged and revised by an amendment adopted at the 1976 General Assembly and ratified by

As noted above, the substance of the General Rules and much of the wording had come from Bresee's 1898 *Manual*. Bresee had introduced them under the caption "Church Membership" and had used in the introductory paragraph the phrase "It is expected" rather than "It is required." The Scripture citations regarding dress and worldliness had been added, as had the prohibition of "membership in or fellowship with oathbound secret orders or fraternities." Bresee's warning against "the indulgence of pride in dress or living" had contained the added words, "the laying up of treasures on earth."

What were known as the Special Rules were not included in the Constitution formulated in 1928. They were placed in a separate section. These provisions paralleled a portion of Bresee's *Manual* of 1898 titled "Special Advices." Included was a statement on the support of the church which urged tithing as the basic financial plan for maintaining local, district, and denominational interests. The 1932 General Assembly adopted a resolution declaring that "storehouse tithing," defined as "faithfully and regularly placing the tithe in that church to which the member belongs," is "clearly both . . . scriptural and practical," a statement printed in the appendix to the *Manual*.[15]

Temperance and prohibition were given a separate paragraph in the Special Rules. It was held that "the Holy Scriptures and human experience alike condemn the use of intoxicating drinks as a beverage. . . . The manufacture and sale of intoxicating liquors for such purpose is a sin against God and the human race." Total abstinence from all intoxicants "is the Christian rule for the individual" and total prohibition of the traffic in intoxicants "is the duty of civil government." Unfermented wine and unleavened bread alone could be used in the sacrament of the Lord's Supper.[16]

The Special Rules also carried a strong statement on marriage and divorce in which it was declared that "the marriage covenant

the districts as required for constitutional amendments. For this reason, they are given in greater detail here than would otherwise be expected; *Manual*, 1980, pp. 37-40.

15. Ibid., p. 268.

16. Ibid., p. 44. The statement that "the Holy Scriptures and human experience alike condemn the use of intoxicating drinks as a beverage" was later (1976) changed to read, "The Holy Scriptures and human experience *together justify the condemnation* of the use of intoxicating drinks as a beverage" (*Manual*, 1980, p. 50, emphasis added).

is morally binding so long as both shall live, and, therefore, may not be dissolved at will." Persons divorced under civil law where "the scriptural ground for divorce, namely, adultery" does not exist and who are subsequently remarried "are living in adultery, and are unworthy of membership in the Church of the Nazarene." Ministers of the church were "positively forbidden" to solemnize marriages of persons "not having the scriptural right to marry."[17] The statement that people remarried after divorce not occasioned by infidelity "are living in adultery" caused some uneasiness that eventually led to its modification.[18]

The appendix also reported a judiciary action on divorce to the effect that one who married a person previously divorced "unscripturally" would be barred from church membership even if his individual case otherwise met the requirements for such membership.[19]

Several other ethical items were included in the appendix to the 1932 *Manual*. A somewhat legalistic[20] interpretation was given to the prohibition against membership in oathbound secret orders when it was ruled that Nazarenes might not maintain insurance policies with such organizations even though "the fees are paid for this purpose only and there is no fellowship with the organization."[21]

On the other hand, it was ruled that a person employed in a store either as clerk or manager who was obliged to sell tobacco would not be "violating the letter *[sic]* of the Manual."[22]

A resolution that had been adopted by the 1928 General Assembly was included in the *Manual* appendix to the effect that "this General Assembly [goes] on record as being unqualifiedly opposed to our people's patronizing promiscuous bathing places."[23]

---

17. Ibid., pp. 44-45.

18. *Manual*, 1972, pp. 49-51. The Special Rules were rewritten extensively in the 1976 statement of the church's ethical and behavioral standards; *Manual*, 1980, pp. 45-56.

19. *Manual*, 1932, p. 261.

20. When legalism is defined as concern for the act without regard for the motive.

21. *Manual*, 1932, p. 261.

22. Ibid. Not the spirit but certainly the letter of the *Manual* would be violated.

23. Ibid., p. 263.

The 1932 General Assembly rejoiced that while "there may be some difference on minor points of activities as a church, we are a united people on the essentials of our holy religion." There seemed to be "no disposition on the part of the church to lower its standard in doctrine and practice."

There was still need for caution, however. The church must not, it said, "in any way yield to the subtle influence of the spirit of this modern age relating to the questions of Sabbath desecration, immodesty in dress and behavior, seeking for worldly pleasure or honor, and disregard for our church law and standard of right." Special concern must also be given to "maintain a proper reverence for the house of God . . . that it shall always be known as a house of prayer and worship." No part of the church building "shall ever be used for social or entertainment gatherings, or as a place of banqueting."[24]

In addition to official positions on Nazarene life-style, there were generally honored extensions of the published standards. The feminine use of "makeup," lipstick and rouge, was almost universally taboo. In some areas, wedding rings were condemned— although a 1944 ruling by the Board of General Superintendents declared that the statement concerning "the wearing of gold as adornment does not apply to the plain band wedding ring," a position reaffirmed in a 1947 meeting.[25]

Changing attitudes toward some of these particulars were to lead to occasional defections, both to the left and to the right. The church was forced to face the issue of extreme interpretations of its standards in the early and middle 1950s when it repudiated extreme positions and settled on a moderate, albeit still conservative, course.

The Special Rules, together with occasional actions taken by a General Assembly regarding matters of individual behavior, were an effort to close what might be considered loopholes in the General Rules. The General Rules did contain specifics governing conduct. But they tended to deal more with broader principles. In 1976, the church would revise both General and Special Rules, declaring its purpose to "relate timeless biblical principles to con-

---

24. Ibid., pp. 277-78.
25. Minutes, Board of General Superintendents, meetings of Jan. 8, 1944, and June 17, 1947.

temporary society." As "an international expression of the body of Christ," the church accepts its responsibility "to seek ways to particularize the Christian life so as to lead to a holiness ethic." The particulars given are to be understood as "guides and helps to holy living."[26]

C. Holiness Preaching and Experience

Not only was the character of the church as a holiness body seen in its statements of doctrine and in its guidelines for conduct, but it was also evident in the emphasis placed on preaching and experiencing the grace of entire sanctification. All Nazarene ministers were and are required to give testimony to a personal experience of sanctifying grace. By the same token, all Nazarene ministers were and are expected to be holiness preachers.

A rather typical pattern had developed in which the morning worship hour on Sunday was usually given to some aspect of the doctrine, experience, or life of holiness. Concerned members of the congregation were invited to come for prayer at the conclusion of the sermon. Most revival series opened with several sermons on entire sanctification, often as related to concern for the conversion of others. Midweek services typically made time for personal testimonies, many of which were to experiences of sanctifying grace.

An examination of sermons and sermon outlines in the *Preacher's Magazine* during the 1930s reveals that most holiness preaching was topical in form. Few ministers who submitted material had developed the art of expository preaching, although many topical sermons were biblically based. The preaching tended to emphasize the "triumphal" aspects of Christian experience; rarely was there serious grappling with the perplexing problems of relating humanity to holiness. There was more concern for the moment of experience than for the continuing life. Yet the public preaching of entire sanctification led a continuing stream of believers into the grace.

The pattern for experiencing entire sanctification was simple, although it might be stated in various ways. Christians were urged to acknowledge their need of a deeper work of grace and to respond to its offer by coming to the altar at the front of the sanctuary for prayer. They were taught to consecrate their persons,

---

26. Cf. *Manual*, 1980, p. 47.

talents, possessions, and relationships to God with "no strings attached." They were instructed to ask specifically for the sanctifying fullness of the Holy Spirit. A final step was appropriating faith, which might be presented either as a determined grasp of God's promise based on one's conviction of the completeness of his consecration, or as a spontaneous reaction at the end of a process of "dying out." Whatever the conception of faith, it was to be sealed by a "witness of the Spirit," an inner assurance or rest that God had responded to the prayers offered by the impartation of His Spirit's fullness.

II. AN EVANGELISTIC CHURCH

Closely related to self-perception as a holiness church was a constant emphasis on revivalism. Holiness cannot be separated from the urge to evangelize. This was the underlying motivation for missions, at home and abroad. While the church's missionaries manned hospitals in Africa and China and conducted schools on a number of fields, the primary thrust of missions in the Church of the Nazarene was evangelism and church building.

At home, the prevailing pattern in the local churches was to conduct at least two revivals or evangelistic campaigns each year, from 10 days to three weeks or even longer in duration. In the fall of 1933, a total of 126 ministers—a number of them accompanied by singers and musicians—were listed in the *Herald of Holiness* as evangelists.[27] In addition, pastors often exchanged meetings or called district superintendents or other denominational officials to minister to their congregations.

The revival emphasis was consistently stressed in the church's official organ. Editor Wiley opened the Silver Jubilee Anniversary number of the *Herald of Holiness* with a lead editorial on "The Christ of History." It is the Christ of history who raises up men and movements for the specific purpose of evangelism, he wrote. "We believe that this is true of the movement known as the Church of the Nazarene." It was not by mere chance that "a new spiritual life suddenly burst through the encrustments of ecclesiastical formalism, in the East and the West and the South." Nor was it mere chance that "those who were animated by the same Spirit were

---

27. HH, vol. 22, no. 40 (Oct. 18, 1933), pp. 31-32, "Evangelists' Slates."

soon brought together in organic unity." The growth of the church was evidence that the Christ of history had led and was leading on.[28]

In the same issue, General Superintendent Williams wrote an article on "The Next Twenty-five Years." The purpose for which the church exists, he said, is threefold: To give the gospel to the whole world; to make God more real to the world; and to carry on a program of "real and effective Holy Ghost evangelism." Williams continued, "Altars are to be kept filled with hungry souls seeking personal contact and reconciliation with God. Revivals are to be held that will reach communities with real personal salvation." The church must never become an organization functioning just for itself. "It must reach out beyond itself and save the world from sin and spiritual darkness."[29]

Wiley returned to the same theme a month later. "Evangelism must be our constant watchword," he wrote. "This is the world's need." Human programs can never change the hearts of men. "Only Christ can save America. Only Christ can speak peace to a perplexed and troubled world."[30]

J. B. Chapman added his eloquent voice to the theme. "New eras of progress in our movement have usually been marked by a revival of evangelistic interest," he wrote. In spite of the stringency of the times economically, many ministers were announcing their entrance into the field of evangelism. "Our people will respond," he wrote, "and our work will reach out into new proportions and into new fields."[31]

Kansas City District Superintendent N. B. Herrell described "A District Superintendent's Inventory" during the Silver Anniversary Year. One of his major points was:

> Evangelism is our watchword and song. It is the message of angel, prophet, priest and king. It gives life to our services, and strength to our departments. It is the glory of Christ and the hope of the church. The Church of the Nazarene is the evangelistic movement of today and our responsibility is measured by our opportunity. Second blessing holiness evangelism is the crying need of the church and the only hope of the world.[32]

---

28. HH, vol. 22, no. 31 (Oct. 25, 1933), p. 1.
29. Ibid., p. 3.
30. HH, vol. 22, no. 35 (Nov. 22, 1933), p. 5.
31. Ibid., p. 7.
32. HH, vol. 22, no. 28 (Oct. 4, 1933), p. 14.

Professor A. S. London, a lay Sunday School evangelist based in Oklahoma City, wrote on "The Searching Passion in Sunday School Evangelism" in which he averred that "a compassionate concern should be the constant attitude of every saved man and woman toward every unsaved boy or girl. Compassion for our unsaved pupils and friends as manifested in broken hearts is our secret in accomplishing our task."[33]

"News of the Churches" was consistently news of successful revival meetings. Pastor Arthur C. Morgan wired from Henryetta, Okla., that Jarrette and Dell Aycock had just closed their sixth and best campaign with the Henryetta church with more than 125 seekers. Twenty-two persons joined the church, bringing the net gain in membership for the year to 113.[34]

The Toronto, Ohio, church reported a four-Sunday tent revival in July, 1933, with Evangelist Earl Stillion in which there were "some two hundred seekers"; and Evangelist Howard W. Sweeten was with Pastor L. G. Milby in First Church, Champaign, Ill. "Good crowds with good interest and seekers are becoming happy finders every night, about forty in the last three nights" was the report.[35]

Indianapolis Ray Street Church telegraphed that the church had just closed a "wonderful revival" with Evangelists Holland and Lela London and Haskell and Deletta London in which there were 250 seekers, 25 new church members, and 1,164 present in Sunday School the last Sunday.[36]

Not all evangelism was relegated to special services. Pastors were expected to be soul winners and were asked to report annually the number of persons coming to pray at the altars of the church in response to evangelistic invitations. By tradition, the Sunday evening service was the "evangelistic service" of the week. Pastor Raymond Browning of Columbus, Ohio, reported that "not a single Sunday night this year [1933] has gone by without souls praying through at the altar in our church."[37]

---

33. Ibid., pp. 12-13.
34. Ibid., p. 23.
35. Ibid.
36. Ibid.
37. HH, vol. 22, no. 33 (Nov. 8, 1933), p. 21.

III. Interchurch Relationships

Both in its Articles of Faith and in frequent pronouncements in its publications, the Church of the Nazarene stood staunchly on the conservative side of the controversy over "modernism" that dominated the 1920s and persisted into the '30s in American church life.

Yet the extremes of fundamentalism and the apparent lovelessness of many of its adherents repelled most Nazarenes. While L. A. Reed in his popular *Herald of Holiness* column "Religious News of the Week" expressed sympathy for conservative Presbyterians in their futile defense of J. Gresham Machen,[38] Managing Editor D. Shelby Corlett a month earlier distinguished Nazarenes from "the fundamentalists." He deplored fundamentalism's dogmatic adherence to premillennialism, rejection of entire sanctification, and "the manner in which some of these leaders assume the position of judges over God's heritage"—the last of which was deemed "absolutely disgusting."[39]

General Superintendent J. B. Chapman early sensed the dangers of an ultraconservative attitude both for theology and for the prosecution of the work of the church. In "The Menace of the Reactionary," a front-page *Herald* article, Chapman noted that the early leadership of the church had been young in years. By 1933, the preponderance of the leaders had reached the age of 50. This, said Chapman, "speaks well for counsel, but constitutes a menace for war."

"Many of our captains have sailed the sea gloriously, but they want to slow down to come into harbor so their ships can dock without shock. Such leadership constitutes a menace," Chapman continued. There is danger in leadership "verbally aggressive, but passionately ultraconservative and reactionary."

It was not youth in years for which he pled, Chapman wrote, but for an aggressiveness and adaptability that rejects the "subtle pessimism which passes for 'carefulness'" and adopts "plans so big and so absorbing that we shall all have to get up an hour earlier every morning and work an hour later every night to even get a part of [the] plans executed."[40]

---

38. HH, vol. 24, no. 9 (May 18, 1935), p. 14.
39. HH, vol. 24, no. 5 (Apr. 20, 1935), p. 4.
40. HH, vol. 22, no. 8 (May 17, 1933), p. 1.

While fully aware of the dangers of theological liberalism, Nazarenes were not antiecumenical in attitude. A statement from the Federal Council of Churches on the social ideals of Christianity was reprinted in the *Herald of Holiness*[41] and an FCC statement on marriage and divorce was quoted in full with approval[42] as was the FCC's "Summons to Spiritual Advance" for 1934.[43] At the same time, the issue that carried the FCC's "Summons" reprinted an article from the *Pentecostal Herald* by G. W. Ridout blasting the "social gospel."[44] An item later that year called the social gospel "Another Half-gospel" and criticized it for trying to "cure the individual by offering a remedy for society at large."[45]

Yet the Nazarenes tended to hold aloof from councils and associations of churches. As late as 1957, the General Board deemed Nazarene membership in the National Association of Evangelicals "inadvisable" and voted to continue "our traditional policy of kindly cooperation without affiliation" with the National Holiness Association. The church did, however, accept membership in some of the units of the NAE and many Nazarenes worked with local, county, or state affiliates of the NHA. The church later affiliated with the NHA as a denomination.

Nazarene scruples relating to the NHA centered in what had been the association's early opposition to organized holiness, and its operation of a foreign missionary program. It was felt that competition for missionary funds would develop, and Nazarene money would be siphoned off into the NHA overseas work. Both of these objections tended to lose their force with the passing of the years.

Reluctance to affiliate denominationally with the National Association of Evangelicals centered around two quite different considerations. One was a theological stance thought to be specifically opposed to the Wesleyan concept of entire sanctification. When the NAE was organized in 1942, three of the four largest member churches were Pentecostal (the Assemblies of God; the Church of God of Cleveland, Tenn.; and the Church of the Four Square Gospel), and the fourth was the National Association of Free Will Bap-

---

41. HH, vol. 21, no. 50 (Mar. 8, 1933), pp. 4-5.
42. HH, vol. 22, no. 10 (May 31, 1933), pp. 11-12.
43. HH, vol. 22, no. 49 (Feb. 28, 1934), p. 32.
44. Ibid., p. 17.
45. HH, vols. 23, no. 40 (Dec. 22, 1934), p. 4.

tists. A second qualm, a bit more nebulous, was the feeling of R. T. Williams and J. B. Chapman that the association was formed to take an adversary stance toward the Federal Council of Churches. The Nazarenes, as J. B. Chapman was fond of saying, were at their best when preaching a positive gospel and not when fighting others.[46]

IV. SOCIAL AWARENESS

Nazarene awareness of social and economic issues was not extensive, although in May of 1933 Editor Wiley cited the social concerns of late 19th-century revivalism,[47] a theme most ably developed by historian Timothy Smith in *Revivalism and Social Reform.*[48] Nazarenes were not immune to the dynamics that led American evangelicals into what David Moberg titled *The Great Reversal,*[49] a tendency that reached its lowest point during the period from 1930 to 1960. Richard Lovelace traces the process that led evangelicals to equate social action with theological liberalism back into the 19th century, even before the Civil War. Divergent views among evangelicals regarding slavery led large segments of the American church to affirm that the gospel should deal only with "spiritual matters" and not engage in social applications of its message except as they might relate to personal morality. The widespread acceptance of premillennial dispensationalism led to despair for social improvement short of the return of Christ and the establishment of His millennial kingdom. The result was a view of prophecy that was "evangelistically active but socially passive." From the era of Dwight L. Moody on, much of the financial support for evangelical causes came from wealthy Christian lay people whose political commitments were totally conservative and devoted to laissez-faire capitalism.

Even more decisive was the early 20th-century polarization between evangelicals and "social gospellers" with liberal theologi-

---

46. PGB, 1957, pp. 9-10. The point concerning Nazarene reluctance to engage in polemics was mentioned by Dr. Samuel Young, meeting of the History Commission, June 7, 1982.

47. HH, vol. 22, no. 10 (May 31, 1933), p. 5.

48. Cf. chap. 1, fn. 1.

49. David Moberg, *The Great Reversal* (Philadelphia: Lippincott, 1972). Cf. the earlier work of Carl F. H. Henry, *The Uneasy Conscience of Modern Fundamentalism* (Grand Rapids: William B. Eerdmans Publishing Co., 1947).

cal orientation. The fundamentalist controversy of the 1920s tended to identify evangelism with fundamentalism and social action
with liberalism.[50]

The depression of the early '30s did tend to push economic
concerns to the fore. Early in 1933, Wiley quoted with approval a
statement from the FCC *Bulletin* to the effect that "economic ex-
ploitation, wherein the acquisitive instinct has not alone outstripped but submerged the sense of social responsibility, is bearing
and eating its own bitter fruit today."

Wiley viewed much of the misery of the depression as "the
consequence of greed fostered by an unchristian commercial system" and recalls that it was "against the rich who hoard up ungodly gains that the apostle James hurls his anathemas." Said
Wiley, "It is this spirit of covetousness that makes fertile soil for the
ungodly Red propaganda."

The economic situation of the day, the editor continued, "demands some sort of a Christian readjustment that will guarantee
employment and a just wage to every deserving individual." The
deadliest damage "this unchristian system produces is the breaking
down of courage and self-respect, initiative and hopefulness."[51]

The labor movement was much in the public mind during the
troubled '30s with the National Labor Relations Act of 1935 and
the Fair Labor Standards Act of 1938. The rights of workers to
organize and the obligations of employers to accept collective bar-
gaining were firmly established. The Council of Industrial Organizations (CIO) was set up in the middle 1930s in competition
with the older American Federation of Labor (AFL).

Nazarenes, like their brethren in other evangelical circles,
were slow to relate to the labor movement, although most of them
belonged to the laboring class. The widespread practice of scheduling union meetings on Sunday turned off many. Others were
repelled by the violence that erupted on occasion on picket lines
during strikes. The class hatred and bitterness often generated during labor disputes was felt to be out of harmony with the spirit of
Christian love.

An exception worthy of note was the work of Paul Coleman,

---

50. Richard E. Lovelace, *Dynamics of Spiritual Life: An Evangelical Theology of
Renewal* (Downers Grove, Ill.: InterVarsity Press, 1980), pp. 375-79.
51. HH, vol. 21, no. 43 (Jan. 18, 1933), p. 2.

pastor of Flint, Mich., First Church from 1932 until his death 20 years later. Coleman was able to win the confidence of both labor and management to the extent that he was often called upon to serve as mediator and conciliator in the seething Michigan labor market.

Not all Nazarenes were happy with the estrangement between the spiritual and the social. Managing Editor D. Shelby Corlett commented on a statement by "a man of some reputation in our church" to the effect that "we as a denomination have been very zealous in pressing the claims of personal salvation but that we have done nothing for society as a whole."

Corlett agreed that as a whole, Nazarenes had done little to enforce the responsibilities of Christian citizenship. "What concerted effort have we ever put forth to arouse our church to support some outstanding moral legislation, or to cooperate with those good agencies now at work in an endeavor to raise the moral tone of our nation?" he queried.

Even the church's own standard for membership had been largely ignored, a standard that required "seeking to do good to the bodies and souls of men; feeding the hungry, clothing the naked, visiting the sick and imprisoned, and ministering to the needy."

"What have we done to overcome racial prejudices," Corlett asked, "to support movements in correcting economic and social evils, to teach the absolute sinfulness of war, to support clean government, etc., etc.?" Perhaps the unnamed critic was correct, he concluded: "We have done nothing for society as a whole."[52]

During the early and middle 1930s, General Superintendent Chapman answered questions in a column in the *Herald of Holiness* titled "The Question Box," a practice he had started during his eight-year stint as editor before elevation to the general superintendency in 1928. Asked early in 1934 about his views on capital punishment, Chapman wrote with balance and clarity:

> While the State has the right to demand "an eye for an eye, a tooth for a tooth," and a life for a life, if I were revising the criminal laws of America today I believe I would make life imprisonment with no hope or plan for pardon the punishment for capital crimes, and I would speed up the processes of trials

52. HH, vol. 24, no. 1 (Mar. 23, 1935), p. 4.

and would make punishment as sure and as speedy as possible.[53]

The growing problem of divorce and remarriage was a concern to Nazarenes at the beginning of their second quarter-century. An example of this concern was a reprinted article from the *Free Methodist* commenting on two Reno divorces with subsequent remarriages in the family of President Franklin Roosevelt.[54]

Both Fascism and Communism were objects of expressed concern with the "Red menace" occupying the center of the stage. Adolf Hitler had become chancellor of Germany on January 30, 1933. Leland Stowe's *Nazi Means War* was quoted with the comment that "while Hitler declares that Germany does not want war, the psychology of the German nation is being directed to warlike ends." Hitler has the "Kaiser Mind." He doesn't want war until he is ready for it.[55]

Two months later, notice was taken of the actions of the Hitler-appointed bishop of the "Nazi church." Under personal orders from "der Fuhrer" pastors of Protestant churches and Roman Catholic priests not in sympathy with the national program for paganizing the church were being arrested. Fifteen hundred had already been taken into custody. This was said to be "an interesting item to those who are watching the 'signs of the times.'" In spite of the antagonism between Germany and Russia at the time, readers were warned to watch the relations between those two nations.[56]

The underlying atheism of Marxist communism drew chief concern from Nazarene observers. Editor Wiley noted that "nothing can possibly be more opposed to the spirit of Christ, or the type of society which Christianity seeks to build, than the Godless system commonly known as Communism." The appropriate action in meeting the menace, however, was considered to be not political but moral and spiritual—"as the early Church met the paganism of the first century, by a superior type of life, by resolute and unflinching adherence to the truth of God, and by Divine anointings with the Holy Spirit." Wiley concluded, "Christians must meet and

53. HH, vol. 23, no. 7 (May 5, 1934), p. 13.
54. HH, vol. 23, no. 23 (Aug. 25, 1934), p. 12.
55. HH, vol. 23, no. 11 (June 2, 1934), p. 15.
56. HH, vol. 23, no. 23 (Aug. 25, 1934), p. 14.

overcome by the blood of the Lamb and the word of their testimony."[57]

This was followed a week later by a warning of efforts to promote the cause of communism in the United States. The rejection by the labor movement of efforts to infiltrate its ranks is mentioned with appreciation. "Genuine holiness hates iniquity in proportion as it loves righteousness."[58]

Throughout 1935, a number of very strong statements were made. E. Stanley Jones' *Christ's Alternative to Communism* was noted with the comment that the only way to bring such an alternative into existence would be through divine intervention as "during the millennium."

In the meantime, however, the church could not ignore social problems. Along with the effort to make better individuals by regeneration must go efforts to purge society of its evils. An editorial in the *Herald of Holiness* affirmed: "While we work for the salvation of the individual drunkard, we must also do our utmost to overthrow the liquor traffic and endeavor to rid the world of that which makes drunkards; and such must be our attitude toward every social evil."[59]

Indeed, the repeal of prohibition was the major social concern of Nazarenes during this era. The question had been prominent in the presidential election campaign of 1932. The Republican National Convention opened in Chicago on Tuesday, June 14, as the Eighth General Assembly of the Church of the Nazarene was in its third day in Wichita, Kans. Tuesday afternoon, the assembly passed a resolution addressed to the convention and ordered it sent at once. The resolution commended the Republican party "for its stand in the years past for the enforcement of the Eighteenth Amendment." It went on to state the church's position "unanimously favoring the retention and rigorous enforcement" of prohibition and its opposition "to all measures to resubmit or repeal this supreme moral enactment in our basic law." Further, support was pledged to "the political party that evidences the moral courage needful to leadership in this great issue."[60]

---

57. HH, vol. 23, no. 18 (July 21, 1934), p. 3.
58. HH, vol. 23, no. 19 (July 28, 1934), pp. 3, 6.
59. HH, vol. 24, no. 14 (June 22, 1935), p. 4.
60. GAJ, 1932, p. 46.

The Democratic Convention did not meet until June 26, but the party position with respect to the repeal of prohibition was well known. Nevertheless the Resolutions Committee of the General Assembly with R. Wayne Gardner as chairman and A. K. Bracken as secretary prepared a resolution addressed to the convention. The resolution put the Church of the Nazarene, "representing a constituency of some 300,000," as unanimously on record as "unqualifiedly opposed to the repeal or modification of the Eighteenth Amendment." The Democrats were urged "to take a righteous stand for the enforcement of prohibition as it is now enacted in the Constitution and in the Laws of the United States."[61]

A third resolution was adopted Thursday morning commending President Hoover on his stand at the convention "on law enforcement and prohibition by the adoption of the law enforcement plank now in [the] presidential platform."[62] The commendation went for nothing, however, and the Democratic landslide in November is attributed to Hoover's "washing out of the prohibition issue in his acceptance speech" at the Republican convention.[63]

During the summer of 1932 and into early 1933 the *Herald* carried on an unremitting campaign in favor of the temperance cause. As far as political results were concerned, the effort was fruitless. In February, 1933, the lame duck Congress then sitting voted the Twenty-first Amendment repealing prohibition. Repeal was ratified by late fall—the final vote necessary coming from the Utah House of Representatives at 3:30 p.m., December 5, 1933.

After repeal became a fact, the recurrent theme in the *Herald of Holiness* through 1934 and 1935 was, "Repeal has failed," pointing out the evils that had been set loose. "The Eighteenth Amendment is lost!" mourned P. P. Belew, superintendent of the Georgia District. "America has retreated from an ideal! The wheels of civilization have reversed! Satan has scored a great victory! By the use of every known strategy the wets have prevailed in one of the most invidious attacks made against law and order!"[64]

---

61. Ibid., p. 51.
62. Ibid., p. 52.
63. HH, vol. 21, no. 36 (Nov. 30, 1932), p. 4.
64. HH, vol. 22, no. 47 (Feb. 14, 1934), p. 12.

Summary

In 1933, its Silver Anniversary, the Church of the Nazarene was a small denomination, thinly scattered across the United States with a handful of congregations in Canada and the British Isles. But its ideals were high and its self-understanding reasonably clear. The Nazarenes were committed to what they conceived to be scriptural holiness both in theory and in practice. They held their mission in the family of churches to be somewhat elitist, but totally given to carrying the gospel of full salvation to all whom they could reach. Their social concerns were real if not extensive, and there was special interest in issues of temperance and public morality. They moved into their second quarter-century with faith and determination.

3

The Lean Years

The second 25 years of Nazarene history spanned a period of unprecedented worldwide change. Modern history's deepest economic depression was followed by the holocaust of World War II. Both brought vast social and political changes around the world. With prophetic insight, Methodist lay missionary-statesman John R. Mott said early in 1933, "The next quarter of a century will be the most crucial period in the history of the world."[1]

I. Depression and the New Deal

The Silver Jubilee came at a critical time. The world was wallowing in unparalleled economic decline, the Great Depression that followed the boom of the 1920s. It began in the United States on the "Black Thursday" of October 24, 1929, when the New York stock market virtually collapsed. Hundreds of thousands of investors, large and small and most of them operating on borrowed funds, were wiped out.[2]

In quick succession, the bottom dropped out from under agricultural prices; factories closed as ability to buy their goods dried up; per capita annual income declined drastically; unemployment soared from 1.6 million to 12.8 million, from 3 percent to 25 percent of the labor force. Weekly wages for workers still employed in

---

1. Cited as "a recent statement," HH, vol. 22, no. 31 (Oct. 25, 1933), p. 29.
2. Cf. standard histories such as Arthur S. Link and William B. Catton, *American Epoch: A History of the United States Since 1900,* 4th ed., 3 vols. (New York: Alfred A. Knopf, 1973), 2:101 ff.; James T. Patterson, *America in the Twentieth Century: A History* (New York: Harcourt Brace Jovanovich, 1976), pp. 197 ff.; and John A. Garraty, *The American Nation: A History of the United States,* 4th ed. (New York: Harper and Row, 1979), pp. 648 ff.

industry fell from an average of $25.00 in 1929 to $16.73 in 1933. America's banking system began to show signs of unusual stress late in 1931 following the summer collapse of Europe's economy.

When the 1932 presidential campaign got under way in the United States, President Herbert Hoover's administration was at its lowest ebb. Like most Americans, the president had assumed that the crash represented only an unusually severe dip in the business cycle. When the crisis worsened, attempts to meet it were too little too late.

The landslide election of Franklin Delano Roosevelt in 1932 and his inauguration as president on March 4, 1933, signalled a series of bold moves to stabilize the shattered economy—not all of them successful. Two days after his inauguration, the president closed all banks for a four-day period. Within four hours after a special session of Congress convened on March 9, the Emergency Banking Act was passed. Only the strongest banks were allowed to reopen and then under Treasury Department supervision.

A series of other measures followed. The Federal Deposit Insurance Corporation was established to restore public confidence in the banking system. A Civilian Conservation Corps was set up to give employment to young men under army supervision. A Home Owners Loan Corporation was given funds to buy home mortgages from banks with low interest, long-term repayment. A new Public Works Administration for large-scale projects was funded with $3.3 billion. The Federal Emergency Relief Administration made grants to the states for assistance to individual families, and the Civil Works Administration set up an emergency work relief program for the winter of 1933-34. The Tennessee Valley Authority and the National Recovery Administration pretty well completed the steps initiated during the first "100 days" between Roosevelt's inauguration and the June 16 adjournment of the special session of Congress.

Other moves followed during Roosevelt's first term. The first New Deal was followed by a second New Deal. The Works Progress Administration, the Social Security Act (from which at first ministers and church employees were excluded), and the National Labor Relations (Wagner) Act were all designed to offer relief to the beleagured laboring man. Income taxes on larger incomes were sharply increased.

Rural America benefited from the Rural Electrification program and other steps which almost doubled farm income between 1932 and 1935. On the other hand, drought conditions in the lower Midwest led to the beginning of the Dust Bowl in 1934 that spread until it covered 50 million acres of farm and grazing land and forced the migration and resettlement of thousands of small farmers—many of them Nazarenes from the rural churches of the Dakotas, Kansas, eastern Colorado, and the Texas and Oklahoma panhandles.

Nazarene reaction to it all was mixed. Like their fellow citizens, virtually all Nazarenes were affected by the hardships under which their nation and their world labored. Nazarene strength had been centered pretty much in rural mid-America where the collapse of the agricultural enterprise was most keenly felt. Urban Nazarenes were chiefly blue collar workers, and thousands lost their jobs.

Many were deeply suspicious of the remedial steps being taken in Washington. The slaughter of farm animals and the plowing under of crops to raise prices was widely condemned. Some followed the more radical dispensationalists in seeing the mark of the beast in the Blue Eagle of the NRA. Not entirely with tongue in cheek, J. G. Morrison wrote to his friend and later his successor as Foreign Missions secretary, Pittsburgh District Superintendent C. Warren Jones, "Someday when the democratic Utopia gets to working right there's going to be a house for every family, a hen for every pot, a diamond for every finger, and a pension and a government job for every good democrat."[3]

Roosevelt's leadership in the repeal of the prohibition amendment prejudiced many evangelicals, including many Nazarenes, against him. The president's sponsorship of a bill permitting the brewing and sale of beer with 3.2 percent alcohol content led some to comment that they were "96.8 percent" with the president. The partial success of many of the administration's measures and the gradual improvement of the economy resulted in a larger degree of acceptance for the New Deal.

The general reaction of the church to the suffering of its members and others in the community was one of deep compassion

---

3. J. G. Morrison letter to C. Warren Jones, June 27, 1934 (Archives, Department of Foreign Missions, correspondence). Cf. "Christian Youth and the New Deal" for a more balanced view of the changes taking place, HH, vol. 24, no. 31 (Oct. 19, 1935), pp. 14-15.

compounded with a certain sense of helplessness. A number of congregations established limited funds supported by special offerings taken during their midweek service to partially offset the most pressing needs. Personal acts of compassion were legion as help was given and received on an individual basis. Biblical promises relating to the supply of basic human needs were cherished and often quoted. Prayer and dependence on God took on new meaning for pastors and people alike, and adversity proved for many the occasion for a tested and proven faith.

II. The Silver Anniversary Observance

Despite the dark clouds of economic privation, the Silver Jubilee was observed with fitting notice. The December 28, 1932, issue of the *Herald of Holiness* carried a front page editorial by Editor H. Orton Wiley titled "A New Year's Wish." The lead was a quotation from 3 John 2: "Beloved, I wish . . . that thou mayest prosper and be in health, even as thy soul prospereth."

"We are living in times of wide-spread perplexity," Wiley wrote, "the effect of which is to bring spiritual men and women closer to God in dependence and fellowship." The world distress of the times is at base "a moral question." The commercialism which exploits and uses men to make money to satisfy the greed of the few and provide for luxurious display is, Wiley said in quoting Joseph Fort Newton's strong words, "Nothing but organized atheism. It is not only unchristian, it is unhuman."

"We are just entering the Silver Jubilee year of the Church of the Nazarene," the editor wrote. The plan was to make the year one of praise and thanksgiving for God's "marvellous blessings over the period of a quarter of a century." Nazarenes should review the past with a view to "re-estimating and revaluing its blessings. . . . We doubt not we shall find that God has given us health and prosperity beyond that accorded to many others—certainly far beyond what we deserve."[4]

The following week, Wiley reviewed the labors of the first 25 years. It had not been without its hardships. Often it was a case of making bricks without straw. "Our colleges have had to build the

---

4. HH, vol. 21, no. 40 (Dec. 28, 1932), p. 1.

wagon while carrying the load. . . . The missionary cause, whether at home or abroad, has labored under tremendous pressure, and the Publishing House has faced the difficulties incident to business in such abnormal times as these."

But for the time, the call is to "straighten our backs and lift up our heads. This is the year of jubilee! Let us cast our burdens upon the Lord for He will sustain us. Let us enter His gates with thanksgiving, and celebrate the year with praises to God." In a burst of eloquence unusual for Wiley, he wrote:

> Let the voice of the aggrieved be stilled by fresh spiritual adjustments; let those occupied with trifles climb to higher altitudes for broader vision; let those borne down unduly by care and anxiety seek to attain a new level of faith in God; let the whiners and complainers take a vacation in the mount of transfiguration; and let everyone, preacher or layman, old or young, seek to make this a year of spiritual enrichment and renewed strength.
>
> If ever a people had just cause for shouting the high praises of God, it is the Church of the Nazarene. God has given us a year of jubilee in order that our labors *for* Him, may not obscure our communion *with* Him. And we doubt not, if the year be spent in joyfulness and praise, that its close will witness marked advances in every department of the work.[5]

General Superintendent Chapman published "A Silver Anniversary Address" in the same issue. He observed that the work of the church after its first quarter-century would be quite different. The early growth, from slightly more than 10,000 to almost 120,000 members, had largely come about by bringing together the converts and reaping the results of the independent holiness evangelism that marked the latter part of the 19th and early part of the 20th centuries.

In spite of the fact that "come-outism" had been discouraged and many had urged the holiness people to "stick to their old churches," a large group of more or less independent holiness preachers and people all over the country had come into being. "This polyglot ministry and unorganized people constituted the raw material which it was the task of the Church of the Nazarene to utilize and make effective," Chapman observed.

The resulting denomination was not split off a parent organization, but "a fusion and union of individuals and minor bod-

5. HH, vol. 21, no. 41 (Jan. 4, 1933), p. 2.

ies who otherwise would not have been one people." The scattered adherents who had been gathered into the Church of the Nazarene were not "pressed together in the cold and held in place by frost." Rather, they were drawn together by a common doctrine and experience and "welded in the fires of Pentecost."

This "first major task" had been accomplished. Now it was time to "go out into the green timber and gather material for further building." The way to do this is to "pray down pentecostal revivals." Members must be taken into the church at the rate of 10 percent of the present membership every year—a rate the Nazarenes were so far comfortably exceeding—"in order that the 'mossbacks' will not become the dictators of a policy of conservatism and passivism that shall write 'Ichabod' over our door."[6]

In May, the general superintendents issued a proclamation specifying October 25 as the Silver Anniversary Day and the month of November as "the special period during which to celebrate the Silver Anniversary of the Church of the Nazarene in all our churches." It was to be "a month of special thanksgiving to God for His mercies in the past, and a month of special prayer for His continued favors upon us."[7] The biblical slogan for the anniversary celebration was "Speak unto my people that they go forward."

The proclamation named General Superintendent R. T. Williams and Youth Executive Secretary D. Shelby Corlett respectively chairman and secretary of a Silver Jubilee Anniversary Committee to draw up specific plans for the month-long celebration.

The committee responded with a week-by-week emphasis. October 29 was set aside as Rally Day with the goal of 200,000 in attendance at Sunday School. An offering received that day was to be used to liquidate local indebtedness to the publishing house—of which there was a considerable amount outstanding—and to satisfy other pressing local obligations.

November 5 was designated Church Appreciation Day. Emphasis was to be placed on the role of the church in bringing the gospel and continued inspiration to its members and its community.

The week preceding November 12 was set aside as a time of

---

6. Ibid., pp. 5-7. New Nazarenes received in 1932 were 24 percent of the membership. In 1933 and 1934 the rate was 20 percent each year. In 1935, it was 16 percent (GAJ, 1936, pp. 207 ff.).

7. HH, vol. 22, no. 7 (May 10, 1933), p. 16.

special devotion to God. "The deepening of the devotional life of the entire church is the most effective protection against every danger, such as formality, legalism, Pharisaism, worldliness, and sin," said Chairman Williams.

November 19 was designated a "great missionary day." Special prayer was urged for solution to the vast financial problems posed by fluctuating exchange rates since the United States had gone off the gold standard.

November 26, the last Sunday of the anniversary month, would witness an offering in every local church for the General Budget. A goal of $100,000 was suggested. The subsequent report showed receipts of slightly over $40,000.[8]

Williams closed his outline of the celebration events with words of challenge:

> I feel to praise God devoutly for the way He has helped the Church of the Nazarene through these financial storms. It is marvellous that we have not gone bankrupt. Great factories, banks, and mighty commercial organizations have gone to the wall after being in existence for a half a century and some longer. It is wonderful that God has helped us—a young church—to weather this storm as successfully as we have. We must not let down, we must do better and tighten the lines and improve every situation. A little sacrifice on the part of every Nazarene and our friends on November 26th will give us a glorious ending of these twenty-five years and make it possible to build in a greater and more effective way across the coming years.[9]

Nazarenes were heartened by reports of spiritual advance on many fronts. The *Herald of Holiness* and the missionary monthly *Other Sheep* carried news of local victories and gains in membership both at home and abroad. Buildings were dedicated, and revivals were reported.

At year's end, the church had received 19,161 members by profession of faith in the United States, Canada, and the British Isles, and had made a net gain of 9,887 worldwide.[10] Sixty-seven

---

8. HH, vol. 22, no. 42 (Jan. 10, 1934), p. 16.
9. HH, vol. 22, no. 28 (Oct. 4, 1933), p. 6.
10. The year 1933 saw a membership loss of 255 on foreign mission fields, chiefly due to losses in Africa (101), Cape Verde Islands (45), China (63), and Japan (85). The statistics of the Department of Foreign Missions at this period were not always accurate, and frequent disparities are noted between the annual

new churches were organized during the year with an addition of five on foreign fields.

Looking back over the 10 years previous (1923-33), General Church Secretary E. J. Fleming noted a total net increase of membership in the United States, Canada, and the British Isles of 61,274 members. The percentage of increase for 1933 (9.7) was the highest annual percentage gain for the decade with the exception of 1930, which had witnessed a net increase of 11.3 percent. The other side of the picture was that despite the membership gain, continued financial hardships had reduced total giving for the year by over $300,000.[11]

III. Financial Pressures

The year of the Silver Jubilee celebration, 1933, turned out to be the lowest point of the depression in the church's finances. Per capita giving had peaked in 1926 at $50.66. From there it plummeted to $23.55 for 1933. It was to be 10 years before the per capita climbed back to the level it had reached in the 1920s, and then only in depreciated dollars.

Of the total giving five years before in 1928, $3.17 per capita had gone for general interests and $3.41 for district expenses. General giving topped at $4.62 per capita in 1929. By 1933, it had bottomed out at $1.63, with $1.54 for district concerns. It should be noted, however, that general interests actually received a slightly larger percentage of the church's total income in 1933—7.71 percent in comparison with 6.25 percent in 1928.[12]

The 1932 General Assembly, apparently influenced by the general expectation that the depression would be of short duration, mandated general projects requiring a budget of $192,000 per year, of which $120,000 was earmarked for foreign missions. When receipts for the first quarter of 1933 averaged a meager 68 percent of the required amount, with no reserves, consternation reigned at

---

reports published in the *Herald of Holiness* and figures given in the departmental report to the General Assembly. Compare HH, vol. 22, no. 42 (Jan. 10, 1934), p. 16-17 and GAJ, 1936, p. 290 for an example.

11. HH, vol. 22, no. 42 (Jan. 10, 1934), p. 17.

12. PGB, 1936, p. 113. Per capita figures for total giving are taken from GAJ, 1980, p. 307.

headquarters. Cuts were made across the board.[13] Heroic efforts at fund raising and sacrificial response from church members reduced the shortfall for the year to approximately $10,000.[14]

Two events proved particularly crucial for the finances of the church. One was the banking panic and "holiday" of March, 1933. The Fidelity National Bank of Kansas City, in which general funds had been deposited, closed March 3 and went into bankruptcy receivership. The church's small ($8,593) but vitally important working fund was frozen. A mere 5 percent was made available within a week. General Superintendent Williams had foreseen the trouble coming, and on the eve of the national bank closing Publishing House Manager M. Lunn had drawn out a substantial amount of publishing house money in cash which he was able to share with headquarters.

It was July 22 before an additional 57 percent of general treasury funds was released when the Union National Bank took over Fidelity's assets and liabilities.[15] Ultimately, the full amount was recovered but in seriously depreciated dollars.

The situation in the spring of 1933 was critical. A total of $22,000 in checks had been mailed to overseas mission stations and must in some way be covered. The general superintendents acted immediately.

In 1932, at the suggestion of San Francisco layman George Kramer, a "Reserve Army" had been formed under the initiative of General Superintendent Williams and Publishing House Manager M. Lunn.

The "army" was to be composed of 10,000 persons each of whom would volunteer to send $1.00 not more than five times in any one year to meet emergencies at headquarters. The money was to be over and above general budgets, and no local church was to be credited with the giving. The Nazarene Publishing House subsidized all expenses in collecting and accounting for the funds so that all receipts were clear and available for immediate use in resolving whatever emergency prompted the call. The first appeal for volunteers to sign up for the Reserve Army had been issued September 14, 1932.

---

13. PGB, 1934, p. 90.
14. Ibid., pp. 90-91. The Publishing House contributed $1,000 to ministerial relief during the year.
15. PGB, 1934, pp. 73, 90.

When the banks closed, an immediate call was sent out to members of the Reserve Army. "On account of the bank moratorium, which ties up the funds for our Foreign Mission fields, the Church is faced with what we consider its greatest emergency," Williams said in issuing the call. Missionary credit in foreign fields would be ruined if the checks issued were to return unpaid. Missionaries would be left "stranded and hungry." Only prompt response by volunteers of the Reserve Army would "save our faithful missionaries."[16]

The call to the Reserve Army was backed up by stirring appeals for an Easter Emergency Offering on April 16. "Only by sacrifice can we continue," the church was told. "The program of salvation and relief at home and abroad must go on. We cannot give up and quit. To continue means self-denial, sacrifice, sharing. There is no other way."[17]

The effort paid off. General treasury receipts had been $9,688 in January and $7,878 in February. The amount rose to $16,142 in March and $30,392 in April. As a result, J. G. Morrison, who wore the hat of general treasurer for about 18 months during this period as well as heading the Foreign Missions Department, was able to report at the end of the year, "We owe no one but ourselves. . . . We have completed the year without outside loans. When we recall some of the gigantic debts which sister denominations have been forced to incur, during this year, this record furnishes at least a grain of comfort."[18]

The second event which severely impacted general finances occurred in April, 1933, when the United States went off the gold standard. As a result, U.S. currency was devalued by approximately 40 percent.

The consequences were particularly serious for foreign missions. Foreign exchange fluctuated wildly. In terms of American dollars, an exchange that had been favorable suddenly became anything but. The cost of living for overseas workers soared.

Compounding missionary problems was the determination at

---

16. HH, vol. 21, no. 51 (Mar. 15, 1933), p. 27.

17. HH, vol. 21, no. 50 (Mar. 8, 1933), p. 31. Cf. letters J. G. Morrison and M. Lunn to R. T. Williams, Aug. 10, 1932; J. G. Morrison and M. Lunn to members of the General Board, April 21, 1933; (Archives, R. T. Williams correspondence).

18. PGB, 1934, pp. 89-90.

headquarters not to go into debt for current operations. In the light of the long struggle ahead to regain a measure of fiscal adequacy, the decision was a wise one. But it meant that all who were supported by general funds were placed on drastically reduced stipends.

Home Mission and Church Extension funds were virtually eliminated. Overseas support was cut by one-third. The value of the dollar in foreign exchange markets continued to fall until it reached levels 50 and 60 percent below those prior to the April devaluation. The net result was the loss of almost two-thirds of the available funds in mission field treasuries.

Money was borrowed from the Nazarene Publishing House to stave off fiscal disasters in India, Guatemala, and Peru. Reporting as Foreign Missionary secretary early in January, 1934, Morrison said, "Now the question confronts us, what shall be done for the coming year. The regular monthly receipts do not warrant appropriations much in excess of the current year's remittance of two-thirds. But more must be appropriated or rigid adjustment downward must be effected."[19]

There was a marked difference in the effects of the depression at home and abroad. Overseas, dollars were not only more scarce; they were worth less as inflation eroded their value. In the United States and Canada, however, a mitigating circumstance was the "deflation" of the currency. Dollars were more scarce, but they were worth more in terms of buying power as commodity prices went down. As contrasted with the weakened dollar abroad, dollars at home bought much more. Prime steak sold for 10 cents per pound. Carrots were a penny per bunch. Day-old bread was priced at one cent per loaf. Yet suffering was real, and the compassionate ministries of the church and her members were taxed to the limit.

IV. THE CHALLENGE OF FOREIGN MISSIONS

The General Board meeting in January, 1934, faced the paradox of commendable growth in membership along with extreme economic hardship. While many denominations were noting net losses or were barely holding their own, the Nazarenes, as we have

---

19. Ibid., p. 70.

seen, had just recorded their second best annual membership gain in 10 years.[20]

The first report heard by the board was that of Morrison as Foreign Missions secretary. In what was actually an understatement, Morrison said, "The work of spreading holiness in mission fields, has, during the past twelve months, passed through unusual vicissitudes." A whole series of financial and administrative problems challenged the leadership of the church.

Always eloquent, Morrison saw the spiritual aspects of overseas missions as presenting unparalleled opportunities.

> This year has witnessed the finest ingathering of souls on mission fields that has ever been witnessed in their history. Each one is ablaze with revivals. The "break" in flint-hearted India, longed for, prayed for and toilsomely labored for these thirty years, has come. Campmeetings and revivals there are scenes of wholesale conversion and sanctification. Japan, in spite of her imperial politics, is the scene of a gracious awakening from end to end. China, amid its anarchy, banditry, turbulence, war and horror, clamors for Christ. South Africa is only limited in its soul-saving efforts by men and means. Latin America is awake to salvation possibilities—this is her day. The opportunities in British West Indies are limitless.[21]

A. Gazaland

One financial crisis had been successfully resolved in regard to the Gazaland field in Portuguese East Africa. In 1929, the Nazarenes had purchased a fine group of buildings at Manjacaze from the Methodist Episcopal church, then in the process of withdrawing from the field. This step was actually necessary to insure the continuation of the mission in Portuguese East Africa. Government regulations required ownership of permanent property in order to operate a mission, and Nazarene beginnings had been in leased facilities. The value of the property was estimated at $40,000. The Methodists were asking $25,000 but accepted an offer of $17,500. A down payment of $5,000 was made, with the balance to be paid in annual installments of $5,000 each for two years with the balance the third year.

However, in 1930, the financial situation worsened, and the

---

20. Hudson, *Religion in America*, p. 378; HH, vol. 22, no. 24 (Jan. 10, 1934), pp. 16-17.
21. PGB, 1934, p. 65.

payment due could not be made. Suffering themselves, the Methodists pressed for payment. It seemed that the property would be lost and along with it the Gazaland field. The Methodist board then agreed to reduce the indebtedness by $2,500 on condition that $5,000 be paid on September 1, 1933, and the remainder on September 1, 1934.

Prompt action by R. T. Williams in soliciting gifts beyond regular budgets from the New England, New York, Washington-Philadelphia, Pittsburgh, Ohio, and Chicago Central districts— where he held the spring and summer assemblies—enabled the treasurer to make the September 1, 1933, payment on schedule. With another call to the Reserve Army, the last $5,000 was paid on time in 1934.[22]

Morrison's list of other "outstanding needs" was staggering, to say the least. Japan, China, India, Palestine, Syria, Africa, Cape Verde, the British West Indies, Mexico, Guatemala, Peru, and Argentina were all pleading for help. The unspoken plaint became known as characteristic of J. G. Morrison, "Can't we do just a little bit more?"

B. The Problem of the "Irregulars"

The missions executive had other problems to present to the board. One of these was the number of "irregulars" raising all or part of their own expenses and going to the mission fields without authorization and sometimes without the knowledge of the Department of Foreign Missions. In a number of cases, their maintenance had fallen back on the missionaries and the department.

Morrison cited several examples. A former district superintendent and his wife were in Japan with the intention to remain permanently; an unmarried woman who had made her own way to Africa developed a large tumor and had to be operated on in the Raleigh Fitkin Memorial Hospital in Bremersdorp; a young Nazarene couple went to Peru supported by outside offerings from church friends and were planning to apply for commission as regular missionaries; the son of a missionary couple in China was en route by ship to the Orient, leaving behind creditors who were pressing the department for payment of his debts; two women had been commissioned and sent respectively to India and Peru with

---

22. Ibid., p. 66.

the understanding that they would raise their own support, funds for which had dwindled away to almost nothing with their keep falling back on the department. Morrison commented:

> These irregulars provide a puzzling problem. They in effect deprive us of the constituted methods of choosing our missionary workers, and by a self invoked train of circumstances force themselves upon us. If we recognize and commission them after they have reached the field, we might as well abandon our constituted machinery for selecting our missionary force, for as soon as the fact becomes noised around that every one who transports himself to one of our fields will soon be received, commissioned and supported, we will have half a dozen knocking at the door of every Nazarene Mission within a short time.[23]

C. Retired and Furloughed Missionaries

Another pressing problem was the support of furloughed and retired missionaries. The church had up to that time made provision for the support of furloughed missionaries for only three months of their year in the homeland. In some cases, the families had been unable to secure pastorates or other employment. The O. P. Deales from China, the A. D. Fritzlans from India, and the Frank Fergusons from Argentina represented typical cases of urgent need.

Particularly pressing were the needs, present and anticipated, of single women—some of whom had served abroad for many years: Nellie Ellison, Myrtle Pelley, Bessie Seay, Maude Cretors, and Eva Carpenter. It was to be many years before any sort of solution would be found for this problem.

D. Personnel Adjustments in 1933

In spite of the grim financial situation throughout 1933, Morrison had been able to work out a number of adjustments in foreign missionary personnel. Maude Cretors, Ora Lovelace, and Mrs. Lula Schmelzenbach and her family had been brought back from Africa. The Fergusons furloughed from Argentina. Mrs. Ethel McHenry came home from Peru, her husband, Guy, to follow early the next year. Margaret Stewart was sent to India; and the C. S. Jenkinses, who had served in Africa since 1920, returned to the field. Travel funds for both Miss Stewart and the Jenkinses were

---

23. Ibid., p. 69.

raised by the missionary societies on the New England and New York districts.[24]

E. The Easter Recovery Offering

As Easter, 1934, approached, the general superintendents made an appeal for an "Easter Recovery Offering." The General Board in January had approved a 10 percent advance in May if finances would permit. The proclamation setting the Easter Offering mentioned the general feeling that the world was on the way to economic recovery. But the church could rely not only on economic improvement but more on the blessing and inspiration of God. "We have done well; but we can do better. In fact, we must do better, if we hope to keep the smile of God upon the church," a front-page article in the *Herald of Holiness* read.[25]

Morrison, who had been so urgent at the General Board meeting in January, went public with his appeal directed toward the Easter Recovery Offering. Three nurses at the Fitkin Memorial Hospital in Africa had suffered a health breakdown. The request from China to mortgage the Bresee Hospital in order to continue its operation had of necessity been refused. Prescott Beals, India field superintendent, was asking whether or not he must close the boys and girls schools there for lack of funds. Replacements and furloughs were desperately needed on several fields.

Dr. David Hynd wrote from Africa that missionary cutbacks had tested and proved the sincerity of African pastors. Reduced from $10.00 per month support to $1.00 per month from Kansas City, these men "evinced the same spirit as the apostles of old."[26]

"Oh, pray; trust God; give," Morrison pled; "the need is great; the time is short."[27]

The Easter Recovery Offering netted approximately $40,000, of which $12,900 came from the Women's Foreign Missionary Society. As a result of this limited success, the month of May saw the General Budget still $6,000 short and plans for a May advance held in abeyance.[28]

---

24. Ibid., p. 67.
25. HH, vol. 22, no. 47 (Feb. 14, 1934), p. 1.
26. OS, vol. 21, no. 9 (Mar., 1934), p. 11.
27. HH, vol. 22, no. 49 (Feb. 28, 1934), p. 11.
28. HH, vol. 23, no. 7 (May 5, 1934), p. 24; no. 11 (June 2, 1934), p. 22.

F. Missionary Personnel in 1934

During 1934, Morrison was able to work out other arrangements. Six missionaries were furloughed home, some on leaves long overdue: the Kauffmans from Palestine, the Eckels from Japan, and Myrtle Pelley and Dora Carpenter from Africa. Leighton S. and Gertrude Tracy retired after 30 years in India. Lacking an adequate pension, Tracy pastored a small church in New York until his health broke and he was unable to continue.

As replacements, John and May McKay were returned to India. Dr. Hester Hayne was sent to the hospital in China, and Dr. and Mrs. H. C. Wesche were secured from the National Holiness Association to work there also. Bertie Karns, who had previously served in Japan, went to China as teacher for the missionaries' children.

In Peru, Rev. and Mrs. Clifford Bicker, already on the field with another mission, were commissioned as Nazarene missionaries, and Rev. and Mrs. Ira B. Taylor began their first term of service in the Bible Training School there. Rev. and Mrs. Charles H. Wiman, who had served two years in Japan, were also sent to Peru, Wiman to supervise the field. Estella MacDonald was sent to Africa, and Russell and Margaret Birchard began their work in Guatemala.

In spite of what had been done, the unmet needs were staggering. There was urgent need to get the Fergusons back to Argentina and the Kauffmans back to Palestine, but no funds were in sight for either couple. A missionary couple needed to be sent to the Cape Verde Islands to supplement the work and eventually replace aging John J. Diaz. Africa needed two nurses and a missionary couple for Portuguese East. India and China both seriously needed additional help. Added to this was the fact that furloughs were overdue for a number of missionaries, some of whom had served long beyond their normal terms. "We confront a genuine emergency," was Morrison's summary understatement.[29]

---

29. PGB, 1935, pp. 65-70. Cf. also Lucile Taylor, *Tribes and Nations from the South* (Kansas City: Nazarene Publishing House, 1960), p. 36; Russell and Margaret Anderson Birchard, *Richard Simpson Anderson: Pioneer Missionary to Central America* (Kansas City: Beacon Hill Press, 1951), p. 92.

G. Expansion in India

The year 1935 saw a major expansion of the Nazarene field in India. The work had been concentrated in the Buldana area in central India where Marathi is the language. Adjoining to the southeast was an area equal in size and population and previously served by the Methodist Episcopal church.

When the Methodists decided to withdraw from this particular field, they offered their property for sale to neighboring mission boards. The General Board at its January, 1935, meeting voted to offer $10,000 for the property of the mission, which was promptly refused. A subsequent offer of $15,000 was accepted, and a payment of one-fourth of the total was made, the balance to be paid in three equal annual amounts.

Field Superintendent Prescott Beals reported that the buildings on the main station in Basim would be adequate for mission needs for several years to come. One building would be converted into the long-proposed Reynolds Memorial Hospital for women and girls. Another was suitable for a Bible training school. Several residences for missionaries were included.[30]

An automobile accident in India in November, 1935, took the lives of May Tidwell McKay and her son John T. ("Buddy"), 6 years old. Mrs. McKay had been a missionary for 15 years and had acquired outstanding skill with the language. The McKay family had just returned to the field after a year of furlough in the United States. John, May, Buddy, and two Indian Christians were en route from Basim to Buldana to help in a camp meeting when the blowout of a tire threw their car out of control and into a tree. Mrs. McKay and Buddy died almost immediately. John and the other passengers were injured but not seriously. The funeral was held in the Buldana church. Beals wrote, "I have never seen more people gathered in and outside the church than on this occasion."[31]

H. Crisis in Japan and China

Financial pressures had drastically limited the supervision of overseas fields by the general superintendents. Only the British West Indies and Mexico had been visited. Problems and challenges in

---

30. Letter, J. G. Morrison to general superintendents, April 25, 1935, archives; PGB, 1936, p. 83.
31. HH, vol. 24, no. 42 (Jan. 4, 1936), pp. 9-10.

Japan and China seemed to make a trip imperative, and J. B. Chapman was chosen to go.

Problems in Japan had been aggravated by the presence of two of the "irregulars" whose activities Missions Secretary Morrison had lamented. One was a former missionary who had returned to the field on her own. The other was a former district superintendent. Neither was amenable to direction from the Department of Foreign Missions. The irreconcilable conflict their presence had created resulted in confusion among the Japanese Christians.

Chapman's solution was to set up the southern portion of the Japan field as a Regular District electing its own superintendent at the assembly and assuming basic self-support. It was to be known as the Kwansai District. The less-developed northern portion of the field, including Tokyo, was to be the Kwanto District.

It had been five years since General Superintendents Goodwin and Williams had visited Japan. There were then 9 churches with approximately 800 members. Now Chapman found 33 churches with over 1,600 members. Thirteen of the churches were entirely self-supporting. During the five years, the Nazarene work had only three ordained Japanese ministers. Chapman ordained 14 more and reported an additional 14 licensed ministers.[32]

The division of the field into two districts proved to be temporary. The rising tide of nationalism and anti-American sentiment in Japan brought government pressures on churches with American connections. In order to present a united front, the two districts were merged with Nobumi Isayama as superintendent. Actually, the division had not been a wise move in the first place. The threat of war and the forced merger really saved the field from even more severe morale problems than it had suffered.

In China, Dr. and Mrs. Chapman found the Nazarene work centering around the walled city of Tamingfu, approximately 300 miles southwest of Peiping. The territory served by the church was 100 miles in length, varying from 30 to 50 miles in width. The mission compound, enclosing some 16 acres, contained the 100-bed Bresee Memorial Hospital, four missionary homes, and buildings for boys and girls schools and the Bible school. Fourteen

---

32. Letter, J. B. Chapman to J. G. Morrison, Oct. 12, 1935, archives; HH, vol. 24, no. 36 (Nov. 23, 1935), p. 5.

missionaries manned the station, hospital, and schools. But more than half of the workers were long overdue for furloughs, and replacements were difficult to arrange.[33]

I. The Cape Verde Islands

A long-anticipated move realized in 1935 was the reinforcement of the Cape Verde Islands with a new missionary couple, Everette and Garnet Howard. The field had been worked by John J. Diaz and his wife since 1900. Both were elderly and failing in health. Diaz had long pled for reinforcements. He had been an effective evangelist but had been able to organize only two small churches and had enlisted almost no nationals as ministerial helpers. When the depression first hit, Morrison and the general superintendents had actually discussed closing the field.[34]

The Howards sailed from New York on October 26, 1935, en route to Portugal for language study and then on to the islands in March, 1936. Both proved effective missionaries and within four years had gained six national ministers and organized another church and five outstations with 139 full members and an additional 160 probationers and 300 in Sunday Schools.[35]

J. The Thin Line Holds

When the quadrennium ended in 1936, Nazarene foreign missions had survived the financial crunch, battered but intact. Some gains had been recorded. The number of missionaries had actually increased from 65 to 69, and the number of national workers from 367 to 403.[36] Evelyn Fox, Carl and Velma Mischke, Estella Mac-Donald, Elizabeth Cole, and Lawrence and Laura Ferree had been dispatched to Africa. Margaret Stewart and Ralph and Orpha Cook were sent to India. Russell and Margaret Birchard had begun their work in Guatemala. Clifford and Ruth Bicker joined the Nazarene mission in Peru, and Ira and Lucille Taylor and Charles H. and Maud Wiman were sent to Peru as additional missionaries.

---

33. HH, vol. 24, no. 40 (Dec. 21, 1935), pp. 5-6.

34. Letter, J. G. Morrison to J. W. Goodwin, May 8, 1931 (Archives, General Board, staff correspondence).

35. PGB, 1936, pp. 84-85; GAJ, 1940, pp. 344-45. See Basil Miller, *Miracle in Cape Verde: The Story of Everette and Garnet Howard* (Kansas City: Beacon Hill Press, 1950).

36. GAJ, 1936, p. 290.

The Howards landed in the Cape Verde Islands, while Amanda Mellies and the L. S. Tracys retired from India.

V. HOME MISSIONS AND MINISTERIAL RELIEF

Similar if less extensive financial problems beset the Department of Home Missions, Church Extension, and Evangelism. Secretary D. Shelby Corlett reported that minimum aid had been given the Arizona, Manitoba-Saskatchewan, and Rocky Mountain districts; and to New England for work in the Maritime Provinces of Canada. Local congregations in New Orleans; Reno, Nev.; Las Vegas, N.M.; and Salt Lake City were also assisted in minimal amounts.[37]

The plight of the church's evangelists was particularly trying. These ministers, without regular salaries and depending on calls from local churches for revival meetings, were sorely pressed financially. The quadrennial address of the general superintendents in 1932 had noted that many evangelists had been forced out of the field for lack of financial support. Pastors were holding their own revival meetings or were exchanging with fellow pastors. Some churches had shortened their meetings with corresponding reduction in support. Except for the few evangelists well enough known to be called for camp meetings, summers and the midwinter holidays were particularly difficult times.[38]

Evangelist C. W. Ruth, a veteran with over 50 years in the field, urged local churches to plan for revival meetings in spite of the lack of prospects for adequate finances. Good meetings carry their own cost, he argued.

As pressing as the problem of retired missionaries was the problem of retired ministers in the homeland. Their cause was ably represented by Ministerial Relief Secretary E. J. Fleming. Fleming noted that the church had assumed responsibility for the partial support of more than 60 aged ministers or their widows at stipends ranging from $5.00 to $20.00 per month.

Monthly appropriations to these men and women had been cut by 20 percent the year before. Even so, only a $1,000 gift from the Nazarene Publishing House and an overdraft of department funds had enabled the secretary to care for the most pressing

---

37. PGB, 1934, pp. 74-75.
38. GAJ, 1932, p. 183.

needs. Without any sort of Social Security and little state or local welfare, the plight of the elderly minister was pitiful indeed. Said Fleming:

> Perhaps the saddest phase of the life of an aged minister is the dawning revelation that comes to him and his companion, when, clothed in threadbare garments and eating his bread of poverty, he discovers that the church in whose service he so eagerly engaged, and to whose growth he so enthusiastically contributed, and for which he was so inadequately remunerated, has been so slow, so backward, to provide for the very simple needs of his declining years. . . . The *apparent*—we say, *apparent*—ingratitude of the church, the *apparently* begrudging manner in which his appeal for help is received, make him feel like a mendicant supplicating at the back door for a meager handout.[39]

No magic solutions were found for the fiscal problems of the denomination, but the gradual improvement of the economy in general and the continued growth of church membership helped relieve some of the pressure. The recovery began in 1934 as giving for general interests by the churches rose from $183,629 in 1933 to $211,314, an increase of over 15 percent. The increase the following year, the last fiscal year before the 1936 General Assembly, was smaller—to $218,965, a percentage of 3.62. At the same time, district interests received almost 9 percent more in 1934, and increased another 8 percent in 1935. Per capita giving stood at $24.47 for 1934 and $25.55 in 1935.[40]

VI. THE *HERALD OF HOLINESS*
AND THE PUBLISHING HOUSE

Late in 1933, H. Orton Wiley submitted his resignation as editor of the *Herald of Holiness.* Wiley had come to the *Herald* from the presidency of Pasadena College in 1928. He was never entirely happy in Kansas City. His family found the climate oppressive. In some ways, he was not cut out for editorial work. Many of his editorials, while a delight to the scholarly, tended to be above the heads of the majority of his readers. He had followed J. B. Chapman, a first-rate theological mind in his own right but also a master communicator.

---

39. PGB, 1934, p. 63.
40. GAJ, 1936, pp. 184, 193, 234; HH, vol. 22, no. 24 (Jan. 10, 1934), p. 16; HH, vol. 23, no. 42 (Jan. 5, 1935), pp. 16-17; vol. 24, no. 42 (Jan. 4, 1936), p. 16.

When in June, 1933, after five years of struggling through a rugged financial crisis, Orval J. Nease, Sr., resigned the presidency of Pasadena College, Wiley was easily prevailed upon to return.

Instead of accepting Wiley's resignation from the *Herald* office, an arrangement was worked out whereby the day-to-day operation of the paper was turned over to D. Shelby Corlett, then secretary of the Department of Home Missions, Church Extension, and Evangelism, and executive secretary of the youth organization. Corlett became managing editor under an agreement that split the salary. Wiley was to furnish "a certain amount of editorial matter each week."

This was to have been "a temporary arrangement," but it lasted two and a half years until the General Assembly of 1936. Wiley would have been willing to continue the plan and was, in fact, reelected for another four-year term as editor. However, a resolution was passed by the assembly requiring the editor to reside in Kansas City, and Wiley resigned to remain with the college.[41] Corlett was a natural choice to succeed him.

With the selection of Corlett as managing editor of the *Herald,* administration of the Department of Home Missions passed to J. G. Morrison, bringing both foreign and home missions under his capable administration.

At the publishing house, sales volume reached its depression low in 1932 when it stood at $218,000, the lowest figure since 1927. Each following year, however, the amount increased until it reached $290,000 in 1936. An amazing record of collection of accounts was established, largely credited by Manager Lunn to "the loyalty of our people."[42] A small discount offered for cash didn't hurt.

Publishing house support during these pressure years was a vital part of the economics of the general church. During the 1932-36 quadrennium, more than $4,000 was contributed in free literature. The subscription price of the *Herald of Holiness* was dropped from $1.50 to $1.00. The sum of $5,000 was given to the Department of Ministerial Relief. An additional $40,000 went to the General Board to be used to undergird the General Budget. In addition, $60,000 in notes held by the publishing house against

41. PGB, 1934, p. 18; GAJ, 1936, pp. 75-76.
42. GAJ, 1936, pp. 331-32, 334.

the General Board were cancelled. Other miscellaneous donations to church interests amounted to almost $5,000.[43]

At the same time, Lunn clearly recognized that expansion needs of the house would require use of its surplus for its own work. The support the house had given the church had been at the expense of rigid economies and ultraconservative practices in regard to its own needs. Lunn therefore recommended and the General Assembly of 1936 approved an expansion for the publishing business "as demands and finance warrant."[44]

VII. CRISIS IN THE COLLEGES

No report from the Department of Education was printed in the *Proceedings of the General Board* for January, 1934. The omission is not readily explained unless it be that Wiley, who had been serving as educational secretary on a part-time basis, had recently moved to Pasadena. Department reports for 1932 and 1934, presented to the January meetings of the board in 1933 and 1935, reflect little of the severe financial pressures weighing on the colleges.

The church had developed no satisfactory method of underwriting current expenses for its schools. The educational work was neither exclusively a district interest nor a general concern, and the later "education budgets" were then almost unknown. Financial campaigns were conducted by the school administrators across their zones for buildings and debt liquidation, but current income depended on tuition and fees, whatever profit might be derived from dormitory and dining hall operations, and rather spasmodic offerings from local churches.

The financial collapse deprived many otherwise qualified students of a college education or drove them to tuition-free public institutions. With the shrinking of student bodies to their lowest ebb in 1932 and 1933, current financial support virtually dried up.

The 1935 report of the Department of Education to the General Board rather indefinitely said, "Practically every college enjoys an increased enrollment."[45] Actually, the tide had turned. Figures compiled from college records by the Department of Education 23

---

43. Ibid., p. 241.
44. Rawlings, "History of the Nazarene Publishing House," pp. 58-63.
45. PGB, 1935, p. 89.

years later reveal a substantial increase in both college level and total enrollments. The six colleges reported a total of 697 students for the 1932-33 school year. The following year, the comparable figure was 926, a healthy 33 percent increase. The 1934-35 reports indicated 1,191 college-level students in the six schools, a further increase of 29 percent—with Bresee College beginning to function as a junior college. The last school year before the 1936 General Assembly saw 1,210 college-level students in Nazarene schools. The growth is explained in part by some improvement in the economy without a comparable increase in the college-age job market. Denied access to jobs, larger numbers of young people opted for continued education.[46]

But while school enrollments were gradually improving, college administrators and faculty members continued to suffer financially. Education in the church came fourth in priority after local, district, and general interests. Teachers in most of the schools received the larger part of their salaries in the form of notes signed by students covering unpaid accounts. Many of those notes were never paid off.

Bertha Dooley, then professor of English at Northwest Nazarene College, reported that faculty members there moved into the dormitories where they were given board and room on a transfer of credit. The school week was extended to six days in order to save a month at the end of the school year. Faculty salaries for those outside the dormitories were $5.00 per month.[47]

Pasadena, Eastern Nazarene, and Trevecca teetered on the verge of bankruptcy. Back at Pasadena after his five-year stint in Kansas City, Wiley found an indebtedness of $100,000—an almost crushing load. J. T. Little, former superintendent of the Southern California District, was persuaded to become financial secretary, and Erwin G. Benson became field secretary. Through their combined efforts, most of the unsecured indebtedness was wiped out by the end of 1935. At the same time, a "living endowment" plan

---

46. The statistics are from Philo, "Historical Development," p. 267.
47. Bertha Dooley, *Northwest Nazarene College* (Nampa, Ida.: Northwest Nazarene College, 1938), p. 53; and Philo, "Historical Development," p. 140; cf. also Albert F. Harper, paper, 1976, "The Administration of President Gilmore," pp. 8-10. President and Mrs. Gilmore and their daughter moved into a dormitory in the fall of 1932 (F. C. Sutherland, "History of NNC," 1962, pp. 53-55).

that had been tried earlier at Trevecca was adopted as a means of raising operating funds. Givers were asked to contribute $1.00 per month, the income that would be derived from an endowment of $200 at 6 percent.

Eastern Nazarene College had been faced in October of 1932 with an ultimatum from the bank holding its large mortgage, demanding $15,000 by December 15 to forestall foreclosure. A heroic campaign raised the necessary funds. The school year ended with a net operating loss of $22,000 as compared with $13,000 the previous year. Another ultimatum from the bank demanded payment of overdue interest by March 20, 1934, on a debt of $100,000. Again, heroic giving by church members throughout the zone saved the day.[48]

Eastern's financial crisis peaked in the 1935-36 school year. The strain proved too much for President R. Wayne Gardner, who had borne the burdens of administration for six strenuous years. His health broke, and he resigned at the close of the school year. The board tapped G. B. Williamson, then pastor at Cleveland First Church, for the post, and with some reluctance he accepted.[49]

Only Trevecca actually went through bankruptcy. The campus and its furnishings were sold at public auction for $25,000 in 1932, and the college was moved to an abandoned school for blacks located just outside the city of Nashville on White's Creek Road. The buildings were occupied under a lease with option to buy. Enrollment was down to 70.

Not only was money for purchase of the property not forthcoming, but also the title was found to be clouded. The college was forced to move again and opened in the fall of 1934 in the facilities of Nashville First Church in downtown Nashville. Here it received its present name, Trevecca Nazarene College, and survived until the nucleus of its present campus was obtained in 1935. Only the leadership of layman A. B. Mackey, who had joined the faculty in 1925, saved the institution.[50]

The trustees at Northern Bible College in Red Deer, Alberta, Canada, asked part-time President Charles E. Thomson to give his

48. Cameron, *ENC: First Fifty Years,* pp. 231-39.
49. Ibid., pp. 258-79.
50. Wynkoop, *Trevecca Story,* pp. 138-63.

full time to the college in 1935. He had pastored the Red Deer church up to that time.[51]

An upheaval in administration at Northwest Nazarene College in the summer of 1935 saw Reuben E. Gilmore removed as president and Russell V. DeLong recalled in his place. DeLong had headed the college previously from 1927 to 1932.[52]

VIII. AMENDING THE CONSTITUTION

One constitutional amendment was ratified in November, 1934. It had the effect of adding to the Articles of Faith a statement directly countering the widely prevalent doctrine of eternal security or "once in grace, always in grace." The article had been adopted by more than the required two-thirds vote at the Wichita General Assembly in 1932, and had been presented to the district assemblies for their consideration and necessary ratification by two-thirds of the assemblies.

The amendment added to Article VII on Free Agency the statement: "We believe that man, though in the possession of the experience of regeneration and entire sanctification, may fall from grace and apostatize and, unless he repent of his sin, be hopelessly and eternally lost."

The amendment was received with some degree of indifference, probably because what it proposed seemed axiomatic to most Nazarenes. One district (Alberta) voted it down. Eight (Abilene, Arkansas, Kentucky-West Virginia, Michigan, Mississippi, New Mexico, North Pacific, and Ohio) took no action. Four (Dallas, Nebraska, San Antonio, and Tennessee) considered the amendment and tabled the motion to adopt. The amendment was ratified with only 1 district more than the required 28 voting approval. Actually the amendment made no change in Nazarene theology. It merely made explicit in the Article of Faith what had been taken for granted.[53]

---

51. Dorothy Thomson, *Vine of His Planting* (Edmonton, Alberta: Commercial Printers, 1961), p. 19.
52. Harper, "Administration of President Gilmore."
53. GAJ, 1936, pp. 168-72.

IX. THE CRUSADE FOR SOULS

The Crusade for Souls launched in 1935 grew out of an impassioned plea by General Superintendent Emeritus Hiram Reynolds for worldwide revival. Reynolds made his appeal at a January meeting of the district superintendents. It was to be one of his last public appearances.

A Crusade for Souls Committee was appointed consisting of the three general superintendents and District Superintendents Samuel Young, E. O. Chalfant, P. P. Belew, B. F. Neely, J. N. Tinsley, and A. F. Sanner. R. T. Williams was chosen chairman and D. Shelby Corlett was named secretary.

A crusade resolution was drawn up by the committee recommending that during 1935 the Church of the Nazarene throughout the world "give herself unstintingly to a special effort to promote an intensive revival in an endeavor to reach the vast unchurched masses."[54]

Leaders on each district were urged to plan whatever seemed to them the most effective method for implementing the crusade. A special period of holiness emphasis from May 12 to Pentecost Sunday, June 9, was recommended. The church was exhorted to engage in earnest and intercessory prayer for "the mighty outpouring of the Spirit of God" in order to make the programs effective.[55]

March 8 was designated a world day of prayer. A Crusade for Souls sacrifice offering was called for on Easter, April 21. The summer months were to be marked by home mission crusades. September 29 was the crusade rally day. The crusade Thanksgiving Offering was set for November 24 and a victory watchnight service for December 31.[56]

H. Orton Wiley noted that the crusade appeal was met "with hearty response on the part of our people." The crusade was an emphasis that got right at the heart of the human problem: "We are now well within range of the Great Commission."

Organizations are essential, Wiley said, but may become formal and lack in both meaning and inspiration. Financial problems

---

54. HH, vol. 23, no. 44 (Jan. 19, 1935), pp. 6, 32.
55. Ibid.
56. HH, vol. 23, no. 49 (Feb. 23, 1935), p. 32.

are ever present, "but these are not our primary or basic difficulties." As the church seeks first the kingdom of God, all needful
things will be added. "We must have a revival. To our Lord has
been given all power, both in heaven and earth. Nothing can with-
stand His Spirit. He calls upon every soldier of the cross to go
forward."[57]

Pastor H. V. Miller, then of Chicago First Church, and George
J. Franklin of Gary, Ind., led the Chicago Nazarenes in a seven-
week campaign featuring prayer meetings three times a day, with
intensive prayer before and after the evening services. Miller said,
"We ate revival, slept (some) revival, talked revival, thought revival, shouted, prayed, believed revival." As a result, "The cause of
spirituality has won in old First Church and today there is a deeper
tone of spirituality than for years past."[58]

Other local churches reported crusade revivals. James Cubie
wrote from Morley, England, that the district assembly there had
been followed by a crusade revival series with the Pilgrim Revival
Party headed by Maynard James and Jack Ford of the Calvary
Holiness Church. "There has not been a barren service, until at the
close of the second week there had been fifty seekers for pardon or
purity."[59]

The same issue of the *Herald of Holiness* that carried word of
the Morley revival printed a report from Superintendent Harry A.
Wiese of the China mission. Since the Chinese language had no
equivalent for "crusade," the effort in China was dubbed the "Save
Soul Movement," a takeoff on Chiang Kai-chek's "New Life Movement."[60] An eight-day campaign at the Tamingfu headquarters resulted in 401 individuals testifying to "receiving definite help at
the altar, thus closing one of the greatest meetings ever held in
Tamingfu."[61]

Overall numerical results of the effort were not immediately
visible. In the biennium 1932-34, Nazarenes racked up a membership gain worldwide of 21,007, an increase of 19 percent. The
record for the biennium 1934-36 was 15,260 members gained, a
growth rate of 12 percent. But the qualitative results appear to

---

57. HH, vol. 23, no. 52 (Mar. 16, 1935), p. 3.
58. HH, vol. 24, no. 14 (June 29, 1935), pp. 8-9.
59. HH, vol. 24, no. 11 (June 1, 1935), pp. 24-25.
60. Ibid., p. 32.
61. HH, vol. 24, no. 14 (June 29, 1935), pp. 8-9.

have been positive and helpful, and the overall increase for the quadrennium was a substantial 40 percent.

SUMMARY

When General Secretary E. J. Fleming came to gather the statistics for his report to the 1936 General Assembly, he discovered that the church had had its best growth since the quadrennium ending in 1923. The 40 percent gain worldwide, from 99,127 to 138,879, had been exceeded only twice since 1911—during the years immediately preceding World War I (1911-15, growth rate 54 percent) and the years immediately following (1919-23, growth rate 45 percent). Nor has the 40 percent gain been approximated since.

Geographical growth (the number of local churches) did not keep pace with numerical increases. The quadrennium began in 1932 with 1,940 churches worldwide and ended with 2,387, an increase of 23 percent. This meant that local Churches of the Nazarene increased in average membership from 51 in 1932 to 58 in 1936.

During the same period, Sunday Bible schools increased from 202,908 to 270,531 or 33 percent; NYPS membership grew from 35,155 to 56,964 (62 percent); and the WFMS went from 24,880 to 37,452, an increase of 51 percent.

Commented the general superintendents in their quadrennial address to the General Assembly: "These gains have been, according to our judgment, large enough to save us from stagnation and reactionism, but not too large for assimilation."[62]

The only negative items were financial. Annual giving for district concerns dropped from $171,641 to $151,569, a decrease of 12 percent; and for General Budget from $233,907 to $215,644, a decline of 8 percent. But the corner was turned in 1934, and gradual increases in giving for general church interests would prevail from then on.

The paradox of the lean years was in the fact that the four years of greatest financial pressure were at the same time the years of greatest growth both geographical (number of churches) and numerical (in church membership) to be achieved during the second quarter-century of Nazarene history.

---

62. HH, vol. 25, no. 15 (June 27, 1936), p. 7; GAJ, 1936, p. 157.

Woodbridge, Noll, and Hatch, in their 1979 volume, *The Gospel in America*, state that "the Great Depression stole attention from spiritual concerns. Liberal and evangelical churches alike suffered losses in both membership and self-confidence."[63] No doubt many turned their attention from spiritual concerns to the hard realities of the economic struggle. Many of the churches the authors designate as liberal did indeed lose membership and self-confidence.

On the other hand, the loss of human securities worked to turn still others—and in considerable numbers—to a deeper trust in God. They found support in the faith and encouragement of fellow Christians. A quick survey of denominational statistics for the 10 years from 1931 to 1940 as reported in the *Yearbook of American Churches*[64] reveals that a number of evangelical churches made substantial gains. For the 10 years of the 1930s, both the Nazarenes and the Assemblies of God gained 82 percent in net membership. The United Lutheran church added 67 percent. The Seventh Day Adventists and the Southern Baptists grew by 37 and 34 percent respectively. Difficult times, of themselves, do not seriously threaten the spiritual mission of the Church. They may, in fact, prove a stimulus to greater faith in moral and spiritual realities.

---

63. John D. Woodbridge, Mark A. Noll, and Nathan O. Hatch, *The Gospel in America* (Grand Rapids: Zondervan Publishing House, 1979), p. 80.

64. *Yearbook of American Churches*, ed. Herman C. Weber (New York: Association Press, 1933) and *Yearbook of American Churches*, ed. Benson Y. Landis (Judson Heights, N.Y.: Yearbook of American Churches Press, 1941); statistical tables.

4

The Gathering Clouds of War

A slow climb out of the depression marked the years 1936 to 1939. In the United States, Roosevelt's second term in the White House was supported by a Congress overwhelmingly Democratic. The president interpreted his 1936, 10-million-vote margin of victory over his Republican opponent as a mandate for further social reforms. The period was marked by a downturn in the economy in late 1937 and the rapid growth of the labor movement. The multiplicity of recovery programs launched by Washington escalated the bureaucracy and greatly enlarged the power of the executive branch of the government.

Ominous signs from abroad began to appear. Adolf Hitler denounced the Versailles treaty with respect to German disarmament and began military conscription in Germany in March, 1935. In November of 1936, Germany and Japan forged an alliance, and late in September of 1938 the Munich Pact permitted the partition of Czechoslovakia. Within a year, World War II had begun.

I. THE NINTH GENERAL ASSEMBLY

The Ninth General Assembly met in Kansas City in June, 1936. It was preceded by conventions of the Women's Foreign Missionary Society and the Nazarene Young People's Society.

The missionary organization convened Thursday morning, June 18, under the gavel of its first and only president, Rev. Mrs. Susan N. Fitkin. The convention was held in the still unfinished Municipal Auditorium assembly room in the midst of a heat wave marked by temperatures exceeding 100° that lasted for over 40 days during the summer of 1936.

The women's organization was able to report a 43 percent increase in membership since its last convention, with over 4,000 of its members on foreign missionary districts. Treasurer Emma B. Word noted that the women had raised a total of $415,274 for the General Budget during the four years of the quadrennium with another $18,276 going for foreign missions specials.

The convention made virtually no changes in its choice of leadership. Mrs. Fitkin was reelected president, and her close friend and colleague Mrs. Paul (Ada) Bresee, daughter-in-law of P. F. Bresee, was reelected executive vice-president. Mrs. Bertha Humble of Villa Grove, Ill., and Mrs. C. Warren Jones were the only additions to the council.[1]

The NYPS Convention, chaired by its General President G. B. Williamson, began Thursday evening in Edison Hall. The convention marked the end of D. Shelby Corlett's tenure as executive secretary of the organization, a position he had held from its inception. In his place, the convention elected Sylvester T. Ludwig, president of Bresee College. Williamson was elected president for a second term, and the council for the new quadrennium was composed of Corlett, Milton Smith, J. George Taylorson, M. Kimber Moulton, and Oscar J. Finch, all young ministers and all destined to play important roles in the church in the years ahead. Although Nazarenes had from the earliest days sought a balance between ministerial and lay leadership in their governing boards and councils, the ideal was not approximated in the NYPS until late in the second 25 years.

The youth group had recorded a 62 percent increase in its membership to a total of 56,964. Eleven district organizations had more than doubled their memberships. The general society had taken an active part in both the Silver Jubilee of 1933 and the 1935 Crusade for Souls. While not primarily a fund-raising organization, the NYPS had contributed a total of $49,362 for General Budget purposes during the preceding four years.[2]

The General Assembly itself opened on Sunday, June 21, with the customary services of worship and inspiration. It had been

---

1. GAJ, 1936, pp. 293-99; *Manual*, 1936, pp. 274-75.
2. GAJ, 1936, pp. 361-67.

planned to hold the sessions in the new Music Hall of the city auditorium. Only two weeks before the date, it became apparent that the facility would not be ready, and the assembly was moved to the 3,000-seat Ararat Temple, just two blocks north of the auditorium.

General Superintendent R. T. Williams preached a Communion sermon in the morning and directed participation in the sacrament of the Lord's Supper. A 2:30 afternoon service featured Uncle Bud Robinson whose "Good Samaritan Chats" were printed weekly in the *Herald of Holiness* and who was universally loved as the church's ambassador of goodwill. The evening sermon was preached by Henry Clay Morrison, a holiness Methodist minister and president of Asbury College in Wilmore, Ky. Capacity crowds attended each service.

The general superintendents' quadrennial address was given Monday night by J. B. Chapman. Chapman reviewed the history of the church and reported the major developments of the preceding four years. Most of the concerns expressed by the general superintendents had to do with the church's missionary program both abroad and at home. They recommended special consideration to finding more adequate support for the colleges and urged a better plan for aid to retired and incapacitated ministers and their dependents.

Concern was expressed for continued spiritual growth. "We warn our ministers against formality and professionalism, and our people against spiritual apathy. . . . Our task demands reality in our religion. We must not be content with appearances and professions."[3]

Although the address of the general superintendents did not mention it, there was widespread concern among the delegates for more adequate supervision of overseas missions. A combination of limited finances and the heavy administrative load carried by the three active general superintendents had resulted in but one overseas trip late in the preceding quadrennium and that in response to what were virtually crisis situations in both Japan and China.

The result of this concern was action to elect four general superintendents with the stipulation "that the Board of General Superintendents be authorized and required to designate one of

3. Ibid., pp. 153-60.

their number from time to time adequately to superintend the Foreign Mission Fields."[4] The salary and expenses of the fourth general were incorporated in the budget of the Foreign Missions Department.

An additional factor was the age (68 years) and physical frailty of John W. Goodwin. Goodwin had served as general superintendent for 20 years and was 2 years short of the then-prevailing 70-year age limit for reelection.

When the first ballot was taken for four general superintendents, the three incumbents were handily reelected. For the fourth spot, J. G. Morrison, the dynamic and tireless Foreign and Home Missions secretary, received 162 ballots out of the 324 necessary to elect. The next highest was H. V. Miller with 97 votes. Morrison was elected on the fifth ballot.

In many ways, Morrison was a "natural" for the post. He had served in the Department of Foreign Missions as its executive for 10 years. He had been general treasurer for about 18 months and had doubled as home missions executive since 1934. He was an effective preacher, well and favorably known throughout the church. While never stepping out of his place, his voluminous correspondence shows him to have carried an unusually heavy administrative load in the overseas mission of the church. One liability was his age—65 at the time of election, the oldest person ever to be elected to the position for the first time.

E. J. Fleming and M. Lunn were quickly reelected as general secretary and general treasurer respectively. As noted earlier, H. Orton Wiley was reelected as editor of the *Herald of Holiness.* However, he chose to remain as full-time president of Pasadena College, and Managing Editor D. Shelby Corlett was then chosen editor.[5]

When the General Assembly finally adjourned near midnight on Monday, June 29, the ministerial and lay delegates headed back to their labors in a period that would see the burden of depression replaced by the critical developments leading to World War II.

---

4. GAJ, 1936, p. 46; cf. also PGB, 1936, p. 34.
5. GAJ, 1936, p. 78.

II. C. WARREN JONES
AND FOREIGN MISSIONS

For the remainder of 1936, Morrison functioned both as general superintendent and executive of the Foreign Missions Department. As the January, 1937, General Board meeting drew near, careful consideration was given to the choice of Morrison's successor in the missions department.[6]

Prominent in the consideration was the superintendent of the Pittsburgh District, C. Warren Jones. Jones had been a member of the General Board since 1928 and had served in the Department of Foreign Missions. He and Mrs. Jones had gone to Japan as missionaries in 1920-21 but had been forced to return home by Jones's severe illness. The department nominated Jones, and the board unanimously elected him. He was to serve in this capacity until retirement in January of 1949.

Jones was also elected Home Missions secretary and secretary of the General Stewardship Committee, and after Fleming's resignation he became general church secretary—diversions of time and effort that occasioned some concern and were finally ended.

The successor to Jones on the General Board was New England District Superintendent Samuel Young. Young was assigned to the Department of Foreign Missions and the following year was chosen its representative on the Finance Committee—a choice of major importance for the fiscal policies of the church. He served in these capacities with the General Board until elected general superintendent in 1948.

For his part, Jones stepped into an awesome responsibility. He was immediately confronted with a shortfall of $30,000 in foreign mission funds. The amount had been budgeted in January of 1936, but General Budget receipts had been far short of anticipated amounts.

The number of missionaries abroad had escalated from 69 in 1935 to 90 in 1936. There had been a tendency to do what needed to be done in faith that the church would come up with the necessary money. In a modest understatement, the general superintendents explained to the church, "The forward program for foreign

---

6. Cf. letter, J. G. Morrison to Ada Bresee, Sept. 11, 1936 (Archives, Department of Foreign Missions, correspondence).

missions [has] advanced faster than funds [have] come in to carry it."[7] The 10 percent anticipated increase in general receipts turned out to be 6.68 percent, and all available reserves had been used up.

The Finance Committee of the General Board took a careful look at the total situation. The source of the problem was not hard to find. The district superintendents at their conference in January, 1936, had agreed to raise a total of $255,230 in General Budget funds. But when their district assemblies met and considered local and district interests as well as general needs, the actual amount underwritten for the General Budget shrank to $238,303. Final receipts were $17,000 short of even the budgeted amount.

The departments of the General Board had submitted asking budgets for 1937 totalling $255,060. The Finance Committee cut the amount allocated for expenditure to $240,000. The foreign missions allotment was cut from $175,340 to $166,340 and the home missions portion from $19,000 to $14,000. The committee also took the rather extreme step of recommending a postponement of foreign visitation by the general superintendents until after the 1938 board meeting, and of cancelling furlough plans for personnel then on the field. An additional $10,000 was allowed the Department of Foreign Missions with the provision that it be appropriated only after the funds were in hand.

A call was made to the Reserve Army to raise additional money—only the sixth call in five years.[8]

As it turned out, sufficient funds came in to permit Dr. Goodwin to visit Mexico, Peru, and Guatemala during 1937—the last trip cut short by Goodwin's serious illness with ptomaine poisoning, prompting an emergency flight back to his home in Pasadena.[9]

More significantly, Dr. Chapman was able to go to India, Palestine, Syria, the Cape Verde Islands, and the British Isles. Chapman had planned to visit India when he went to Japan and China the year before, but the financial crunch made it inadvisable at that time.

The year's delay enabled the doctor to arrange to take Mrs. Chapman and their two sons, Harold and Paul, on the 10-month

7. HH, vol. 25, no. 46 (Jan. 30, 1937), p. 1.
8. HH, vol. 25, no. 45 (Jan. 23, 1937), p. 7.
9. PGB, 1937, pp. 103-13.

trip without additional expense to the church. It was a healing experience for the family, still suffering from the unexpected death of their son and brother Brilhart in March in New York City. With the completion of this trip, Chapman had visited all the mission fields of the church except Mexico.[10]

Chapman's stay in India was particularly helpful. He visited the churches, talked with the national pastors as well as the missionaries, and after a six-weeks study decided to organize the field as a self-governing district. The first district assembly was held in November, and six national pastors were ordained as elders. One of the men newly ordained, Samuel J. Bhujbal, was elected district superintendent.

Chapman had been a consistent advocate of the policy of encouraging mission churches to work toward self-support and to become fully functioning organizations. As he said in reviewing the developments in India in his report to the General Board in 1939, "As early as possible in every place, we must make initial organizations, and as fast as the boldest can recommend, we must pass on responsibility to the nationals." With prophetic insight, he added, "There is no assurance that a foreign church can continue to operate long anywhere. . . . It is too late to begin on this matter when the bars [against foreigners] are lifted. We must begin voluntarily and must proceed amidst many obstacles."[11]

Shortly after Chapman's visit and as a result of his urging, Reynolds Memorial Hospital was opened at Basim. Dr. Orpha Speicher had reached the field in December, 1936. By June, 1938, her language study completed, she began the medical work with one missionary nurse to assist her. As envisioned, one of the buildings on the Basim station that had been taken over from the Methodists three years before was converted into a hospital building.[12]

Another appeal for funds was made to the district superintendents' conference immediately following the 1937 General Board meeting. An additional $20,000 was pledged in increases for General Budget, subject to acceptance by the 1937 district assemblies.

---

10. PGB, 1938, p. 82; HH, vol. 26, no. 26 (Sept. 11, 1937), pp. 6-7; no. 49 (Feb. 19, 1938), p. 25; PGB, 1939, p. 75.
11. PGB, 1939, pp. 76-77; Prescott L. Beals, *India Reborn: The Story of Evangelism in India* (Kansas City: Beacon Hill Press, 1954), p. 49; DeLong and Taylor, *Fifty Years of Nazarene Missions,* 2:36-39.
12. DeLong and Taylor, *Fifty Years of Nazarene Missions,* 2:38.

The effort paid off, for total giving for general interests increased from $230,064 in 1936 to $285,866 in 1937.[13]

The improvement in finances was to be short-lived. A general economic recession hit the United States in the latter part of 1937. General giving fell by $5,000 in 1938 and recovered but slightly in 1939.[14]

Late in January, 1938, Dr. Morrison sailed for Argentina and visited the British West Indies on the way home. His subsequent report to the General Board had the effect of exonerating both the character and leadership of West Indies Mission Superintendent J. I. Hill, who had operated under a cloud of suspicion for three years.[15]

In spite of continued financial pressures, the years 1936 through 1939 saw seven overseas fields substantially reinforced with new missionary personnel in addition to missionaries returning from furlough.

A long period of political turmoil began in China when the Japanese invaded from Manchuria in July of 1937. By fall, the city of Tamingfu, where the Nazarene field headquarters and Bresee Memorial Hospital were located, was being bombed by Japanese planes. Although the mission compound was not hit, all missionaries except Superintendent Harry Wiese were evacuated. A temporary period of calm during the Japanese occupation permitted the missionaries to return in 1939.[16]

Two years after the invasion of China, Japan Missionary Superintendent William A. Eckel mailed a letter from Manila to Kansas City which he did not dare mail from Japan. In it, he related the pressures building up on foreigners in the island kingdom and the threat posed to Christianity by the rising tide of Japanese nationalism. New legislation was pending that would require the Church of the Nazarene in Japan to operate under one head—in effect

---

13. PGB, 1937, p. 111; HH, vol. 25, no. 45 (Jan. 23, 1937), p. 3; HH, vol. 26, no. 42 (Jan. 1, 1938), pp. 14-15.

14. Statistics for the Church of the Nazarene tend to lag behind actual conditions, since they are based on figures reported to district assemblies held from April to October during the year in question. District assembly reports are, in turn, for the 12 months preceding the assembly.

15. PGB, 1938, p. 82; 1939, pp. 78-84; cf. correspondence and other materials in archives concerning the status of Hill and the field, 1925-1938.

16. DeLong and Taylor, *Fifty Years of Nazarene Missions,* 2:84-86; PGB, 1938, pp. 80-81.

dissolving the Kwansai and Kwanto district division set up during Chapman's visit two years before.[17] While Kansas City tended to minimize Eckel's fears, subsequent events proved them fully justified.

III. LEADERSHIP LOSSES

The years leading up to World War II proved to be a time of extensive and rather significant leadership changes in the Church of the Nazarene. The entire church mourned the passing of the "grand old man" of Nazarene foreign missions, General Superintendent Emeritus Hiram F. Reynolds. Reynolds died July 13, 1938, at the age of 84 after an illness of 19 weeks. To the very end of his life, he was an ardent promoter of the cause of Christ worldwide. He had been an active general superintendent for 25 years and a very busy emeritus for 6 years.[18]

General Church Secretary E. J. Fleming paid Reynolds a justified tribute when he said at the funeral, "Some say that Dr. Bresee was the founder of the Church of the Nazarene, but when I think of its beginnings I always say Dr. Bresee and Dr. Reynolds were the founders. He was just as potent in the founding of this church as any other man that lived."[19] And J. G. Morrison said of Reynolds, "The original missionary policy, that was for years the governing fundamental law of all our mission fields, was beaten into shape by this itinerant and apostolic General Superintendent from the first-hand, white-hot facts gathered by himself by actual contact with the problems of the mission stations."[20]

Even more shocking was the death of General Superintendent Morrison 15 months later. Morrison returned to Kansas City on October 19, 1939, from a three-month trip to Africa during which he visited every part of the largest Nazarene mission field. There he had the pleasure of ordaining eight nationals as ministers in the

---

17. Letters, Mar. 11, 1939, W. A. Eckel to C. Warren Jones; J. G. Morrison to J. B. Chapman, Apr. 14, 1939; Chapman to Morrison, Apr. 17, 1939 (Archives, Department of Foreign Missions, correspondence; J. G. Morrison correspondence).

18. HH, vol. 27, no. 18 (July 16, 1938), p. 4; Amy N. Hinshaw, *In Labors Abundant*; Mervel Lunn, *Hiram F. Reynolds: Mr. World Missionary* (Kansas City: Nazarene Publishing House, 1968).

19. HH, vol. 27, no. 23 (Aug. 20, 1938), p. 2.

20. Ibid., p. 5.

church, the first so distinguished in the 30-year history of the African mission.[21]

Morrison's return was delayed by the outbreak of war in Europe. The only available passage was aboard a Japanese ship sailing from Cape Town to Rio de Janeiro by way of Buenos Aires. He took advantage of the stopover in Argentina to spend 10 days with Missionaries Cochran and Lockwood.[22]

Morrison was able to secure passage via Pan American Clipper planes back to the United States. When he arrived, he was ill from what was thought to be food poisoning and dysentery. He spent almost a week in the hospital for observation, and for three weeks afterward had been up, working a limited schedule, and preparing his report on the Africa trip—a paper he finished in first draft on Thanksgiving morning, November 23.[23]

Just the day before, Morrison had written Iowa District Superintendent Hardy C. Powers cancelling a church dedication scheduled for November 26, saying, "I feel much better and am getting quite completely recovered from the ailment that I contracted in South America, but I am on a very rigid diet and this keeps me so desperately weak and frail that I am afraid I would not be of much service to you if I should come."[24]

Dr. and Mrs. C. Warren Jones paid the Morrisons a visit in the early afternoon of Thanksgiving Day. The two men talked briefly about the missionary concerns so close to both of them, and Morrison reported that he was feeling better. After the Joneses left, Morrison was lighting a fire in the fireplace when he dropped over dead from a massive heart attack.[25]

Morrison had been a Nazarene only 18 years when he died at age 68. As a Methodist minister throughout most of his career, he had founded the Laymen's Holiness Movement in the Dakotas and, in 1922, led most of his followers into the Church of the Nazarene. After a four-year stint as district superintendent and a brief period (1926-27) as president of Northwest Nazarene College, he was called to Kansas City where he served for 10 years

---

21. DeLong and Taylor, *Fifty Years of Nazarene Missions,* 2:199.
22. Letter, Morrison to C. S. Jenkins, Oct. 20, 1939; archives.
23. PGB, 1940, pp. 71-76.
24. Letter, Nov. 22, 1939, Morrison to Powers; archives.
25. Letter, M. Lunn to J. W. Goodwin, Nov. 27, 1939; archives.

chiefly as Foreign Missions secretary prior to election as a general superintendent in 1936. He was, as J. B. Chapman called him, truly "an apostle of achieving faith."[26]

Morrison's death was the first loss of a general superintendent in office since the passing of E. F. Walker in 1918, some 21 years before. It was to be the first of a series that within 10 years would claim the lives of all the members of the Board of General Superintendents then serving and two others elected at the General Assembly held seven months after Morrison's demise.

The General Board meeting in January, 1938, heard plans for a Mid-quadrennial Sunday School Convention scheduled for the following June at Bethany, Okla. The plans were drawn and presented by Edgar P. Ellyson, who had served as Church Schools secretary and editor in chief of the department since 1923.

Immediately after the board meeting, under gentle pressure from the general superintendents, the aging Ellyson submitted his resignation to take effect July 1 of that year. Plans were worked out for Dr. and Mrs. Ellyson to continue writing for the department without reduction in salary until after the General Assembly of 1940.[27]

Ellyson had made a substantial contribution to church schools in his 15-year tenure. The growth of Sunday School literature both in variety and volume was phenomenal. The number of schools had increased from 1,149 to 2,313 with enrollments zooming from 88,846 to 277,250 and average weekly attendance going from 49,000 to 160,860. Periodical publications increased in volume from 142,400 to 357,100 per week. Ellyson had been responsible for overseeing and editing a total of 11 church schools publications. He had introduced a graded curriculum up through the junior level (9-11 years).

Ellyson's post was offered to J. Glenn Gould who declined. Orval J. Nease, former president of Pasadena College and pastor of Detroit First Church, was then nominated and accepted.

The June, 1940, convention preceding the General Assembly became a time for recognition of the services of Ellyson and in-

---

26. HH, vol. 28, no. 42 (Dec. 30, 1939), p. 31; cf. Ramon P. Vanderpool, "The Life and Ministry of J. G. Morrison" (B.D. thesis, Nazarene Theological Seminary, 1955). Chapman's reference is to Morrison's most significant book titled *Achieving Faith* (Kansas City: Nazarene Publishing House, 1926).

27. Letter, J. G. Morrison to J. B. Chapman, Jan. 14, 1938; archives.

duction of Nease as his successor. Over 1,200 attended as delegates and visitors, and the 1,400-seat Bethany Municipal Auditorium was filled to overflowing for the night sessions.

Bethany-Peniel President A. K. Bracken paid Ellyson a well-deserved tribute at the Friday afternoon appreciation service:

> Dr. Ellyson is known as a theologian. When in the early days of our movement we needed sound and sane leadership and thinking, no one made a greater contribution than did Dr. and Mrs. Ellyson. He is known as a teacher, a spiritual adviser and counselor. He has done outstanding work in his administration of the Sunday School work. We have always had full confidence in his orthodoxy.[28]

IV. FLEMING AND THE NMBA

As well as serving as general church secretary, E. J. Fleming had been secretary-treasurer of what was first known as the Mutual Benefit Society, set up by the General Assembly of 1919. This was a quasi-insurance program in which members agreed to pay a stipulated sum when notified of the death of another member. The proceeds of these assessments, also in a stipulated amount, were then paid the beneficiaries of the deceased member.

At first it was thought the society could operate simply as a benevolent organization. However, it soon became clear that it was in fact an insurance plan and would have to come under state insurance department supervision.

In 1923, the Mutual Benefit Society was put under a board of directors elected by its membership rather than by the General Assembly, and in 1933 the name was changed by the directors to the Nazarene Mutual Benevolent Association.

By 1938, it became clear that the organization was operating on an unsound financial basis. Because younger persons could purchase standard life insurance at cheaper rates, the average age of society members was going up, with increasing death rates, dwindling reserves, and the clear danger of bankruptcy.

The officers and directors faced a hard choice. (1) They could attempt to continue until overcome by insolvency; (2) they could

---

28. PGB, 1938, pp. 66-68, 95; 1939, pp. 112-13; HH, vol. 27, no. 16 (July 2, 1938), pp. 2-3; HH, vol. 27, no. 17 (July 9, 1938), pp. 2-15; letters, J. G. Morrison to R. T. Williams, Jan. 20 and Feb. 2, 1938; archives.

dissolve the association, a move virtually impossible without voluntary or involuntary receivership under court orders; or (3) they could reorganize as a legal reserve insurance company. Opting for the third alternative, the association leaders proceeded to reconstruct their rate and benefit structure on an actuarial basis. The reorganization plan was presented to the insurance departments of the states of Missouri, Arkansas, and Nevada and was approved by all three as sound and equitable to those affected.

Older members, particularly, were bitterly disappointed. Benefits were cut to as little as 20 percent of former levels, and rates were adjusted upward correspondingly. Older persons had little choice, since new policies elsewhere were prohibitive in cost. Eventually, 97 percent of those above age 50 stayed in; 80 percent of the membership as a whole. They were told that while the old arrangement was only 18 percent solvent, the new association was "120 percent solvent" with a surplus that "per dollar of liability is greater than the old line companies."

The association officers made a sincere effort to build its membership beyond the 5,000 already enrolled, for whom $5 million in protection was pledged. Ads were placed in the *Herald of Holiness* presenting the NMBA as "By Nazarenes . . . for Nazarenes."[29]

Fleming and the directors fully expected the approval of the church leadership and hoped to continue advertising through the *Herald* and presenting their appeal as a Nazarene organization. Of the general superintendents, Goodwin was noncommital, Morrison was in favor, but Williams and Chapman were adamantly opposed. Doubtful of the success of the new arrangement, they feared implication of the church both legally and morally in the event of bankruptcy.

The Williams-Chapman view prevailed, and the Board of General Superintendents passed a motion at a meeting on August 21, 1939, requiring that the term "Nazarene" be deleted from the name of the organization. No general officer of the church could serve as an official of the association. The offices must be moved from the church headquarters. No platform presentation in district assemblies could be made in behalf of the reorganized association. Notice of this action was published in the October 28 issue of the *Herald of Holiness.*

---

29. Frequently throughout 1937 and early 1938.

M. Lunn, who had been elected president of the new organization, chose to remain as manager of the publishing house and as general treasurer and resigned his position in the association. Fleming, on the other hand, felt committed to the project and resigned as general church secretary effective October 1, 1939. The association changed its name to the Christian Mutual Benevolent Association and moved its offices to Carson City, Nev. There it continued to do business until bought out by the Woodmen of the World.[30]

Fleming had served his church well: 20 years as a pastor, and 20 years as its general secretary. Not all the district secretaries or headquarters workers appreciated his insistence on accurate statistics. But in his long service as secretary of the Department of Ministerial Benevolence, his personal concern for the elderly ministers and widows he served endeared him to many. When Rev. Mrs. Edna Wells Hoke died at age 61 in 1936, Fleming wrote the bereaved minister-husband:

> My dear brother, your heart is heavy with sorrow. A few more years and the dear Lord will call you to that home also. A few more years and all of us will be remembered no more by those who follow on. But while we tarry and continue our labors and, while you gather up the broken strands and seek to find a new course in life, the dear Master will walk by your side. No doubt you will find it very difficult to know just which way to turn and what to do, but He who loves you will walk by your side, and you, with your hand in His, will be able to go forward.[31]

V. Other Changes

Just four months before the 1940 General Assembly, General Superintendent J. B. Chapman lost his wife. Maud Frederick Chapman died on the 37th anniversary of their marriage, February 18, 1940, in Oklahoma City, the victim of double pneumonia that followed an attack of influenza.

---

30. Correspondence, R. T. Williams to J. G. Morrison, June 26, 1939; Williams to J. B. Chapman, July 11, 1939; Chapman to Williams, July 11, 1939; Williams to Chapman, July 21, 1939; Fleming letter of resignation to Board of General Superintendents, Aug. 15, 1939; Fleming to Board of General Superintendents, Aug. 21 and 28, 1939; Minutes, Board of General Superintendents, Aug. 21 and 28, 1939; HH, vol. 28, no. 33 (Oct. 28, 1939), p. 11; Fleming to Williams, Sept. 5, 1940 (Archives, R. T. Williams correspondence).
31. HH, vol. 25, no. 38 (Dec. 5, 1936), p. 26.

Mrs. Chapman had been very much a part of her husband's life. As R. T. Williams noted at the funeral, "The heart-searching messages that have come from Dr. Chapman's heart and lips have been inspired to no small extent by that overflow spirit of Sister Chapman. She was a Spirit-filled woman and lived a Spirit-filled life."[32]

Chapman's second marriage two years later to Missionary Louise Robinson reinforced his already strong missionary interests and helped spark the extensive missionary expansion which took place at the end of World War II.

General leadership was not alone in changes during the 1936 to 1940 years. Over half the district superintendents who came to the 1940 General Assembly were new in office. Some names of men appear on the superintendents' list who were to take large places in the future: John L. Knight, Abilene; Paul Pitts, Alabama; Dowie Swarth, Alberta; I. C. Mathis, Dallas; Earle W. Vennum, Florida; Glenn Griffith, Idaho-Oregon-Utah; Hardy C. Powers, Iowa; Oscar Finch, Kansas; Elbert Dodd, Louisiana; Cecil C. Knippers, Mississippi; R. C. Gunstream, New Mexico; D. I. Vanderpool, Northwest; Roy H. Cantrell, Ontario; O. L. Benedum, Pittsburgh; and Raymond Browning, Southeast Atlantic.

VI. NAZARENE COLLEGES TO THE EVE OF WORLD WAR II

Debt liquidation was a first order of business for Nazarene colleges during the years leading up to the outbreak of the Second World War. At the same time, increasing enrollments as financial conditions improved somewhat increased the pressure for more adequate dormitories, library holdings, laboratories, and other physical facilities. Total enrollments grew from 2,239 in 1936 to 2,658 in 1939-40.[33]

A. New Administrations

Three of the colleges entered the new quadrennium in 1936 with new presidents: Gideon B. Williamson at Eastern Nazarene College, A. B. Mackey at Trevecca, and Harold W. Reed at Bresee.

---

32. HH, vol. 28, no. 50 (Feb. 24, 1940), p. 3; vol. 29, no. 2 (Mar. 23, 1940), pp. 28-29.
33. GAJ, 1940, p. 392.

Williamson gave his first attention to reducing the horrendous debt ENC was carrying in 1936. So successful was he that the indebtedness of the school, secured and unsecured, was reduced from over $130,000 to $85,000 by 1940.[34]

When Mackey assumed the reins at Trevecca, the college was operating on a seven-acre campus leased from the Methodist Board of Education with option to buy. The facility had been a college for blacks and included an administration building and two dormitories. When the option expired, Trevecca was able to make a required down payment of $4,000. On his own, Mackey purchased an additional 40 acres of farmland adjoining the campus, later to be transferred to the college. The college registered a 20 percent increase in enrollment and reduced its total indebtedness by over $10,000 in the first year of Mackey's administration.[35]

Under Reed's leadership, the curriculum at Bresee was expanded to four years in 1938. However, it became clear by the end of the quadrennium that the support territory of the college was too small to maintain a full college program. With Presidents Bracken (of Bethany-Peniel) and Reed present, the Department of Education in its January, 1940, meeting recommended a merger of the two colleges. When the respective boards of control approved, the merger was consummated, and Bresee College concluded 35 years of educational work.

Several of Bresee's faculty and many of its 125 students transferred to Bethany. Reed joined the staff at Pasadena College and enrolled in a doctoral program at the University of Southern California.[36]

B. Economic Progress

Bethany itself added a 100-bed dormitory (later expanded to 175 beds) and called it Bud Robinson Hall. The building also accommodated the college dining hall and a modern kitchen. The facility was occupied in 1936. Three years later the men's dormitory was doubled in size to accommodate 85 men. In recognition of the

---

34. GAJ, 1940, p. 391; Cameron, *ENC: First Fifty Years,* pp. 288-89.
35. GAJ, 1940, p. 392; Wynkoop, *Trevecca Story,* pp. 163 ff.; HH, vol. 29, no. 12 (June 1, 1940), p. 9.
36. PGB, 1940, pp. 53-54; GAJ, 1940, p. 391; Roy Cantrell, "History of Bethany Nazarene College" (D.R.E. diss., Southwestern Baptist Theological Seminary, Fort Worth, 1955), pp. 196-206; Philo, "Historical Development," pp. 47-48.

Bresee merger, a new wing of the Administration Building constructed in 1940 was named Bresee Hall. The enrollment moved from 391 in 1937 to 450 in 1940. Assumption of Bresee College liabilities left the indebtedness at approximately the same figure.[37]

Pasadena College reported a debt reduction from $82,253 to $38,400 with a campaign in progress in 1940 to liquidate an additional $10,000. In the meantime, college enrollment increased from 370 to 556 in four years.[38]

Northern Bible College officially changed its name to Canadian Nazarene College (Western) in February, 1940; reduced its indebtedness by $6,000 while adding another $6,000 in buildings and equipment; had its high school department accredited by the province of Alberta; and reached a high enrollment of 93 during the quadrennium.[39]

C. The Relocation of Olivet

Olivet experienced the most dramatic changes of all the colleges during this period. T. W. Willingham, president since 1926, resigned at commencement time in 1938, and A. L. Parrott was chosen his successor.

Early Sunday morning, November 19, 1939, fire of undetermined origin completely destroyed the Administration Building of the college. The building was the largest on the campus and housed 32 classrooms, the college library, the science laboratories, a music hall, chapel, administrative offices, and "college museum."

In addition to the loss of the building was the destruction of three grand pianos, eight upright pianos, the larger part of the school's orchestra instruments, and 7,000 library books. All equipment in the chemistry, zoology, and physics laboratories was lost with the exception of an armload of microscopes valued at $3,000 carried out by one of the students. The total loss was estimated at $100,000, insured to only one-fourth of that amount.

The college had the largest enrollment of its history to that date, 398 students, up from 304 the preceding year. Later in the

---

37. Cantrell, "History of Bethany," pp. 153-55; HH, vol. 29, no. 12 (June 1, 1940), p. 4.
38. GAJ, 1940, p. 392; HH, vol. 29, no. 12 (June 1, 1940), p. 8, the annual education number, gives slightly different data for some of the colleges.
39. GAJ, 1940, p. 391; HH, vol. 29, no. 12 (June 1, 1940), p. 4; vol. 28, no. 51 (Mar. 2, 1940), pp. 28-29. The designation "Western" was soon dropped.

week, classes were carried on in improvised classrooms. Within hours, President Parrott and the Executive Committee of the board met to assess the situation and plan reconstruction or relocation. There was strong feeling on the Executive Committee in favor of relocation.

Sentiment was sharply divided both in the board and in the community when the options were made known. Many local people had a large investment in the presence of the college in their community and could not be reconciled to the idea of a move. Parents had purchased lots and built homes to be near the college. For the town itself, the presence of the college was its chief reason for being. Almost everyone in the community had large financial and emotional stakes in the continued operation of the institution.

Others felt that the fire was a clear signal for relocation. For one thing, it became apparent that no loan of a size sufficient to rebuild at Olivet could be obtained. The college attorney advised the board that long-term financing in any considerable amount was completely out of the question.

Possible sites for relocation were considered in the following two months at Des Moines; Decatur, Ill.; and Indianapolis. The choice fell instead on the campus of the former St. Viator College at Bourbonnais, a suburb of Kankakee, Ill., some 80 miles north of Olivet, which was up for sale. The final action to relocate was taken at a board meeting held in Danville, Ill., on February 6, 1940. The vote to buy the Bourbonnais property was 32 in favor and 9 opposed.

The decision met with strong local protest. Three well-known Olivet constituents drafted a long telegram to General Superintendents Williams and Chapman the week following the board's decision. Jacob A. Hirshbrunner was postmaster of the town and had long been a member of the District Advisory Board. J. H. Dennis was a Nazarene minister well known in southern Illinois. Louis Mellert was a substantial farmer whose fields backed up to the borders of the town. The three stated that they represented "Olivet citizenry and surrounding community."

Their message predicted loss of support and possible loss of the college if the projected move were allowed to go through. "People heartbroken," they said. "Men of keen financial ability predict an impossibility to finance new location."

The telegram went on to remind the generals that money had

been pledged for a new church in Olivet. They claimed that a new Administration Building could be built there for the cost of repairs alone at the Bourbonnais campus. The college would be trading a sympathetic community at Olivet for an area 90 percent Roman Catholic at Bourbonnais with a Catholic church and nunnery located on the same property. The move, they speculated, was prompted by the "selfish motive of a few."[40]

The appeal was unavailing and none of the dire predictions of Hirshbrunner, Dennis, and Mellert came about. The new campus encompassed 53 acres of land. Buildings included a four-story Bedford limestone and fireproof Administration Building; a dormitory housing 250, also of fireproof Bedford limestone; a gymnasium; a dining hall; a heating plant; and three other structures. The educational facilities had been planned for a college of 1,000 enrollment. The total property was at that time valued at over $1 million. Nearby Kankakee, a city then of 30,000, was highly industrialized and offered many opportunities for student employment.

The financial stipulations were well within reach. Proceeds from the fire insurance at Olivet paid off the indebtedness on the old campus. The purchase price of the Bourbonnais property was $200,000, with a down payment of $25,000 to be made October 1. The balance of the purchase price was financed at 4 percent interest, with interest only the first five years. Then $5,000 per year on the principal was due for the next five years, after which the college would pay $10,000 per year until the total was paid. A vigorous financial campaign was launched across the educational zone, and the indebtedness was actually lifted in four years.

The college was given possession June 1, 1940, and the move was made during the summer. The name of the school was officially changed to Olivet Nazarene College at the time of transition. The disaster of fire turned out to be an opportunity for the Central Educational Zone to build what came to be the largest Nazarene college, located on a well-equipped campus.[41]

---

40. Original telegram, Chapman file; archives.
41. Letter, Board of Trustees of Olivet College to Board of General Superintendents, dated Feb. 7, 1940; archives; HH, vol. 28, no. 38 (Dec. 2, 1939), p. 4; vol. 29, no. 8 (May 4, 1940), pp. 16-17; no. 12 (June 1, 1940), p. 7; no. 16 (July 6, 1940), pp. 27-28; GAJ, 1944, p. 275; and Philo, "Historical Development," p. 107.

D. Accreditation of Northwest Nazarene College

Northwest Nazarene College scored a notable achievement with its full accreditation in 1937. It was the first Nazarene college to be so recognized. In his first term as president, 1927-32, R. V. DeLong had secured the accreditation of the first two years of college work as a junior college. When he returned in 1935 for a second term, he set about to secure full recognition from the Northwest Association, the regional agency whose accreditation was recognized by the other regional associations and was therefore tantamount to national accreditation. A warm, personal relationship between De-Long and Frederick E. Bolton, chairman of the accreditation committee of the association, didn't hurt the school's prospects.[42]

Enrollment at NNC increased from 238 to 406 from 1937 to 1940, and Morrison Hall, a women's dormitory housing 100 girls, was completed in 1940.

E. Intercollegiate Athletics

Early in 1939, an issue was raised with the general superintendents relating to intercollegiate athletics at Northwest Nazarene College. NNC teams began playing basketball with other nearby colleges on a trial basis during the second year of President Gilmore's incumbency. The program had become well established and had won approval of the college's Board of Regents.

The new departure, however, appeared to be in conflict with an action taken back in 1922 by the then General Board of Education and later reaffirmed by the Department of Education and the General Board in January of 1934. Intercollegiate athletics "as commonly practiced in colleges" was deemed "out of harmony with the beliefs and practices of the Church of the Nazarene." The statement stopped short of outright prohibition of intercollegiate athletics, but most of the colleges had considered competition with other schools to be off limits.[43]

General Superintendent Williams was not disposed to involve the general leadership in the question as it related to NNC. He did, however, write J. G. Morrison, who was serving as secretary of the

---

42. Taylor, "Handbook of Historical Documents," p. 156; GAJ, 1940, p. 391; HH, vol. 29, no. 12 (June 1, 1940), p. 6; Sutherland, "History of NNC," pp. 60-69.

43. PGB, 1935, pp. 89-90; letter, H. Orton Wiley to J. W. Goodwin, May 11, 1938; archives.

Board of General Superintendents, that "I think it might be well for us to formulate some sort of a kind, gracious statement to Dr. De-Long and exhort him just a little bit in a very kind, unofficial way to be on the lookout and to eliminate this difficulty as soon as he possibly can."[44]

Morrison wrote DeLong in this vein February 14. He received a forthright reply. DeLong replied that should the general superintendents or the General Board be disposed to solve problems of what he deemed a "purely administrative" sort, NNC could request rulings concerning activities in some of the other colleges considered wrong at Northwest: "Three-act-comedy plays; mixed bathing beach parties; roller skating rinks (which our students have been prohibited from using); wearing of jewelry; attending professional baseball games and matched college football games."

Assuring Morrison that the college had no disposition to do anything "the General Superintendents do not want," but asking the opportunity of bringing to their attention "some facts which maybe they have not thought of," DeLong went on the offensive. "I have been acquainted with Northwest Nazarene College for thirteen years and I am sure there never was a more wholesome or a more spiritual student body than we now have," he wrote. Scores of students were attending the missionary band prayer meeting on Tuesday afternoons. The prayer and fasting service each Thursday noon was attended by 200 or more. Fully 95 percent of the students were professing Christians, including practically all the student leaders. Both the faculty and the administrative council were convinced that the school was doing the best work it had ever done.[45]

The upshot of the discussion was the submission of memorials (now known as resolutions) from the Ohio District delegation and from the Arizona district assembly to the 1940 General Assembly. The somewhat ambiguous wording of the Ohio memorial was adopted and printed in the appendix of the *Manual* in each successive edition until 1964: "We recommend that it be definitely provided that schools and colleges of the Church of the Nazarene engage only in intra-mural athletics."[46]

---

44. Letter, R. T. Williams to J. G. Morrison, Jan. 23, 1939; archives.
45. Letter, R. V. DeLong to J. G. Morrison, Feb. 21, 1939 (Archives, J. G. Morrison correspondence).
46. GAJ, 1940, p. 154; *Manual*, 1940, p. 278.

The issue was not resolved until 1964 when the General Board was authorized to adopt policies establishing what were deemed the necessary controls over intercollegiate athletics.[47]

SUMMARY

In the four years leading up to the 1940 General Assembly, the Nazarene growth rate established a trend that was to prevail from that time on. The peak growth rate, excluding the very early years, had been attained in the 1933-36 quadrennium when the church added 40 percent to its total membership and increased the number of local congregations worldwide by 23 percent. In the next four years, the growth rate declined to 24 percent in membership and 18 percent in number of churches.

Worldwide in 1940, Nazarenes numbered 172,144 worshiping and working in 2,813 congregations. Sunday School enrollment and attendance kept pace with church membership during this interval, also. The WFMS recorded an 8 percent increase in numbers, and the NYPS showed a growth rate of 13 percent.

The situation was reversed in economic matters. Total giving for all purposes rose over the four years from $3,330,926 in 1935 to $4,944,266 in 1939, an increase of 48 percent. General Budget giving during the same period increased from $215,644 to $286,122, or 33 percent. The lower percentage growth in general funds was to occasion concern later.[48] The years immediately ahead were to be times of severe testing. The ravages of depression and a slow recovery were to be followed by the trauma of the most destructive war in history.

---

47. The same Department of Education policy statement that placed strictures on intercollegiate athletics also warned against "dramatics and other forms of literary entertainment out of harmony with the beliefs and practices of the Church of the Nazarene"; and the 1940 General Assembly adopted a statement, "Relating to Dramatics in Schools and Colleges," which affirmed that "there is danger in the excessive use of dramatical productions in our schools and colleges" and resolved that "this practice be carefully restricted and greater emphasis be placed on the spiritual exercise that leads to sound Christian experience" (Manual, 1940, p. 278; PGB, 1935, p. 89).

48. Annual statistical summaries, HH, vol. 23, no. 42 (Jan. 5, 1935), pp. 16-17; vol. 28, no. 42 (Dec. 30, 1939), pp. 16-17.

5

The Church
in a World Aflame

The road to Pearl Harbor was not without some early warning signs. Both Japan and Germany had made sinister moves: Japan against China in 1937, and Germany against Austria in 1938. When Germany and Russia signed a nonaggression pact and Germany invaded Poland in August and September of 1939, Great Britain, Canada, and France declared war. World War II, destined to change the life of man on earth, had begun.

Americans were torn between conflicting motives: to keep out of war, and to prevent the victory of the Axis powers. The German blitzkrieg of early 1940 was followed by the surrender of France and the British retreat from Dunkirk. The American debate intensified.

President Roosevelt quickly called for $4 billion for national defense. Warned of German efforts to construct an atomic bomb, he instituted a top-secret atomic research program. Hitler's all-out attempt to bomb and starve Britain into surrender in the summer of 1940 failed, but the German submarine blockade made serious inroads into England's military capacity.

When Winston Churchill replaced Neville Chamberlain as Britain's prime minister in May, 1940, he immediately appealed for 50 American destroyers left over from World War I. Forbidden to sell the ships by neutrality laws, Roosevelt arranged to trade the destroyers for leases on British naval bases in Bermuda and Newfoundland. This was but the beginning of a vast lend-lease program by which military equipment was supplied to Britain and her allies.

In September, 1940, as sentiment began to harden in the United States, Congress passed the first peacetime conscription law in American history. Although isolationist pressure was strong, 800,000 reservists and 1.2 million draftees were called to the colors. Japan signed a mutual-assistance treaty with Berlin and Rome, and a European war moved a long step toward becoming a global conflict.

Meanwhile, President Roosevelt announced his decision to run for a third term as president. The campaign of 1940 tended to cast Wendell Wilkie and the Republicans in the role of antiwar proponents against the interventionist sentiment in the Democratic camp. Roosevelt won without trouble, although by a smaller majority than in either 1932 or 1936. He lost no time in moving more solidly behind the Allied cause.

The submarine war in the Atlantic intensified, and America was soon committed to naval action against the Germans. Still it would have been almost impossible to overcome the strong "America First" sentiment and bring about an open declaration of war.

The Japanese attack on Pearl Harbor December 7, 1941, changed all that. On December 8, the United States declared war on Japan, and three days later Germany and Italy declared war on the United States. The American people were united by Axis aggression, and World War II finally included all its combatants.

It is difficult to exaggerate the changes that resulted from America's involvement in World War II. The last vestiges of economic depression vanished. Vast dislocations of population took place. Twenty-five million men and women enlisted or were drafted into the armed forces, including 30,000 Nazarenes. Every area of life was profoundly affected.

I. The Church Looks Ahead

The General Assembly of 1940 met in June in Oklahoma City. The presidential campaign was in full swing. News of the fighting in Europe was on the front page of every daily paper. Talk of war and the future was muted in the public sessions of the assembly but dominated the halls and foyers of the convention and assembly sites.

The Women's Foreign Missionary Society began its General

Convention in the arena of the Oklahoma City Municipal Auditorium Thursday morning, June 13. The convention marked the 25th anniversary of the organization, and it was reported that $25,000 had been raised in 1939 and 1940 for Bible training schools in overseas fields.

The entire statistical report was encouraging. By the time the general society was 25 years old, it numbered 2,049 local senior societies and 388 young women's organizations, with district organizations on all districts. The total membership of the senior societies had reached 44,857, an increase of 6,801 during the preceding four years. A total of 5,670 of the members were on the foreign fields. The young women's department enrolled 6,940 at home, an increase of 1,130 during the quadrennium, and had a modest membership of 177 abroad.

The society as a whole had raised over three-quarters of a million dollars for world missions during the quadrennium, a 68 percent increase over the preceding four years. The Prayer and Fasting League had registered an increase of 5,226 members in the four years to total 34,419 and had raised $239,591 for missions.[1] Mrs. Susan N. Fitkin, president of the society from its beginning, was unanimously reelected for the coming quadrennium as was Mrs. Paul Bresee as executive vice-president.

The General Convention of the Nazarene Young People's Society began Thursday evening in the Hall of Mirrors of the auditorium. The thousand seats proved quite inadequate for the numbers attending. The convention elected a new general president, Pastor M. Kimber Moulton of First Church, Baltimore. Moulton had been a member of the council for the previous four years as well as prominent in youth activities in the east. Sylvester T. Ludwig was reelected general secretary of the organization.

The General Assembly itself drew what was then a record 8,075, including delegates and registered visitors. Retiring General Superintendent J. W. Goodwin preached the Communion sermon on Sunday morning, June 16. R. T. Williams preached in the afternoon service, and in the evening J. B. Chapman delivered a sermon on "Christ and the Bible" destined to become a much-quoted classic.

Williams had been given the responsibility of preparing the

---

1. HH, vol. 29, no. 11 (May 25, 1940), pp. 3-4.

quadrennial address of the general superintendents, which he presented Monday night. He noted the "unprecedented world conditions" which had prevailed throughout the preceding four years. Despite it all, some notable gains had been achieved. The church must face its future with courage, love, and a greater faith in God.

The future for the church was seen to be not without its dangers. Williams listed eight: (1) The danger of losing sight of the central theme of holiness as the heart of the Atonement; (2) professionalism; (3) substituting creeds and programs for the presence and power of the Holy Spirit; (4) institutionalism; (5) departmental independency; (6) legalism; (7) overorganization and excessive overhead; and (8) failure to maintain a balance between episcopacy and congregationalism.

Williams called on the assembly to take action in a variety of areas. He and his colleagues were concerned that the church have a clear voice addressed to problems of war and politics; that it raise high standards of ministerial ethics; that it provide more adequately for retired ministers; that it give attention to strengthening its work abroad by more careful selection of missionaries, more adequate equipment of the fields, and stronger supervision; that it take definite steps toward the establishment of a graduate seminary for more adequately educating its ministry; and that it continue to emphasize the necessity of deep spirituality and to foster the work of evangelism.[2]

The assembly faced the necessity of electing two new general superintendents. Morrison had died in office nine months before; and Goodwin, who had been limited by age and illness, was retiring. The two eligible incumbents were reelected with huge margins: Williams with 96.3 percent of the first ballot, and Chapman with 97.9 percent.

Orval J. Nease, 48, then executive editor and secretary of the Department of Church Schools, was elected on the fourth ballot. Nease had gone from the pastorate of Columbus, Ohio, First Church to the presidency of Pasadena College in 1928. Leaving the college in 1933, he pastored Detroit First Church for five years until elected Church Schools executive secretary and editor. His

2. GAJ, 1940, pp. 203-24; HH, vol. 29, nos. 15-16 (June 22, 29, 1940), pp. 17-32.

two years in Kansas City had given him a wider exposure to the church.

Howard V. Miller, whose 46th birthday occurred during the General Assembly, was elected on the fifth ballot. Miller came to the general superintendency after six years as pastor of the Hartford, Conn., church, nine years as a district superintendent, a nine-year pastorate in Chicago First Church, and a year as dean of religion at Northwest Nazarene College. He was a graduate of Colgate University and had been a Baptist pastor before entering the experience of entire sanctification and joining the Church of the Nazarene in 1922.[3]

C. Warren Jones, who had served as general secretary since the resignation of E. J. Fleming the year before, was elected to a full term in that office. M. Lunn was continued as church treasurer by an almost unanimous vote. D. Shelby Corlett was continued as *Herald* editor, and J. Glenn Gould, pastor of Cleveland First Church, was elected editor of church schools periodicals.

In the organization meeting of the General Board immediately following the General Assembly, C. Warren Jones was reelected Foreign Missions secretary and M. Lunn was given four additional hats: publications secretary and manager of the Nazarene Publishing House, church extension secretary, ministerial relief secretary, and temporary educational secretary.[4]

The General Assembly adopted a modest beginning for a ministerial pension plan in establishing the Nazarene Ministers' Benevolent Fund. The plan had been drawn up by a panel appointed by the General Board: R. T. Williams, chairman; M. Lunn, secretary; and members L. A. Reed, E. E. Hale, and T. W. Willingham.

Income for the fund was to be from General Budget allotments, a portion of the operating surplus of the publishing house, any specifically designated offerings, gifts, donations, bequests, or legacies, and investment income. The chief source of revenue, however, was to be in the form of contributions from local churches equal to 1 percent of their total giving excluding money raised for buildings.

---

3. Bill J. Prince, "Comparative Study of the Lives and Homiletical Style of Charles G. Finney and Howard V. Miller" (B.D. thesis, Nazarene Theological Seminary, Kansas City, 1955), pp. 40-57.
4. PGB, 1941, p. 20.

Ministers, missionaries, or their widows, would be eligible for assistance from the fund based on years of service, need, number of dependents, other sources of support, and "the record of the applicant's co-operation in this plan and the general program of the church." The plan envisioned both permanent relief—stipends at the rate of $10.00 per year of full-time service but not to exceed $240 annually—and emergency assistance to active ministers not to exceed $50.00 for sickness, surgery, or accidents.

The plan was to be administered by the Department of Ministerial Relief of the General Board and to begin formal operation May 1, 1942. Subject to a number of modifications, it still forms the basic program in the United States in addition to national Social Security for the support of retired Nazarene ministers.[5]

Facing the reality of British and Canadian involvement in the war, and the prospect of United States entrance, the assembly adopted a statement prepared by San Francisco Pastor J. G. Taylorson. Titled "War and Military Service," the resolution recognized the commitment of the church to peace. On the other hand, it affirmed, "Evil forces and philosophies are actively in conflict with . . . Christian ideals." Thus there may arise "such international emergencies as will require a nation to resort to war in defense of its ideals, its freedom and its existence."

Since the supreme allegiance of the Christian is to God, the church does not "endeavor to bind the consciences of its members relative to participation in military service in case of war." It does, however, "believe that the individual Christian as a citizen is bound to give service to his own nation in all ways that are compatible with the Christian faith and the Christian way of life." Because some of its members have conscientious objections to "certain forms of military service," the Church of the Nazarene "claims for conscientious objectors within its membership the same exceptions and considerations regarding military service as is accorded members of recognized noncombatant religious organizations."

The general church secretary was instructed to set up a permanent register in which members of the church prior to their nations' entrance into war could record their convictions as conscientious objectors.[6] As it turned out, the number of official regis-

---

5. GAJ, 1940, pp. 89-92.
6. Ibid., pp. 158-59.

trants was not large; but the church did offer its members the protection provided under law for those who by reason of conscience would refuse to bear arms.

II. War and the General Church

Nazarene leadership was quick to respond to the shock waves the bombing of Pearl Harbor sent around the world. In the first issue of the *Herald of Holiness* to go to press following that fateful Sunday of December 7, 1941, Editor D. Shelby Corlett wrote an editorial titled "We Are at War." It was a balanced call for responsible citizenship combined with a plea that the church continue to be the church. Corlett said,

> In a time of war the church will be tempted to divert its efforts to the promotion of the war. To this temptation the church must not yield. The church must be the church in time of war, just as in time of peace. The chief message of the church is the final triumph of God's plan. The church, even in war time, should be one place where the people will find a light of hope and peace amid the darkness of war and confusion; a place where the comfort of the gospel may be brought to sorrowing and fearing souls, where the star of hope is permitted to shine with a brightness and inspiration that will give people a faith in God and in the ultimate triumph of righteousness that they will have courage to overcome in the conflicts of life. As the Church of the Nazarene we must be everlastingly at our task—we must go all out for the saving of sinners, the reclamation of backsliders and the entire sanctification of believers.[7]

The annual Superintendents' Conference met January 7-8, 1942, under a sense of destiny—keenly conscious of the serious situation facing both the world and the church. With uncertainty about the precise shape of coming events went a strong conviction that the church must not fail in its distinctive role in human life.

The general superintendents made an appeal for "a period of importunate prayer encompassing the month of March and climaxing with Easter Sunday, April 5, 1942." They were concerned about the conservation and increase of church membership. They cautioned the educational institutions of the church to use the improving economic conditions to pay off their debts and set their financial houses in order. They pled for "the paralleling of our

---

7. HH, vol. 30, no. 40 (Dec. 20, 1941), p. 3.

co-operation with our nations in their response to liberty's call, by a mobilization of our all for God and humanity through sacrifice and service."[8]

The General Board, meeting immediately after the superintendents' conference, also faced the issues posed by world conflict. Sylvester T. Ludwig, soon to become president of Bethany-Peniel College, spoke for the Nazarene Young People's Society—which, with the Sunday School, was most directly affected by the conditions brought about by war:

> There is only one fear we need to have regarding our work during 1942. That is "inner fear" which freezes us into inactivity. The temptation will come—amid war, blackouts and restrictions—to pull into our shell and say, "There isn't much we can do anyway." Nothing could be more pleasing to the enemy of man's soul than for us to go into a "spiritual bomb cellar" and there, away from the conflict of sin, repose in comparative safety. And those of us who are leaders must set the pace. If we retreat, God have mercy on us. This generation of youth will never forgive us for such spiritual cowardice.[9]

An immediate casualty was the cancellation of the Mid-quadrennium Church School Conference scheduled for July, 1942. This was in compliance with government requests for limiting unnecessary travel in the interest of national defense.[10]

A. The Servicemen's Commission

Even before United States involvement in the war, the NYPS General Council had established a free literature fund to provide the *Herald of Holiness,* the *Young People's Journal,* and the *Young People's Standard* to Nazarene service personnel whose names and military addresses were supplied by the pastors. A personal letter from Ludwig's office accompanied the first mailing of the publications. Later the devotional quarterly, *Come Ye Apart,* was substituted for the *Journal.* [11]

When Ludwig resigned as NYPS general secretary in June of 1942 to become Bethany-Peniel's president, Bethany professor John L. Peters was elected to take his place. Peters had been chosen a member of the General Council at the convention in Oklahoma

---

8. HH, vol. 30, no. 44 (Jan. 19, 1942), pp. 4-5.
9. PGB, 1942, p. 84.
10. Ibid., p. 57.
11. Ibid., p. 83.

City two years earlier. He was much concerned about his peers in service and had himself applied for a commission as a chaplain. Peters suggested a permanent Servicemen's Commission both to carry on the free literature program and to establish stronger ties with service personnel and chaplains. The Board of General Superintendents responded by naming Peters along with C. Warren Jones, D. Shelby Corlett, J. Glenn Gould, and M. Lunn as members of the commission.

Peter's appointment as a chaplain came through early in 1943, and he resigned the NYPS post. Ludwig was asked to again carry the NYPS work as acting general secretary until the next convention.

The Servicemen's Commission not only picked up the free literature program, it became the coordinating agency for members of the Nazarene ministry serving as military chaplains. Nazarene chaplains were provided as much free literature as they could distribute, and each was given a field Communion set. At their request, they were supplied with songbooks, Sunday School quarterlies and supplies, libraries of religious books, and birthday folders. A system was set up to contact Nazarene pastors near military bases in the States and to supply them with the names of personnel from Nazarene churches and Sunday Schools stationed there.[12]

B. Nazarene Military Chaplains

The number of Nazarene ministers in the chaplaincy grew rapidly. The first four to become active duty chaplains were Edward J. Mattson, Elbert L. Atkinson, Alfred Minyard, and Archel R. Meredith. Before the war ended, 46 Nazarene chaplains were on active duty. By 1960, a total of 60 Nazarene ministers had held commissions as chaplains. Others have been commissioned and continue to serve in peacetime.

One Nazarene chaplain, Gilbert J. Spencer, graduate of Olivet Nazarene College in 1941 and pastor of the Aurora, Ill., church until he entered the military in March, 1943, was killed in an explosion on Luzon in the Philippines while conducting a service; and Byron Dale Lee was killed in action in Korea later. Mark R. Moore was wounded in the Battle of the Bulge in Belgium and held

---

12. PGB, 1944, pp. 80-81.

as a prisoner of war in Germany. R. Wayne Gardner was critically injured in an accident in a combat area.

Bronze Star medals were awarded William T. Armstrong, Elbert L. Atkinson (with five service stars), Everett D. Penrod (two Oak-Leaf Clusters), and Wilford N. Vanderpool. John T. Donnelly received the Guadalcanal star, Alden D. Grimm a Presidential Citation and the French Croix de Guerre with palm leaf, and Joseph S. Pitts the Philippine Liberation medal.[13]

The chaplains not only fulfilled their duties in the service but were instrumental in helping establish or encourage Nazarene work in Alaska, Hawaii, the Canal Zone, Australia, Okinawa, and in Italy and Germany—as well as extensive rebuilding in Japan and Korea.[14]

III. Missions in a World at War

As might have been expected, the involvement of the United States in war and the worldwide spread of the conflagration created severe problems for the church's mission abroad.

A. China and Japan

The China field had, indeed, been in chaos even before the Japanese army invaded from Manchuria in 1937. The Nazarene field around Tamingfu was quickly overrun by the Japanese. While the headquarters compound itself escaped extensive damage, other mission properties were not so fortunate. A large church building at Ch'ao Ch'eng, 30 miles away, was levelled by a Japanese bomb.

When the invasion began, the missionaries were evacuated to the coast. Only Mission Superintendent Harry Wiese remained in Tamingfu when the Japanese first occupied the area. During the occupation, other missionaries were permitted to return.

Since the United States and Japan were not at war until the

---

13. Letter, Beulah Garrett, secretary to Servicemen's Commission Director Ponder Gilliland, to Chaplain Samuel R. Graves, Jr., dated Mar. 17, 1960, archives; HH, vol. 34, no. 15 (June 25, 1945), p. 8; no. 20 (July 30, 1945), p. 3; PGB, 1946, pp. 87-88; 1947, p. 99.

14. Lauriston J. DuBois, ed. and comp., *The Chaplains See World Missions* (Kansas City: Nazarene Publishing House, 1946); Robert William McNeely, "The Work and Message of Armed Service Chaplains from the Church of the Nazarene" (B.D. thesis, Nazarene Theological Seminary, Kansas City, 1953).

end of 1941, American missionaries were at first treated with a modicum of consideration. However, as tensions grew between the two countries, in October, 1940, the American consul asked all personnel not absolutely essential to return to the United States. Thus by March, 1941, all of the missionaries had been evacuated except medical Dr. Henry C. Wesche, Bresee Hospital superintendent; Arthur Moses, the business manager; Rev. and Mrs. L. C. Osborn; Miss Mary Scott; and Rev. J. W. Pattee. When a Chinese Christian woman doctor was secured for the hospital in July, Dr. Wesche followed Mrs. Wesche and daughter Mary to the United States.

The morning of December 8 (December 7 east of the international date line) Japanese soldiers occupied the Tamingfu compound and interned the five American missionaries they found there. Within four months, the Osborns and Pattee were repatriated on the famous refugee ship, the *Gripsholm*. A year and a half later, Moses was sent home. Mary Scott was held in a large concentration camp in Weishen, Shantung, until American paratroopers were dropped into the area August 17, 1945, and the long ordeal was over.[15]

Missionary Dr. Evelyn Witthoff and Nurse Geraldine Chappell sailed for India from San Francisco on the *President Grant* in November, 1941, one month before the attack on Pearl Harbor. They reached Manila on December 7, and the following day were placed ashore with the other passengers while the ship set sail for safer waters.

Within two weeks, Manila was an embattled city. On January 1, the Japanese army entered the city. All American and British citizens were rounded up and taken to Santo Tomas University, whose 40 walled acres were to be the home of 4,000 internees for the next three years.

Dr. Witthoff worked in the camp hospital and Miss Chappell in the children's unit. Food grew progressively more scarce and living conditions more harsh until returning American forces entered Manila in January, 1945, and reached the interment camp

---

15. DeLong and Taylor, *Fifty Years of Nazarene Missions*, 2:84-87; John W. Pattee, *Hazardous Days in China* (Pasadena, Calif., n.d.), pp. 72-82; Mary L. Scott, *Kept in Safeguard* (Kansas City: Nazarene Publishing House, 1977); letter, Dr. Henry C. Wesche to R. T. Williams, Oct. 16, 1941, archives.

early the next month. The Nazarene medical missionaries were at last able to return home, later to reach India where Dr. Witthoff served until 1973 and Nurse Chappell until 1978.[16]

The rising tide of nationalism in Japan itself, prior to Pearl Harbor, had placed all foreigners under suspicion. Americans were particularly marked. Christianity was suspect as a religion antagonistic to Shinto, the state religion. Early in 1939, regulations were issued requiring all missionaries to submit copies of their sermons to the local police in order to receive authorization to preach. All foreigners were required to obtain permits to remain in the country. These residence permits were good for only one year and were to be carried at all times. Any travel required specific passes.

In the spring of 1940, Rev. and Mrs. William Eckel were warned to leave the country by a Japanese friend who had close connections with government officials. By a small miracle, they were able to secure passage and returned to the States, leaving behind all their personal belongings except what they could carry with them. Misses Bertie Karns and Pearl Wiley, the only other Nazarene missionaries in Japan, were also able to get home—Miss Karns on the last ship to sail before the attack on Pearl Harbor.

Hiroshi Kitagawa and Nobumi Isayama, longtime Japanese Nazarene leaders, were allowed to make the trip to the 1940 General Assembly in Oklahoma City. There, in consultation with the general superintendents, it was decided to merge the Kwanto and Kwansai districts which had been set up in 1936. Kitagawa and Isayama were supplied with funds sufficient to support Nazarene national workers for the following three years.

Further pressure by the Japanese government forced the union of the four holiness bodies having missionary work in Japan: the Scandinavian Alliance Mission, the World Missionary Society of the National Holiness Association, the Free Methodist church, and the Church of the Nazarene. The resulting group mustered a membership total of 5,000—large enough to come within the minimum limit set by the authorities.

Bishop Tsuchiyama of the Free Methodist church, a graduate of Pasadena College, was named moderator of the united or-

---

16. Evelyn M. Witthoff, M.D., and Geraldine V. Chappell, R.N., *Three Years Internment in Santo Tomas* (Kansas City: Beacon Hill Press, n.d.); DeLong and Taylor, *Fifty Years of Nazarene Missions*, 2:28-29; OS, vol. 29, no. 7 (January, 1942), p. 3.

ganization; Hiroshi Kitagawa became director of the educational work, and Isayama served as superintendent of the Nazarene segment. Later, all Christian bodies in Japan were required to operate under the name *Nippon Kirisuto Kyodan*—the Christian Church of Japan.[17]

The war brought widespread destruction to Japan, and buildings owned by the Church of the Nazarene did not escape. Eight of the 10 church buildings in Tokyo were destroyed. Throughout the rest of the country, 18 other Nazarene churches lay in ashes, leaving only 10 intact.

On the eve of the war, the church had 83 national workers and 41 organized churches with a total membership of 1,551. Forty Sunday Schools enrolled 1,616 with an average attendance of 1,086. After the war, Eckel was able to find only 33 national workers and 22 organized churches with 1,237 members. Sunday Schools numbered 20, but both enrollment and attendance were swelled by U.S. service personnel to 1,185 and 1,260 respectively.[18]

B. Other Fields

Other mission fields suffered in lesser degree during the war years. Travel became difficult and dangerous. Foreign supervision was impossible except in the Western Hemisphere, and there only to a limited degree. Furloughs were cancelled, and though money became more plentiful, problems of logistics made extensive reinforcement of the fields difficult. Nineteen missionaries were brought home or interned in China, and four were returned from Japan. Other fields received reinforcements sufficient to hold the total missionary force to 93 in 1944 as compared with 94 in 1940.[19]

One tragic loss during the quadrennium was the drowning of

---

17. Letter, William Eckel to C. Warren Jones, Mar. 11, 1939, archives; Eckel, *Japan Now* (Kansas City: Nazarene Publishing House, 1949), pp. 93-96; Juliaette Tyner and Catherine Eckel, *God's Samurai: The Life and Work of Dr. William A. Eckel* (Kansas City: Nazarene Publishing House, 1979), pp. 52-56; DeLong and Taylor, *Fifty Years of Nazarene Missions,* 2:61-64; PGB, 1941, pp. 103-5; HH, vol. 29, no. 45 (Jan. 5, 1941), p. 4; OS, vol. 29, no. 6 (December, 1941), p. 2.

18. The membership figures are taken from the quadrennial reports of the Department of Foreign Missions for 1940 and 1947 published in GAJ, 1944, pp. 244-45, and 1948, chart, p. 235. DeLong and Taylor, *Fifty Years of Nazarene Missions,* 2:64, give ministers and members before the war as 35 and 2,500, and after the war as 26 and 1,800.

19. Cf. PGB, 1942, pp. 57, 67.

Missionary Glenn Grose, returning from a meeting at a leper colony near his mission in Africa.[20] The loss was particularly painful for the work of the mission. Grose had earned a master's degree in Portuguese in order to be better qualified for teaching on the Moçambique field. The educational task had to be taken up by national leaders.

C. New Fields

Two new fields were opened for Nazarene foreign missionary work during the 1940-44 quadrennium and a beginning made in Alaska.

1. *Puerto Rico*

Missions executive C. Warren Jones had been approached by a young Puerto Rican evangelist, J. R. Lebron-Velazquez, during the 1941 annual meeting of the American Bible Society in New York, about bringing an independent holiness group of which he was the leader into the Church of the Nazarene. Velazquez was pastor of the *Iglesia del Salvador* (Church of the Savior) in San Juan, Puerto Rico, and president of a Council of Christian Churches comprising about 22 congregations with a total membership of slightly over 1,000.

General Superintendent and Mrs. Howard V. Miller visited the island in the fall of 1943 to investigate the situation. As it turned out, many of the congregations and their pastors chose to retain their independent status. However, Velazquez and Frank Fournier, pastor of the largest group at Mayaquez, together with four other churches, united with the Church of the Nazarene. Velazquez was named superintendent. Although he returned to independent work in 1952, the accession provided a small but important nucleus for later Nazarene work in Puerto Rico.[21]

2. *Nicaragua*

In the fall of 1943, Nazarene work was begun in Nicaragua, the third republic of Central America to be entered. Harold and Evelyn Stanfield were the pioneer missionaries. Their efforts met

---

20. PGB, 1942, p. 36; DeLong and Taylor, *Fifty Years of Nazarene Missions,* 2:206.

21. OS, vol. 30, no. 9 (March, 1943), pp. 10-11; PGB, 1944, pp. 10-12, 37; GAJ, 1944, p. 241; J. R. Lebron-Velazquez, "Puerto Rico," in Edith P. Goodnow, ed., *New Missionary Frontiers* (Kansas City: Nazarene Publishing House, n.d.), pp. 98-112; Carol Gish, *Missionary Frontiers at Home* (Kansas City: Nazarene Publishing House, 1960), pp. 28-32.

ready success, and within four years there were eight missionaries, 12 national workers, five organized churches, and five additional preaching points. A Bible training school had been built at San Jorge, and the work had spread across the border into Costa Rica.[22]

3. *Beginnings in Alaska*

In 1936, medical Dr. R. G. Fitz and Mrs. Fitz, who had served in China for 16 years, retired and took up a homestead just outside the city of Fairbanks, Alaska. One of their first moves was to gather a congregation for religious services. About 15 persons met in the open air in June in front of the Fitzes' unfinished cabin. Later, the little group moved into a rented house in the city, and in July, 1938, the first Church of the Nazarene in Alaska was organized with 13 charter members.

Albert and Bernice Morgan assumed the pastorate in 1940 and supervised the erection of the first permanent church building. Nazarene servicemen stationed in the Fairbanks area and other military personnel converted and sanctified in the services were an important factor in establishing the church in the community. The General Board contributed approximately $50,000 during the early years.[23]

Mrs. Morgan wrote in April, 1943,

> Our new Nazarenes are enthusiastic and faithful. Sometimes our congregation is almost entirely in khaki. We have a wonderful team of soldier leaders in the musical program. A gifted sergeant at the piano who makes the piano ripple with music. A Spirit-filled and unusual sergeant song leader. A soldier quartet known as the Ambassadors composed of a first lieutenant, two sergeants and a corporal. We advertise our church as "the church with an oldfashioned altar." God has been giving us souls.[24]

IV. A PUBLICATION LANDMARK

The years 1940-43 saw the fruition of 20 years of scholarship in the publication of H. Orton Wiley's long-awaited three-volume *Chris-*

---

22. PGB, 1944, p. 64; GAJ, 1944, p. 241; 1948, p. 239 and statistical chart, p. 233.
23. GAJ, 1944, p. 238; DeLong and Taylor, *Fifty Years of Nazarene Missions,* 3:34; Richard S. Taylor, *Our Pacific Outposts* (Kansas City: Beacon Hill Press, 1956), pp. 7-11.
24. Bernice Bangs Morgan, circular letter, Apr. 29, 1942, archives.

tian Theology. Wiley had been asked in 1919 to prepare a systematic theology for use in the course of study for licensed ministers and to "serve as a standard of doctrine in connection with the literature of our church."[25]

Wiley had been educated at the College of the Pacific and the Pacific School of Theology where he earned an M.Th. degree and where his mastery of theology was recognized with an honorary S.T.D. in 1928. He had taught systematic theology in connection with his service as president of Northwest Nazarene College from 1916 to 1926 and at Pasadena College both from 1926 to 1928 and from 1933 on.

Wiley's thought is deeply rooted in the history of Christian doctrine. His method is to develop the biblical background for each of the themes he treats, then to sketch the historical development of the doctrine through the Christian centuries, and finally to state his constructive position. He cites long passages in smaller type at the bottoms of the pages, giving supporting material from a wide variety of sources.

Volume 1 was published in the summer of 1940. It contains two major parts: an introduction dealing with the province of theology, and the doctrine of the Father.

Volume 2 came out the next year. It concludes the doctrine of the Father and moves on to the doctrine of the Son and the doctrine of the Holy Spirit.

Volume 3 was published in 1943 and concludes the doctrine of the Holy Spirit with a chapter on Christian ethics and the life of holiness. Volume 3 also deals with the doctrine of the church and concludes with the doctrine of last things, where Wiley espouses a modified premillennialism.

The three volumes, with an extensive bibliography and index, total 1,468 pages.

A 461-page *Introduction to Christian Theology* followed in 1946. The material was taken from the larger three-volume work but arranged and adapted by Paul T. Culbertson, Wiley's faculty colleague at Pasadena College. It was designed as a text for introductory courses in theology and "to present Christian doctrine in a

---

25. Introduction by J. B. Chapman in H. Orton Wiley, *Christian Theology,* 3 vols. (Kansas City: Nazarene Publishing House, 1940), 1:5.

brief, yet substantial form for the general use of the laity of the church."[26]

Not only have Nazarenes profited from Wiley's theological efforts, holiness people in all denominations have given the three volumes wide acceptance, and Wiley has come to be recognized as the spokesman for the Wesleyan position in general theological circles. Yet Wiley does not write as a theologian for other theologians. He writes, as Carl Bangs has pointed out, as a minister for other ministers because "faith seeks understanding. A biblical faith called for a faithful theology."[27]

Nor did Wiley engage the rising neoorthodox theology of the 1930s and 40s, or other theological movements that made these decades such an exciting time in Christian thought. He did recommend William Temple's *Nature, Man, and God* for reading by his mature students, and he read Barth, Brunner, and the Niebuhrs, Reinhold and Richard; but he did not interact with them in his published work. The currents of thought were too recent for their full significance to be seen, and Wiley contented himself with citing the earlier recognized authorities of his day.

Another publication first was the 1941 launching of *Come Ye Apart*, a devotional quarterly introduced as "A Guide to Holy Living for Use in Individual and Family Devotions." The first issue was dated January 1 and included the following panel of contributors: J. B. Chapman, Bud Robinson, Mrs. S. N. Fitkin, Jarrette Aycock, G. B. Williamson, Paul Updike, Howard W. Jerrett, Raymond Browning, C. B. Strang, J. G. Taylorson, Lloyd B. Byron, N. B. Herrell, Ed. K. Hardy, together with excerpts from P. F. Bresee and a cover poem by Lon Woodrum.[28]

The publishing house property was enlarged during 1941 with the purchase of three pieces of property across Troost Avenue for $21,166, and the completion of a one-story addition to the plant at a cost of $17,787. The Beacon Hill Press (now Beacon Hill

---

26. (Kansas City: Nazarene Publishing House, 1946), p. 3.

27. *Our Roots of Belief: Biblical Faith and Faithful Theology* (Kansas City: Beacon Hill Press of Kansas City, 1981), p. 70. The material in the book was presented as the H. Orton Wiley Lectures in Theology, Point Loma College, San Diego, October, 1977.

28. HH, vol. 29, no. 39 (Dec. 14, 1940), p. 25. The first printing of 10,000 was sold out before the end of January.

Press of Kansas City) imprint for trade and special editions or publications was adopted at this time also.[29]

During the quadrennium ending in 1944, the publishing house contributed almost $86,000 to the Department of Ministerial Relief. The progress of the house well earned J. B. Chapman's accolade in the quadrennial address of the general superintendents at Minneapolis in 1944: "The Nazarene Publishing House is the greatest single asset of our denomination today, and our ministers and people are behind it with all it takes to make its continued prosperity a certainty, under the blessings of God."[30]

V. EDUCATION IN WAR YEARS

Nazarene colleges shared the general dislocation brought about in American education by the war. Even before Pearl Harbor, the beginning of the military draft was a portent of things to come. The availability of deferments from military service for bona fide ministerial students helped to some degree.

Actually, total enrollments held fairly steady, but the balance shifted sharply between men and women as more and more men were called into service and increasing financial resources made the attendance of more women possible. The seven colleges enrolled a total of 2,019 students in 1940-41. The figure for 1941-42 was 2,038. By 1943-44, it had risen to 2,156.[31]

Three of the colleges inaugurated new presidents during the quadrennium. C. E. Thomson, president at Canadian Nazarene College for 21 years, returned to the pastorate in 1941—to be followed for a year by Ernest Armstrong as acting president and William C. Allshouse in 1942.

S. T. Ludwig, for six years the executive secretary of the NYPS and before that president of Bresee College for nine years, replaced A. K. Bracken as president of Bethany-Peniel College; and Lewis T. Corlett, dean of religion at Bethany for the preceding eight years, was called to Northwest Nazarene College to succeed Russell V. DeLong.

Bethany also continued its practice, initiated with Bailey M.

---

29. PGB, 1942, pp. 49-51.
30. PGB, 1944, p. 48; GAJ, 1944, p. 142.
31. GAJ, 1944, p. 273.

Hall, of employing a businessman as its chief financial officer. When Hall resigned in 1941, banker John Stockton took his place. Pasadena College hired J. Bruce Deisenroth, Oakland businessman and longtime treasurer of the Northern California District, as its business manager in 1940.

Constantly improving economic conditions enabled all of the colleges to pay off their accumulated indebtedness. The most outstanding example was Olivet, which paid off in four years the entire debt on the campus it occupied in 1940. At the same time it increased its enrollment from the high of 352 in its former location to 710 at Kankakee in 1944.

Fire seriously damaged the chapel and fine arts building at Eastern Nazarene College in May of 1941, and gutted the administration and classroom building at Trevecca in March, 1943. Both losses were replaced with more adequate facilities within the year. Trevecca also completed its McClurkan Memorial Building and Alumni Chapel in 1943.

Northwest Nazarene College dedicated a women's dormitory, Morrison Hall, in September, 1940, and Williams Library in 1943 in spite of stringent limitations on building imposed by the wartime situation.

The Southern California District constructed a 31,000-square-foot combination camp meeting auditorium and gymnasium on the campus of Pasadena College. Seating 3,000 persons as an auditorium, the structure was finished just in time for camp meeting in the summer of 1944.

Both Pasadena and Eastern Nazarene colleges achieved full regional accreditation in 1943, joining Northwest Nazarene as fully accredited institutions of higher education.[32]

Nor was lay training in the local churches neglected. Nazarene Sunday Schools had had a "standard teacher training course" planned and outlined under the aegis of E. P. Ellyson in 1923 and initiated in 1925. In the late 1930s the youth and missions leaders began to show interest in lay training courses. There was also the

---

32. Cf. PGB, 1944, pp. 68-69; GAJ, 1944, pp. 274-75; HH, vol. 30, no. 6 (Apr. 26, 1941), p. 3; no. 8 (May 10, 1941), p. 20; and frequent reports from the colleges in HH, passim; Cantrell, "History of Bethany," pp. 49-71, 207-13; Thomson, *Vine of His Planting*, pp. 22-24; Cameron, *ENC: First Fifty Years*, pp. 290-304, 316-28; Sutherland, "History of NNC," pp. 64-73; Knott, *History of Pasadena College*, pp. 72-83; Wynkoop, *Trevecca Story*, pp. 175-80.

growing feeling that the entire membership, not just "leaders," need training.

Again, R. T. Williams led the way. He pointed out that the basic concept of the Christian life is service, not leadership per se. The result was the appointment by the General Board in 1941 of a Committee on the Correlation of Religious Education. The older Leadership Training Course was renamed and supplemented to become Christian Service Training. R. R. Hodges, a layman who had previously taught at Bresee College in Hutchinson, Kans., and who had headed the leadership training work of the Church Schools Department since 1936, was named the director—a post he was to hold until 1948.[33]

VI. THE PASSING OF PIONEERS

Three Nazarene pioneers died in 1941 and 1942. C. W. Ruth, associated with P. F. Bresee as his assistant in the beginning days in Los Angeles, became ill at a meeting of the National Holiness Association at Wilmore, Ky., and died at Asbury College there in May, 1941, at the age of 71.

Leighton S. Tracy, 60, who had retired in 1934 after a distinguished 30-year career on the mission field in India, died in September, 1942. Most of his last eight years were spent in pastoring a small congregation in New York City.[34]

The completely unique Reuben (Uncle Bud) Robinson died on November 2, 1942, at the age of 82 at his home in Pasadena, Calif. Uncle Bud had travelled as an evangelist for over 50 years. He did, indeed, become "a legend in his own time."

Born in January, 1860, in White County, Tennessee, Robinson was raised on the plains of Texas. He was converted as an illiterate cowboy and ranch hand at age 20 and joined the Methodist church. Sensing a call to preach, he taught himself to read and write with the New Testament as his chief textbook and a barn door as a slate.

Cowboy Bud immediately began to preach wherever he could

---

33. Kenneth S. Rice, "The History and Significance of Leadership Training and Christian Service Training in the Church of the Nazarene" (D.R.E. diss., Southwestern Baptist Theological Seminary, Fort Worth, 1956), pp. 148-93; PGB, 1941, pp. 14-15; 1942, pp. 80-81.
34. GAJ, 1944, pp. 111-16.

gather a few to listen. Ten years after his conversion, through exposure to the strong holiness ministry of W. B. Godbey, the young exhorter was sanctified while hoeing corn. With an ever widening circle of influence, Bud moved his wife, the former Sally Harper, and two daughters to Peniel, Tex. Under the banner of the National Holiness Association, he began a coast-to-coast ministry.

Robinson first encountered the Church of the Nazarene when he held a meeting for P. F. Bresee in Los Angeles. In the spring of 1908, he invited Bresee to Peniel to organize the first Church of the Nazarene in the state of Texas with 103 charter members, the Robinsons among them.

Four years later, the Robinsons moved to Pasadena, Calif., and located near Pasadena College where Bud continued a practice he had begun in Peniel of helping young people find the kind of education he had himself not known. He and his wife helped put approximately 115 students through college.

Robinson himself was an unceasing student. He had a prodigious memory and could quote almost one-fifth of the English Bible. His had an inimitable sense of humor, and he kept his congregations alternately in laughter and tears. He became one of the best-known writers in holiness circles with a weekly column in the *Herald of Holiness* titled "Good Samaritan Chats," and 15 books, all characterized by the down-to-earth good sense and the good-natured humor that characterized his preaching. For 52 years his theme had been "holiness" and, for the last 30 years, "the *Herald of Holiness*" had been added. Although ill and suffering during much of 1942, he was able to attend day services at the 1942 Southern California District camp meeting where he secured his 53,000th subscription for the *Herald.* Uncle Bud Robinson left a legacy of inspiration to the church with his whimsical writing and his undying enthusiasm for the gospel that had transformed his life.[35]

VII. Crisis in Leadership

The Board of General Superintendents faced the most severe internal crisis in its history during the 1940-44 quadrennium. The prob-

35. J. B. Chapman, *Bud Robinson: A Brother Beloved* (Kansas City: Beacon Hill Press, 1943), pp. 75-85; George C. Wise, *Reverend Bud Robinson* (Louisville, Ky.: Pentecostal Publishing Co., 1946), pp. 93-95; Basil Miller, *Bud Robinson: Miracle of Grace* (Kansas City: Beacon Hill Press, 1947), pp. 199-207; Corbett, "Man of Many Friends," *Our Pioneer Nazarenes*, pp. 44-49.

lem itself was compounded by a series of misunderstandings and failures in communication. It involved areas of administration and discipline in which there were no explicit guidelines.

The question concerned the discipline of a ministerial student who held a district minister's license but had never up to that time served as pastor or evangelist. It was initiated by the violation of a pastoral confidence, and it led to an action against one of the members of the Board of General Superintendents by the remaining members of the board.

In the fall of 1941, ugly rumors began to circulate with regard to the handling of a moral problem in his family by newly elected General Superintendent Orval J. Nease. The whole issue is probably best summarized by the statement of Dr. Nease himself: "I treated the matter as a family rather than a public affair."[36]

In his subsequent efforts to offset the rumors and clear his name, it is probably true that Nease underestimated the compassion of the church for a father dealing with a thoroughly penitent son who on one occasion had fallen into an act of sin. Some of his explanations, easily misinterpreted, actually aggravated the situation.

The crux of the matter was the installation of the son as pastor of a church in Little Rock, Ark. When the problem and its sequel became known, it seemed to many that normal church discipline was being circumvented and that Nease was guilty of malfeasance in office.

Early in April, 1942, Nease met with the other generals in Fort Wayne, Ind., and discussed the entire matter with them. It was decided to demand the son's resignation from his pastorate. Following the meeting, under date of April 15, Williams, Chapman, and Miller wrote Nease absolving him of personal involvement in "any immoral act or sin" but censuring him sharply for having "grievously erred officially and administratively in the handling of this case in the matter of discipline, giving the appearance of protection to a member of your family that might endanger the ethical standards of our church."[37]

---

36. Undated statement from Orval J. Nease in the Chapman file for 1942, archives.

37. Unsigned carbon of letter in Nease file, archives, dated Apr. 15, 1942. When Nease quoted the first part of the statement as exoneration and did not

As the summer wore on, the situation became more tense. Some of the district superintendents cancelled preachers' meetings and tours scheduled with Nease, and at least three objected to having him hold their district assemblies.

Even before the Fort Wayne meeting, Chapman and Miller had come to feel that a request for Nease's resignation was the only solution. Williams held out for six months against the idea. At last he consented. On July 22, 1942, the three wrote Nease, "We believe it will be in the best interests of the Church for you to step aside from the General Superintendency by way of a resignation. We trust you will cooperate with this united judgment of the three other General Superintendents of the Church."[38]

Nease replied that he must have time for prayer and consideration. He repeatedly sought another meeting with his colleagues, a confrontation which did not come off until the General Board meeting in January, 1943. The other men again pressed for a resignation.[39]

Nease apparently agreed. But shortly after he reached his Pasadena, Calif., home, he had changed his mind. He wrote Williams on March 12 that he had been receiving letters from "prominent district superintendents and pastors all over the denomination, nearly one hundred in number," urging him "to hold steady." He reminded Williams of a remark the senior general superintendent had made to him in Fort Wayne: "When I don't know what to do, I don't do anything." Nease concluded, "I believe that this is sound advice for me now and that is the course I shall follow."[40]

On April 29, 1943, the other three general superintendents addressed a note to the district superintendents: "This is merely to bring to your attention information which we feel you should know. Doctor Nease has finally given us his reply to our request that he resign. He declines to do so." At the same time, acting as a majority, they reassigned to themselves the district assemblies that

cite the censure of the second part, the other general superintendents withdrew the statement (letters, R. V. Starr to O. J. Nease, June 18, 1942; J. B. Chapman to O. J. Nease, July 22, 1942, archives).

38. Unsigned carbon of letter in archives.

39. Letter, O. J. Nease to R. T. Williams as chairman of the Board of General Superintendents, dated Aug. 4, 1942; Nease to H. V. Miller, Sept. 24, 1942; and Oct. 14, year date not given but apparently 1942.

40. Letter, O. J. Nease to R. T. Williams, Mar. 12, 1943, archives.

had been slated for Nease through the balance of 1943 and the spring of 1944. They had gone to the limit of their authority.

Here matters stood until the General Assembly in Minneapolis in June, 1944. A month before the assembly, Nease wrote the district superintendents stating that he would have "sought release long since" except that "such a withdrawal under pressure" would have been a confession "of that of which I am not guilty." He went on to state his hope that "a Christian way could be found to satisfy the existing confusion"; but if not, rather than permit the "unrest" to continue, he said, "My name should not be considered for reelection."[41]

The potential for division was keenly felt by the other generals. Decisive leadership is always liable to provoke adverse reactions. Some seemed to take partisan positions as an opportunity to register opposition to the majority on the Board of General Superintendents.

Williams, Chapman, and Miller went to Minneapolis resolved to accept reelection if by a margin of as little as a single vote, but with the mutual agreement that they could not serve if Nease were reelected.[42]

The atmosphere of the General Assembly was troubled and tense as the time approached for election of the general superintendents. When the first ballot was reported, Williams, Chapman, and Miller were easily reelected although with conspicuously lower percentages than in previous elections.[43] Nease received 221 votes, 39.5 percent of the total. G. B. Williamson was next with 126 votes, and Hardy C. Power polled 62 votes.

When the second ballot was reported, Nease had dropped 3 votes to 218, Williamson had pulled up to 211, while Powers went down to 52. The third ballot gave Nease 203, Williamson 289, and Powers 39.

After the tellers reported the third ballot, Nease—who had

---

41. Mimeographed letter dated May 15, 1944, addressed "My Dear Brother," archives.

42. G. B. Williamson, personal interview, July 17, 1976.

43. In 1932, Williams received 95.8 percent of the vote; in 1936, 97.1 percent; in 1940, 96.2 percent; and in 1944, 84.4 percent. Chapman's votes for the four same assemblies were 96.7 percent, 98.5 percent, 97.9 percent, and 91.5 percent. This was Miller's first reelection vote. He received 77.6 percent of the ballots cast.

not presided in any of the preceding four days of assembly sessions—spoke as a matter of personal privilege. "The Church of the Nazarene, of which I am a part, can make it without me," he said, "but I cannot make it without the Church. . . . I do not want, in any way, to embarrass the onward progress" of the church. "Therefore," he concluded, "I ask that company of friends who have so splendidly expressed their confidence by voting for me, to look in another direction."[44]

The members of the assembly and visitors stood in applause. With rare foresight R. T. Williams observed in an aside to those near him on the platform, "He will be reelected in four years, and the church will be healed."[45]

The atmosphere of the gathering was transformed. The ballotting continued. Williamson drew 298 votes on the fourth ballot, Nease 130, and Powers came back up to 81. After a recess, ballot No. 5 showed Williamson with 189, Powers 146, and Nease 85. On the next ballot, Powers pulled ahead and on the eighth ballot was elected the fourth general superintendent. The next morning, Nease was in the chair and took his rotation through the remainder of the assembly.[46]

A number of changes were to come from the distress of the preceding three years. In part at the urging of H. V. Miller, the general superintendents began to function as a board.[47] An even more immediate outcome was the adoption by the General Assembly of 1944 of a statement subsequently printed in each edition of the *Manual* of the church: "The office of any General Superintendent may be declared vacant, for cause, by the unanimous vote of the remaining members of the Board of General Superintendents, supported by a majority vote of all the District Superintendents."[48]

SUMMARY

Nazarenes came to their 1944 General Assembly at Minneapolis from a war-weary world. Because of travel restrictions in effect, the

---

44. GAJ, 1944, p. 66.
45. Samuel Young, personal interviews, Feb. 16, 1977, and Aug. 7, 1980.
46. GAJ, 1944, pp. 66-76.
47. Letter, H. V. Miller to R. T. Williams, Mar. 29, 1944, archives.
48. GAJ, 1944, p. 129; *Manual*, 1980, Par. 313, pp. 149-50.

assembly drew the smallest number of visitors of any General Assembly since 1919.

The tide of war had clearly turned the year before on both the European and Pacific fronts. The battle of Midway in June, 1942, had given the American navy control of the central Pacific. Guadalcanal was taken in February, 1943; and by June, 1944, American forces were on the verge of victory at Saipan and Guam in a relentless ocean advance toward Japan. The battle of the Philippine Sea had almost completed the destruction of the Japanese navy and reduced the Japanese air force to a fanatical band of kamikaze or suicide pilots.

June 6, just 11 days before the WFMS and NYPS conventions began, was D day in western Europe. Before the assembly adjourned on June 23, the Allies had a million soldiers in Normandy poised for their final strike at Germany. Eleven months of hard fighting lay ahead, but victory was assured.

The somber shadow of war lay over the assembly and was reflected in the comment of J. B. Chapman in presenting the quadrennial address of the general superintendents that the war was "a carnage forepicturing the great Armageddon."[49]

Despite the turmoil and dislocation of war, Chapman pointed to 74,898 professions of regeneration or entire sanctification at the altars of the church, with a net gain in church membership of 24,761 in the United States, Canada, and the British Isles. Another 987 were added on the mission fields.

Geographical growth was indicated by the addition of 477 congregations to bring the worldwide total to 3,290. The rate of growth in membership for the four years was 15 percent, the lowest figure since the 11 percent recorded in the four-year period ending in 1919.

Church schools enrollment rose slightly, but average attendance dipped from 198,394 per week to 193,829—a consequence, no doubt, of the unsettled conditions of the times. Youth membership likewise increased less than 2 percent, to 45,120. The WFMS gain was 17 percent to 40,975 members in the domestic districts.

In spite of the stringent controls on building materials, Naza-

49. GAJ, 1944, p. 136.

renes managed to build 464 new church buildings in the four years, completing one approximately every three days.

The financial picture reflected war-boom economic conditions. Giving for schools and colleges soared from $269,918 to $660,645 in comparison with the preceding four years, a 144 percent increase. Giving for foreign missions rose from $731,923 in the 1936-40 period to $1,389,824 for 1940-44, a 90 percent gain.

In fact, the increase in missionary giving moved C. Warren Jones to write a confidential airmail-special delivery letter to General Superintendent Williams saying, "We have a new type of trouble. . . . We have too much money, so much that if it ever leaks out to our people we will be two-thirds ruined."[50]

The cause of the alarm was indeed a new type of "trouble"—a working balance of $261,000 in the foreign missions fund and $40,000 surplus in home mission funds. Little time was lost in setting up a reserve. It was a reserve that postwar spending soon depleted, creating another financial crisis in missionary funding in 1948-49.

Chapman concluded his 1944 survey with the words, "The church is, we believe, better organized than ever before, and better able to carry through whatever projects it may deem wise to adopt."[51]

---

50. Letter, C. Warren Jones to R. T. Williams, May 28, 1943, archives.
51. GAJ, 1944, p. 140.

6
Entering the Postwar World

Neither the auxiliaries—the Women's Foreign Missionary Society and the Nazarene Young People's Society—nor the General Assembly meeting in Minneapolis in June, 1944, were disposed to make extensive changes in organization.

The WFMS reelected Susan N. Fitkin, president since the founding of the national organization in 1915, for what was to be her last term. Missionary Margaret Stewart, Mrs. W. W. Tink, and Mrs. R. V. DeLong were the new council members.

The NYPS reelected its national president, M. Kimber Moulton, and chose Lauriston J. DuBois, the young pastor at Newton, Kans., as its executive secretary.

The General Assembly itself chose Sylvester T. Ludwig, president of Bethany-Peniel College, to be the new general church secretary, and the General Board picked him to head its Departments of Home Missions and Education. Other department heads remained the same.

Two actions of long-range significance were authorization of a graduate theological seminary for the church and the appointment of a Radio Commission to develop a radio outreach for the denomination.

Nazarenes leaving Minneapolis had no way of knowing what lay ahead. The two most experienced general superintendents, Williams and Chapman, would not live out the quadrennium, and with their passing would come a new era in the church's top leadership. Within 11 months the war in Europe ended; in August, 1945, the world plunged into the atomic age, and three weeks later the war in the Pacific was over.

Seven months after the General Assembly, at which he had

delivered the masterful Communion sermon, General Superintendent Emeritus John W. Goodwin died in his Pasadena, Calif., home. He was a highly inspirational preacher and had shared the top leadership of the church for 25 years to the time of his retirement. But it was the loss of the two men in active leadership that shocked the church and inaugurated a new era in its general superintendency.[1]

I. Facing a New Age

The death of President Roosevelt in April, 1945, followed four months later by the shattering of Hiroshima and Nagasaki and the subsequent end of the greatest war in history, moved Nazarenes—as it did all church people—with a deepening sense of destiny.

General Superintendent Chapman wrote an editorial he called "In Our Day of Triumph" which was printed on the first page of the *Herald of Holiness.* "Throughout the Allied Nations tonight the sound of praise is heard," he said. "Our people are happy, and the religious among them are full of praises to God." But the hour not only called for praise, it called for prayer. The victors should pray for themselves that they "may be worthy of the victory God has given . . . and prove this worthiness by devotion to God and the highest ideals of national, community, home, and individual life." Those who rejoice in the prospect of the safe return of loved ones should pray in deepest sympathy "for those whose loved ones are not coming home at all." The sorrow of those who have loved and lost may be made even greater by "the unbridled joy of those who have loved and won."

With true statesmanlike understanding, Chapman urged prayer for former enemies. "The Germans, the Italians and the Japanese were once our friends. Let us pray that they may be our friends again." We will not harm them by hating them, for hate can ruin us: "Let us drive it from our hearts and minds as we would drive the plague from our houses."

But it was the future that concerned the writer. Men were talking about "re-educating" the people of the former "aggressor nations." But the word "educate" must be given a Christian content if it reaches the heart of the subject. Chapman continued:

---

1. HH, vol. 33, no. 47 (Feb. 5, 1945), p. 3; no. 52 (Mar. 12, 1945), pp. 1-6.

We must evangelize the world to make it safe for democracy. . . . It is of no use to look at the past and speculate on what might have been if we had gone more swiftly with the Gospel message. Our call is to look forward and meet the demands of the Great Commission today, tomorrow and the day after that. In our day of triumph, let us pray. And having "sung a hymn," let us turn with greater faith and greater courage to taking Christ to the nations through the medium of the Gospel.[2]

Not all gatherings of church leadership are decisive or significantly influential for the future, but the Superintendents' Conference of January, 1946, certainly was. The meeting had at first been cancelled by reason of wartime travel limitations. When conditions eased in the fall of 1945, the conference was reinstated. Fifty-four of the 60 district superintendents met with the general superintendents in Kansas City First Church. George Frame of the British Isles District, absent for 10 years because of the impossibility of civilian wartime travel, was present.

Despite encouraging reports from the sickroom of R. T. Williams, the absence of the senior general superintendent, his first time to miss such a convocation, added to the sense of crisis experienced by the group. What attitude would the church take as it faced the shambles of a postwar world?

It was given again to J. B. Chapman to speak for the church's leadership. His keynote address would never be forgotten by those who heard it. He titled the message "All Out for Souls":

All Out for Souls—I want to propose these words as a battle cry and a slogan for a new crusade. I would have us think of all that we have as a trust to be exercised, rather than as a heritage to be enjoyed. I would have us think of our responsibilities, more than our privileges. I would account ourselves as having just now received the tools for service, rather than to think of anything past or present as a finished feat. We are now just like the farmer who has obtained his machinery and motor power, and to whom the fields look for the harvest. . . .

Ours is a vitally spiritual approach. Even though we are dogmatic as to doctrine, our effectiveness is in our life, rather than in our attitude in pointing out the way of life or even in analyzing life itself. We preach holiness, but we must also be holy and help others to become so. We champion the cause of oldtime religion, but we must exemplify this kind of religion and promote it by the same means that our fathers used. . . .

---

2. HH, vol. 34, no. 25 (Sept. 3, 1945), p. 1.

Chapman went on to say that many are more concerned with symptoms than they are with the disease. He pled for the realization that now, as always, "out of the heart are the issues of life." The need of the church is not more legislation. The "one indispensable point" is "a passion for the souls of men":

> Brethren, I was born in the fire, and I cannot endure the smoke. I am a child of the bright daylight, and mists and fogs and depressing gloom are not to my liking. I want to go all out for souls. The revival I seek is not the product of the labors of some personality-plus evangelist. Such a revival is too detached and impersonal to meet my needs or to answer my prayers. I want that kind of revival that comes in spite of the singing, the preaching, the testimonies and the human attractions and distractions. I want that kind of revival because it takes that kind to really revive me.
>
> I want a revival that, like a summer shower, will purify the atmosphere of our churches everywhere, and which will awaken the dormant forces of our people, young and old. I want something so general and so divine that it will be uncontrollable. Something that will reform and regenerate drunkards and save respectable worldlings. Something that will bring in the youth and the little children. Something so attractive that it will break over into the circles of the pleasure-loving. Something that will set people on their back tracks to make restitution for wrongs committed. Something that will bring God to bear upon our domestic problems to save our people from the twin evils of divorce and race suicide. Something that will inject old-time honesty, veracity, purity and other-world mindedness into our preachers and people. Something that will make this namby-pamby, soft-handed, compromising, cringing sort of holiness as obsolete as Phariseeism was on the day of Pentecost.[3]

The deep emotion with which Chapman spoke as well as the clarity of his call made a profound impression. While he did not live to see it, the church's response to his plea to go "All Out for Souls" was the Mid-Century Crusade for Souls, plans for which were approved by the 1948 General Assembly.

II. The Changing Leadership

Hardy C. Powers, the man elected to replace Orval Nease, was a Texan whose family had settled in southern California. Powers

---

3. HH, vol. 34, no. 45 (Jan. 21, 1946), pp. 3-4.

attended Pasadena College and pastored for five years in the area before moving to First Church, Council Bluffs, Ia., in 1930. He became district superintendent of the Iowa District in 1936. He had served on the General Board for four years and was widely known throughout the church as a strong preacher in revival meetings, camp meetings, and preachers' conventions.

Powers was to serve a total of 24 years as general superintendent until his retirement in 1968. During that time, he was chairman of the Board of General Superintendents for 10 years by virtue of his role as senior general superintendent after the death of Miller in 1948.

Powers became noted for his insight in the choice of people for responsible positions in the church. He was a major force in transforming the general superintendents into a board in fact as well as in name. As G. B. Williamson said of him, "He saw clearly that God's people wanted and needed the guidance that a Board of General Superintendents molding variety into unity could provide. To such a purpose and policy Dr. Powers dedicated all the 24 years he served as a leader, trusted and beloved."[4]

A. R. T. Williams Stricken

The problems developing within the Board of General Superintendents before the 1944 assembly had taken a heavy toll of the strength of R. T. Williams. He was, by gifts and temperament, the leading administrator for the general church and had been for 28 years. He was suffering from high blood pressure and severe digestive problems for which the only remedy offered was extended rest.[5]

Williams felt almost a sense of rejection as a result of the loss of votes at the General Assembly. A year after the assembly, while he was in his Kansas City office for a few days, G. B. Williamson, at that time pastor of Kansas City First Church, visited with him. Reporting the visit to Mrs. Williamson later, the pastor said, "He is a wounded man."[6]

---

4. HH, vol. 61, no. 16 (Aug. 2, 1972), p. 20; cf. Corbett, *Pioneer Builders,* pp. 24-27.
5. Letters, R. T. Williams to Mrs. Bullock, Dallas, Dec. 1, 1943; to H. B. Anthony, Columbus, Ohio, Dec. 13, 1943, archives.
6. G. B. Williamson, interview, July 17, 1976.

Driven by a strong sense of responsibility, Williams carried his slate of district assemblies through the fall of 1944 and in the spring and fall of 1945. He presided at the 1945 General Board meeting in January although anxious friends noted signs of great weariness at times when he was out of public view. To spare his strength, he drove to most of his assignments at a leisurely pace, finding it the most restful mode of travel. Mrs. Williams accompanied him most of the time.

Williams' fall assemblies were in the Southeast—in North and South Carolina, Georgia, Florida, Alabama, Mississippi, and Louisiana. Because the distance there was great, and she was very tired from the summer schedule, Mrs. Williams decided not to go.

Williams' conduct of the assemblies, his morning talks, and his ordination services were of the same high order they had been for almost 30 years.

After the Florida assembly the third week of October, on the way to Alabama, Williams had agreed to preach for Pastor Bruce Hall in First Church, Columbus, Ga., Sunday morning, October 21. He arrived in Columbus on Saturday night. Pastor Hall had arranged for a hotel room and was to pick him up Sunday morning for breakfast at 8:00.

When Williams awakened early in the morning, he was conscious that something had happened to him. He was unable to stand. By the time he had to get up, however, he felt a bit better and dragged himself out of bed and began to shave.

When Hall arrived, he found Dr. Williams unable to speak. The pastor quickly summoned Nazarene physician J. M. Wilson, who rushed him to the hospital. Mrs. Williams was summoned and hurried to Columbus, together with her son, R. T. Williams, Jr., then pastor of Oklahoma City First Church.

As word spread, a vast volume of prayer went up all over the church. The crisis seemed to come on Tuesday night, and the following day there were signs of improvement.

When the patient's strength would permit him to leave the hospital, Mrs. Williams rented a small house in a quiet residential section of Columbus, and Dr. Williams was moved to the temporary home where he was to convalesce for five months from October to March. A great outpouring of concern and affection came from around the world by telegram and letter. There were encouraging developments as the patient's strength increased. There were hopes of full recovery, although his speech never did fully clear up. He was able to ride, to walk, and even to drive.

As spring approached, Williams longed for his cottage at Tuscumbia, Mo., in the foothills of the Ozarks. By the middle of March, Dr. Wilson consented to the trip, and Dr. and Mrs. Williams, together with their son R. T., Jr., and his wife, arrived at the cottage at noon on Thursday, March 21, exactly five months to the day after the stroke that laid him low.

Friday night, March 22, about midnight, another cerebral hemorrhage occurred. R. T., Jr., who had returned to Oklahoma City, was summoned again, and word was flashed to the older son, Reginald, an attorney in Salem, Ore., who with his wife arrived Sunday afternoon.

Dr. Williams' condition steadily worsened. He never spoke after the second stroke, although he recognized members of the family and seemed conscious up to the end. At noon, Monday, March 25, 1946, Roy T. Williams entered the more excellent glory. He had celebrated his 63rd birthday just six weeks before. It was true of R. T. Williams as Henry Ward Beecher had remarked, "When the sun goes below the horizon he is not set; the heavens glow for a full hour after his departure. And when a great and good man sets, the sky of the world is luminous long after he is out of sight. Such a man cannot die out of this world. When he goes he leaves behind him much of himself."[7]

How much of himself Roy Williams left the church in which he gave his life can scarcely be exaggerated. No other individiual did more to shape the Church of the Nazarene and hold it together through stormy years than did he. The 30 years he served as general superintendent—longer than any other man has or likely ever will—were crucial, formative years. He held the church together. No uniting group ever pulled out, despite the travail of hammering out a common life.

Williams served in the general superintendency longest with Hiram F. Reynolds, John W. Goodwin, and James B. Chapman. All were great and good men, and each in his own way made an indispensable contribution to the developing life of the denomina-

---

7. Quoted, Helen Smith Shoemaker, *I Stand by the Door: The Life of Sam Shoemaker* (New York: Harper and Row, Publishers, 1967), p. 220.

tion. But it was R. T. Williams who was the administrator par excellence.

Those who worked with Williams testify that he carried 90 percent of the administrative burden of the church. When difficulties arose, it was Williams who was consulted first, and his colleagues almost always did as he advised. He had an uncanny ability to size up a situation. And his correspondence with troubled persons who wrote him freely reveals a deep compassion and understanding.

Williams sometimes seemed slow to make a decision; but once it was made, he rarely turned back. His understanding of the financial concerns of the church was unsurpassed. He tended to be conservative in spending the church's money and always insisted on the highest standards of accountability.

Williams viewed the Church of the Nazarene as an American church with missionary endeavors; the missionary vision of the church was largely generated by H. F. Reynolds and J. B. Chapman. He rarely went abroad. But when missionary commitments were made, it was to Williams that his colleagues looked for guidance in providing the necessary funds.[8]

Nazarene polity provides that in case of a vacancy in the office of general superintendent, the district superintendents shall elect a successor. As a matter of practice, this has been done only when the vacancy has occurred in the first two years of a quadrennium.

A vote was taken in the weeks immediately following Williams' death, and 50 out of 57 ballots cast fell to Gideon B. Williamson, who until just the year before had been president of Eastern Nazarene College and at the time was pastor of Kansas City First Church. Williamson, it will be recalled, had received the next highest number of votes at the 1944 General Assembly when Hardy Powers was chosen. He was inducted on April 23, 1946, into the office he was to fill with distinction for 22 years.

Williamson was born November 26, 1898, near New Florence, Mo. The family had its roots in the Church of God (Holiness), centered at College Mound, Mo. Williamson graduated from John

---

8. Williamson interview, July 17, 1976; personal interview, Dr. Samuel Young, Feb. 16, 1977; personal interview, P. H. Lunn, Nov. 6, 1980; cf. also Williamson, *Roy T. Williams: Servant of God;* memorial issue, HH, vol. 35, no. 8 (May 6, 1946); GAJ, 1948, pp. 146-47, 154-55.

Fletcher College at Oskaloosa, Ia., where he joined the Church of the Nazarene. His pastoral ministry began at Farmington, Ia., followed by pastorates at Austin Church in Chicago, and Cleveland, Ohio, First Church. From there he went to the presidency of Eastern Nazarene College and briefly to Kansas City First Church. He was an outstanding biblical expositor and a strong and able administrator.[9]

B. J. B. Chapman's Death

James B. Chapman was 18 months younger than Williams. They had first met as young men in their 20s when both joined the Church of the Nazarene at Pilot Point, Tex., in 1908.

Chapman was then president of the Western Council of the Holiness Church of Christ which united with the Church of the Nazarene at Pilot Point, and Williams was ordained during the assembly there. Later, Chapman served as dean while Williams was president of Peniel University, and Chapman succeeded Williams in the presidency in 1913, a post he held for five years.

The two men were strikingly different but complemented each other ideally. Chapman had been editor of the *Herald of Holiness* for six years when he was elected general superintendent in 1928. In the 18 years they shared the responsibilities of the general superintendency, the two balanced each other to a degree that Nazarenes have always thought to have been providential. Neither would have been what he was without the other. As H. V. Miller said of them in his quadrennial address at the St. Louis General Assembly in 1948, "We would hardly suppose that there could be two men differing so greatly in personal temperament yet whose composite living and leadership could have afforded a church a greater contribution."[10]

Sixteen months after the passing of Roy T. Williams, James B. Chapman died in his sleep at his Indian Lake home near Vicksburg, Mich., just a month before his 63rd birthday. As G. B. Williamson wrote in the *Herald of Holiness* after Chapman's death, "When the history of the first forty years of the Church of the Nazarene is written, there will be three names that will stand out

---

9. HH, vol. 35, no. 7 (Apr. 29, 1946), pp. 5, 16; vol. 57, no. 19 (June 26, 1968), pp. 3-4; Corbett, *Pioneer Builders*, pp. 31-35.
10. Williamson interview, July 17, 1976; GAJ, 1948, p. 155.

in the front row alone. They will be Phineas F. Bresee, Roy T. Williams, and James B. Chapman"[11] Bresee, said Williamson, laid the foundation; Williams built on it a firm structure; Chapman added beauty—"stained glass windows."[12]

Chapman had carried an unusually heavy schedule during the first six months of 1947 without taking time off for rest and relaxation. He had suffered a light heart attack 10 years previously in India, but the fact was not widely known. Early in July, he and Mrs. Chapman made their way to their home on the shores of Indian Lake for some much-needed rest.

The hoped-for rest did not immediately materialize. Remodeling work on the house had been held up by lack of materials. It took several days of hard work and inconvenience before the Chapmans were able to get settled in.

The last two weeks of the month provided more leisure. Three of the children and seven grandchildren were at the lake enjoying vacations in their own cottages. Chapman had always been close to his family and enjoyed being with his grandchildren.

Occasional evenings were spent on the lawn with family and friends in fellowship and conversation—always lively when Dr. Chapman was in the group. The Michigan district assembly began Tuesday evening, July 29, in the nearby camp meeting auditorium with General Superintendent Hardy C. Powers in the chair. The Chapmans attended the opening service and visited with friends afterward. Dr. Chapman spent a brief time with Powers, making a date for breakfast together the next morning. It was an appointment he was not to keep.

During the night, Mrs. Chapman heard her husband breathing heavily. She went to the bedside, but he was gone without a struggle and without saying a word. It was 2:10 a.m., Wednesday, July 30.[13]

Chapman's biographer, *Herald of Holiness* Editor Shelby Corlett, whose daughter Marion was the wife of Chapman's son, Dr. Paul Chapman, was at the lake at the time and at the bedside within minutes. Said the editor, "He looked like he might still be

---

11. HH, vol. 36, no. 29 (Sept. 29, 1947), p. 7.
12. Williamson interview, July 17, 1976.
13. Letter, July 30, 1947, S. T. Ludwig to the district superintendents; archives.

asleep, so peaceful and normal was the expression on his face."[14] But the one G. B. Williamson rightly described as "One Man in a Century" was indeed gone, and only the worn and tired body was lying on the bed.[15]

Chapman was a philosopher-theologian with the soul of a poet and a rare gift of communicating truth by the written and spoken word. He was by any measure an intellectual giant. He had a dry wit that enlivened his preaching and a way with epigrams that made him eminently quotable. He read widely and wrote prodigiously. He authored almost 30 books or booklets and hundreds of editorials. Even after his election as general superintendent, he continued to write the "Question Box" in the *Herald of Holiness,* and Editor Corlett and his successor, S. S. White, printed a short editorial from Dr. Chapman on the front page of the *Herald* from the time Corlett took over as editor in 1936 until two years after Chapman's death.[16]

III. The Generals Become a Board

The dual loss within less than a year and a half tokened a marked change in leadership style within the Board of General Superintendents. Toward the end of his first term, H. V. Miller articulated some of his observations and concerns relating to the office in a letter to Dr. Williams. He acknowledged the influence of the Nease problem as they approached the 1944 General Assembly, but related his discussion more generally to what he called "a tacit restlessness relative to composite leadership," a restlessness, he says, which was "intensified by the fact of the common knowledge that the Board meets but once a year as such."

While he had no specific remedies to offer, Miller did argue for the need for more regular meetings of the general superintendents and the need to convey to the church that "the General Superintendents were speaking from time to time as a body."[17]

Shortly after the January General Board meeting in 1944, Williams sent a memo to Chapman and Miller. It was titled "Policy for

---

14. D. Shelby Corlett, *Spirit-filled,* p. 195.
15. HH, vol. 36, no. 29 (Sept. 29, 1947), p. 6.
16. Cf. Corlett, *Spirit-filled;* memorial issue, HH, vol. 36, no. 29; GAJ, 1948, pp. 147-48 and 155-56; personal interview, G. B. Williamson, July 17, 1976.
17. Letter, H. V. Miller to R. T. Williams, Mar. 29, 1944; archives.

General Superintendents." It reflected the position Williams had held throughout the 1930s and from which he felt Chapman had departed at the Superintendents' Conference in his unilateral plea for immediate action to start a seminary.[18] The general superintendents were "to speak and act as a body rather than as individuals on matters that concern the church." Whatever differences in judgment occur, "that fact is to be kept from the general public in the interest of solid and united leadership." "No one should express a disagreement with another," he said, "except to that individual or to the whole Board."

Both in matters of administration and in the interpretation of law or doctrine, "the Board should speak as a Board and not as individuals." When requests for funds come, or other matters arise that would affect the church as a whole, "no individual General Superintendent should express his own view, but refer the matter to the Board." This would also apply to matters of foreign jurisdiction. Each general superintendent represents the board, and his report should come back to the board to be presented in a united front to the church. An August meeting should be held as well as the traditional January meeting. Here was a long step toward policies that were to become the accepted norms in the years ahead.[19]

At the very beginning, the general superintendents collectively had been called a board as early as 1911.[20] In 1923, a section in the *Manual* was titled "The Board of General Superintendents," and the first stipulation was, "The General Superintendents shall organize as a Board, and arrange for, and assign to, the members thereof the particular work over which they shall have special jurisdiction."[21]

The number of general superintendents remained at three from 1908 to 1928, when it was increased to four with the addition of J. B. Chapman to the three who had served together since 1916—R. T. Williams, H. F. Reynolds, and J. W. Goodwin. On the retirement of H. F. Reynolds in 1932 and through the depths of the depression, the number was reduced again to three with the arrangement that the general superintendent emeritus could and

---

18. Cf. infra, pp. 205-6.
19. Williams file, archives.
20. *Manual,* 1907, p. 44; *Manual,* 1908, p. 47; *Manual,* 1911, pp. 64-65.
21. *Manual,* 1923, p. 85.

would be assigned occasional duties. Back up to four in 1936, the number was increased to five in 1948.

While board terminology was used, as Miller noted, the group met regularly only once a year in connection with the meetings of the General Board. There was much consultation in person and by mail between meetings, but opportunities for extended periods of discussion and deliberation were lacking. The dominant personalities of Williams and Chapman and the fact that Goodwin lived in southern California militated against a board philosophy. During the 1930s, Goodwin would often write, "Whatever you brethren think."

By 1948, the picture had changed radically Goodwin, Williams, and Chapman had been removed by death within the span of three years. H. V. Miller lived only six months after his third election in 1948, and Orval J. Nease died two years into his second term in 1950. Hardy C. Powers had served only four years, and G. B. Williamson only two years. The result was a total change in the personnel of the general superintendency in a period of six years.

We have noted Miller's feeling about the "restlessness relative to composite leadership" expressed in 1944. Powers shared that thinking and Williamson readily concurred. The addition of Samuel Young to the group in 1948 gave another impetus to the board concept.

In addition to changing personalities and concepts of leadership, the reference to the general superintendents of ever increasing responsibilities added to the need for board action. As the church and its General Assemblies grew in size, there was more and more the tendency to delegate responsibility and authority to "the Board of General Superintendents."

With increasing need for collective action, the group began to meet more frequently and to devote more time to the meetings. The election of the fifth general in 1948 reduced the work load of each and made available the time for more and longer meetings. The growing availability of air travel and the fact that four of the five elected in 1948 lived in Kansas City facilitated interaction among the men.

The loss by death of four general superintendents in office within four years (Williams, 1946; Chapman, 1947; Miller, 1948; Nease, 1950) led the General Board to a conscious effort to ease the pressures. A greater allocation was provided for their expenses. It was not until Powers' day that the general church began to pay the generals' long-distance telephone bills. The policy was adopted of once a quadrennium sending the general's wife with him on trips for foreign supervision.

After World War II, the general superintendents began to take a more definite interest in and supervision of the foreign mission fields. Although the General Assembly of 1928 had given complete supervision of overseas work to the generals and had provided that each field was to be visited twice a quadrennium,[22] the intervening depression and war years had made implementation of such a policy all but impossible. The practice of visiting each field at least once a quadrennium was begun after the cessation of hostilities.[23]

IV. New General Officers

By the fall of 1944, Mervel Lunn had come to the conclusion that it was time to separate the work of the publishing house manager from that of the general treasurer. Each position was a full-time job. Lunn had held the dual office for most of the preceding 16 years. In October, he offered his resignation as general treasurer.

With customary thoroughness, Lunn outlined his reasons in a letter to the general superintendents. The general treasurer was then handling four times as much money as he had been accountable for three years earlier. The publishing house business was also growing at the rate of 20 percent a year. There was also an obvious need to expand the work of the general treasurer to include screening and acceptance of annuity funds and solicitation of wills and bequests. There was additional need for someone related to the headquarters organization to oversee hiring of clerical help for the expanding departments of the General Board.

No doubt with a smile, Lunn wrote, "While I don't generally admit it, I am in all honesty compelled to admit that at my age it is

---

22. *Manual,* 1928, p. 109; personal interview, Dr. Samuel Young, Feb. 16, 1977.
23. Williamson interview, July 17, 1976.

now necessary to conserve my strength. I cannot consistently work overtime as has been the practice in the past."[24]

Lunn's logic prevailed. The general superintendents accepted his resignation as general treasurer and nominated another layman, John Stockton, at the time business manager of Bethany-Peniel College.

Stockton was eminently fitted for the role. He was a 45-year-old businessman who had begun a career in banking in 1922 in Oklahoma City. He had served with the Home Owner's Loan Corporation during the depression and was employed by the bank commissioners of the state of Oklahoma. He was later manager of the Enid Production Credit Association for four years, and in 1941 became business manager of the college. Stockton held the post of general treasurer for 25 years until his retirement in 1970.[25]

Another significant change saw Albert F. Harper chosen editor in chief of Sunday School literature and executive secretary of the Department of Church Schools. J. Glenn Gould, who had occupied that office since the election of Orval Nease to the general superintendency in 1940, had never enjoyed living in Kansas City and the Midwest. When he resigned in July, 1945, to become pastor of the college church and professor of theology at Eastern Nazarene College, the General Board chose Harper to be his successor.

Harper came to the office splendidly equipped for the almost 30 years he was to serve. He was a graduate of Northwest Nazarene College and earned a Ph.D. at the University of Washington. He had been dean of the college at Northwest Nazarene for six years, and for four years was head of the department of philosophy and taught theology at Eastern Nazarene College. At the time of his election, he had just been named dean of theology at Olivet, a post he never actually occupied, and was serving a second term on the General NYPS Council. He amply fulfilled the prediction of S. T. Ludwig, "His well furnished mind and devoted consecration of talent will give the church constructive leadership for many years to come."[26]

Harper quickly made some significant changes. He insisted

---

24. Letter, M. Lunn to Board of General Superintendents, Oct. 19, 1944; archives.

25. Corbett, *Pioneer Builders*, pp. 75-77.

26. HH, vol. 34, no. 27 (Sept. 17, 1945), p. 4; no. 24 (Aug. 27, 1945), p. 11.

that the story papers published for church schools be related to the curriculum. The purpose was to give teachers "added resource material and . . . to strengthen the emphasis which teachers are trying to get across at any given time." He supervised development of new periodicals to give help for teachers using the graded materials and developed workbooks for pupil use.[27]

Carrying the responsibility for promotion as well as editorial work, Harper brought Erwin G. Benson to the department as field man and editor of the new *Church School Builder,* a magazine for all church school workers. He pushed the development of boys' and girls' clubs as a denominational alternative to the scouting programs a number of the larger churches were supporting. Called the Caravan program, it included Nazarene Braves for boys 9-11; Trailblazers for boys 12 and over; Nazarene Indian Maidens for girls 9-11; and Pathfinders for girls 12 and above.[28]

By 1958, Sunday School enrollment had grown from the 350,279 it showed when Harper took office to 758,000—a growth rate over twice that of church membership for the same period. During the same interval, average weekly Sunday School attendance increased from 213,190 to 399,612, a healthy 87.4 percent.

V. Expansion in Kansas City

For some 32 years the Nazarene Publishing House and the denominational headquarters personnel had occupied portions of the same buildings on Troost Avenue. The steady growth of the publishing interests and the expansion of the General Board departments led to severe overcrowding that became particularly critical during the war years.

Measured by total net sales, the publishing house business had held to a fairly level figure during the period from 1937 through 1940. However, during the war years and with improving economic conditions, sales soared from $354,773 in 1940 to $644,193 in 1944. The increase in business demanded space for larger inventories and for additional equipment and employees. Manager Lunn had planned well, and as war clouds gathered, had

27. PGB, 1948, p. 76.
28. GAJ, 1948, pp. 277-79.

purchased new machinery, added some building space, and had put up-to-date equipment in place.

In the fall of 1944, a large stone mansion across Troost Avenue on the corner of 30th Street went on the market. Lunn was quick to see the possibilities. He negotiated for its purchase and arranged to transfer it to the General Board as a headquarters property.

The building was a three-story structure with full basement. It was quickly refurbished, and the rooms on the ground floor were designated for the missionary office and offices of the general treasurer and general secretary. The second floor provided offices and a conference room for the general superintendents.

The third floor, the former ballroom of the mansion, was a large area seated as an auditorium for General Board meetings and where the superintendents' conferences might be held. The auditorium also served as a chapel for headquarters and publishing house personnel and later for the seminary. The annual meeting of the General Board in January 1945, was held there, and Editor Corlett remarked, "It seemed to be the universal opinion of those who were in the building for the first time that it is a valuable and needed addition to our property holdings here in Kansas City."[29]

It was to be less than 10 years until the major headquarters relocation of the 1950s became an urgent necessity.

Publishing house sales continued to soar in postwar years, from $644,192 in 1944 to $1,157,284 in 1948. Space, paper, machinery, and personnel were in continual short supply. Purchase of the headquarters building across the street provided momentary relief, but by 1948 the house was faced with the urgent need for further expansion.

In 1947, a retail store was opened in the building just south of the main plant on Troost Avenue to serve the members of the nine churches in the Kansas City area as well as the street trade. Branches were opened in Pasadena, Calif., and Toronto, Ontario, Canada, and depositories were located on the campus of Hurlet College in Glasgow, Scotland, and in Sydney, Australia.[30]

Meanwhile, the publications list was expanding with the addition of the holiness classics series in 1944 featuring abridged editions of such volumes as Bishop Foster's *Christian Purity*, Asbury

---

29. HH, vol. 33, no. 46 (Jan. 29, 1945), p. 3.
30. GAJ, 1948, pp. 258-71.

Lowrey's *Possibilities of Grace,* and J. A. Wood's two volumes on *Purity and Maturity* and *Perfect Love,* the first of others to follow.[31]

Several Church Schools periodicals were launched in 1946: in addition to the *Church School Builder* there were three teachers' quarterlies, *The Beginner Teacher, The Primary Teacher,* and *The Junior Teacher;* and a periodical for children's workers called *The Junior Society Leader.*

The NYPS also launched a new monthly magazine for young people in October of 1946 called *Conquest.* Edited by NYPS General Secretary Lauriston J. DuBois and Office Editor Dorothy Davidson, the magazine was a pleasing mix of fiction, poetry, inspiration, college material, and Bible games. The first number was dedicated to the memory of Dr. R. T. Williams, who for most of its existence to that point had sponsored the General NYPS. By 1948, *Conquest* had reached 15,000 subscriptions.[32]

VI. EXPANSION OVERSEAS

The last year of the war and the three years immediately following witnessed the rapid expansion of Nazarene work in overseas areas. A substantial part of these developments was a direct result of contacts made by Nazarene chaplains and service personnel. Also, it was possible to move into new fields because of the church's share in the rapidly improving economy.

A. The Pacific Area

A number of significant steps were taken in the Pacific basin.

1. *Alaska*

We have seen the beginnings of Nazarene work in the Fairbanks area through the efforts of Missionary Dr. R. G. Fitz and his family dating back to 1936, and Alfred and Bernice Morgan from 1940. The main Fairbanks congregation was almost exclusively composed of American settlers and servicemen and their families. However, services specifically for Eskimos were added by the Morgans and Vivien Chaffee and by 1943 were drawing between 30 and 40 each Sunday.[33]

---

31. HH, vol. 33, no. 18 (July 17, 1944), p. 3; no. 24 (Aug. 28, 1944), p. 15.
32. HH, vol. 35, no. 29 (Sept. 30, 1946), p. 4; *Conquest,* vol. 1, no. 1 (October, 1946), 64 pp. plus cover.
33. Letter, Bernice Morgan to C. Warren Jones, Nov. 11, 1943 (Archives; Department of Foreign Missions, correspondence); PGB, 1945, pp. 85-87.

In 1944, Lewis and Muriel Hudgins were sent to Nome, far west on the Bering Sea just 138 miles from Russia. Hard work and sheer persistence enabled the Hudginses to dig out a predominantly Eskimo congregation, erect a two-story parsonage, a church large enough to seat 300, and a fellowship hall. General Superintendent Hardy Powers visited Nome in November, 1945, and reported:

> Our missionaries, Rev. and Mrs. Lewis Hudgins, are tireless workers. Their resourcefulness is amazing. We started there with practically nothing except two workers whose hearts were aflame with a holy passion to get the news of full salvation to the Eskimo. A housing shortage exists in Nome, hence they were forced to improvise living quarters and a place of worship. By purchasing army buildings and otherwise, they are now in the process of constructing a substantial church and parsonage that will be a credit to our church in that area. I found our standing in the community good and God is honoring the Holiness message and hungry natives are praying through to victory at our altars.[34]

Most of the finance was provided by a special NYPS offering. The General Council set a goal of $10,000. The final tally on the offering was $19,267.[35]

Anchorage, the largest and fastest-growing city in Alaska, was the site of the third Church of the Nazarene in Alaska. The Morgans had urged the purchase of property there as early as 1943. The arrival of Rev. and Mrs. Matt R. Korody and their four children in May, 1949, was the occasion of an actual beachhead. Using the front room of the parsonage at first, then a rented hall, next a basement church, and finally the superstructure, the church moved forward rapidly, establishing a solid and permanent work.

Other workers followed and other churches were born: in Seward with Rev. and Mrs. L. C. Hopkins in 1950; in Ketchikan with Rev. and Mrs. Clark H. Lewis in 1951; in Juneau, the territorial capital, beginning in 1951 with Glen and Fran Widmark and organized in 1953 by Rev. and Mrs. J. Melton Thomas; in Sitka with Trueman and Sally Shelton in 1955; in Kenai with Pastor Gene Smith; a second church in Anchorage in the Homesite area with

---

34. PGB, 1946, pp. 62-63; cf. Taylor, *Fifty Years of Nazarene Missions,* 3:31-37; R. Taylor, *Our Pacific Outposts,* pp. 9-15.
35. HH, vol. 33, no. 39 (Dec. 11, 1944), p. 15.

Arden Sickenberger as pastor; and a church in the Totem Park area of Fairbanks with Rev. and Mrs. Charles C. Powers.

In spite of the vast distances involved, Alaska has had a district organization since 1952. In the early stages of what eventually came to be known as Overseas Home Missions administered by the Department of Home Missions of the General Board, the work was supervised by members of the Board of General Superintendents.

In April, 1951, Dr. Powers gathered the pastors of the four Alaskan churches operating at that time for a preliminary conference in Fairbanks. Chaplain Conley Pate of the U.S. Army and Dr. Fitz also attended. A District Advisory Board was chosen, budgets were assigned, and arrangements were made for a delegated district assembly to be held in 1952.

By 1958, Alaska had 10 Nazarene churches with 395 members, 725 in Sunday School each week, total annual giving of almost $115,000, and property valued at just short of one-half million dollars.[36]

2. *Hawaii*

The immediate occasion for Nazarene beginnings in Hawaii was a letter from O. J. Wooldridge, Jr., of Kilgore, Tex., a sailor in the U.S. Navy stationed in Hawaii. Wooldridge wrote his former pastor, Leo Baldwin, in 1944 and said, "What is the matter with the Church of the Nazarene? Why aren't they in Hawaii? Many churches are there but no Nazarene churches."

Baldwin was then pastoring a church in Kansas City. His response was to contact Foreign Missions Secretary C. Warren Jones, who showed him a file of letters from other Nazarene servicemen in Hawaii pleading for their church to come to the islands. Baldwin himself became burdened, and in January, 1946, he was commissioned to open a Nazarene work in Honolulu. He served as District Superintendent from 1946-51.

The Baldwins sailed for Hawaii in May. They were met by a Nazarene couple from Annapolis, Md., Mr. and Mrs. William Henck. The Hencks had lived in the islands for six years and were to be of immeasurable help in starting the new work. The loan of

---

36. Cf. Taylor, *Fifty Years of Nazarene Missions,* 3:31-46; R. Taylor, *Our Pacific Outposts,* pp. 7-25; PGB, 1947, p. 14; GAJ, 1948, p. 159; GAJ, 1960, statistical charts.

a building owned by the Japanese Holiness church enabled the Baldwins to begin services in June. By September, a residence on Makiki Street had been purchased and was remodeled to provide a chapel. It was dedicated in February, 1947, with 125 persons present.

The first Nazarene church in Hawaii was organized in July with 50 charter members. Within a year, the membership stood at 116. Crowded out of its original quarters, the church purchased an oriental-style theater building in 1952 which was readily remodeled into an attractive church auditorium. With the move to new facilities, the name of the church was changed from Makiki to Honolulu First Church. The congregation from the first has been numerically the strongest on the district.

In September, 1948, Reuben and Mary Jo Welch were assigned to organize a second church in Honolulu in the Kaimuki District. With an initial gift provided by Eureka, Calif., lumberman G. Lynwood Speier, property was purchased and remodeled and the church organized on Easter Sunday, 1949.

In June of 1949, a Sunday School was started in Wahiawa, north of Honolulu in the center of Oahu near Schofield Barracks, by Rev. and Mrs. Norman Moore. The Moores had been in Hawaii studying Chinese under appointment to China when the Communist revolution shut down missionary work there. During the summer a surplus army building was purchased and remodeled, and by October it was in use for church services. The church was organized in March, 1951, with 15 members.

By the spring of 1949, it became evident that Baldwin could serve the work better if he could give full time to starting other churches. In May, he turned the Honolulu church pulpit over to Leo Steininger and moved to Kailua on the northeast shore of Oahu opposite Honolulu.

The Baldwins immediately started services in the front room of their home. By October, the group gathered was ready for a full-time pastor, and Rev. and Mrs. Joseph Clark took over. Within a year, two lots were secured and a converted surplus army barracks became the church building. Later, Pastor Harold Meadows led the congregation in building a commodious permanent building; and when the district assembly was conducted there in 1956, the church reported 47 members, an average Sunday School attendance of 141, and church and parsonage valued at $61,000.

In 1951, forced to the move by the health problems of their son, the Baldwins returned to the mainland and took the pastorate in Chandler, Ariz. Cecil Knippers, then field representative for Bethany-Peniel College, was appointed Baldwin's successor.

Knippers took over the pastorate of the Honolulu Kaimuki Church, and the Welches moved to Hilo on the "big island" of Hawaii to start the fifth church, the first on one of the "outer islands." They held their first service with 40 participants in January, 1952, in a tin-roofed bus shed. The next Sunday, the group met in the cafeteria of the Kapiolani elementary school. Soon a building site was purchased and the congregation moved into its own building in September with 98 persons in attendance at the first service. When the health of their daughter Pamela forced the Welches to return to the mainland, Stanley Ledbetter became the pastor.

The sixth church started as a mission in Honolulu in February, 1953, and was organized as Central Church in August with District Superintendent Knippers serving as pastor, assisted by James Kokada. Rev. and Mrs. J. E. Chastain arrived a year later to take over.

Maui, another of the outer islands, was the location of the next congregation, gathered in the port city of Kahului by Rev. and Mrs. Reeford Chaney. A half-acre corner lot was purchased, and in October, 1954, the district tent was pitched on the lot and services begun in the "tent sanctuary." A church building soon followed, although the church was not fully organized until April, 1956.

Hanapepe on the island of Kauai was the location of the next church. A choice site had been purchased and in January, 1957, Paul and Nancy Schmidt arrived to begin the work. Within six months a fine building was completed, and after a revival meeting conducted by Rev. and Mrs. C. William Fisher in July and August, the church was organized with the Fishers among the charter members. William and Marjorie Fisher, by their practice of donating revival services to home mission churches, had a substantial part in the beginnings in Hawaii.[37]

Nazarenes in the islands have been active in interdenominational projects also. District leaders Cecil Knippers and J. Robert

37. Taylor, *Fifty Years of Nazarene Missions*, 3:47-65; R. Taylor, *Our Pacific Outposts*, pp. 37-47; Leo H. Baldwin, "The Hawaiian Islands—Christianity Comes to Hawaii," in Goodnow, ed., *New Missionary Frontiers*, pp. 33-44; HH, vol. 36, no. 19 (July 21, 1947), p. 15; *Conquest*, vol. 2, no. 6 (March, 1948), pp. 20-25; PGB, 1947, p. 15; GAJ, 1948, pp. 159-60.

Jensen, Kailua Sunday School superintendent, assisted in the formation of Honolulu Christian College in 1953. Dr. J. Paul Gresham, for the previous 18 years dean of Trevecca Nazarene College, became the first dean and later president.

Knippers became a member of the Christian Broadcasting Association and secured time for a half-hour Sunday broadcast on the association's FM station. Five radio stations in the Islands were broadcasting "Showers of Blessing," then just getting started.

By 1958, there were eight churches in the Hawaiian Islands, five on Oahu and one each on Hawaii, Maui, and Kauai. They ranged in membership from 5 at Hanapepe to 130 at Honolulu First, with a district total of 414. The average Sunday School attendance for the district was 715. The combined property values stood at $393,500.[38]

3. *Australia*

Nazarenes had long viewed the continent of Australia as a possible area for expansion. In 1936, Free Methodist evangelist E. E. Shelhamer campaigned in Australia and wrote Nazarene headquarters urging the church to consider sending workers.[39] Even before there were plans for an actual beginning, the NYPS took as its quadrennial project the raising of $50,000 for holiness evangelism on the continent "down under," and General Secretary Lauriston DuBois reported $50,956 raised by General Convention time in June, 1948.

The unfolding story involves a series of providences a human planner would be hard put to duplicate. Meredith T. (Ted) Hollingsworth, a young British-born licensed minister from Little Rock, Ark., was serving in the U.S. Army medical corps in New Guinea when he contracted a tropical disease that necessitated his return to the States. Instead of being flown directly back as his orders first indicated, he was moved to the army medical installation in Brisbane, Queensland, Australia in March, 1944.

Hollingsworth's convalescence was rapid, and during the two months he remained in Brisbane, he contacted a small Christian assembly with a Plymouth Brethren background. There he met

---

38. Hawaii District Minutes, 1958; GAJ, 1960, statistical charts.
39. HH, vol. 25, no. 14, June 20, 1936, p. 11. As early as 1938, on their way home from India on furlough, Prescott and Bessie Beals spent almost two months in Australia preaching and making contacts. They reported, "Already folks interested," OS, vol. 25, no. 10 (March, 1938), p. 7.

35-year-old Albert A. E. Berg, a warrant officer in the Australian army and a lay preacher.

Berg and his fiancée, Marion Russell, together with Mr. and Mrs. Hubert Kilvert, associates in the Mount Pleasant Gospel Hall, were deeply interested in what Hollingsworth told them about the Church of the Nazarene and its position with regard to entire sanctification as a "second blessing." While the Plymouth Brethren theology made no room for the cleansing of the Christian heart, both couples had experienced deep hunger for a closer walk with God. Berg had some intellectual preparation from an encounter with Thomas Cook's book *New Testament Holiness* and had actually been preaching the experience which he himself did not at the time have.

Before Hollingsworth left Brisbane, Berg promised that he would preach holiness until he experienced it and from then on because he had. For his part, Hollingsworth promised that he would do what he could to see the Church of the Nazarene come to Australia. Berg experienced his personal Pentecost in January, 1945; and Hollingsworth, back in the States the preceding June, lost no time keeping his end of the bargain.

Hollingsworth enrolled in Bethany-Peniel College to complete his ministerial studies. After an initial contact with S. T. Ludwig, who was serving as executive secretary of the Department of Home Missions, Hollingsworth prepared a thorough paper he called "The Evangelization of Australia and New Zealand" for presentation to the Board of General Superintendents, who in turn passed it on to the General Board with a recommendation for favorable action.

Hollingsworth was invited to make a personal presentation to the General NYPS Council at its January, 1945, meeting. The council voted unanimously to follow through with plans to raise the $50,000 recommended by the convention the preceding June.

The general superintendents appointed H. V. Miller to oversee the beginnings in Australia. After correspondence with Berg in Brisbane, Miller arranged with the Pittsburgh District in May to license Berg *in absentia* as a minister with local membership in the Warren, Pa., church.

Berg laughingly related later that when news of his church affiliation got around, a friend met him one day and jokingly said,

"Good morning, Brother Berg, how is the Church of the Nazarene this morning? Is he well?"

Berg said, "I could have honestly informed him that we were having 100 percent attendance at all of our services because the Church of the Nazarene in Australia was just there under my hat."[40]

This situation was not to continue long. Four hundred miles to the south, in Sydney, A. C. Chesson, copastor of an independent congregation, with his son Ralph, and a young Methodist home missionary, Harold Madder, had long been praying for a holiness church in Australia. Berg and Chesson had been friends; and when Chesson came through Brisbane on an evangelistic tour, the two met and Chesson learned about Berg's new affiliation and for the first time heard about the Church of the Nazarene. Within a month, Chesson had made his decision and committed himself to membership and ministry in the new church. He, too, was received into membership and licensed as a minister *in absentia* by the Louisiana District.

A third ministerial couple, Douglas and Maysie Pinch, were working among the aborigines in Coraki, New South Wales. Berg had been sending Nazarene literature to friends he thought might be interested, Pinch among them. Pinch had long been convinced that only the fullness of God's work in redemption would stabilize the Christian experience of those with whom he worked. He became the third to seek membership and license in the Church of the Nazarene.

Another soldier, newly discharged from the Australian army, made a fourth recruit. Arthur A. Clarke had previously had several years of pastoral experience in Baptist churches in the Sydney area. In December, 1945, Chesson invited Berg to come to Sydney for a series of holiness meetings. During this time he met with Clarke. The following April, Clarke and Pinch joined Berg in Brisbane for an Easter convention, and Clarke made his commitment to the new work.[41]

---

40. Letter, A. A. E. Berg to W. T. Purkiser, Aug. 17, 1979.
41. Cf. the series of articles by Hollingsworth in *Conquest*, vol. 1, under the general title "Advance in Australia," Introduction, no. 5 (February, 1947), p. 31; "Albert Berg: Our First Australian Nazarene," no. 6 (March, 1947), pp. 34-40; "Alfred Chesson: Man of Prayer," no. 7 (April, 1947), pp. 37-40; "Douglas Pinch: Missionary to the Aborigines," no. 8 (May, 1947), pp. 39-45; "Arthur Clarke: Soldier," no. 9 (June, 1947), pp. 28-31.

Meanwhile Dr. Miller and his fellow general superintendents decided to send E. E. Zachary, superintendent of the Kansas District, to Australia as district superintendent. Zachary and his family arrived in Brisbane in October, 1946, and were met by the little band of warmhearted ministers who had committed themselves to the Church of the Nazarene.

Within three weeks, Zachary held a revival for the small group Chesson had gathered in Sydney and organized them into the first Church of the Nazarene in Australia on November 3, 1946, with 20 charter members. A. A. Clarke was called to be the first full-time pastor of the church.

A second group which was meeting in the Zachary residence in Brisbane and gathered largely through the prior labors of Berg, was organized in January, 1947, with 17 charter members.

Chesson meanwhile moved to Adelaide in South Australia, 1,000 miles west of Sydney. Before the end of 1947, District Superintendent Zachary organized the small band that had been gathered there into another church.

The first church among the aborigines was the mission of Douglas and Maysie Pinch on the coast 70 miles south of Brisbane. It was organized in July, 1947, with a chapel and parsonage furnished through the financial assistance of the faculty and students of Bethany-Peniel College.

A fifth church came into being in Melbourne, halfway between Sydney and Adelaide, and capital of the province of Victoria. Erle E. Spratt, graduate of a prominent Bible institute, had experienced entire sanctification through the testimony of Albert Berg and the Nazarene literature Berg had supplied him. When he returned to Melbourne, where he had lived and worked, a fellow institute student, Stanley Simmons, attempted to salvage him from the "heresy" into which he had fallen. The result was that Simmons and his wife were also sanctified.

In January, 1948, Zachary and Weaver W. Hess, who was in Australia for six weeks of evangelism, went to Melbourne for a revival meeting. At the end of the campaign, a church of 12 members was organized with Spratt as pastor. In September, Spratt accepted a call to Adelaide, and Simmons took over as pastor.

The Northmead church in a suburb of Sydney was an outgrowth of the earlier church in the city. It grew out of the concern of a layman, Edward Clucas, who was a member of the Campsie church in Sydney. He became concerned for his own neighborhood, rented a hall for services, and became the lay pastor. After a revival conducted by District Superintendent Zachary, the sixth Nazarene church was organized at Easter, 1948.

A first district assembly was held in Sydney in April, 1948, with Zachary presiding. Berg was invited to the General Assembly in St. Louis in June, 1948, both to represent the young churches in Australia and to enable him to get better acquainted with the church he had joined.

In the fall of 1948, Zachary made his last trip to Australia as superintendent. Australian immigration laws made it virtually impossible for him to gain permanent residence. With him was General Superintendent H. V. Miller, who was to hold the second district assembly and ordain five Australian ministers as elders in the Church of the Nazarene: A. A. E. Berg, A. C. Chesson, A. A. Clarke, W. D. Pinch, and Harold R. Madder. Berg was elected district superintendent, a post he held until his death in 1979.

From the very beginning, it was evident that a Bible college in Australia was indispensable. In January, 1952, the General NYPS Council voted to raise $25,000 to establish such a school, and Dr. Richard S. Taylor was appointed principal. Taylor had been a successful pastor and evangelist and had earned a doctorate in theology at Boston University. Dr. and Mrs. Taylor sailed for Australia in October, 1952, and school was opened on a six-acre campus with adequate existing buildings in Thornleigh, a suburb of Sydney, in March, 1953.

The church in Australia continued modest growth through the 1950s until by 1958 there were 12 congregations located in four of the five continental states: Queensland with 6, New South Wales with 4, Victoria with 1, and South Australia with 1. The 12 churches reported 350 members with an average of 746 attending Sunday School each week. The congregations ranged in size from 8 members at Quilpie to 53 at Adelaide Croydon Park.

District Treasurer C. A. Garratt reported that the district had reached 46 percent self-support. When E. E. Zachary returned to hold the 10th anniversary district assembly in 1958, he was able to say, "The progress they have made since the first district assembly in 1948 is thrilling." Zachary was particularly impressed with the spirit of evangelism he found among the preachers and their people.[42]

Typical of Australia, the number of church members does not adequately reflect the strength of the churches. Some strong new pastors had joined the ranks, among them some of the first graduates of Australian Nazarene Bible College. Included in the ministerial roster, in addition to those mentioned above, were R. G. C. Allder, Raymond M. Box, Will E. Bromley, E. M. Carless, Malcolm B. Hancock, E. W. Hill, Stanley Lavender, Charles Lee, Peter A. Robinson, Max W. Stone, J. E. Straw, Gavin E. Thompson, and John N. White,[43] the last named destined to be Berg's successor as district superintendent.

4. *The Philippines*

Nazarene missions in the Philippine Islands began in fact 20 years before they began in name. The story starts with the conversion of a 27-year-old Filipino student in Seattle First Church, Marciano Encarnacion by name. Encarnacion had come to the United States to study pharmacy and planned to take his work at the University of Washington in Seattle. Lacking a year of high school by American standards, he enrolled in the academy at Northwest Nazarene College during H. Orton Wiley's strongly mission-centered administration there. After completing his senior year, he returned to Seattle and enrolled in the School of Pharmacy at the university. Upon graduation in 1926, he returned to his homeland.

Encarnacion's career as a pharmacist was actually tentmaking to support a lay preaching and witnessing ministry, chiefly in his own hometown of Cabanatuan, north of Manila in the heart of the island of Luzon, and not far from Baguio City. Here a small group of believers gathered, with other converts scattered from Baguio City to Manila.

Chaplain Josiah E. Moore, Jr., was attached to the American army of liberation in the Philippines late in World War II. He had learned of Encarnacion through contacts with Salvation Army officers, and met the druggist in his store in Baguio City. Encarnacion happily related the work of the years and urged Moore to visit his people in Cabanatuan.

Moore, however, was under orders to be transferred, but Bond

42. HH, vol. 47, no. 14 (June 4, 1958), p. 6.

43. Cf. Taylor, *Fifty Years of Nazarene Missions*, 3:67-86; R. Taylor, *Our Pacific Outposts*, pp. 96-122.

Woodruff, another Nazarene chaplain, was told of developments and was able to follow up. With permission from General Superintendent Powers, Woodruff officially organized the first Church of the Nazarene in the Philippines in the home of Encarnacion's sister, Mrs. Espina, in May, 1946, with 29 charter members and installed Encarnacion as pastor.

Another chaplain serving with the liberation forces in the Philippines in 1945 was Joseph S. Pitts. His unit soon moved on to Japan, but Pitts was deeply stirred by the spiritual needs he sensed while in the Philippines. Pitts was also to play a key role later in reestablishing contact with the surviving church in Japan.

Out of the armed services and back in the United States, Pitts talked with General Superintendent Powers at the 1947 district assembly at Urbana, Ohio, about what he had found in the Philippines and the urgent need for missionaries. Before the conversation ended, Powers said, "If you will go, I'll send you."

For eight months, Pitts struggled with the issue. Finally, he wrote Powers that he would go if no one else could be found. The answer came, "Get ready, you are going to the Philippines." The Pitts family landed in Manila on February 10, 1948. They were met by Encarnacion who took them to the sole Nazarene congregation in Cabanatuan.

Within six months, Pitts moved to a suburb of Baguio City, the justly famous "summer capital" of the Philippines, where Nazarene field headquarters were later established.

Following a lead from the United States, Pitts journeyed to Iloilo City, on the island of Panay, 300 miles south of Manila, where he found a group of holiness people interested in joining the Church of the Nazarene. In July, he organized a church there with 45 charter members including five or six young people called into Christian service. Iloilo City was later to become a second Nazarene center in the islands.

A revival with a small independent church in Bacalag resulted in another Nazarene congregation, and a wartime contact of Chaplain Pitts led to Sunday School and preaching services in Aringay. The migration of a member of the Cabanatuan church to the island of Mindoro was the beginning of a church there.

After two years alone, the Pitts family was reinforced by the arrival of John and Lillian Pattee. The Pattees had seen nine years of service in China and had been forced out by the communist takeover of the mainland. With the arrival on the field of Adrian and Willene Rosa and Miss Frances Vine in 1952, the Fitkin Memorial Bible College was begun near Baguio City with an initial enrollment of 35 students. The Bible college has followed an innovative program with three years of study, a year in the field as pastor or evangelist, followed by a final year at school before graduation.

By 1958, the field reported 11 missionaries, 20 national workers, 16 churches and preaching points (of which 5 were fully organized churches), with 538 members and a Sunday School enrollment of 1,554. Vacation Bible schools enrolled 1,300, and the college had 54 students.[44]

When General Superintendent Hugh C. Benner visited the Philippines in 1958, he found a spirit of revival in the Bible college that was reaching out into the local congregations. He reported that the missionaries said "that such a deep and powerful moving of the Holy Spirit has not been experienced in the Philippines prior to this revival."[45]

5. *Return to Japan*

When General Douglas MacArthur's occupation forces moved into Japan in the summer of 1945, the unit to which Chaplain Pitts was attached was not far behind. Before he left Manila, Pitts had been contacted by a general's aide, Baldwin Eckel, son of Missionary William Eckel. Young Eckel gave him a map of Tokyo with the location marked of one of the Nazarene churches there, and also the names of the pastor, Rev. Okuba, and the district superintendent, Nobumi Isayama.

Arriving in Japan, Pitts discovered that the church had been burned, and no one knew the whereabouts of Okuba. He did find a Methodist school, however, where he learned the former address of Isayama.

Pitts was finally able to find Isayama and his wife, living in the back of an unburned Nazarene church right at the edge of an area that had been totally destroyed by American fire-bombs. He was

---

44. Joseph Pitts, *Mission to the Philippines* (Kansas City: Beacon Hill Press, 1956); Grace Ramquist, *No Respecter of Persons* (Kansas City: Nazarene Publishing House, 1962), pp. 105-17; DeLong and Taylor, *Fifty Years of Nazarene Missions,* 2:99-104; R. Taylor, *Our Pacific Outposts,* 48-64; PGB, 1947, p. 15; GAJ, 1948, p. 160; Field Statistics, 1958, OS, vol. 46, no. 3 (March, 1958), pp. 8-9.
45. PGB, 1959, p. 62.

also able to meet a handful of other Nazarene pastors who were in touch with Isayama, and to give them much needed encouragement and help.[46]

Other Nazarenes attached to the military were of great assistance in reestablishing contact with the Japanese church. Dr. Howard Hamlin, assistant chief of the surgical section and chief of the orthopedics division of the Forty-ninth General Hospital in Tokyo, made a large contribution toward advancing Nazarene interests in Japan. Lt. Doyle Shepherd, who with his wife Mattie was to give 21 years of service as a missionary in Japan, was active in mission work in connection with his service in the military. Other chaplains and servicemen took great interest in helping Japanese Nazarenes reestablish their shattered and scattered churches. Their attendance at services of the Japanese churches and gifts of money and labor in rebuilding bombed-out buildings proved of inestimable value.

Lt. Col. and Mrs. Robert H. Shaw established the foundation for the work of the Church of the Nazarene on the northern island of Hokkaido where Shaw was stationed as economics officer. In Yokohama, the church property was the gift of Nazarene servicemen. Majors Engleman and Barmore and Captain Luce and their wives were the moving force.[47]

Dr. Hamlin was particularly helpful. He had asked for assignment to Tokyo with that thought in mind and arrived there in November, 1946. His rank as lieutenant colonel and an additional assignment as War Department consultant until October, 1948, gave him a position of influence in the American military government of the country.

When William Eckel was able to get back into Japan in January, 1947, Hamlin managed to get him the perquisites of an army line officer, including the purchase of an automobile—1 out of 30 shipped to Japan by the army post exchange, for which there had been 3,000 applications.

Hamlin was the first Nazarene contacted by Japanese workers from the Oriental Missionary Society operating a growing school at Chiba that later became a major Nazarene educational venture

---

46. Cf. Joseph S. Pitts, "The Road to Tokyo," in DuBois, ed. and comp., *Chaplains See World Missions,* pp. 9-30.

47. HH, vol. 40, no. 44 (Jan. 9, 1952), p. 23; no. 49 (Feb. 13, 1952), p. 23.

in Japan. He was also instrumental in securing the site for missionary headquarters in Tokyo from the Mitsubishi family for $1,500—a property that was later to sell for $1.5 million when the headquarters was relocated.[48]

But the sustained labor of gathering scattered churches and rebuilding on prewar foundations fell to William Eckel. The Eckels had fled Japan in 1940 shortly before the outbreak of war. With no prospect of resuming his missionary work in the immediate future, Eckel accepted appointment as superintendent of the Rocky Mountain District. He was serving in that office when Japan surrendered. His 24 years (1916-40) as a missionary in Japan had given him a superb mastery of the language and made him, as his friends observed, "more Japanese than the Japanese."

It took six months to get necessary clearances, but in January, 1947, Eckel landed in Yokohama to be met by Lieutenant Shepherd and Nobumi Isayama and to start the work that would occupy most of his next 19 years.

Encouraged by Eckel's first reports from Japan, the General Board in January, 1948, requested General Superintendent Hardy C. Powers and General Treasurer John Stockton to make a trip to Japan to survey the field. On the basis of their report and recommendations, added missionary personnel were authorized. Harrison and Doris Davis were the first reinforcements to arrive in 1950, followed by Merril and Myrtlebelle Bennett and Hubert and Virginia Helling two years later. Bartlett and Grace McKay arrived in 1954 and Maurice and Jeannette Rhoden in 1956.

Postwar conditions made it possible for the church to obtain ownership of property to be held by a newly incorporated nonprofit organization, the Japan Nazarene church. By 1955, eight years after his return, Eckel could report ownership of "about forty-five nice pieces of property in many sections throughout the country. On every piece of property today has been built a church, a parsonage for the national pastor, a kindergarten, or all three."[49]

A significant move occurred when property was purchased in Tokyo for a theological college, and Nippon Nazarene Seminary

---

48. Cf. Howard H. Hamlin, *The Challenge of the Orient* (Kansas City: Beacon Hill Press, 1949); personal interview, Dec. 11, 1981.
49. William A. Eckel, *The Pendulum Swings* (Kansas City: Beacon Hill Press, 1957), p. 118. The manuscript was prepared in 1955 although the book was published in 1957.

was dedicated at the beginning of school in April, 1952. Dr. Eckel was president; Hiroshi Kitagawa, vice-president; Harrison Davis, dean; and the faculty included Doris Davis, Aishin Kida, Susumu Okubo, Makoto Oye, and Yoso Seo. Merril and Myrtlebelle Bennett were added to the faculty the second term.[50]

By 1958, a total of 12 Nazarene missionaries labored in Japan, with 100 national workers. The field reported 101 churches and preaching points with 4,160 members; 69 Sunday Schools enrolled 4,421; 15 vacation Bible schools registered 793 students. There were 16 day schools enrolling 1,357, while 22 students were in the seminary.[51]

6. *A New Try in China*

The defeat of Japan and withdrawal of Japanese troops from China left the Nazarene field in Shantung Province firmly in the hands of the Chinese Communists and inaccessible to any Western missionary work. A new field in Kiangsi Province 750 miles south of Tamingfu, previously occupied by the Methodist church, was offered and accepted.

The new field had a population of over 3 million, with 200 professing Christians. Nazarene work was begun in two centers in 1947 manned by Harry and Katherine Wiese, John and Lillian Pattee, Dr. Rudolph and Lura Fitz, Michael and Elizabeth Varro, Mary Scott, and Ruth Brickman. A Bible school was started in October, 1948.

The work came to an abrupt and cruel end. Chinese Nationalist forces were in constant retreat before the Communists from the north. In December, 1948, the women missionaries and the children were ordered evacuated. By spring of 1949 it became clear to all that the Nationalist cause on the mainland was lost, and in May the remaining missionaries withdrew.

The last information to come out of China was compiled in 1949. It reported 48 organized churches in north China with 43 other stations having regular worship; 5,000 communicants; 7 ordained national ministers and 30 licensed nationals. In Kiangsi in south China, the Nazarene missionaries left 3 organized churches

---

50. Cf. HH, vol. 34, no. 32 (Oct. 22, 1945), p. 2; PGB, 1949, pp. 101-6; DeLong and Taylor, *Fifty Years of Nazarene Missions,* 2:65-70; Eckel, *Japan Now,* pp. 103-12; Tyner and Eckel, *God's Samurai,* pp. 57-90.
51. Foreign missions field statistics, 1958.

with 3 other regular preaching points, 4 ordained nationals and 5 licensed national ministers, 70 church members and 200 probationers, and 6 Sunday Schools with 300 enrollment.[52]

B. Italy

Meanwhile, halfway around the world, Nazarene servicemen attached to the occupation forces that liberated Italy in 1945 made a contact that resulted in the starting of Nazarene work on the European continent.

Albert Carey and Charles Leppert were invited to a Friday night prayer meeting for English-speaking military personnel, held by a translator for the Allied army of occupation in Florence. Their clear testimony to entire sanctification and representation of the Church of the Nazarene drew the attention of the interpreter, Alfredo Del Rosso.

The 55-year-old Del Rosso, a native of Poggibonsi, near Florence, had been converted in the Evangelical church in Sienna at the age of 17. He later studied theology in the Waldensian seminary for two years where he came into the experience of entire sanctification at the age of 24. After a stint in the Italian army in World War I, rising to the rank of captain, he began to preach in the Baptist church first in Rome and later in Civitavecchia.

After seven years as a Baptist minister, Del Rosso's holiness emphasis led him first into the Apostolic church (of Welsh origin) and later into independent mission work. The rise of Fascism in Italy resulted in persecution, and until the outbreak of World War II Del Rosso evangelized in Switzerland, England, France, Denmark, Sweden, and Norway—in the process gaining facility in some 14 European languages. World War II saw him back in the Italian army as a major until 1943, when he was able to escape the area still held in German control and make his way to Florence. There he worked with the Salvation Army and preached in various evangelical churches in the Florence area as well as in his own independent mission.

At the time he met the American soldiers, Del Rosso had four small mission organizations in Florence, Rome, and Civitavecchia, each with a constituency of about 30 persons. Carey and Leppert

---

52. PGB, 1948, p. 68; DeLong and Taylor, *Fifty Years of Nazarene Missions,* 2:87-93.

arranged for him to receive Nazarene literature, and Del Rosso began translation of the *Manual* into Italian. In January, 1946, he wrote asking affiliation with the Church of the Nazarene.[53]

It took a little over a year to work out arrangements for General Superintendent H. V. Miller to visit Italy on his way back from missionary supervision in India and the Near East. Miller was impressed with Del Rosso and recommended to the General Board in January, 1948, that he be brought to the General Assembly the following June and that the church take steps to accept his work as the start of a Nazarene mission field in Italy. In August, 1948, Del Rosso's ministerial ordination was recognized, and his four missions with their national pastors became part of the Church of the Nazarene.

Del Rosso centered his efforts on the city of Rome, and within a year had established five preaching points in the capital. Building restrictions were stringent, and it was not until 1953 that property could be purchased and a building constructed. In 1952, the field was placed under the jurisdiction of the Department of Foreign Missions, and Earl and Thelma Morgan were sent as missionaries.

By 1958, Italy reported six national pastors and 16 churches or preaching points with 445 members.[54]

C. In the Americas

1. *Bolivia*

The Nazarene mission in Bolivia officially dates from 1945, although holiness work had begun with the labors of Ninevah and Eula Briles in 1922. The Brileses had gone to Bolivia under the sponsorship of an independent mission board. They were forced to return home in 1932 when funds failed. They joined the Church of the Nazarene and pastored until 1945 when the Department of Foreign Missions asked them to return to Bolivia. They quickly gathered their former converts and before the end of the year had organized three churches, all in the vicinity of the capital of La Paz.

---

53. Letter, Alfredo Del Rosso to S. T. Ludwig, Jan. 3, 1946, Ludwig file, archives.

54. Minutes, Board of General Superintendents meeting of Jan. 3, 1948; Carol Gish, *Mediterranean Missions* (Kansas City: Nazarene Publishing House, 1965), pp. 117-28; Grace Ramquist, *And Many Believed* (Kansas City: Nazarene Publishing House, 1951), pp. 121-26; Olive G. Tracy, *The Nations and the Isles* (Kansas City: Nazarene Publishing House, 1958), pp. 143-79; PGB, 1948, pp. 54-55; DeLong and Taylor, *Fifty Years of Nazarene Missions*, 2:277-80; Missionary Howard Culbertson, letter to author, Nov. 19, 1983.

The work in Bolivia grew rapidly. In 1946, work was begun in La Paz itself where two more churches were soon added. In 1946, Ronald and Sarah Denton were sent as missionaries but had to transfer to Argentina a year later because of the health of their young son. The Armstrongs, Jack and Janet, arrived in 1950, and Earl and Mabel Hunter transferred from Guatemala in 1952 where they had served since 1946. Frank and Mary Van Develder served two years in 1955-57.

A unique but extremely valuable feature has been the operation of day schools in connection with each of the local churches. To help supply the need for workers, a Bible school was opened in La Paz in February, 1953, and two years later a 20-acre property was purchased for the school with Alabaster funds.[55]

By 1958, the field had 35 national workers, 22 churches and preaching points, 856 members, and 1,542 enrolled in Sunday School. There were four American missionaries. The Bible school enrolled 34 students.[56]

2. *Cuba*

The roots of Nazarene missionary work in Cuba go back to 1902 when a trio of missionaries representing J. O. McClurkan's Pentecostal Mission landed in Cuba on the way to Colombia. Unable to gain entrance to the country of their destination, they stayed to labor in Cuba. The husband and wife of the team returned to the States in 1905, and Leona Gardner remained alone to labor on, most of the time supporting herself by teaching school.

When the Pentecostal Mission joined the Church of the Nazarene in 1915, attempts were made to reinforce the lone missionary but without permanent success. When the Nazarenes officially closed the field in 1920, Miss Gardner remained on her own until offered an assignment in Guatemala in 1925. For 20 years the church was without representation on the island.

In 1945, the General Board decided to reenter Cuba. Lyle and Grace Prescott, who had been in the Virgin Islands for a year, were transferred to Cuba. Their first work was in Trinidad, where Miss Gardner had served so many years. In May of the next year, how-

---

55. For "Alabaster" see NFMS, *Ten Years of Alabaster* (Kansas City: Nazarene Publishing House, 1958).

56. Alice Spangenberg, *South America: Eucalyptus Country* (Kansas City: Nazarene Publishing House, 1967), pp. 97-119; DeLong and Taylor, *Fifty Years of Nazarene Missions,* 2:256-60.

ever, they moved to Havana and opened work there. General Superintendent Powers organized the Havana church in December with 17 members. John and Patricia Hall were sent as reinforcements in 1947 and remained until forced out by the Castro takeover in 1959. Ardee and Faith Coolidge followed in 1952, and Howard and Modena Conrad in 1957.

By 1958, Cuba had six missionaries, 17 national pastors, 37 churches and preaching points, with 256 members and 1,256 enrolled in Sunday School. A Bible school enrolled 15 students.[57]

3. *British Guiana (now Guyana)*

A year after the reentry of Cuba, an independent work established by William C. Rice in British Guiana was accepted into the Church of the Nazarene and formed the nucleus of early Nazarene work in that portion of South America. Rev. Lelan Rogers, superintendent of the Nazarene mission on the island of Trinidad, and Mrs. Wavy Rogers were the only missionaries of the church in British Guiana until 1952 when Donald and Elizabeth Ault arrived. Two years later, Herbert and Alice Ratcliff were sent to British Guiana, and David and Elizabeth Browning, who had served in British Honduras (Belize) since 1944, were transferred to British Guiana in 1955. Wayne and Elwanda Knox replaced the Aults when because of illness they returned to a pastorate in the United States in 1957.

British Guiana, and its neighbors, Dutch and French Guiana, differ from the rest of South America in that their prevailing culture is not rooted in Spanish or Portuguese influence, and the prevailing religion is not Catholicism but Hinduism with a mixture of Islam. The population is not large, and low altitude and oppressive heat make it a difficult locale for North Americans.

By 1958, British Guiana reported 6 missionaries, 13 national workers, 15 churches or preaching points, and 388 members. However, 49 Sunday Schools were being conducted with 3,272 enrolled, and 12 vacation Bible schools enrolled 992 in 1958. Six students from British Guiana were attending the area Bible school in Trinidad.[58]

---

57. DeLong and Taylor, *Fifty Years of Nazarene Missions,* 2:313-17; OS, vol. 34, no. 11 (May, 1947), p. 6; vol. 35, no. 1 (July, 1947), p. 3; PGB, 1947, p. 69.

58. Spangenberg, *Eucalyptus Country,* pp. 19-29; DeLong and Taylor, *Fifty Years of Nazarene Missions,* 2:53-55.

4. *The Spanish Department*

The first need of any foreign language mission is to have the Bible available in a current edition. Soon coming into focus is the further need for literature dealing with Bible doctrines and interpreting the Christian life. The Shirley Press in Africa had early met this need on the largest foreign mission field of the Church of the Nazarene. But the growth of Nazarene missions in Mexico and Central and South America where Spanish is the common language soon made Spanish publication a necessity.

With almost as many Spanish-speaking as English-speaking people in the world, there was still very little evangelical literature available and no holiness material. As early as 1928, a General Assembly committee on publishing interests had recommended that Nazarenes begin publishing a monthly magazine, Sunday School literature, and holiness books in Spanish.[59] In 1944, the Latin delegations at the General Assembly again asked for a Spanish department. The request was referred to the General Board. Nothing came of it until 1946 when the January meeting of the General Board approved the organization of a Spanish Department to be set up as a branch of the Nazarene Publishing House and jointly sponsored by it and the Department of Foreign Missions. Nine months later, the Spanish Department began functioning under the direction of Honorato Reza.

Reza was a Mexican national, converted as a boy of 12 and educated in one of the day schools operated by the Church of the Nazarene in Teloloadan and the Nazarene Seminary in Mexico City. As a teenager he attracted the attention of General Superintendent J. W. Goodwin, who long held jurisdiction over the Mexican districts. Enlisting the help of NFMS President Susan Fitkin, Goodwin invited young Reza to come to Pasadena College and arranged for him to live in the Goodwin home while attending college.

After graduation from Pasadena, Reza attended the University of Mexico City where he earned a graduate degree. At the time of his selection to head the Spanish Department, he was an ordained minister pastoring a Spanish-speaking congregation in Los Angeles and teaching in Pasadena College. He was eminently

---

59. GAJ, 1928, p. 243.

qualified as a translator and proved to be an able administrator of a growing department.

The early production work was done with a special linotype machine manned by Moises Castillo, the son of a United Brethren pastor in Puerto Rico. By October 1 the department was publishing a 16-page semimonthly magazine, *El Heraldo de Santidad*, featuring translated articles from the English *Herald of Holiness* as well as primary Spanish materials. By 1948, C. Warren Jones was able to report that *El Heraldo* had a circulation of 6,000, more than twice as many as any other Protestant publication in Spanish.

The production of Spanish Sunday School literature began in January, 1946, with the 80-page *El Sendero de la Verdad* ("The Path of Truth") similar to the English *Bible School Journal*, and a four-page giveaway leaflet, *La Antorcha Dominical* ("The Sunday Torch"). Both Sunday School publications had a circulation of 7,000 by 1948 and were being distributed in 24 different Spanish-speaking countries as well as to Latinos in the United States.

Within a year, the department had also translated *The ABC's of Christian Doctrine, The ABC's of Christian Living*, and *The ABC's of Holiness*, booklets by *Herald* Editor Corlett, as well as a series of tracts.

Spanish translations of the *Manual*, Wiley and Culbertson's *Introduction to Christian Theology*, and Spanish songbooks followed in quick succession. *El Heraldo*, the Sunday School literature, and the *Introduction to Christian Theology* have from the beginning enjoyed wide circulation among evangelicals outside the Church of the Nazarene.[60]

At the end of his first year as director of the Spanish Department, Reza wrote:

> Yes, we have a tremendous responsibility. There are millions of souls in Latin America and among the Spanish-speaking people of the United States who are looking to us for the message of holiness. Our task is definite and distinct. Our publications are not just another enterprise. They are THE needed publications for the advancement of God's kingdom. We are not so much interested in "getting the market" as we are

---

60. DeLong and Taylor, *Fifty Years of Nazarene Missions*, 2:77-80, 117; GAJ, 1948, pp. 157-58, 240; PGB, 1947, p. 77; Williamson interview, July 17, 1976; personal interview, Honorato T. Reza, Dec. 8, 1981.

in helping the people worship the Lord "in the beauty of holiness."[61]

Reza reported in June, 1952, that a believer in southern Mexico found a copy of *El Heraldo de Santidad*. He read it through with great interest and presented it to the group of converts with whom he worshipped. They endeavored to get in touch with the sponsoring organization without result until one of them learned the name and address of Superintendent David Sol of the South Mexico District. Sol met with the group, preached to them on a number of occasions, and they became members of the Church of the Nazarene.[62]

VII. In the Continental United States

Two significant movements in outreach to ethnic groups in the United States developed in the 1944-48 quadrennium; and a retirement home for missionaries was established in Temple City near Pasadena, Calif.

A. Among the Blacks

A scattering of Nazarene churches with predominantly black membership had sprung up in several areas in the United States. Each of these was attached to the particular district in which it was located. But no organized plan had been made to push holiness evangelism among blacks in America until the General Assembly of 1944 adopted a recommendation from the Department of Home Missions to the effect that such work be started.

As H. V. Miller expressed it four years later in the quadrennial address of the general superintendents to the St. Louis General Assembly, "It is not to our credit that a church with our professed soul passion should have so long neglected the evangelization of the fourteen millions of colored people in the United States."[63]

In September, 1944, the general superintendents issued a policy statement they called the "Policy Covering the Setup and Organization for Colored Work." It provided for a new "Colored District of the Church of the Nazarene." R. T. Williams was to have jurisdiction, and S. T. Ludwig was to be the secretary.

---

61. HH, vol. 36, no. 35 (Nov. 10, 1947), p. 12.
62. OS, vol. 39, no. 6 (June, 1952), inside cover.
63. GAJ, 1948, p. 158.

The program's success depended chiefly on the initiative of the district superintendents in whose areas there were concentrations of black people. An annual conference for superintendents of those districts on which there were black Nazarene churches was to be held. Reports from black pastors would be heard at the conference. Nazarene work among blacks was assigned to the supervision of the Department of Home Missions.

When Dr. Williams died, jurisdiction of the black work passed first to J. B. Chapman and at his death to Hardy C. Powers. The conference directed by the policy statement was first called in 1947 at Meridian, Miss. It was a miniconference in truth, its participants being General Superintendent Powers; S. T. Ludwig, who doubled as secretary of the "district" and executive of the Home Missions Department; Cecil Knippers, superintendent of the Mississippi District; and three black ministers. Five widely scattered churches were reported.

By the second year, the numbers had increased. Several district superintendents and pastors were present. Black work was being sponsored on 10 districts: Alabama, Chicago Central, Florida, Indianapolis, Louisiana, Mississippi, Northern California, Southern California, West Virginia, and Wisconsin.

The 1948 General Assembly took up the matter of work among blacks again and resolved "to put on an intensive evangelistic campaign to organize this quadrennium at least one hundred churches among the colored people if and when leaders are available."[64] The leadership was not available, and few new black churches were organized.

The 1949 conference on Nazarene work among blacks held in November listed 12 black ministers serving in the church. Three were to bear a large part of the leadership load in the years ahead: R. W. Cunningham of Institute, W.Va.; Clarence Jacobs of Indianapolis; and Warren A. Rogers, then of Detroit.

In 1948, Roy F. Smee became full-time executive secretary of the Department of Home Missions and took an active interest in developments. Plans were already under way for opening a Bible training school for blacks at Institute, a suburb of Charleston, W.Va., where a black Nazarene church was already operating.

With General Board assistance, a church building was con-

---

64. Ibid., p. 129.

structed to accommodate the congregation in a sanctuary and Sunday School classrooms, as well as the Nazarene Bible Institute with chapel, library, and classrooms. An affiliation was worked out with West Virginia State College for the Colored immediately across the street in which students could supplement their work taken at the Bible institute.[65]

Edwin E. Hale, an experienced white churchman and chaplain during World War II, was appointed the first president in June, 1948, and before the end of the year school was begun. Hale served as president until 1955, when he resigned to take a pastorate. He was succeeded by R. W. Cunningham, who had doubled as pastor of the Institute church and teacher in the school from its beginning days, ably assisted by Clarence Bowman. The school continued to function until 1970 when it was merged with the Nazarene Bible College that had been established in Colorado Springs.

In 1953, the Gulf Central District was set up to provide more direct supervision for and assistance to the black Nazarene churches. Its territory included 12 states: Alabama, Arkansas, Florida, Georgia, Kentucky, Louisiana, Mississippi, North Carolina, South Carolina, Tennessee, Texas, and Virginia. The district officers were all white men: Leon Chambers was appointed superintendent; Alpin Bowes, Smee's assistant in the Home Missions office, was secretary; John Stockton, general treasurer of the church, was treasurer; and General Superintendent D. I. Vanderpool, who had taken over jurisdiction from Powers in 1950, continued as the general having jurisdiction. All but Chambers were based in Kansas City.

The effect of the new arrangement was to place the black churches and pastors in a new relationship to each other and to their district organization. The sixth annual black conference became the first district assembly of the Gulf Central District. There were still only five churches, but an additional eight missions were reported with 171 average attendance in Sunday School each week. Black churches and pastors located outside the Gulf Central area continued to belong to the districts in which they were located.

This arrangement was to last until 1972 when the rising tide of

---

65. HH, vol. 37, no. 26 (Sept. 6, 1948), p. 13.

integration sentiment and a changing social climate in the states covered by the Gulf Central District pointed to the wisdom of dissolving the district as a separate entity and returning the churches to the geographical districts in which they were located.[66]

By 1958, when Chambers resigned from the superintendency to be followed by Warren Rogers, he was able to report 15 organized churches and a total of 12 black ministers.

B. North American Indian Missions

Sporadic efforts by Nazarene workers among American Indians, particularly in Oklahoma, date back as far as 1910 when C. B. Jernigan organized a camp meeting among the Ponca Indians south of Ponca City, Okla. Twenty-five years later, J. W. Short, superintendent of the Western Oklahoma District, held a series of revivals among the 122,000 Indians in the state, and D. G. Ogburn campaigned among Indians in Yuma, Ariz., and Zuni, N.M.

In 1944, the General Board authorized establishment of the North American Indian District and placed it under the supervision of the Department of Foreign Missions. Dowie Swarth, the enthusiastic Dutchman who had superintended the Alberta District for five years and the Arizona District for two years, was put in charge.

Swarth had 11 organized churches in his far-flung territory: 6 in Oklahoma and 5 in New Mexico, Arizona, and California. Practically all of the churches depended for pastoral supervision on the Anglo pastors of nearby churches.

The vast distances separating the stations created an isolation that was in part overcome by the division of the district into zones in 1947. The churches and mission stations in Oklahoma constituted the Eastern Zone. The Central Zone embraced the missions in New Mexico and eastern Arizona. Western Arizona and California comprised the Western Zone.

Swarth was phenomenally successful in enlisting help. By the

---

66. Taylor, *Fifty Years of Nazarene Missions,* 3:148-56; PGB, 1945, p. 25; HH, vol. 34, no. 29 (Oct. 1, 1945), pp. 5, 8; vol. 37, no. 16 (June 28, 1948), p. 13; GAJ, 1948, pp. 158-59; Minutes, meeting of Board of General Superintendents, June 15, 1948; Carol Gish, *Missionary Frontiers at Home.* For an intimate picture of an outstanding black Nazarene minister cf. Warren A. Rogers with Kenneth Vogt, *From Sharecropper to Goodwill Ambassador* (Kansas City: Beacon Hill Press of Kansas City, 1979).

time of the first district assembly in May, 1945, in Albuquerque, N.M., First Church, he had eight missionaries working under his direction. Three years later, as reported by H. V. Miller at the 1948 General Assembly, the district was operating 34 mission stations besides outstations with 40 missionaries including nine teachers and a trained nurse. There were 15 church buildings, 16 parsonages, besides some 10 other properties with an estimated value of $123,600. There were 584 full church members, approximately 1,000 in Sunday School each week, and district organizations for both WFMS and NYPS.[67]

In 1948, the C. Warren Jones Indian Training and Bible School was established on a 480-acre property near Lindrith, N.M., about 100 miles northwest of Albuquerque. The property was given to the church by the Emmanuel Orphanage and Bible School that had previously occupied the site. The school was moved to a more accessible location just south of Albuquerque in 1954 under the supervision of G. H. Pearson. Pearson had been the director for the previous two years in Lindrith and served for the first two years in Albuquerque. He succeeded Swarth as district superintendent in 1956.

By 1958, the district reported 48 missionaries with 16 national workers supervising 44 churches and mission stations with 1,053 members and 1,568 enrolled in Sunday School. The Bible school enrolled 33 students, and three dispensaries treated 3,338 patients.[68]

C. Casa Robles

Caring for retired missionaries had been an unsolved problem for Nazarene leadership for many years. In 1940, the Southern California District initiated a move to establish a retirement home for missionaries in the area. Four years later, the General Assembly instructed the Department of Foreign Missions to take necessary steps to establish such a home.

A "founding commission" was set up with Southern California District Superintendent A. E. Sanner as chairman, Pasadena College President H. Orton Wiley as secretary, and including

---

67. Dowie Swarth with John C. Oster, *Ever the Pioneer: The Romance of Home Missions* (Kansas City: Nazarene Publishing House, 1978), pp. 70-78; DeLong and Taylor, *History of Nazarene Missions,* 2:136-38; GAJ, 1948, p. 158.
68. Foreign missions field statistics, 1958.

WFMS President Mrs. Susan Fitkin, Southern California District WFMS President Mrs. Paul Bresee, and Los Angeles First Church Pastor M. Kimber Moulton.

After two years of study, a site was purchased in Temple City, six miles south of Pasadena. Five separate purchases were made to put together a four-acre property. Existing buildings provided five cottages, and a larger structure was remodeled into a central facility and residence for the superintendent. The many native oaks on the property suggested the name "Casa Robles," "House of the Oaks." The property was dedicated in February, 1946, by General Superintendent J. B. Chapman.

The first superintendent of the facility was Rev. V. P. Drake, 1946-52. He was succeeded by A. E. Sanner, who had just retired as superintendent of the (by then) Los Angeles District.

Additional cottages were added, each a one- or two-bedroom home with completely modern facilities. Retired missionaries with 20 years of service are eligible for permanent residence; and as space is available, missionaries on furlough are accommodated. The home was particularly helpful in assisting the relocation of the missionary contingent forced out of China by the communist take-over there.[69] By 1958, 21 cottages had been built and 18 retired missionaries were in permanent residence.

VIII. EDUCATIONAL EXPANSION

The years immediately following World War II saw dramatic expansion in the educational work of the church. During the war years, the six colleges in the United States and Canadian Nazarene College had used the improved economic conditions of their constituencies to pay off accumulated indebtedness. While other non-public colleges and universities had lost 37 percent in enrollment during the war years, Nazarene institutions had gained 17 percent.[70]

---

69. Four-page unpublished paper by A. E. Sanner, superintendent of Casa Robles from 1952 to 1966, dated Mar. 31, 1979; personal interview, A. E. Sanner, Apr. 3, 1981; PGB, 1946, pp. 16, 34; 1947, pp. 37-38; OS, vol. 34, no. 9 (September, 1947), p. 3; telephone interview, G. H. Pearson, Nov. 10, 1981; telephone interview, Louise Robinson Chapman, Nov. 10, 1981.

70. PGB, 1945, p. 63.

The end of hostilities in August, 1945, with generous educational benefits provided for veterans, launched a period of growth that saw the college-level enrollments soar 97 percent in four years, from 1,945 in 1944-45 to 3,841 in 1947-48. Building had been at a virtual standstill and facilities had been full even before the war. While many returning veterans were married and living off campus, dormitory facilities were still crowded to the limits as were classrooms, libraries, laboratories, and other academic facilities.

The year 1945 witnessed the beginnings of two new educational institutions, the first established by Nazarenes since Canadian Nazarene College was started in 1921.

A. Hurlet Nazarene College

The struggling group of Nazarenes in the British Isles had made two earlier attempts to establish a training college for ministers and Christian workers, both of them under the leadership of founder George Sharpe. The first of the early efforts was a casualty of World War I when the Pentecostal Bible College closed its doors in 1916 after three years of operation. The second, begun in 1920 in Sharpe's home and later moved to Parkhead church, survived through a relocation until 1928.

George Frame became superintendent of the British Isles district in 1940. One of his many problems during the war years was lack of manpower for the churches, despite some notable accessions to the ministry in this period. Frame was determined to attempt a remedy. After a two-year search, he was able to find a property in West Hurlet near Glasgow, and Hurlet Nazarene College came into being in 1945 with the capable Frame in the dual role of district superintendent and principal of the college (1945-54).

Annual grants from the Department of Education in Kansas City in the amount of $1,500 to $2,000 aided materially in the early years, and the NYPS took on a special project to raise $10,000 in 1949 to apply on the indebtedness.

The student enrollment in Hurlet was disappointingly small. It fell to 6 in 1950, but climbed to 16 in 1953. The small faculty was reinforced by the arrival of J. Kenneth Grider in 1951 who combined teaching with doctoral studies at the University of Glasgow.[71]

It was only after the 1955 merger of Calvary Holiness church with the Church of the Nazarene that the school began to operate on a viable basis. Then both Calvary's Beech Lawn College and the Hurlet campus were sold to provide a more adequate campus at Didsbury near Manchester, and British Isles Nazarene College began to function under the presidency of Hugh Rae.[72]

B. Nazarene Theological Seminary

Nazarene educators had felt the need for graduate theological education for many years. Two of the early "universities"—Peniel in Texas and Nazarene University in Pasadena, Calif.—had organized Bachelor of Divinity programs, but resources were far too limited to be effective and they were later dropped. Four of the colleges had added fifth year studies in theology leading to a Bachelor of Theology degree; and when H. Orton Wiley returned to Pasadena in 1933, he soon set up a graduate program leading to the degree of Master of Arts in religion. In 1941 Northwest Nazarene College instituted a Master of Theology program. But a full-fledged seminary offering a standard three-year graduate curriculum had been a persistent dream.

At the 1940 General Board meeting in January, H. Orton Wiley as education secretary urged that the church plan for the establishment of a central theological seminary of graduate rank immediately after the coming General Assembly. The Department of Education followed up with a recommendation that the General Board ask the General Assembly in June to give serious consideration to such a school and that the board appoint a committee of three to investigate a suitable location and project an estimate of the costs involved in such a venture. In accepting the recommendation, the board appointed Samuel Young on the East Coast, A. E. Sanner in the West, and R. V. Starr in the Midwest as a "Committee on Location for Theological Seminary."[73]

At the adjourned meeting of the General Board just prior to

---

71. Ford, *In the Steps of John Wesley,* pp. 56-72, 87; Taylor, "Historical Documents," p. 175; PGB, 1948, p. 45.

72. Mitchell, *To Serve the Present Age,* pp. 62-65.

73. PGB, 1940, pp. 21, 52, 86.

the June assembly, the committee reported in favor of Kansas City as the location for a central theological seminary and indicated its judgment that an annual subsidy of not less than $15,000 would be necessary for the beginning years with a faculty of four. It was understood that this amount made no provision for the purchase of property.[74]

At its convention just prior to the General Assembly, the NYPS voted a recommendation to the assembly that a theological seminary be established near headquarters in Kansas City in the fall of 1940.[75]

R. T. Williams in the general superintendents' quadrennial address to the General Assembly joined the chorus:

> Definite steps should be made toward the establishment of a seminary. The hour may not be here yet, but is not far distant, when such will be essential to the best interests of the church. Ministers who have completed college and university courses, feel the need of work in this specialized field for highest efficiency. Many have sought seminary work in an atmosphere that has undermined their usefulness. The loss to the church from those who take seminary work in institutions unfavorable to the fundamental principles of our denomination is too heavy. We need to train our men in our own institutions for our own peculiar, God-given task.[76]

The assembly's committee on education unanimously recommended that the body authorize the establishment of the seminary in Kansas City "near headquarters" and elect a Board of Trustees empowered to proceed with view to opening in the fall of 1940.

The committee's report did not reach the assembly floor until shortly before adjournment on the second Monday. Perhaps picking up the note of caution in Dr. Williams' words, "The hour may not be here yet," the assembly tabled the matter, and there it rested for the next four years.[77]

It was at the District Superintendents' Conference in January of 1944 that the matter of a seminary next surfaced. General Superintendent J. B. Chapman was the keynote speaker and delivered an address he called "A Nazarene Manifesto." In it, he argued that "we should set in now—right now—to build a seminary for

---

74. PGB, 1941, pp. 7-8.
75. GAJ, 1940, p. 192.
76. Ibid., p. 222.
77. Ibid., p. 192.

the training of our preachers." It must be a "real seminary" on a truly graduate level with "high standard courses."

Chapman predicted a first-year enrollment in such a school of 100. "I cannot further argue it here," he said, "but I feel so sure I am right about this matter that I do not anticipate any adverse argument on the question."[78]

Chapman may not have anticipated an argument, but he did receive a pointed letter from the Senior General Superintendent R. T. Williams, strongly objecting to unilateral advocacy of a move that should have had prior consultation with other members of the Board of General Superintendents and mutual agreement among them.[79]

The "Nazarene Manifesto" was seconded with regard to the seminary in a paper presented to the conference by R. V. DeLong, then superintendent of the Northwest Indiana District. The result was that the conference passed a motion asking the Board of General Superintendents to appoint a seminary commission to report to the 1944 General Assembly in June.[80]

The commission consisted of R. V. DeLong, chairman; another district superintendent, E. O. Chalfant of Chicago Central; M. Kimber Moulton, Los Angeles First Church pastor and general president of the NYPS; and two laymen: Harlan Heinmiller, Detroit General Motors executive; and M. Lunn, manager of the Nazarene Publishing House and general treasurer of the church.[81]

The Department of Education, meeting just after the Superintendents' Conference, listed several points for consideration by the seminary commission: that the school be located in Kansas City, appropriately housed; that its funds be provided from general sources without direct appeals to the church at large; that only graduate courses be offered, with uniform and standard entrance requirements; that tuition be free; and that the school open, "if possible," in the fall of 1945.[82]

---

78. Quoted, Taylor, "Historical Documents," pp. 176-77.
79. Letter, R. T. Williams to J. B. Chapman, copy to H. V. Miller, Feb. 3, 1944; reply, J. B. Chapman to R. T. Williams, Feb. 16, 1944 (Archives, R. T. Williams correspondence).
80. Cf. Taylor, "Historical Documents," p. 177.
81. Minutes of the Board of General Superintendents, meeting of Jan. 7, 1944; PGB, 1944, p. 20.
82. PGB, 1944, p. 47.

Spearheaded by DeLong, the commission made a thorough study of seminary programs and consulted the American Association of Theological Schools, the accrediting agency for seminaries. The administrators of the seven colleges were polled. A list of 10 recommendations was drawn up and presented to the General Assembly in June.

The first recommendation was "that a Nazarene Seminary, which shall be a graduate institution, be authorized by this General Assembly and that steps be taken to organize and create such an institution."[83]

Other recommendations included provision for the election of a Board of Trustees; referred the naming and location of the seminary to the Board of General Superintendents and the seminary board; provided for the nomination of the president by the general superintendents; and instructed that the president and all professors be in the experience of entire sanctification.

Financial stipulations doubled the amount suggested by the committee four years previously and provided that the seminary be financed for the quadrennium with a current budget of $30,000 annually: $15,000 from the earned surplus of the Nazarene Publishing House, and $15,000 from the General Budget. In addition, $100,000, or approximately 50 cents per church member, was to be raised in an appeal to the churches to provide for grounds, building, and equipment.[84] The entire report "was adopted . . . amid applause from members of the Assembly."[85]

The assembly proceeded to elect a seminary Board of Trustees: one member from each of the educational zones, and six members elected at large, with three being laypersons. The board in turn elected as its officers: chairman, Hugh C. Benner, pastor of Kansas City First Church; secretary, L. A. Reed, pastor, Chicago First Church; and treasurer, M. Lunn. Three members of the first board became administrators or faculty members of the institution: Benner, DeLong, and Reed.

The board asked the General Assembly to select a name for the school and offered two suggestions: Bresee Theological Semi-

---

83. GAJ, 1944, pp. 49-50.
84. Ibid., pp. 49-51.
85. Ibid., p. 48.

nary and Nazarene Theological Seminary. The choice went hands down to Nazarene Theological Seminary.[86]

The general superintendents and the seminary trustees moved promptly after the assembly. By September they had elected the chairman of the Board of Trustees, Hugh C. Benner, president of the seminary.

The 45-year-old Benner was born near Marion, Ohio, and was an alumnus of Olivet with a master's degree in history from the University of Southern California. He had taught at Eastern Nazarene College, Trevecca, and Pasadena College, and for 15 years had pastored leading churches in the West, Northwest, and at Kansas City.

His was a staggering task. At the time of his election, as he recalled, "we had nothing but an idea—not a faculty member, not a student, not a word of a catalogue, not an outline of a curriculum, not a book, a brick, or a dollar."[87]

Benner energetically started to work to change all that while continuing as pastor of Kansas City First Church until June, 1945, only three months before the seminary was to open its doors. His first task was the selection of a faculty. Working closely with the Board of General Superintendents, he nominated an outstanding group of men—all ordained ministers and seasoned churchmen and educators:

Stephen S. White, a University of Chicago Ph.D. and dean of theology at Olivet Nazarene College, was chosen as professor of systematic theology.

Mendell L. Taylor, Ph.D., University of Oklahoma, and dean of Bethany Nazarene College, became professor of church history.

Ralph Earle, Th.D., Gordon Divinity School, and professor of biblical literature at Eastern Nazarene College, was named professor of biblical literature.

Russell V. DeLong, Ph.D., Boston University, district superintendent in Northwest Indiana, became professor of philosophy and religious education and later dean.

Louis A. Reed, M.A., University of Southern California, pastor of Chicago First Church, was selected as professor of preaching and the pastoral ministry.

---

86. Ibid., pp. 100, 102.
87. GAJ, 1948, p. 299.

President Benner was also to serve as professor of church administration, Roy E. Swim of the Department of Church Schools was named part-time professor of biblical languages, and Dr. H. Orton Wiley, president of Pasadena College, was listed as occasional professor of biblical interpretation.[88]

In the summer of 1947, Delbert R. Gish, Ph.D., Boston University, was added to the staff as full-time professor of philosophy of religion. Albert F. Harper, who had become Church Schools editor and executive secretary in 1945; and S. T. Ludwig, general church secretary, taught courses part-time in religious education and church administration. Before the quadrennium ended, a Department of Missions and Evangelism was set up under the direction of Dean DeLong, and veteran India Missionary Prescott L. Beals became the first resident missionary teacher.

In 1948, White was elected *Herald of Holiness* editor and became a part-time professor. Lauriston DuBois began to teach practics part-time in 1950, and when Lewis Corlett became president in 1952, he added J. Kenneth Grider, a recent Glasgow University Ph.D. in theology, and James McGraw, in practics, to the faculty.

Harvey E. Finley, a Johns Hopkins University Ph.D., came to teach Old Testament language and literature in 1954. The seminary gained a full-time librarian in 1955 in the person of Eleanor L. Moore. In 1956, DuBois became a full-time professor, and the following year W. T. Purkiser, Ph.D., University of Southern California, was added to teach biblical theology and literature.

While still carrying his church responsibilities in 1944-45, Benner managed to visit each of the six liberal arts colleges in the United States where he presented the seminary program to the faculties and ministerial students. A list of 150 prospective students was drawn up.

February 18, 1945, was designated Seminary Sunday, and each local Nazarene church was requested to receive and send in an offering for capital expenses of the school. By July 1, almost two-thirds of the churches had responded with $73,000 in cash.[89]

Plans were made to set up the library and classrooms in the

---

88. Minutes of the Board of General Superintendents, meeting of Jan. 12, 1945; GAJ, 1948, p. 300.

89. Undated report of Hugh C. Benner to the Board of General Superintendents and Seminary Board of Trustees; archives.

recently purchased headquarters building on the corner of 30th and Troost, as well as in the facilities of the Nazarene Publishing House across the street. The first piece of property purchased by the seminary was a small hotel at 30th and Harrison, adjoining the headquarters building. The structure offered 35 rooms for dormitory purposes, as well as an apartment for the manager and space for a cafeteria. It was bought with all its furnishings for $42,000 and renamed Nazarene Seminary Hall.

Library resources were a specially critical point of need. Members of the faculty visited used bookstores in Boston, Chicago, St. Louis, and Kansas City, selecting books of particular value for their respective fields and ordered books in print from the publishers. By the time classes began in September of 1945, a working library of 5,000 volumes had been gathered, and before the end of the quadrennium the collection numbered 12,000. The old carriage house of the residence serving as headquarters was refurbished to provide quickly outgrown library space.

The seminary was approved by the government for selective service deferment in May and began operations on September 19, 1945, with the first chapel service September 20, just one year to the day from the election of the president.

While expectations of early enrollments varied widely, the more sober predictions were an initial student body of 25 with 50 as the top registration by the end of the quadrennium. The actual enrollment for the two semesters of the first year was 60, with 101 the second year, and 135 by 1947-48. The result was serious overcrowding of facilities that were extremely limited.

President Benner's frantic appeal to the 1948 General Assembly for a campus and buildings went unanswered for five years. The assembly did respond with an increase in current annual operating funds from $30,000 to $50,000 and did approve an annual offering in the churches for buildings and equipment.[90]

Classrooms and the area used for chapel were anything but adequate. Chapel was held in the largest room available, the former ballroom of the old mansion that served as headquarters. It was located on the third floor and was reached by a narrow, winding stairway. In a pinch it could seat 150. Classes were held wher-

---

90. GAJ, 1948, pp. 300-306.

ever space was available in buildings on both sides of Troost Avenue—a thoroughfare that carried 30,000 commuters per day and that must be crossed at risk of life and limb by seminary students and faculty changing classes.

Through it all, student and faculty morale was high. Many of the students had served in the pastorate or in church-related work and were strongly motivated. A high tide of spiritual blessing and inspiration was sought and maintained in chapel and classroom, and high academic standards were set.

The first graduates received their diplomas in May, 1947. They were nine in number, men who had entered with at least a year of graduate work elsewhere. General Superintendent J. B. Chapman was the commencement speaker, his last appearance in such a service.

A year later, the first three-year class of 37 graduated. President Benner noted that the 46 graduates during the first quadrennium of seminary history was a number nearly as large as the predicted high enrollment had been.[91]

Alumni from the early days have taken a large place in the leadership of the church in recent years.

An innovation originating in the seminary was a conference on evangelism sparked by R. V. DeLong as head of the school's Department of Evangelism. The first was held in Kansas City in January, 1947, for two days prior to the annual superintendents' conference. The meeting was cosponsored by the Southern California, Chicago Central, Tennessee, New England, and Dallas districts.

All of the general superintendents and almost all of the district superintendents, 150 evangelists, hundreds of pastors, and scores of laymen attended. The conference registered 551 participants, but evening crowds reached 1,200. Long feeling themselves the forgotten servants of the church, many evangelists expressed appreciation for the emphasis given their distinctive ministry. One evangelist wrote, "I have been associated with the holiness movement for fifty years. I saw, heard, and felt at the Conference on Evangelism more than in any other two days of my life."[92]

---

91. Ibid., p. 301.
92. Ibid., p. 305; HH, vol. 35, no. 45 (Jan. 20, 1947), p. 7; no. 46 (Jan. 27, 1947), p. 22.

C. The Colleges

Four of the seven colleges in the United States and Canada changed top leadership during the 1944-48 quadrennium. S. T. Ludwig, who had been president of Bethany-Peniel College for two years, was elected general secretary at the 1944 General Assembly. He was followed at Bethany by Kansas District Superintendent Oscar J. Finch. When Finch resigned in 1947, his successor was Roy H. Cantrell.

Cantrell was a graduate of Asbury College and Seminary in Wilmore, Ky., and had taught at Eastern Nazarene College as well as pastoring in New York State and putting in eight years as district superintendent in Ontario, Minnesota, and Kansas.

When the trustees of Kletzing College, formerly John Fletcher College, of Oskaloosa, Ia., made an abortive attempt to turn the school over to the Nazarenes, Cantrell had been picked as its president. The Kletzing move was blocked by the school's chief financial backer, and Cantrell went instead to Bethany to begin an outstanding 25-year administration.[93]

William Allshouse had guided the destinies of Canadian Nazarene College during most of the war years. When he resigned in 1946, A. E. Collins, Alberta district superintendent, became acting president for one year. Collins was followed by L. Guy Nees who served until 1949.

G. B. Williamson ended his nine-year tenure as president of Eastern Nazarene College in 1945 to replace Hugh C. Benner as pastor of Kansas City First Church. He was followed at ENC by the school's dean of theology and college pastor, Dr. Samuel Young, who was president until elected general superintendent in 1948.

Olivet Nazarene College had been led through its momentous move to Bourbonnais, Ill., and through the difficult war years by A. L. Parrott. When Parrott left in 1945, his successor was layman Grover Van Duyn, assistant state superintendent of schools for the state of Illinois. Van Duyn remained as Olivet's president until 1948.

The college enrollment bulge has already been mentioned. Many of the additional students were returning veterans. The Servicemen's Readjustment Act of 1944, the so-called GI Bill, pro-

---

93. For the Kletzing proposal, cf. HH, vol. 35, no. 6 (Apr. 22, 1946), pp. 14-16; PGB, 1946, p. 42.

vided that World War II veterans who were not over 25 years of age at the time they entered the service and who had served for 90 days or more were entitled to at least one year of education at government expense. The Veterans' Administration paid the student's tuition, fees, books, and other supplies up to a total of $500 per year and $60.00 per month to single or $85.00 to married students for living expenses.

Hundreds of Nazarene servicemen, including a number of chaplains, took advantage of these provisions. Their presence on college campuses added a seriousness of purpose and an enhanced measure of dedication to the student bodies. Many were called to ministerial or missionary work. Many were married. Their maturity was a stabilizing factor in student life.

The rapid increase in numbers of students put severe strains on campus facilities, particularly housing. Building had been almost impossible for four years, and the backlog of need was staggering. All of the colleges undertook to provide added dormitory space, for both men and women. "Temporary" facilities in government surplus barracks, quonset huts, and mobile homes were hastily provided at Olivet, Bethany, Pasadena, and Northwest.

Canadian Nazarene College added eight acres to its campus in 1946, the gift of the city of Red Deer, and completed an Administration Building in 1947.

ENC added a wing to Munro Hall, the women's dormitory, the first building there in 14 years.

Trevecca completed the rebuilding of the Administration Building in 1945, a project begin two years earlier, and added a dormitory, Tidwell Hall, to its campus in 1947.[94]

D. Spanish Nazarene Bible and Missionary Training Institute

Leaders on both sides of the Mexican-American border soon saw the need for training for Spanish-speaking young people preparing for church-related service. A start had been made in 1942 when Spanish Bible classes were offered as an extension division of Pas-

---

94. Cf. Cameron, *ENC: First Fifty Years*, pp. 339-52; Cantrell, "History of Bethany," pp. 213-19, 224-25; Knott, *History of Pasadena College*, pp. 82-85; Sutherland, "History of NNC," pp. 74-77; Thomson, *Vine of His Planting*, pp. 24-25; Wynkoop, *Trevecca Story*, pp. 188-98, 245, 267.

adena College. However, the response was limited and the effort was soon abandoned.

In the meantime, the Spanish work on both sides of the Monterrey-Texas border was burgeoning. A small Bible school campus owned by another denomination came on the market in San Antonio, and Texas-Mexican District Superintendent Fred Reedy persuaded the General Board to purchase the property.

In 1947 the Spanish Nazarene Bible and Missionary Training Institute (later, the Seminario Nazareno Hispanoamericano) was opened with Pasadena College graduate Hilario Peña as director. A faculty of five was gathered, and school began in September with 26 students drawn from three Latin American countries, Mexico, and the southwestern United States.

In 1952, Missionary Edward Wyman became the director, and by 1958, the institute enrolled 40 students under a faculty of six.[95]

IX. "SHOWERS OF BLESSING"

The 1944 General Assembly also authorized the general superintendents to appoint a commission of five to study the feasibility and to report to the General Board on the establishment of a "Radio Voice of the Church of the Nazarene." A number of pastors and churches locally had been conducting radio programs, as for example Agnes Diffee in Little Rock, Ark., and J. E. Williams at Long Beach, Calif., First Church. But the denomination as a whole had not entered this field.

The generals responded by selecting M. Lunn; S. T. Ludwig; John Stockton, Bethany-Peniel business manager and soon to become general treasurer; Haldor Lillenas, songwriter, musician, and director of the Lillenas Publishing Co.; and Hugh Benner, then still pastor of Kansas City First Church.

The commission soon acted to begin raising funds for a projected broadcast. They set up the Nazarene Radio League, and T. W. Willingham, former president of Olivet Nazarene College and at the time superintendent of the Missouri District, was chosen executive director. He in turn chose Stanley N. Whitcanack as office manager. Ray H. Moore, minister of music at Detroit First

---

95. DeLong and Taylor, *Fifty Years of Nazarene Missions,* 2:126-28; foreign missions field statistics, 1948; PGB, 1958, pp. 76-77.

Church, was selected as director of music. Offices were established on the third floor of the publishing house building.

Individuals were urged to "vote" for a coast-to-coast broadcast by pledging $1.00 per month. July 1, 1945, was envisioned as a beginning date, and the "ballots" were to be in by April 1 in order that necessary preparations might be made. A little over $16,000 per month was pledged, and the general superintendents authorized the commission to proceed with definite arrangements.[96]

The first half-hour broadcast of "Showers of Blessing" was aired June 17, 1945, with General Superintendent H. V. Miller as the speaker. The program was carried by 37 stations.[97] Music for the first eight programs was recorded by the Orpheus Choir of Olivet Nazarene College under the direction of Walter B. Larsen. Moore's Detroit First Church choir recorded music for the next four programs, after which a Kansas City-based "Showers of Blessing" choir picked up the music. A total of 27 different speakers were featured during the first year of broadcasting, with R. V. DeLong and L. A. Reed gradually emerging as the favorites.[98]

The half-hour format was continued through December of 1946. By the end of the first year, the number of stations had increased to 75 and by the end of 1946 the number stood at 87.[99] Through 1946, all air time was purchased through the Kansas City office, and a deficit of over $19,000 was accumulated.[100]

The director and the commission faced some hard choices. Their solution to their problem was three-pronged: to reduce the program length to 15 minutes; to use one principal speaker; and to adopt a local sponsorship plan for securing air time.

The reduction in the length of the program made it easier to obtain free air time and more favorable time slots. Sponsorship by churches in the community almost eliminated the cost of air time. R. V. DeLong, then dean of the seminary, began an extended stint as the principal speaker.

Within a year and a half, most of the deficit had been liq-

---

96. HH, vol. 33, no. 49 (Feb. 19, 1945), p. 3; vol. 34, no. 8 (May 7, 1945), p. 13.
97. Mimeographed information sheet from Nazarene Radio League, dated Dec. 7, 1967, archives.
98. Ibid.
99. PGB, 1947, p. 98.
100. GAJ, 1948, p. 314.

uidated. A gratifying number of stations accepted the program on a sustaining basis, without charge for air time. The 1948 General Assembly voted to put the radio commission in the General Budget for $50,000 per year administered through the Department of Home Missions.

The result was continued growth until by 1958, "Showers of Blessing" was airing on 340 stations in 44 states and with 50 outlets abroad that carried the program overseas; 194 were "sustaining" stations.[101]

SUMMARY

General Secretary S. T. Ludwig closed his first term in office with a report of substantial gains for the four years in the homeland: an increase of 268 churches to a total of 3,316; and 23,029 increase in membership to a total of 209,277.

After four years of losses during the war in both Sunday School enrollment and attendance, the tide had turned and the period ending in 1948 saw an enrollment increase from 332,753 to 398,940 (19.9 percent) and a growth in average weekly attendance from 194,038 to 251,655 (29.7 percent). More encouraging even was the fact that each of the four years had recorded an accelerating pace of growth, and 1947 showed the largest numerical gain in church schools work in the history of the department with the exception of the 1938 banner year.[102]

The NYPS showed a slight decrease, explained by the fact that honorary members were no longer included in the totals. WFMS membership grew by 20 percent to 64,193.

Building activity had been intense. A total of 501 new churches had been built or bought; 512 parsonages had been added. The dollar values of church and parsonage property rose from $18.7 million to $37.5 million, while the ratio of indebtedness to property value fell from 13.3 percent to 11.9 percent.

Per capita giving throughout the church rose steadily: to $64.74 in 1944; $75.54 in 1945; $82.33 in 1946; and $90.28 in

---

101. Ibid., pp. 156-57; PGB, 1959, p. 106; HH, vol. 36, no. 50 (Feb. 23, 1948), pp. 2-7.
102. GAJ, 1948, p. 276.

1948. Giving for general interests was up from $960,949 in 1944 to $1,407,065 in 1947.

Although foreign missionary activity had been widespread during the preceding four years, numerical results were disappointing. Organized churches on foreign mission fields had increased from 242 to only 260 while their membership grew only slightly from 11,644 to 11,756. The quadrennium had been a time of sowing. The reaping was to come.[103]

---

103. Ibid., pp. 188-93.

7

The Mid-Century Crusade for Souls

A look back at church growth patterns for the preceding 16 years (1932-48) revealed a gradually declining rate of growth in Nazarene church membership in the United States, Canada, and Great Britain. In the quadrennium ending in 1936, Nazarenes had added 40 percent to their membership. The quadrennium ending in 1940 saw the rate drop to 23.9 percent. The period ending in 1944 recorded a 15.3 percent increase, and the rate for the four years ending in 1948 was 12.3 percent.

Part of the attempt to cope with this declining rate in fulfilling the church's mission to the world was a Mid-Century Crusade for Souls with emphasis on visitation and personal evangelism throughout the denomination. While the crusade did not reverse the pattern, it did check the trend. The growth rate moved up to 15.9 percent for the period ending 1952 and stood at 15.4 percent by the time of the General Assembly of 1956.

I. LAYING THE GROUNDWORK

The WFMS and NYPS conventions prior to the General Assembly both selected evangelistic themes for their gatherings. The missionary society theme was "That They Might Know Him." The young people chose "I Am Debtor."

The missionary society heard the last report of its founding president, Mrs. Susan N. Fitkin. Mrs. Fitkin had led the national organization for 33 years. She was 78 years old and in failing health. Her report revealed her enduring vision of the place and importance of the women's organization:

> The W.F.M.S. came into existence thirty-three years ago. It has been the God-ordained instrument, not only for missionary intercession and information, but for raising millions of dollars for that sacred cause. . . . Through our regular monthly meeting we are constantly agitating and educating our women to be missionary minded, to know our missionaries by name, to pray for them and each field specifically, and to give sacrificially for every missionary enterprise.[1]

The convention responded warmly to Mrs. Fitkin's report. With her statement that she would no longer be able to serve as president, she was enthusiastically elected general president emeritus. A $50,000 offering for a China Bible Training School in honor of the retiring leader was oversubscribed by $20,000. An ardent supporter of missions to the end, Susan Fitkin died peacefully in her Oakland, Calif., home at the age of 81. In addition to her work as WFMS general president, she had been a member of the General Board for 24 years, longer than any other person had ever served.[2]

Mrs. Fitkin's successor was Louise Robinson Chapman, widow of General Superintendent J. B. Chapman. Mrs. Chapman had been a missionary in Africa for 20 years prior to her 1942 marriage to Dr. Chapman. She was to give 16 years of service to the general WFMS leadership until her retirement in 1964.

The NYPS General Convention also elected new leadership. Seminary Professor Mendell L. Taylor was elected president to succeed Los Angeles First Church Pastor M. Kimber Moulton. Taylor's history of the NYPS, *Nazarene Youth in Conquest for Christ,* dedicated to D. Shelby Corlett as the first general executive secretary, had been a featured presentation of the opening convention service.[3] Lauriston DuBois was reelected for a second term as general secretary. DuBois was an excellent speaker and much in demand for youth-oriented meetings. He had already demonstrated the value of his leadership during the preceding four years.

The opening conventions and the 1948 General Assembly were all held in St. Louis. The General Assembly itself convened in

---

1. Quoted, HH, vol. 37, no. 17-18 (July 12, 1948), p. 25.
2. HH, vol. 40, no. 37 (Nov. 21, 1951)—the memorial issue.
3. (Kansas City: Nazarene Publishing House, 1948).

the beautiful and spacious Kiel Auditorium with the traditional Communion service on Sunday morning, June 20. In contrast with the Minneapolis meeting held four years before under severe wartime travel restrictions, St. Louis drew the largest crowd ever to attend a Nazarene General Assembly up to that time: 625 delegates and well over 9,000 visitors.

All were keenly aware of the loss during the preceding four years of three general superintendents whose experience and service extended back into the founding days of the church: Emeritus John W. Goodwin, who had delivered the Communion address in Minneapolis; Roy T. Williams, whose leadership had spanned 30 formative years; and James B. Chapman, who had joined the church at Pilot Point and whose prepared and printed Communion address scheduled for St. Louis in 1948 was distributed to the congregation the first Sunday morning.

The general superintendents' quadrennial address had been written by H. V. Miller and was presented by him on Monday morning. It was one of the longest quadrennial addresses ever given (23 large printed pages) and covered a wide range of topics.

Miller made much of the 40th anniversary year (1908-48) and stressed the distinction between pioneers and "inheritors." He was concerned that the vitality of the past be preserved for the future:

> No task confronts us requiring more painstaking effort than the passing on to another generation the same ideals and vision and full passion that moved our fathers. Along with line upon line of instruction and precept upon precept of doctrine must come revival tides of God's glory to illuminate and to confirm the truth of our teaching. No one can say the inheritance which is ours is cheap. Its coinage is in the blood, vision, sacrifice of men like Bresee, Reynolds, Williams, and Chapman. God forbid that the vitality of the past should spend itself solely because we of another generation fail to perpetuate it.[4]

The unique task of the church reminded Miller of John Wesley's concern that the people of his Methodist classes should "resolve to be Bible Christians at all events; and, wherever they went, to preach with all their might, plain old Bible Christianity."[5]

Home missions, evangelism, youth training, "our standards" of discipline and behavior, and world evangelism were brought

---

4. GAJ, 1948, p. 162.
5. Ibid., p. 163.

into focus as objects of the church's planning. The church must never "mistake ecclesiastical accomplishment for spiritual reality."[6] While future growth is to be assumed, Miller said, we must "discourage the development of too-large churches and too-large educational institutions."[7]

Still, Miller would not want to "fall prey to the bogey of bigness." He pointed out that "the discriminating choice" had already been made between the two philosophies, "Stay small and keep clean," or "Grow and serve humanity to the maximum and recognize the hazards and dangers implied." The latter "was the choice of our fathers. We need not flinch from the choice they made if we are alert, wise, and discriminating."[8]

In specific goals for the four years ahead, Miller suggested $5 million for world evangelism: $1 million for expansion in the home base and $4 million abroad. In terms of personnel, the goal should be a 50,000 gain in membership and 1,000 new congregations, with 550,000 in Sunday School.

Definite recommendations included the development of a philosophy of education for Nazarene colleges, attention to the development of the church in rural areas in the United States and Canada, consideration to more effective youth training, expansion of publishing interests, adjustments in the Nazarene Ministers Benevolent plan to care for aging ministers, the inclusion of the seminary and radio league in the $1 million to be raised for work in domestic areas, and as a slogan to afford both "divine motivation and pattern for the fulfillment of that motivation . . . CHRIST IS ALL AND IN ALL."[9]

Miller climaxed his address with an unidentified quotation from H. Orton Wiley:

> Once we see the magnificent sweep of the Church of Christ, we shall be delivered from the narrow, petty, and unessential things that harass us only too often. Then also we shall rest with an abiding confidence although the kingdoms of this world should crash about us. Knowing that the church is built upon a foundation which can never be shaken, we rest with firm confidence in the living hope for the church to which we are begotten by the resurrection of Jesus Christ from the

6. Ibid., p. 170.
7. Ibid., p. 172.
8. Ibid.
9. Ibid., p. 176.

dead; and we know that He shall come again and that the kingdoms of this world shall yet become the kingdoms of our Lord and His Christ.[10]

II. NEW HANDS AT THE HELM

Four men had been elected to the general superintendency in 1944; R. T. Williams, J. B. Chapman, H. V. Miller, and Hardy C. Powers. Of the four, Williams and Chapman had died during the quadrennium. Because the Williams death occurred during the first two years of the period, the district superintendents had been asked to elect a successor, and G. B. Williamson had been chosen and installed.

The assembly's Committee on Superintendency recommended the election of five general superintendents for the ensuing quadrennium. The church had had four general superintendents since 1915 with the exception of the depression years when three had served. The election of the fifth was justified by the growth both in church membership and in the number of districts, and by the added foreign supervision requested by both the 1944 and 1948 General Assemblies.

A. General Superintendents Elected

The three incumbents, Miller, Powers, and Williamson, were elected with large votes on the first ballot. The fourth name was Orval J. Nease with 57 percent of the votes, 68 short of election. Next in order were Hugh Benner and Samuel Young. On the second ballot, Nease came within 7 votes of election and on ballot number three was elected.

The assembly reacted with enthusiasm as Dr. and Mrs. Nease were escorted to the platform. An almost palpable sense of relief was evident. A substantial number of the church's leaders had felt that Nease had been unfairly treated four years earlier. His wide and successful evangelistic work and his uncomplaining demeanor during the four intervening years had paved the way for what seemed to many to be personal vindication. Whatever sore spots had remained from the events leading up to the 1944 General Assembly had indeed, as R. T. Williams had predicted, been

---

10. Ibid.

healed. Nease was, in fact, struggling with physical problems at the time, a situation he frankly discussed with his colleagues when the new Board of General Superintendents met for the first time after the election. He was determined, however, to give his best to the assignment and threw himself into his work with enthusiasm.

Benner continued through the second and third ballots as next in line, but Young's vote was rapidly narrowing the gap. On the next three ballots, Benner dropped as Young continued to gain. On the seventh ballot, Samuel Young was elected the fifth general superintendent.

Young was comparatively unknown throughout much of the church, having served almost exclusively in the Northeast. He had been born in Glasgow, Scotland, where he was converted and joined the Parkhead Church of the Nazarene. The family emigrated to the United States when Young was 15 years of age and settled in Cleveland.

Young had begun a career as a cost accountant when he was sanctified and called to the ministry. He graduated from Eastern Nazarene College and earned a master's degree at Boston University. Pastorates at Salem, Ohio, and South Portland, Me., were followed by six and a half years as superintendent of the New England District and five years as college pastor and head of the theology department at Eastern Nazarene College until election as college president in 1945.

Young had been a member of the General Board since 1937 where he had been on the vitally important Department of Foreign Missions and the Finance Committee. He was to make a major contribution on the Board of General Superintendents during his 24 years in office.[11]

B. Other Officers Chosen

Other significant leadership changes occurred during the 1948 General Assembly and at the General Board meeting immediately following. *Herald of Holiness* Editor D. Shelby Corlett had come from Kansas City to the opening session of the NYPS Convention where he was honored as the founding executive secretary of the youth organization. He felt it necessary to return home the following day. When the time came for the election of the editor, H. V.

---

11. Cf. Corbett, *Pioneer Builders,* pp. 36-40.

Miller spoke on behalf of the Board of General Superintendents in appreciation for the faithful service of Dr. Corlett as editor of the *Herald.* On the advice of his physician, he had requested that his name not be placed in nomination.

The assembly passed an appropriate resolution of appreciation and elected Stephen S. White, professor of theology at the seminary, as *Herald* editor. Corlett was able to resume work after a year and served as pastor in Anaheim, Calif., for four years before moving to Northwest Nazarene College in 1953 as professor of Bible and theology.[12]

At the General Board meeting immediately following the General Assembly, C. Warren Jones, missions executive since 1936, indicated his desire for retirement. He was 66 years old. He had carried the burdens of the foreign work through the end of the depression and the hectic wartime and early postwar period. He had seen the missionary force grow from 69 at the beginning of 1936 to 204 in 1948, and the roll of national workers from 403 to 788. Overseas membership had almost doubled, from 14,177 to 24,048 in the same period. The foreign missions budget had ballooned from $160,000 per year to $890,000 and the missions program from 12 fields to 19 in the 12-year interval.

Jones could have served four years longer before reaching the mandatory retirement age of 70. At least partly responsible for his resignation was his concern over mounting deficits in the Department of Foreign Missions which were to result in the severe financial crunch of January, 1949.

Arrangements were made for Jones to carry on until January, 1949, at which time his successor was elected. The choice fell to 34-year-old Remiss Rehfeldt, superintendent of the Iowa District. Rehfeldt had pastored in Burlington and Council Bluffs, Ia., and had been district superintendent for four years. He had just been elected to the General Board. As had his immediate predecessor, Rehfeldt stepped into a staggering financial crisis in the foreign missions program—a crisis that led to an innovative and permanent emphasis on General Budget giving.

The 1948 General Assembly had shown a deepening concern for home mission expansion in the church. It had become clear that

---

12. GAJ, 1948, pp. 94-95.

further development abroad could proceed only as the home base was strengthened.

The Department of Home Missions and Evangelism had been a part-time assignment for executives carrying other tasks. D. Shelby Corlett, J. G. Morrison, M. Lunn, C. Warren Jones, and S. T. Ludwig had all worn the Home Missions mantle in connection with other responsibilities, in most cases full-time tasks.

The net gain in number of churches had dropped sharply during the preceding four years: from 393 in 1932-36; 363 in 1936-40; and 431 in 1940-44, to 268 in 1944-48. While home missions had traditionally been considered a district concern in the Church of the Nazarene, the increasing number of districts and the variety displayed in district leadership made some sort of denominational direction important.

The General Assembly in 1948 referred a proposal for a full-time executive for home missions and evangelism to the Board of General Superintendents and the General Board with power to act. In turn, the general superintendents recommended Northern California District Superintendent Roy F. Smee for the post, and the General Board elected him.

Smee had been Northern California district leader for 17 years and had compiled an impressive record. The number of churches on the district had increased from 36 to 92, and the district church membership had grown from 1,980 to 6,766, percentage gains almost twice those of the denomination as a whole. While gains during the 1930s could be attributed in part to heavy migration from the Dust Bowl region of the Middle West, those of later years were largely in terms of converts who had not been Nazarenes before.

Smee tackled his new job with boundless enthusiasm. He brought in as office manager one of his young pastors, Alpin P. Bowes, and he himself travelled the church extensively urging the importance of starting new churches to add to district membership and strength. While other factors entered the overall picture, the gains in numbers of churches shot up from 268 in 1944-48 to 474 in 1948-52 and to an all-time high of 536 in 1952-56.

One of Smee's most important innovations was the beginning in 1945 of the General Church Loan Fund to assist in financing new buildings. By 1958, the revolving loan fund had passed the $1 million mark.

Early in January, 1950, Miss Emma B. Word, who had long served in the Foreign Missions office and had been secretary-treasurer of the women's missionary auxiliary, resigned "due to health and pressure of work in the office and other things."[13] At that time, it was decided to transfer the WFMS funds to the general treasurer's office instead of handling them in a separate account.

To fill Miss Word's vacancy on the WFMS General Council and to serve as general secretary, the council chose China Missionary Mary Scott, whose tenure in the office lasted 25 years until her retirement in 1975.[14]

A substantial turnover in the membership of the General Board also took place. When the 24-member board met in January, 1949, there were 13 of the members serving for the first time: District Superintendents O. L. Benedum, Harvey Galloway, E. D. Simpson, Paul Updike, Ray Hance, and Edward Lawlor; businessmen Leonard M. Spangenberg and Al E. Ramquist; educators L. T. Corlett and Vernal Carmichael; Medical Dr. J. Robert Mangum; WFMS President Louise Robinson Chapman; and NYPS President Mendell Taylor were all to hold large places in the work of the church in the years ahead.

Later in the quadrennium, Bethany-Peniel College President Roy Cantrell replaced Hugh C. Benner, ineligible to serve by reason of his seminary post. District Superintendent Arthur Morgan took the place of newly elected General Superintendent D. I. Vanderpool; and Olivet Nazarene College's new president, Harold W. Reed, replaced the deceased Selden Dee Kelley.

III. TWO GENERALS DIE IN OFFICE

One of the five general superintendents elected in 1948 lived only six months after the assembly. Howard V. Miller came back in early December from an exhausting and tension-filled trip to Australia and the Hawaiian Islands. While in Hawaii, Miller had suffered an attack of what at the time was thought to be acute indigestion. Returning to his home in Brooktondale, N.Y., for a brief Christmas vacation, he was stricken suddenly with a coronary thrombosis

---

13. PGB, 1950, p. 45.
14. Ibid., p. 46.

and died at 4:30 p.m., Tuesday, December 28, 1948. He was 54 years of age, the youngest general superintendent to die in office.

Miller's younger colleague of three years on the Board of General Superintendents, G. B. Williamson, described him as "a man free from all self-seeking, self-serving designs. He had keen insight, sound judgment, and a fair mind." Williamson recalled the General Assembly six months before: "He was at the zenith of his power in the General Assembly of 1948. The quadrennial report which he wrote and read will doubtless prove to be a directive to the denomination for a generation."[15]

The superintendents' conference was scheduled for the second week of January, and the superintendents were informed that an election would be held to fill the vacancy caused by Dr. Miller's death. The superintendents had traditionally selected the person next highest in the voting at the previous General Assembly. In the 1948 voting, Hugh Benner had been a front-runner. Not all the district superintendents favored the seminary, however, and some were wary of Benner's strong leadership. Others deemed his seminary work too important to be interrupted.

The vote went instead to Daniel I. Vanderpool, superintendent of the Northwest District. The 1948 General Assembly had adopted a constitutional amendment to provide that filling a vacancy on the Board of General Superintendents would require a two-thirds vote of all the district superintendents instead of a simple majority as previously.

Technically, the provision was not law until approved by two-thirds of the district assemblies, certified by the Board of General Superintendents, and published in the *Herald of Holiness.* It was April 10, 1950, before this process was completed. However, the superintendents decided to follow the spirit of the new provision. Vanderpool received 37 votes on the second ballot, well over the majority; and was declared elected on the third ballot with 51 out of 56 votes (6 superintendents were absent), well over two-thirds of the 62 organized districts.[16]

The 47-year-old Vanderpool came from the Missouri holiness group that had nurtured G. B. Williamson and A. E. Sanner. He had been educated, as had Williamson, at Central Holiness Univer-

---

15. HH, vol. 37, no. 48 (Feb. 7, 1949), p. 3—the memorial issue.
16. GAJ, 1952, pp. 215-17.

sity (John Fletcher College) at Oskaloosa, Ia., and joined the Church of the Nazarene there.

After some four years in full-time evangelism, chiefly in Colorado, Vanderpool was elected superintendent of the Colorado District where he served until he became pastor of Denver First Church in 1924. After other pastorates in Pasadena, Calif., and Walla Walla, Wash., he became superintendent of the Northwest District in 1938. Always remembered as a warmhearted, effective preacher of the gospel, Vanderpool served 15 years in the general superintendency until retirement in 1964.

The fourth death in the general superintendency in a little more than four years was the passing of Orval J. Nease, November 7, 1950, at the age of 58.

Shortly after his reelection in 1948, Nease made an exhausting trip to Japan, Korea, China, and the Philippines. Somewhere along the way he picked up a virus that aggravated an already weakened condition. He was forced to miss the General Board meeting in 1949 and labored through the balance of that year and almost all of 1950 with limited strength. Death came at home after a brief illness.

Had he been willing to take sufficient time for a complete recovery, Nease might have lived longer. But his attitude was reflected in a statement he made during this period and recalled by his senior colleague, Hardy C. Powers, "I have only one desire, and that is to spend all I have in the service of God and the church."[17]

General Superintendents Powers, Young, and Vanderpool attended the funeral in Pasadena. Dr. Williamson was en route to Australia and could not be present. The three leaders conferred about the election of a successor. Since the next General Assembly was just a little over 18 months away, they unanimously decided to defer an election until the General Assembly, a decision Williamson had already recommended.[18]

IV. LAUNCHING THE MID-CENTURY CRUSADE

Tied in with the home missions and evangelism emphasis of the 1948 General Assembly was the launching of a quadrennial emphasis labelled the Mid-Century Crusade for Souls.

---

17. HH, vol. 39, no. 41 (Dec. 18, 1950), p. 3—the memorial issue.
18. Minutes, Board of General Superintendents, meeting of Nov. 10, 1950.

One point of impetus for the crusade went back to J. B. Chapman's impassioned plea, "All Out for Souls," at the 1947 January Superintendents' Conference. The superintendents adopted a resolution asking the appointment of a committee to formulate plans for added emphasis on personal evangelism and soul winning for the quadrennium to begin in 1948. The committee was appointed in September by the Board of General Superintendents and reported to the General Assembly with a recommendation "to authorize as a quadrennial project a church-wide plan of visitation evangelism and systematic training in personal soul winning."[19]

A. Visitation and Personal Evangelism

In their October 4 crusade proclamation, the general superintendents took care to explain that the Mid-Century Crusade for Souls with its emphasis on visitation and personal evangelism was not a substitute for the traditional revival meetings and evangelistic campaigns with their public appeal for conversions and commitments to entire sanctification. "It is not to be carried on without the pulpit and the altar; it is rather to assure the evangelist a crowd to whom to preach and some prospects to invite to his altars."[20]

The proclamation quoted a passage from Chapman's book, *The Preaching Ministry:*

> Our tendency to see parts as though they were the whole has led us to suppose a conflict between *personal evangelism* and *mass evangelism.* But the fact is these two forms of soul winning have always been complementary and inseparable. There have been no examples of successful mass evangelism in which personal evangelism did not play a very large and indispensable part, and personal evangelism unattached from gospel preaching has been altogether disappointing. *The two go together.*[21]

The generals saw four features of visitation and personal evangelism that must be present if desired results are accomplished. There must be *inspiration,* an inner motivation and soul burden on the part of the participants. *Organization* with direction by capable leadership is essential. *Continuation* in the sense of adequate follow-up must feature the program. And *preservation,* or what would now be called "discipling," must follow.

---

19. GAJ, 1948, p. 57.
20. HH, vol. 37, no. 30 (Oct. 4, 1948), p. 2.
21. Ibid.

The work of personal evangelism does not stop with conversion, the proclamation explained. The new convert must be instructed, his interest sustained, and help given in hours of temptation. "Adjustment to the church life must be made. The way of holiness must be explained. Membership in the church is to be accomplished." All of this falls within the sphere of the personal evangelist.[22]

B. Crusade Helps

As the crusade was launched, helpful materials were provided. A series of paperback books explained goals and methods. Two were written for study by lay people and recommended for use as Christian Service Training texts. Dr. Shelby Corlett had put together a volume titled *Soul Winning Through Visitation Evangelism* assisted by former army chaplain Neal C. Dirkse and seminarian Carl Bangs, Jr.

A companion to Corlett's volume was one jointly authored by Albert Harper and layman Elmer H. Kauffman who for 20 years had been educational director for the Fuller Brush Company. Kauffman had adapted and successfully used in the work of the church some of the sales methods of his profession. *First Steps in Visitation Evangelism* was an attempt both to motivate and to guide the personal worker in his efforts outside the public services of the church.

At the same time, a book was published to help pastors adapt and use the materials, Lauriston DuBois' *Pastor and Visitation Evangelism.*

In addition to book-length materials, a complete set of printed forms, record cards, and leaflets introduced the church to the outside community. The program began with a community survey, concentrating on an area within one mile of the church location. The survey contact point was an inquiry concerning children for Sunday School. Its emphasis was "aggressiveness without offense."[23]

Later in the quadrennium, three other books were presented: *He That Winneth Souls,* edited by Alpin P. Bowes, featuring illustra-

---

22. Ibid., p. 3.
23. Albert F. Harper and Elmer H. Kauffman, *First Steps in Visitation Evangelism* (Kansas City: Nazarene Publishing House, 1948), pp. 50-102.

tions of personal evangelism in the mid-century crusade with the emphasis on "Go thou and do likewise;" Fletcher Spruce's *Revive Us Again,* outlining techniques for revival; and Evangelist C. William Fisher's *The Time Is Now,* a ringing call for continued commitment to evangelism in the church.[24]

The *Herald of Holiness* for September 12, 1949, was the first of a long series of annual "special" *Heralds* designed specifically for community distribution. It was published with a two-color art cover and featured a series of articles designed both to introduce the Church of the Nazarene as a denomination and to serve as an evangelistic appeal. The publishing house arranged for bulk sales at three cents per copy, and 600,000 of the "'Get Acquainted' Crusade special issue" were printed for wide distribution.[25]

C. The Lamplighters' League

In the meantime, the youth organization added its own thrust in personal witnessing and soul winning in the Lamplighters' League. The league was the product of the fertile minds of two young northern California ministers, Ponder W. Gilliland and Paul Martin. The title was a takeoff from Grace Noll Crowell's lines:

> *I shall light my lamp at faith's white spark,*
> *And through this wild storm hold it high;*
> *Perhaps across the utter dark*
> *Its light will flash against the sky,*
> *Steady enough and clear enough*
> *For some lost one to steer him by.*[26]

The league was totally unstructured and informal: "not an organization, but a movement."[27] It had no membership roll and no officers. It was composed of those who would resolve to deal with one individual a month about his spiritual condition, and who would memorize a list of Scripture references dealing with conversion and holiness. Lauriston DuBois, NYPS general secre-

---

24. C. William Fisher, *The Time Is Now* (Kansas City: Nazarene Publishing House, 1950).

25. HH, vol. 38, no. 26 (Sept. 5, 1949), p. 3. The special was vol. 38, no. 27 (Sept. 12, 1949), 28 pp.

26. *Poems of Inspiration and Courage* (New York: Harper and Row, 1965), p. 57; used by permission. The verse was first published in *The Lifted Lamp* in 1944.

27. PGB, 1951, p. 84.

tary, said, "We have not stressed numbers or tried to bring pressure to bear to get young people to sign the pledge. Hence, we do not keep records of numbers. However, there has been an unusual response. It has been the challenge that our young people have wanted."[28]

D. Crusade Results

It is impossible to know how extensively the offered plans were followed in the local congregations, or how many churches were seriously organized to put the program into action. The consensus was that where it was used, it was successful. Adaptations were, of course, necessary for rural areas and for high-rise apartment complexes in the cities. For example, Willard H. Taylor, then pastor of Chicago's Woodlawn Church, gave detailed suggestions for working around security arrangements in apartment buildings in the inner city.[29]

Overall results are also difficult to assess. Other factors entered the church growth picture. The 15 years immediately following World War II were a time of general interest in religion and of growing church membership particularly in the United States. In 1957, the United States Census Bureau reported that 96 percent of the American people indicated a religious affiliation, an unprecedented number, although doubtless in many instances without much meaning.[30]

Smee's vigorous home mission emphasis had markedly increased the planting of new churches, motivated by the obvious necessity to grow or die. Denominational emphases such as the Mid-Century Crusade for Souls are difficult to sustain over a long period of time. The crusade emphasis gradually lessened during the quadrennium, and the attempt to extend it into 1952-56 under the rubric "Crusade for Souls Now" was not particularly successful.

With all the factors considered, the growth pattern of the church does reflect a reversal of the declining trend in rate of growth that had prevailed since 1936. For the two quadrenniums including and following the Mid-Century Crusade, the growth rate

---

28. PGB, 1950, p. 113.
29. HH, vol. 39, no. 34 (Oct. 30, 1950), p. 14.
30. Cf. Hudson, *Religion in America*, p. 382-83.

climbed back to 15.9 percent in 1948-52 and 15.4 percent in 1952-56 before resuming its slide to 11.2 percent in 1956-60 and to a plateau average of 10.2 percent for the three quadrenniums from 1960 to 1972.[31] In percentage growth, the crusade years 1948-52 represented a 29.2 percent improvement over the quadrennium immediately preceding.

V. FINANCIAL CRISIS
AND THE 10 PERCENT PROGRAM

The General Board faced a severe crisis in the finances of the Department of Foreign Missions in its January, 1949, meeting. After R. T. Williams was incapacitated, ever-optimistic General Superintendent Chapman vigorously pushed missionary expansion. The missions secretary, C. Warren Jones, became concerned about the size of the commitments being made and did everything short of resigning his position to slow the pace.[32]

Jones reflected the size of the expansion in his report to the General Assembly in June, 1948. A total of 160 missionaries had been sent out during the preceding four years. Of the 160 total, 134 were new missionaries, and 26 were missionaries returning to their fields from furloughs. At the same time, the church had opened five new fields and had reentered Japan and China.[33]

A. The Financial Crunch
General church receipts had escalated sharply during the four years ending in 1948 but had failed to keep pace with the lavish outpouring of money necessary to finance the missionary expansion. General Treasurer John Stockton sounded the alarm in no uncertain terms.

Stockton pointed out that until 1946, the General Board had always set its budget at a safe margin below expected income. This was due in large part to the strongly conservative leadership of

---

31. In 1972, in recognition of the internationalization of the church, the general secretary began to include overseas membership in reporting totals. Adding 99,163 members to the 407,476 reported in domestic districts, the total growth rate for the church worldwide was 16.1 percent for 1972-76 and 12.7 percent for 1976-80.

32. Interview, Samuel Young, Feb. 16, 1977.

33. GAJ, 1948, pp. 235-41; HH, vol. 37, no. 17-18 (July 12, 1948), p. 23.

R. T. Williams. However, in January, 1946, the board budgeted $1,765,025, of which 87 percent or $1,540,700 was earmarked for foreign missions. At the same time, the general budgets accepted by the districts totalled only $1,022,575—a shortfall of $742,450.

A somewhat more cautious approach was taken in January of 1947 when the board approved a foreign mission budget of $1,224,522 against expected General Budget receipts of $1,509,208. Only $800,000 was to be definitely allocated by the department; the additional $424,522 could be spent only "if and when the money is received through current income."[34]

In 1948, the General Board voted a total budget of $1,185,325 with an additional $143,000 for buildings and property on foreign fields "if and when." The General Assembly later in the year added an additional $83,942. Of this total of $1,412,277, approximately $1 million was received. Stockton summarized, "This means that, in order to pay the budgets approved in the past three years, we have had to spend $1,011,726.81 more than we have received; and this does not allow for the $143,000 building and property fund." Reserves built up during the war years were totally depleted. The conclusion: "We believe you can easily see that this procedure cannot continue." Stockton's recommendation was that the board "cut every budget to bare necessities; and if more funds are received than are required to pay the budgets, they can be distributed to the Department of Foreign Missions and the Department of Home Missions on a percentage basis of 80 percent to 20 percent."[35]

B. The General Board Response

The response of the board was twofold. Budgets were cut. Both the seminary and the Radio League were cut from $50,000 to $45,000 each. Foreign missions was dropped from $840,000 in 1948 to $700,000 in 1949, with an additional $74,960 "if available." The Church Extension budget was reduced from $22,500 to $10,500; Ministerial Benevolence from $45,000 to $35,000. The total was brought down from $1,269,277 (excluding the foreign missions building and property fund of $143,000) to $1,172,563.

The second response of the board was of more lasting significance. During the postwar years, the percentage of all funds re-

---

34. PGB, 1949, p. 119.
35. Ibid., pp. 118-19.

ceived throughout the church for general interests had been dropping, from a high of 8.39 percent in 1945 to 6.8 percent in 1948. As early as March, 1947, C. Warren Jones had suggested the goal of 10 percent of all church giving for General Budget concerns, approximately 80 percent of which had gone to foreign missions.

C. The 10 Percent Program

The board adopted a resolution proposed by the Department of Foreign Missions urging "steps to develop and intensify the program of the 'life-line' giving of our people by presenting a great challenge to our whole church for sacrificial giving and setting up a goal for each local church equal to the sum of 10 percent or more of the annual total giving of each church for world evangelism."[36]

The first of those steps was a strong presentation of the problem and its proposed solution to the Superintendents' Conference which in 1949 followed the General Board meeting instead of preceding as it often had. Notice had been sent out that the successor to deceased General Superintendent Miller would be chosen at the conference, and an unusually large number of district superintendents had come. Most of the superintendents pledged their districts to accept increases in their general budgets at the assemblies during the year.

Strong emphasis was given the 1949 Easter Offering, and on April 17, Nazarenes laid on the altars of their church a then unprecedented $815,000 for world evangelism.[37]

The 10 percent program for evangelism pointed the way to the principle of proportionate giving that was later to be used to give guidance for other denominational concerns. Its immediate effect was to increase the proportion of total church giving earmarked for General Budget and missionary specials.

Per capita giving for the church as a whole in 1948 had been $101.78. This rose slightly to $104.64 in 1949. However, the per capita portion sent to Kansas City was up from $6.97 in 1948 to $9.15 in 1949, or from 6.85 percent of total giving to 8.74 percent

---

36. Ibid., p. 58; cf. OS, vol. 34, no. 3 (March, 1947), p. 2; and minutes, Board of General Superintendents, meeting of March 17, 1949, when plans were made to urge support for the "Ten Percent Program" at the upcoming district assemblies.

37. GAJ, 1952, p. 227.

of the total. Missions specials in 1949 added another $221,594 to the total.[38]

General Treasurer Stockton's enthusiasm is understandable when he reported seven years later, "Probably the 10 percent giving for world evangelism has done more to raise money for missions during the last few years than anything else." Stockton then listed the year-by-year giving for world evangelism for the preceding six years, increasing from $1,545,243 in fiscal 1949-50 to $2,644,874 in fiscal 1955-56. "You can see from the above record the progress that has been made," he said. "The 10 percent program is not only a good program but I sincerely believe it is God's program for missions in our church."[39]

The increased giving of the church combined with the fiscal responsibility of the General Board's decision to budget only within the limits of fund availability prevented further crises of this sort, at least in the General Budget. A further step was taken later when the board acted to budget on the basis of actual receipts the preceding year rather than on the basis of anticipated income.

Much of the credit for sounder financial policies goes to General Superintendent Samuel Young whose earlier experience as a cost accountant proved a valuable asset during his 24-year tenure on the Board of General Superintendents. Strongly supporting the new move was businessman Leonard M. Spangenberg, long associated with Boston's prestigious Babson Institute. Spangenberg became chairman of the influential Finance Committee of the General Board in 1949, a post he held for almost 20 years.

D. The Alabaster Fund

Coupled with the 10 percent program was the Alabaster fund pushed by the Women's Foreign Missionary Society and its new

---

38. PGB, 1950, pp. 18, 83, 87. For reporting purposes, district percentages soon came to be used. General Treasurer Stockton listed "The Big Ten" and "The Climbing Ten" districts in terms of their records in General Budget giving. Three districts had already passed 10 percent—Northeastern Indiana with 12.96 percent, Northwest Oklahoma with 11.20, and Idaho-Oregon with 10.82 (HH, vol. 40, no. 17 [July 2, 1951], p. 21). A follow-up resolution adopted by the General Board in 1951 stressed the idea of local churches allocating "a tithe of the tithe" for missions, citing Neh. 10:38-39 and Num. 18:25-29 as a biblical basis (HH, vol. 40, no. 28 [Sept. 17, 1951], p. 9). Missions "specials" are funds specified for approved projects above and beyond regular General Budget giving.
39. GAJ, 1956, p. 226.

president, Mrs. Louise Robinson Chapman. The name was taken from the Gospel account of the action of Mary of Bethany who broke an alabaster flask of ointment to anoint Jesus just before His crucifixion (Matt. 26:7; Mark 14:3; John 12:3). Small cardboard boxes were provided for each family into which miscellaneous coins and currency could be dropped. These Alabaster boxes were to be brought to the church periodically and the funds sent to the general treasurer to be used specifically for buildings, property, and physical facilities for missionary work.

Launched in 1948, the fund brought in $64,000 the first full year. Receipts increased each year until by 1958-59, the annual giving had reached $433,000. A tabulation made in 1962 indicated that 352 churches or chapels had been built with the Alabaster money, 154 national workers' homes, 88 homes for missionaries, 74 school or Bible school buildings, 22 hospital or dispensary buildings, and nine cottages at Casa Robles for retired missionaries. In addition, 74 parcels of land for building sites had been purchased. Total receipts in the first 13 years of Alabaster giving added up to $3,681,403.[40]

VI. THE QUADRENNIUM IN EDUCATION

College enrollments in the six colleges in the United States and at Canadian Nazarene College peaked for the quadrennium at 3,921 in 1948 before declining to 3,455 in 1952-53. In the United States, the decline was due in large part to increased selective service call-up of young men for service in the Korean conflict and the call back of reservists into the service. At the seminary, where male students for the most part were allowed ministerial deferment from military service, the enrollment climbed steadily from 101 in 1946-47 to 196 in 1951-52.[41]

A. The Colleges Advance

Financial support for the schools continued to improve. Capital giving for all the colleges rose 68.2 percent to $1,222,100 for the

---

40. Mimeographed publicity memo regarding Louise R. Chapman, Louise R. Chapman file, archives; cf. NWMS, *Ten Years of Alabaster.*
41. GAJ, 1952, p. 300.

four years 1948-52, while current income moved up 53.9 percent to $6,894,148.

All of the colleges in the United States added to their campus facilities during the four years. Bethany-Peniel College began construction of a new science hall, a two-story structure 70 by 125 feet completed in early 1952. Both Eastern Nazarene College and Northwest Nazarene College gained the use of new college church buildings constructed on or near their campuses and available for chapel use. Olivet Nazarene College completed a new 111-room women's dormitory named Williams Hall and constructed at a cost of $400,000. Pasadena College built an 8,000-square-foot, reinforced concrete library building completed in the spring of 1950. Trevecca added Tidwell Hall, a men's dormitory in 1948-49 and broke ground for a new fine arts building in 1951 on the occasion of the college's 50th anniversary.[42]

Four of the colleges changed top administrators. At Canadian Nazarene College, L. Guy Nees resigned in the spring of 1949 to return to the pastorate. His successor, E. E. Martin, died suddenly on Christmas Day, 1951, and the dean of theology, Arnold E. Airhart, was elected president. Airhart served as CNC president for a total of 18 years in two terms of office.

When Eastern's president, Samuel Young, was elected general superintendent in 1948, the college board elected Vice-president Edward S. Mann, a layman. Mann, then 40 years old, was an alumnus of the college and had earned a graduate degree in mathematics. He had been professor of mathematics, college business manager, assistant to the president, and vice-president since 1945. He was particularly gifted in dealing with educational foundations and developed a strong fiscal policy for the school during his 22-year tenure.[43]

At Olivet, Grover Van Duyn was replaced by Detroit Pastor Selden Dee Kelley as president in the summer of 1948. Kelley died suddenly April 9, 1949, at age 51—but not until he had effected a financial turnaround for the institution. His successor was Harold W. Reed. Reed was well qualified. He had served as pastor of some strong congregations, but had earned a Th.D. from the University

---

42. Cameron, *ENC: First Fifty Years,* pp. 381-82; Cantrell, "History of Bethany," p. 225; Sutherland, "History of NNC," p. 75; Knott, "History of PC," pp. 88-89; Wynkoop, "Trevecca Story," p. 202.
43. Cameron, *ENC: First Fifty Years,* pp. 259, 292, 343, 383 ff.

of Southern California, had been president of Bresee College for four years, and dean of theology and vice-president of Bethany-Peniel College. He brought a long and stable administration to the college during his 26 years as president.[44]

The venerable H. Orton Wiley, president of Pasadena College for a total of 21 years, suffered a severe heart attack in April of 1948. The vice-president and dean of the college, W. T. Purkiser, was made acting president for the 1948-49 school year and inaugurated as president at the 1949 commencement, a post he held until 1957.

The first of a series of annual educational conferences was held at ENC in October, 1950. The three-day meeting brought together the presidents, deans, and business managers of the seven colleges in North America and the seminary. The conferences have proved helpful in providing a forum for the exchange of plans and methods, enabling the college administrators to work together more closely to accomplish their shared objectives.

B. Survey and Strategy for Education

The 1948 General Assembly requested the general superintendents to appoint a Commission on Education "to make a comprehensive study of the needs of the education program of the Church of the Nazarene and to formulate both a philosophy of education and a policy in harmony with those needs."[45] The commission returned partial reports to each of the General Board sessions of the quadrennium and wrapped up its work with a report to the adjourned session of the board just prior to the 1952 General Assembly.

The commission's 1950 report revealed wide disparities in the financial and demographic resources of the schools. At the time, a "North Central" zone was being considered, its territory to be carved out of areas then served by Olivet, Bethany, and Northwest. The proposal centered around a school and farm property at Tabor, Ia., conveyed to the church by the Hephzibah Faith Missionary Association in 1949. The plan was to operate a Bible school.[46] The

---

44. HH, vol. 38, no. 14 (June 13, 1949), p. 3.
45. GAJ, 1948, p. 115.
46. PGB, 1950, pp. 59-60; 1951, pp. 46-47. Cf. Paul W. Worcester, *The Master Key* (Tabor, Ia., 1966), pp. 62-63; minutes, Board of General Superintendents, meeting of Mar. 18, 1949.

projected new zone did not materialize until the late 1960s, and then along different lines.

The Central or Olivet Zone served the largest Nazarene constituency, 66,667 members or 29.7 percent of the total denominational membership. Bethany was second with a constituency of 44,485. The Canadian college was serving a constituency of only 2,493. The Olivet and Bethany zones not only had the largest memberships, they also enjoyed the largest financial potential as reflected in church giving.

The problem of student recruitment and financial support was particularly critical for Canadian Nazarene College with only the western Canadian provinces as its zone. While the Canadian constituency gave the largest per capita support to their college, their small numbers raised only about $9,000 annually for educational purposes—as compared, for example, with $127,000 contributed to Olivet, $73,000 to Eastern, and almost $72,000 to Bethany-Peniel. The commission confessed that it had been "unable to find a satisfactory solution to the Canadian" dilemma or, indeed, to the disparity existing between the schools in the United States.[47]

The commission's preliminary statement of a philosophy of education, while not neglecting religious concerns, revealed a strong liberal arts emphasis, stressing the importance of broad basic grounding in general education.[48] The final statement returned to a more traditional understanding of the educational mission of the church in terms of religious commitment. It declared that "the program of the educational institutions of the Church of the Nazarene is to provide the necessary disciplines for training the heart, mind, and life of youth based on two main objectives."

The first of these objectives was "the presentation and emphasis of" the basic creed of the church:

> Our understanding of God as an absolute, infinite, holy personality; of Jesus Christ as the Son of God and Saviour of mankind; of the Holy Spirit as the Third Person of the Trinity and the Executive of the Godhead in the world; of the Bible as God's revealed Word for every generation; of man created in God's "own image" but depraved in his faculties as a result of the Fall, and therefore is now sinful but savable through divine grace. God's plan of salvation requires that the individual be

---

47. PGB, 1950, pp. 125-28.
48. PGB, 1949, pp. 150-52.

born again, sanctified wholly as a second crisis experience, and live a life free from volitional sin while in this present life. Also, in obedience to God, man is called to a life of Christian service to all mankind irrespective of color, race, or social position.

The second main objective was "the challenge to youth to accept Christ in personal experience and to incorporate into thought and deed the fundamental principles and ethical concepts of the divine revelation."[49]

The implementation of these objectives involved making the colleges' offerings "available to the largest number of persons by keeping costs relatively low and encouraging students to exercise thrift and a balanced economy in college life." A strong program must be provided in both curricular and extracurricular areas "to enable youth to recognize and incorporate into life the necessary disciplines for character development and for making a strong spiritual impact on this generation. Adequate biblical and theological courses for training for ministers and an enlightened laity in fundamental biblical and theological truths" should be offered.

The statement on implementation also placed heavy stress on the key responsibility of the faculties of holiness colleges.

The Christian teacher, with a full personal commitment to God, a firm loyalty to truth, a deep personal appreciation for the Bible as God's revealed Word, a clear vision of the value and place of the Church of the Nazarene in current civilization and in history, and a devotion to the objective of guiding youth to personal decision in Christian experiences of regeneration and entire sanctification and the development of Christian character and useful service to mankind, is a continual "must" for realizing the goal for the holiness college.

"The Christian college stands or falls upon the character and emphasis of her teachers," the commission concluded. "The duty of the Christian teacher is to have found his own Christian integration and to be willing and able to explain how he has arrived."[50]

C. Seminary and Headquarters Relocation

A major development at Nazarene Theological Seminary was the purchase of land and construction of an adequate building. For five years the seminary had operated in overcrowded and inadequate quarters shared with the general church offices and the pub-

---

49. PGB, 1953, pp. 23-24.
50. Ibid., pp. 24-25.

lishing house in the 2900 block of Troost Avenue. The area was solidly built up. The character of the surrounding community was changing rapidly. Further expansion at that location seemed quite out of the question. Each of the four interests—seminary, headquarters, radio, and publishing—was seriously overcrowded.

The need for seminary facilities brought the whole matter of a possible relocation to the fore. As early as January, 1948, the General Board had authorized a "Commission on Location of General Interests" to study the feasibility of moving to a different location in Kansas City to establish a "Nazarene Center" that would provide for the seminary, the Radio League, headquarters, and the publishing house. The commission was composed of top-drawer personnel: M. Lunn, publishing house manager; John Stockton, general treasurer; Hugh Benner, seminary president; T. W. Willingham, radio director; and District Superintendents E. O. Chalfant, D. I. Vanderpool, and V. H. Lewis. All were men of vision and deeply committed to finding the best solution within the limits of the church's available resources.

The commission reported in June to the General Assembly, pointing to the deterioration in the area of the present location, its physical limitations, the congestion of a noisy commercial area, and the overcrowded facilities in use. The recommendation of the commission was that all four interests be relocated in the Kansas City area and that an initial offering from the church be authorized to finance the step. The group also recommended the appointment of a permanent commission to carry out the recommendations and supervise the move.

The permanent commission was composed of the members of the first group with the exception of D. I. Vanderpool who had been elected general superintendent in January, 1949, and with the addition of J. B. Deisenroth, business manager of Pasadena College, and District Superintendent Arthur C. Morgan.

A thorough canvass of the Kansas City area was conducted. The commission finally settled on a 21-acre parcel of land belonging to insurance magnate James J. Lynn and located at 63rd Street and The Paseo, approximately four and a half miles south of the Troost Avenue location.

The south 10 acres was set aside for the seminary which would pay half the total cost. The remainder was divided between the publishing house and the General Board, sharing the balance of the purchase cost. In each case, funds were available: from the capital funds accumulated by the seminary, from publishing house surplus already set aside for expansion, and from the operating budget of the General Board.[51] Through the good offices of realtor E. A. Mabes, who negotiated the purchase without charge to the church for commission or expenses, the property was purchased for $89,500. Mr. Lynn later sent a check for $5,000 to the seminary to apply toward the cost of the first building to be erected on the grounds.

The General Board in 1950 approved plans for enlargement of the publishing plant at its present location "for temporary occupancy." The seminary was authorized to proceed with plans for a building or buildings to include a temporary library and adequate for anticipated needs for the following five years. Construction costs were to be held to $300,000. The general superintendents were asked to direct a campaign throughout the church to raise the seminary building funds, and construction was authorized to start when 80 percent of the needed money was in hand.[52]

The seminary building campaign was launched in April, 1950, with the goal to "build the seminary without debt."[53] It took 18 months to raise $180,000 in cash and to secure commitments from the districts to cover the remaining $120,000. The General Board authorized the seminary to proceed with construction in January, 1952, with permission to borrow $75,000 as necessary. Ground was broken and building begun in the spring of 1952.[54]

At the same time, the board authorized the construction of a headquarters building to start as soon as possible. An offer of $75,000 for the mansion property at 30th and Troost was in hand, and $75,000 was available in general funds. Building costs were rising, and economies were possible with the construction of both structures at about the same time.[55] Actual construction of the headquarters building, however, did not get under way until 1953.[56]

---

51. PGB, 1949, pp. 148-50.
52. PGB, 1950, pp. 122-23.
53. HH, vol. 39, no. 7 (April 24, 1950), pp. 9-16.
54. PGB, 1952, pp. 122-23.
55. Ibid.
56. PGB, 1953, pp. 142-43.

VII. PUBLISHING HOUSE DEVELOPMENTS

The publishing house continued to set records for production and sales. Manager M. Lunn reported that gross sales for the four years ending in 1952 had reached $6,260,000 with an all-time high of $1,817,000 for the latest year.

Lunn reviewed the years of his stewardship and pointed out that in each of the 30 preceding years the house had registered a surplus of income over expense. After necessary allowances for depreciation and replacement of equipment, $531,110 had been donated to various church interests: $231,346 to the Nazarene Ministers Benevolent Fund, $102,580 in free literature, $16,000 to the Women's Foreign Missionary Society literature fund, $60,000 to the seminary, $100,000 to the Department of Foreign Missions, and $21,074 to miscellaneous other general interests. A total of $175,000 had been given during the past four years alone.[57]

The year 1950 witnessed the retirement of Haldor Lillenas, who had served for 20 years as head of the Lillenas Publishing Company, the music arm of the publishing house. The house had bought the Lillenas operation and moved it from Indianapolis to Kansas City in 1930. Purchase of the Lillenas interests had vested ownership of 1,535 music copyrights in the publishing house. The addition of other copyrights brought NPH ownership of music copyrights to a number unequalled by any other evangelical music publisher.[58]

Of top significance in terms of the future development of the publishing house was the enlistment of Meredith A. (Bud) Lunn, son of Manager M. Lunn, as assistant manager in January, 1951.[59] The younger Lunn had gone from college into the armed forces during World War II. On demobilization, he took a managerial position with General Motors Corporation. As a young layman seriously interested in the church, Lunn joined the publishing house staff in 1946. Even before his official appointment as assis-

57. GAJ, 1952, pp. 202, 273-76; Rawlings, "History of NPH," p. 79.
58. Fred A. Mund, *Keep the Music Ringing: A Short History of the Hymnody of the Church of the Nazarene* (n.p., n.d.), pp. 14-19; Eleanor Whitsett, *A History of the Lillenas Publishing Company and Its Relationship to the Music of the Church of the Nazarene* (Abstract of a Master of Music thesis presented to the University of Missouri, 1972; Kansas City: Nazarene Publishing House, n.d.), pp. 6-7.
59. PGB, 1951, pp. 42-43.

tant manager, he had become the elder Lunn's right-hand man. When M. Lunn retired in 1960 at the age of 73, there was little question about who would succeed him. The transition of management was in fact "continuity without a ripple."[60]

When relocation of headquarters and the seminary was planned, it was intended that the publishing house would also build on the new property and dispose of the Troost Avenue holdings. However, immediate pressing needs had made building expansion at the main printing plant imperative. A one-story addition 80 by 100 feet was built to accommodate a retail store and offices. The decision was finally made to keep the manufacturing and shipping departments at the Troost Avenue location.

By 1952, in addition to its main holdings in Kansas City, the publishing house operated branches in Pasadena and in Toronto, Ontario, Canada; retail stores in Kansas City and Bethany, Okla.; and depositories for the distribution of literature in Brisbane, Australia; Discovery, Transvaal, South Africa; and on the campus of Hurlet Nazarene College in Glasgow, Scotland.[61]

VIII. MISSIONS MARCHES ON

The headlong pace of missionary expansion immediately following World War II slowed somewhat in the 1948-52 period. The financial crisis of 1949 had a sobering effect on the Department of Foreign Missions and the General Board. Still, reinforcement of individual fields went on apace, and some significant new developments occurred.

Missionaries working under the Department of Foreign Missions increased in number from 204 to 240, and national workers from 788 to 1,006 during the four years. Organized churches in foreign mission fields increased from 249 at the end of 1947 to 581 at the close of 1951, and membership rose from 22,883 to 29,798 in the same period.[62]

---

60. Corbett, *Pioneer Builders,* p. 81.
61. GAJ, 1952, pp. 274-75.
62. The increase in numbers of organized churches is in part accounted for by the fact that prior to 1949, the African field counted no organized churches but listed simply "outstations." In 1949, some 186 outstations were reclassified and reported as organized churches.

A. South Africa European

The missionaries working in South Africa had often urged an effort to evangelize and establish the church among the 2 million Europeans who made their homes in the Republic of South Africa and in Moçambique. The Republic was noted for a strong religious orientation in which reformed theology was the prevailing note. Dutch Reformed minister Andrew W. Murray had been a leading spokesman for the Keswick interpretation of the higher Christian life in South Africa, an emphasis on the fullness of the Holy Spirit for victorious Christian living and service. A number of independent holiness evangelists had labored there, but in no case had they organized the fruits of their labors into permanent congregations.

During the years immediately following World War II, the general superintendents set out to visit all the foreign stations in which the church was working. In 1947, Dr. Hardy Powers spent two months in southern Africa. In addition to visiting the native work, he spent some time investigating the possibility of work among the Europeans.

Powers returned to report his conviction that the time had come to make a serious attempt to establish the Church of the Nazarene among the English- and Dutch-speaking people of the Republic. He viewed the prospect as "one of the most challenging opportunities ever presented to the Church of the Nazarene" in which could lie "the solution to the evangelization of the entire continent of Africa."[63]

Powers noted the revival efforts of the holiness people who had been evangelizing in South Africa. "They are committed to a policy that forbids denominational organization," he said, "but they are facing among many of their people the same problem we faced in this country a few years ago . . . of conserving the fruits of their ministry in churches indifferent or openly antagonistic to the gospel of holiness."[64]

As general superintendent in jurisdiction over the African field, Powers was authorized to move ahead. His choice of a minister for the project was a ·happy one. He contacted 32-year-old Charles H. Strickland. Strickland had been superintendent of the

---

63. PGB, 1948, p. 57.
64. Ibid.

Florida District but at the time was just two years into a pastorate at Dallas First Church. Both Rev. and Mrs. Strickland came to feel that this was God's will for them, and on August 26, 1948, flew to South Africa with their two young sons.

The Stricklands located in a growing suburb of Johannesburg and quickly began to make contacts among the Europeans in the interests of their work. "Showers of Blessing" radio program had been broadcast since early in 1948 and helped prepare the way. Holiness ministers and people were found who were the fruit of the labors of the London-based Africa Evangelistic Band.

South African laws passed in 1921 made the registration of new churches in the country extremely difficult. It would have been almost impossible to secure such registration in 1948. But when Strickland conferred with government officials about the matter, it was discovered that in 1915 pioneer Nazarene missionary Harmon Schmelzenbach had gone to Pretoria, the administrative capital of the Republic, and had registered the Church of the Nazarene with the government for work both among the Bantu and European people. This was 33 years before Strickland arrived!

The progress of the work, conducted both in the English and Afrikaans languages, was no less than spectacular. Within 10 years, a full district organization had been perfected with 23 fully organized churches having 527 members, 18 European missions or Sunday Schools, a total of 1,449 in Sunday School, and a Bible college that had been in operation since 1954 with Floyd and Libby Perkins in charge. By 1958, the school had enrolled 20 students and graduated 11, of whom 8 were in active service on the district. A printing press provided by the Nazarene Publishing House was installed to provide Sunday School literature and gospel tracts in Afrikaans, a campground purchased, and a youth camp established there which in 1958 enrolled 250.[65]

B. Jordan

The Nazarene mission in Jordan was an immediate outcome of the founding of the modern state of Israel in neighboring Palestine in

65. Charles H. Strickland, *African Adventure* (Kansas City: Nazarene Publishing House, 1958); "Report of the District Superintendent," South African District Minutes, 1958. Cf. also PGB, 1950, pp. 24-25; 1951, pp. 59-60; Taylor, *Fifty Years of Nazarene Missions*, 3:115-39; David Hynd, *Africa Emerging* (Kansas City: Nazarene Publishing House, 1959), pp. 136-37.

1948. Great Britain had governed Palestine since 1922 under a League of Nations mandate. The infamous holocaust during World War II in which 6 million Jews lost their lives brought the already growing Jewish desire for a homeland to fever pitch. The Jewish population in Palestine had been increasing rapidly through immigration, legal and illegal, and despite strong British opposition.

When the United Nations voted in the fall of 1947 to divide Palestine into a Jewish state, an Arab state, and a small international zone around Jerusalem, the British announced their decision to surrender their mandate. On May 14, 1948, the British high commissioner left Palestine. The Israelis immediately proclaimed the founding of the state of Israel. Arab armies from Lebanon, Syria, Jordan, Iraq, and Egypt invaded the country and the war of independence was on.

During the fierce fighting that followed, the Israelis lost the Old City of Jerusalem but retained control of the western portion or New City. By the time an armistice was finally reached in January, 1949, Jordan had taken control of the West Bank including Bethlehem and the Old City of Jerusalem, Syria had occupied the Golan Heights east of the Sea of Galilee, and Egypt overran the southwest coastal Gaza strip. But the Israelis held about 50 percent more of the land than the U.N. partition plan had provided, and there was no room for a Palestinian state. Thousands of Arabs from Israeli-occupied sections poured across the borders into Jordan, Syria, and Lebanon, and the festering refugee problem emerged.

Nazarenes had maintained missionaries in Jerusalem since Samuel and Hranoush Krikorian first arrived in the fall of 1921. The work was almost entirely among the Armenian population of the ancient city. During the fighting in 1948, practically all the Armenian Nazarenes fled from Israeli territory into the Old City and on across the Jordan River into the Hashemite Kingdom of the Jordan.

The two-story Nazarene church and day school building in the newer portion of Jerusalem was on the Israeli side, and its congregation was scattered. It was not used for mission purposes for a little over four years, until Alexander and Hallie Wachtel arrived as Nazarene missionaries in September of 1952. Some of the refugees from the state of Israel stayed in the Jordan-controlled Old City of Jerusalem where Rev. and Mrs. Vartkes Keshishian held them together as a congregation worshipping in borrowed quarters.

After the 1948 Arab-Israeli conflict, the Krikorians came home for furlough. On their return to Palestine, unable to gain permission to live in Jerusalem, they made their home in Amman, Jordan, and immediately set about gathering the scattered Armenian Nazarenes. Amman became the district headquarters for the Jordan District, and by 1958 two substantial churches had been built there.[66]

Zerka, some 15 miles north and a little east of Amman, became another Nazarene center with British Nazarene missionaries William and Grace Russell. Here a church and day-school building were erected with Alabaster funds. The school operated a kindergarten and three grades for approximately 200 pupils by 1958. By that time the district had 19 national workers with 111 members in eight churches, two of which were fully organized with missionary and youth societies.[67]

C. Korea

Nazarene missions in Korea root back in the work of independent holiness evangelist Robert Chung. Korea had been the scene of outstanding revival movements under Presbyterian auspices in the early part of the century. There had also been a strong holiness influence in Korean Christianity due originally to the work of the Oriental Missionary Society. The Holiness Church of Korea, the outgrowth of the OMS work, had approximately 550 congregations.

Japanese occupation and annexation of Korea in 1910 at first did little to slow the advance of Christianity. In fact, it strengthened the cause, since Christianity became identified with national resistance to Japan. Strong opposition to the churches from Japanese authorities began in 1935, and World War II forced the evacuation of the remaining foreign missionaries. When the war ended, the southern part of the country (south of the 38th parallel) became free and allied with the Western world, while North Korea

---

66. Tracy, *Nations and Isles,* pp. 67-80; Gish, *Mediterranean Missions,* pp. 73-75.
67. Tracy, *Nations and Isles,* pp. 80-86.

became a totalitarian Communist state. Christians north of the 38th parallel either fled to the south or were forced underground.

Chung (Korean, Chung Nam Soo) was converted in the revival movement that began in 1907. Forced out of Korea by Japanese persecution, he made his way to Los Angeles and later on to Asbury College in Wilmore, Ky.

At Asbury during what totalled a nine-year residence, Chung professed the grace of entire sanctification in a 1916 fall revival conducted by the college president, H. C. Morrison. Gathering some support from independent holiness camps and associations, Chung returned to Korea in 1926 and began an extensive evangelistic ministry. Frequent trips to the United States to raise support made him suspect to the Japanese as an American spy, and during the war he was arrested and tortured. He was finally able to hide out in Seoul until the war's end and South Korea was freed.

On a visit to the United States in 1947, Chung met C. Warren Jones, the Nazarene foreign missions executive. During the conversation, the Korean evangelist expressed an interest in having the Church of the Nazarene organize and preserve the results of his work.

In October, 1948, General Superintendent Orval Nease included Korea in his Oriental itinerary. In Seoul, Nease received Chung's ministerial ordination from the Methodist church and ordained six other Korean preachers as Nazarene ministers. As a result, nine fully organized congregations with more than 800 members became part of the Church of the Nazarene.

In less than two years, on June 25, 1950, North Korean Communists invaded the South and within two days were on the outskirts of Seoul. The Chung family was able to escape and get back to the United States. President Truman ordered U.S. forces into the defense of the South, and the war raged on for three years, ending in a truce in July, 1953. Eighty percent of South Korea was devastated. The Nazarene military chaplaincy suffered its second wartime fatality on July 27, 1950, when Chaplain Byron Lee was killed as enemy planes strafed the unit to which he was attached.

After one visit back to Seoul in 1952, Chung returned in 1953 to gather up what he could of the pastors and their congregations. By July, he had been successful in gaining 12 places of worship, each with a full-time worker. American servicemen stationed in Korea were of major assistance—some chaplains and some officers and enlisted men—Geren Roberts, Henry Stroman, Robert Shaw, Albert Gamble, and Melvin Shoemaker among others.

In May, 1954, Donald and Adeline Owens arrived in Seoul as the first Nazarene missionaries, beginning a 13-year span of service, and Robert Chung returned to the United States to retire. By fall, the Korean Nazarene Bible Training School was opened with 28 students. The first district assembly was held in 1955, and a national superintendent, Park Kee Suh, was elected.

By 1958, the Bible school had graduated five students, Eldon and Marcella Cornett had reinforced the Owenses as missionaries, and the field reported 24 churches and preaching points with 1,563 members and over 1,900 in Sunday School. The Bible school enrollment stood at 27. Within three years, the Bible school property in Seoul would be sold, and the school relocated seven miles from downtown on a good-sized acreage on the main highway from the city to Kimpo Airport. The school, renamed Nazarene Korean Theological Institute, became the missionary center for the growing church.[68]

D. Haiti

On the other side of the world, significant developments were taking place in the Caribbean in the little land of Haiti. As in Korea, Nazarene missions in Haiti stem from an earlier national work.

In 1937, a 25-year-old Haitian law student in Port-au-Prince by the name of Carlos Louis Egen was converted and called to preach. Disillusioned by developments in his church, he left preaching for teaching until 1945 when he was strongly impressed that God was calling him back into the ministry.

After starting an independent work, Egen contacted C. Warren Jones in the Foreign Missions office in Kansas City and asked that the Church of the Nazarene receive him and his work. A visit from General Superintendent Powers in 1946 resulted in Egen and his work being officially recognized two years later and given modest support to help with property rental.[69]

---

68. Ralph Earle, *Fields Afar: Nazarene Missions in the Far East, India, and the South Pacific* (Kansas City: Nazarene Publishing House, 1969), pp. 76-86; DeLong and Taylor, *Fifty Years of Nazarene Missions,* 2:94-98; R. Taylor, *Our Pacific Outposts,* pp. 86-95; Ramquist, *No Respecter of Persons,* pp. 135-42; OS, vol. 36, no. 3 (September, 1948), p. 1; PGB, 1949, pp. 10, 45, 112-13.
69. PGB, 1949, p. 45.

Late in 1948, General Superintendent H. V. Miller made a trip to Haiti. His findings confirmed those of Powers. He described Egen as "a consecrated little bundle of holy energy" and noted that his "somewhat nebulous but real" following in Port-au-Prince and nearby numbered several hundred.[70]

Miller's recommendation was that "as soon as possible" a central building in Port-au-Prince be purchased to house a common meeting place and provide a missionary residence and facilities for a small Bible training school. Miller urged that "a couple should be sent prepared to carry on in organizing and directing the work with the special project in mind of training workers and making the work indigenous from the start. The potentialities," he said, "are there."[71]

In the fall of 1949, General Superintendent Vanderpool visited the Egen work. He found about 500 followers in seven communities with 10 or 12 Haitian preachers. He felt that the door was wide open in Haiti and seconded the call for a missionary couple on the field "to acquaint the people with our doctrine and church polity, and assist in laying a good foundation for our church."[72]

Paul and Mary Orjala were chosen to be the missionary couple and were appointed in January, 1950. They reached the field in October. At the first preachers' conference the following month, 13 congregations were reported with 734 members, 14 preachers, and two elementary school teachers in schools held by two of the churches. Only three of the preachers had more than an elementary school education, although all could read and write both French and Creole with varying degrees of skill.[73] Only one of the churches was fully organized.

---

70. Ibid., p. 107.
71. Ibid.
72. PGB, 1950, p. 81; HH, vol. 38, no. 40 (Dec. 12, 1949), p. 3.
73. Both languages are used and necessary. The official language of Haiti is French, but the majority of the people speak Creole, a "pidgin" adaptation of French. To be effective, the missionaries have had to master Creole as well as French. To create holiness literature in Creole and to teach the people to read and write their language has been a major challenge (Lyle Prescott, *Light in Latin America* [Kansas City: Nazarene Publishing House, 1961], pp. 163-64). For the ministers' conference, cf. Kathleen Spell, *Haiti Diary: Compiled from the Letters of Paul Orjala* (Kansas City: Beacon Hill Press, 1953), p. 28. Orjala proved to be a superb linguist and later earned a Ph.D. on the basis of his linguistic and missionary competence.

Within a year, Orjala had started a Bible school with seven students, one of whom was Joseph Simon, who was to be one of the first graduates and one of the first national ministers ordained in 1960. Egen, who actually had no real holiness background, left the church within 18 months, but all of the preachers and most of the people remained with the Nazarene mission. Egen's chief legacy was a point of entry and raw material with which to build.

Missionary reinforcements soon followed. Charles and Alberta Alstott reached the field in the fall of 1952. Max and Mary Alice Conder, Nazarenes who had gone to Haiti in 1950 with an independent holiness mission, were received as associate missionaries in March of 1953.

The added missionary personnel made possible the relocation of the Bible school. It was put on a full-time basis in foothill property purchased at Freres, 10 miles from the center of Port-au-Prince. A permanent church building was dedicated in Port-au-Prince in March, 1955. Missionaries Brian and Evelyn Vanciel were sent to the field in 1956. Permanent Bible school buildings were dedicated in the fall of 1957 with 20 students enrolled; and Harry and Marion Rich, fresh from a five-year pastorate in Quincy, Mass., arrived on the field as the fourth missionary couple.

By the end of 1958, in addition to the eight missionaries, Haiti reported in with 37 national workers, 3,018 members and probationers, 42 churches and preaching points—indeed what Lyle Prescott could properly call "Harvest in Haiti."[74] In addition to the Bible school, 13 day schools were being operated with 816 students.[75]

E. Uruguay

A start was made in Uruguay in January, 1949, as an outgrowth of the Nazarene mission in neighboring Argentina when Ronald and Sarah Denton transferred to Montevideo. Some three years later, in February, 1952, the first church was organized. An extension division of the Buenos Aires Bible school was opened in Montevideo in 1954. The two students first enrolled, David Corvino and Salvador C. Ramos, both became active pastors.

---

74. *Light in Latin America,* pp. 153-71.
75. Paul R. Orjala, *This Is Haiti* (Kansas City: Nazarene Publishing House, 1961); DeLong and Taylor, *Fifty Years of Nazarene Missions,* 2:318-21.

By 1958, Uruguay Nazarenes numbered 59 with 263 enrolled in Sunday School. They were worshipping in six churches or preaching points served by six missionaries and three national ministers. The Bible school enrollment stood at eight. Uruguay was to remain part of the Argentina District until 1962 when it was organized as a separate district.[76]

SUMMARY

When the quadrennium ended in 1952, Nazarenes could look back on four years of significant progress. The rate of growth in membership had turned up from the 12.3 percent of the preceding four years to 15.9 percent. General Secretary Ludwig reported "steady and substantial growth" with a "net gain in church membership" of 33,488. "With the exception of the quadrennium ending in 1936," he said, "this is the largest gain in church membership we have made in the history of the denomination for a similar period." In numbers of church organizations, likewise, the record was good with a net gain of 474, "the largest gain in any quadrennium since the church was organized in 1908." The year 1951, with a net gain in churches of 152, was "the largest in any one year of our denominational history."[77]

The 198 missionaries at the end of the previous four-year period had increased to 301 by 1952, and the corps of national workers overseas had risen from 882 to 1,006. Membership in foreign fields gained 23.9 percent to 29,798.[78] The foreign missions department began the practice of counting probationers as well as "full members" in their membership figures for 1949 and later years and reported in with an additional gain of almost 22,000.

Some 92,000 of the membership in the United States and British Commonwealth nations were new Nazarenes, a figure offset by losses of over 58,000.[79]

In step with the rising American economy, total church giving had soared to over $83.6 million—up from $62.6 million the pre-

---

76. PGB, 1950, p. 79; W. Howard Conrad, *South America in Perspective* (Kansas City: Nazarene Publishing House, 1974), pp. 180-87.
77. GAJ, 1952, p. 215.
78. Ibid., p. 263.
79. Ibid., p. 219.

vious quadrennium. Per capita giving rose from $90.28 in 1947 to $111.76 in 1951.[80]

Sunday School enrollment was up over 100,000 to almost half a million, and average weekly attendance at home and abroad reached 344,000. The missionary society reported over 90,000 members, and the young people's society figure reached 86,000 worldwide.

Secretary Ludwig commented:

> Four years seems like a long time when you look at it from the beginning of the quadrennium. Now that it has passed, it seems like a few fleeting moments. Much has happened in our national and international life to sober us. Much lies ahead to challenge us. By the grace of God we have been brought to this good hour to pray and plan for wisdom and courage to face the future.[81]

---

80. Ibid., pp. 219-27.
81. Ibid., p. 218.

8

The Struggle over Standards

The 13th General Assembly was held in June, 1952, in Kansas City, the first time in the headquarters city since 1936. The number of voting delegates was two less than the gathering in St. Louis four years before. Total attendance of delegates and visitors was estimated at 10,000.[1]

The preliminary conventions convened as usual three days preceding the Sunday opening of the General Assembly itself. The missionary society convention quickly reelected its general president and its executive secretary, Mrs. Louise Robinson Chapman and Miss Mary Scott. The convention also initiated a name change. The Women's Foreign Missionary Society became the Nazarene Foreign Missionary Society with the relatively unsuccessful purpose of enlisting the men of the church.[2] Korea's Robert Chung preached the closing sermon as the convention ended "on a note of blessing and victory."[3]

The NYPS Convention elected Ponder W. Gilliland, the youthful superintendent of the San Antonio District, its general president. Lauriston DuBois, on whose office as general secretary there was no age limit, was reelected almost unanimously. Financial projects for the young people were to raise $50,000 for Bible schools in Australia and on the South Africa European District,

---

1. HH, vol. 41, no. 47 (Jan. 28, 1953), p. 3.
2. GAJ, 1952, pp. 167-68; minutes of the Board of General Superintendents, meeting of June 19, 1952.
3. HH, vol. 41, no. 19 (July 16, 1952), pp. 8-9; cf. *Proceedings,* Seventh Quadrennial Convention, NFMS, June 19-21, 1952.

and money to put "Showers of Blessing" on New York City radio for two years.[4]

The NYPS theme for the following four years was "By My Spirit" with an annual emphasis on "By My Spirit—Stand" for the first year; "By My Spirit—Speak" for the second; "By My Spirit—Share" for the third; winding up the quadrennium with "By My Spirit—Serve."[5]

While the auxiliaries were having their conventions, Department of Church Schools Executive Secretary Albert Harper sponsored a General Church Schools Convention. This was the first time to have such a convention in conjunction with a General Assembly. With Harper as chairman and keynote speaker, the convention sought to motivate and inform church school workers. Featured speakers included Pastors John Riley, Lawrence Hicks, R. T. Williams, Jr., and William McKee; lay Sunday School evangelist A. S. London; Erwin G. Benson, Church Schools field secretary; and District Superintendent Edward Lawlor of Canada West.[6]

Hardy C. Powers presented the quadrennial address of the Board of General Superintendents on the first business day of the General Assembly. Powers gave a comprehensive summary of progress during the preceding four years. But his major concern was not the "retrospective"; it was "introspective" and "prospective." "Only God can fully and accurately measure the eternal spiritual values involved," he said.[7] A concern for moral and spiritual purity was grounded in the conviction that "the power of the indwelling Spirit alone can keep the church from the taint of evil on every hand."[8]

Powers and his colleagues were aware of a growing tension over the interpretation of the church's behavioral standards reflected in its General and Special Rules. The issue was not a new one. It was brought to something of a point of crisis with the development and rapid spread of television.

Even as Powers spoke, "memorials" (written resolutions presented for formal consideration) from the East Tennessee and

4. GAJ, 1956, p. 293.
5. HH, vol. 41, no. 18 (July 9, 1952), p. 3; cf. Proceedings of the Eighth Annual NYPS Convention, June 19-21, 1952.
6. HH, vol. 41, no. 19 (July 9, 1952), p. 4.
7. GAJ, 1952, p. 205.
8. Ibid.

South Carolina districts were awaiting action which would ban the viewing of television for Nazarenes. Athletics and dramatics in the colleges, the wearing of wedding rings, feminine use of cosmetics, and dress styles deemed to be immodest were other points of issue—not always articulated, but present in the minds of many.

Powers himself was not one to soften the church's positions as stated in its *Manual.* He spoke with clarity of the importance of "a certain minimum of laws and rules" as essential in "establishing denominational identity." "As a result of the sanctified judgment of many holy men of many generations," he said, "such a list is written into our church *Manual.* No man can long retain his self-respect, not to mention the blessing of God, who willfully and persistently ignores these rules."[9]

> But our final and ultimate safety lies, not in a multiplicity of rules, but in strong affections. Jesus said, "If ye love me, keep my commandments," and again, "If a man love me, he will keep my words." . . . Christ, in pointing out this truth to the Apostle Peter, asked him that heart-probing question, "Lovest thou me?" and then went on to declare that upon the purity and strength of the affections for Christ depend the strength and usefulness of the Church.[10]

Hope and safety would lie in "keeping close to God." Revivals are essential. "The energizing touch of God must be upon all we plan and undertake. We must keep the glory down." "In the final analysis," Powers said, "no amount of external safeguards can really protect us, but the love of Christ continually shed abroad in our hearts by the Holy Ghost will keep our hearts pure, our lives transparent, and our hands clean from all evil."[11]

Powers went on to list specific goals for the four years ahead: 75,000 new church members; emphasis on mass evangelism along with a continuation of the Crusade for Souls with its stress on lay involvement in personal soul winning; an all-out effort to win the unconverted members of Nazarene families; the salvaging of losses in church membership; the organization of 1,000 new churches; and the raising of $10 million for world evangelism, with con-

---

9. Ibid., p. 210.
10. Ibid.
11. Ibid., p. 211.

tinued emphasis on the 10 percent plan as a minimum in giving for missions abroad and at home.[12]

If Powers meant by his membership goal new Nazarenes instead of net increase in membership, it was handily exceeded with a total gain of 95,393 during the quadrennium ahead. But the net membership gain was 37,359—due to the kind of losses Powers would have salvaged, a kind of loss that unfortunately went on unchecked. The net gain in number of churches was 595. The $10 million for missions was exceeded by $276,929.[13]

The assembly quickly reelected the four incumbent general superintendents: Powers, Williamson, Young, and Vanderpool. In balloting for the fifth to replace O. J. Nease, Seminary President Hugh C. Benner led all the way and was elected on the third ballot to the post he would hold until retirement in 1968. The five men, with the addition of V. H. Lewis as the sixth in 1960, were to serve together 12 years in all until Vanderpool's retirement in 1964.

The general officers, Ludwig, Stockton, and White, were reelected, and all of the department executives of the General Board were continued in office.

The seminary board met during the General Assembly to choose a successor to President Benner. The choice fell to Lewis T. Corlett, president of Northwest Nazarene College for the preceding 10 years. He was to serve until retirement in 1966. Corlett was a younger brother of D. Shelby Corlett. He had been educated at Arkansas Holiness College and Peniel University and had taken graduate work at Dallas Theological Seminary while pastoring in that Texas city. He had taught in Pasadena and had been dean of religion at Bethany-Peniel College for eight years before his call to NNC.

The 56-year-old Corlett brought to his seminary assignment a distinguished record as a teacher of ministers as well as an educational administrator. He was a man of rare courage. While his special academic field was the teaching of preaching and church administration, he had done significant work in the area of relating human limitations to the ideals of holy living in books on *Holiness*

---

12. Ibid., pp. 207-9. The General Assembly voted to continue the crusade for souls under the slogan "Crusade for Souls Now" albeit, as it turned out, with diminished emphasis.

13. GAJ, 1956, statistical tables, p. 20.

in Practical Living (Beacon Hill Press, 1948) and *Holiness, the Harmonizing Experience* (Beacon Hill Press, 1951).

Corlett stepped into a Herculean task. The new seminary building had been started, but revisions in the plans became necessary. Before the first semester was over, Homiletics Prof. Louis A. Reed died of a sudden heart attack at Richmond, Mo., en route by auto to Chicago,[14] and Corlett had to take over his classes. Building campaign pressures were on, and faculty salaries over the first seven years of seminary operation had not kept pace with the cost of living.

Corlett's wise choices in faculty and administrative personnel, his understanding of the church and its workings, and his insight into the educational process brought the seminary well along toward accreditation during his administration.

I. GAINS IN THE BRITISH ISLES

Two small holiness denominations in the British Isles united with the Church of the Nazarene within a three-year period.

A. The International Holiness Mission

The International Holiness Mission had been started as a layman's movement in 1907 by David Thomas, a prosperous London businessman. It was in turn the outgrowth of an earlier lay movement headed by London lawyer Richard Reader Harris.

In the process of the movement's development, a "superintendent minister" was appointed, and the group of missions that had grown up around the original center in London began to take on the form of a denomination. Associates of Thomas, David B. Jones, and his wife, went to South Africa in 1908, and in 1914 the resulting flourishing mission work was recognized as the South African branch of the International Holiness Mission. The IHM field overlapped that of the Nazarenes, and the missionaries of both churches had enjoyed close fraternal relationships from the earliest days.

The IHM was split in 1934 when four of its gifted young min-

---

14. HH, vol. 41, no. 34 (Oct. 29, 1952), p. 2; no. 38 (Nov. 26, 1952), pp. 14-17. Until 59-year-old Reed's death, the original seminary faculty had remained intact.

isters, Maynard G. James, Jack Ford, Leonard Ravenhill, and Clifford Filer, withdrew over issues of lay leadership and spiritual gifts, and set up the Calvary Holiness Church.[15]

In the meantime, the work in South Africa had outstripped the home church in Great Britain. By 1952, a total of 30 missionaries were working on 11 mission stations and 195 outstations. The field reported 1,863 members and 50 native evangelists. There was a Bible school, a secondary school, and Ethel Lucas Memorial Hospital at Acornhoek, Transvaal, superintended by Dr. T. Harold Jones, son of mission founder D. B. Jones.[16]

The financial burden had become too heavy, and the IHM Executive Council sought a solution in union with a larger church. Already concerned about merger was J. B. Maclagan, a leading minister on the British Isles District who had accepted the position of superintendent minister of the IHM back in 1945. He was a sincere advocate of the union of the holiness denominations in Britain and took the IHM appointment with the intention of working toward that end.

In 1951, Nazarene Superintendent George Frame of the British Isles District made a direct approach to the October convention of the IHM. Exploratory committees were appointed by both the Britain and South Africa branches. In each instance the committees favored merger.

The Nazarene General Board and the Board of General Superintendents approved the negotiations,[17] and in April, 1952, the IHM council and its local churches overwhelmingly voted to become Nazarenes. An October rally in Leeds formalized the union with General Superintendent Powers and Foreign Missions Secretary Remiss Rehfeldt representing the Church of the Nazarene.

Both in Britain and in South Africa the union strengthened the church. The IHM added 27 churches and 885 members to the Nazarene district in the British Isles. Nazarene work had been concentrated chiefly in Scotland and the north of England. The IHM churches were scattered throughout Britain, Ireland, and Wales. Looking back after the union, George Frame said,

---

15. Personal interview, Albert Lown, July 11, 1979.
16. The figures are given by Jack Ford, *Steps of John Wesley*, p. 126; cf. OS, vol. 40, no. 1 (January, 1953), p. 18.
17. Minutes, Board of General Superintendents, meetings of Mar. 3 and Sept. 6, 1952.

The British Isles District as a result of this union now has 62 organized churches and a number of missions. This is a vastly different picture from what it was when I became district superintendent in 1940 with 24 congregations. At that time we had only five churches in England; now we have 39. Three years ago, there was no Church of the Nazarene in London; today we have seven churches in greater London.[18]

The following year, the British Isles District was divided into British Isles North, with Frame as district superintendent, and British Isles South, superintended by J. B. Maclagan. The northern district had 28 churches with 966 members, and British Isles South 37 churches and 1,210 members.

The results of the union in Africa were equally beneficial. Nazarene Field Superintendent W. C. Esselstyn reported that the very first meeting of representatives from the two mission councils in early 1952 was "marked by the blessing of God and a very genuine warmth of fellowship." When the union occurred, Esselstyn reported, "It increases our missionary staff by 32 members, our Bantu workers by nearly 100, our school enrollment by 1,300, and our church membership by more than 2,000, besides adding much to our medical work, to the number of our mission stations, and to the areas of our influence."[19]

B. The Calvary Holiness Church

Leaders of the Calvary Holiness Church, in the meantime, were watching developments with keen interest. There had been sporadic efforts to bring about reconciliation and possible reunion between the IHM and the CHC in the 18 years of their separate existence. The development of the Calvary Holiness Church had been slow and fraught with inner tensions. By 1952, the CHC had reached a place where some solution to pressing problems must be found.

The CHC did not have extensive foreign missionary work as did the IHM in South Africa. A small mission in Pakistan with two missionaries operating in rented quarters, and two missionaries in Colombia, South America, comprised the extent of its overseas work. The CHC, however, did maintain a small college at Staly-

---

18. OS, vol. 40, no. 1 (January 1953), p. 5.
19. Ibid., p. 6; cf. HH, vol. 41, no. 42 (Dec. 24, 1952), pp. 3-4; also PGB, 1953, pp. 107-8, 120.

bridge known as Beech Lawn Bible College in which enrollment had peaked at 16 but had dropped to 6 by 1953.[20]

In addition, there was a drift within the Calvary Holiness Church toward Pentecostalism with some speaking in unknown tongues and heavy stress on divine healing. This, in fact, had been one of the points of tension that had led to the division in 1934 from the IHM. The four leaders who seceded to found the Calvary Holiness Church, while not themselves advocates of glossolalia and staunchly opposed to the doctrine that it is the evidence of the baptism with the Holy Spirit, still felt that if persons spoke in unknown tongues in their meetings, they should not be restrained.[21] Some of the ministers who had come into the movement, CHC historian Jack Ford explained, "put a greater emphasis upon the gifts than the founders had done. By a strange irony the gifts of the Spirit figured as a contributory cause to the end of the Calvary Holiness Church's independent existence as they had done to its origin."

CHC President Maynard James and his close confidant Ford became increasingly concerned lest the church they had labored to found should "exchange its original Holiness emphasis for a Pentecostalistic emphasis on the gifts of the Spirit. For the gifts to be permitted was one thing; for them to become paramount was quite another."[22]

Still another factor was the evidence James and Ford noted of the values derived by their brethren in the IHM from union with the Church of the Nazarene. The union had gone off smoothly, the IHM found its missionary problems solved, its resources increased, and it enjoyed "the enhanced prestige which belongs to a large denomination and participating in that unity with those like-

---

20. Ford, *Steps of John Wesley,* p. 160.

21. Based on the English translation of 1 Cor. 14:39, "Wherefore, brethren, covet to prophesy, and forbid not to speak with tongues." A careful study of the original Greek yields another possible translation much more in harmony with the total context: "Eagerly desire to prophesy, and do not hinder by speaking in tongues." Cf. Harvey J. S. Blaney, "St. Paul's Posture on Speaking in Unknown Tongues," *Wesleyan Theological Journal,* vol. 8 (Spring, 1973), p. 57; Charles D. Isbell, "*Glossolalia* and *Propheteialalia:* A Study of 1 Corinthians 14," ibid., vol. 10 (Spring, 1975), pp. 15-22.

22. Ford, *Steps of John Wesley,* pp. 168-69.

minded which makes its own appeal to those who take the New Testament standard as the pattern of their church life."[23]

It was natural then that the leaders of the CHC should consider the possibility of following the direction of their brethren in the IHM. While negotiations were proceeding between the IHM and the Church of the Nazarene in 1952, Ford had urged in the *Flame*, the bimonthly CHC paper edited by Maynard James, that "we pursue our course in charity toward all God's people, and welcome every opportunity of a deeper unity with our Holiness Brethren."[24]

Thus, in the summer of 1954, James and Ford took the initiative in seeking a meeting with Nazarene District Superintendent Frame. Later Frame and James Maclagan, by that time district superintendent of the British Isles South District, met with the ministers of the CHC to answer their questions about the organization and functioning of the Church of the Nazarene both in Britain and internationally.

Questions were raised about baptism, divorce, premillennialism, the support of the ministry, and in particular, the gifts of the Spirit. While the CHC officially accepted only baptism by immersion and made premillennialism an article of faith, as opposed to the broader stance of the Nazarenes on both these issues, it was the question of "unknown tongues" that was the most difficult.

On November 30, 1954, James wrote Frame, setting forth the position of the CHC on the baptism with the Spirit and speaking in unknown tongues. He strongly disavowed any view that "speaking in other tongues" is the initial evidence of the baptism with the Holy Spirit. He recognized that tongues speaking had "led to strife, spiritual pride and division." He affirmed that the proofs of a Spirit-filled life are purity of heart, the fruit of the Spirit, perfect love to God and men, and power for effective service.

James, however, did add a proviso: "We do not deny that there may be a genuine gift of 'tongues' in operation today, and so we dare not adopt the unscriptural attitude of forbidding to speak in another tongue *provided* we are *sure* it is really of the Holy Spirit." He recognized that this position "may not express the official Naz-

---

23. Ibid., p. 169.
24. Ibid.

arene attitude." But if he and his colleagues could be given "freedom of conscience" at this point and "confidence be reposed in [them] as ministers of Christ to do all in [their] power to further the interests of Scriptural Holiness," then they would "gladly welcome the fusion of the C.H.C. into the Church of the Nazarene and would count it a privilege to serve as ministers in its ranks."[25]

At the January, 1955, general meetings in Kansas City, Frame and Maclagan met with the Board of General Superintendents to discuss the merger. They reported that the CHC had 27 congregations with approximately 700 members 16 years and older plus a junior membership. There were 12 ordained ministers. All but 3 of the CHC congregations had tentatively endorsed the union.[26] They also communicated the substance of James's letter regarding unknown tongues. The general superintendents voted authorization for the Advisory Boards of the two British Isles districts to consummate the union,[27] an action confirmed by the General Board in its subsequent meeting.

As negotiations proceeded, all the issues were ironed out. The mission in Pakistan would be discontinued. The two lady missionaries there transferred to another mission board and so carried on their work. Samuel and Gwladys Heap, the CHC missionaries in Colombia, joined the Church of the Nazarene and served until retirement in 1975 in Peru, Guatemala, and Panama.[28] Two other CHC missionary couples who were in Britain at the time of union also became Nazarene missionaries: Robert and Grace Brown, who worked in Barbados and Guyana until retirement in 1980; and Edward and Margaret Cairns, who served in Belize (British Honduras) from 1958 to 1972.

The *Flame* would be continued as an independent holiness journal aimed at circulation outside the church. Hurlet Nazarene College and Beech Lawn Bible College properties would both be sold and a combined institution established in another location.[29]

The union was officially consummated under the gavel of General Superintendent Samuel Young in Manchester on June 11, 1955. Young had just concluded the district assemblies of the two

25. Ibid., pp. 171-72. The emphases are in the original. Cf. fn. 21 supra.
26. Minutes, Board of General Superintendents, meeting of Jan. 5, 1955.
27. Ibid., meeting of Jan. 8, 1955.
28. Cf. PGB, 1956, p. 58.
29. Ford, *Steps of John Wesley,* pp. 173-74.

Nazarene districts. He reported that "there was much prayer and careful deliberation on the part of both groups. The Holy Spirit himself seemed to be their true leader."[30]

One problem arose out of the merger, an extreme shortage of pastors. Several of the CHC ministers backed away from becoming Nazarenes. All of the congregations except one were located in the British Isles South area, and District Superintendent Maclagan was hard put to assimilate the churches and supply them with ministers.[31] The membership of the British Isles South District moved from 1,324 to 1,977 and the number of churches from 38 to 62, largely as a result of the merger.

Hurlet Nazarene College and Beech Lawn Bible College were consolidated the following year and became British Isles Nazarene College. New property was purchased in the suburbs of Manchester.[32] The new location made it possible to establish a working relationship with the University of Manchester. Hugh Rae, who had succeeded George Frame as president of Hurlet in 1954, became president of the new institution, a post he held until 1966.[33]

II. A Middle Course on Standards

The same period that brought reinforcements in Britain witnessed a minor defection in the United States. The issue was the interpretation of the ethical standards of the *Manual*. While precipitated by what was interpreted as a too liberal action of the 1952 General Assembly in regard to television, the underlying concerns were much broader.

A. The Nature of the Issue

Any organization with high standards of conduct for its membership faces the perpetual problem of legalism in the interpretation of its positions. The Church of the Nazarene had not been free from tensions in this area from its very beginnings.[34]

---

30. HH, vol. 44, no. 18 (July 6, 1955), p. 3.
31. PGB, 1956, p. 58.
32. Cf. letter, G. B. Williamson to Superintendents Frame and Maclagan, July 5, 1956; copy in minutes of the Board of General Superintendents.
33. Taylor, "Historical Documents," p. 176.
34. Cf. Smith, *Called unto Holiness*, "Union and Liberty—One and Inseparable," pp. 205-23.

There were sectional differences, and not all of them based on a north-south division.

A few district superintendents refused to recommend to their churches any pastor whose wife wore a wedding band, despite two rulings by the Board of General Superintendents that the plain band did not constitute the "wearing of gold" in the meaning of the *Manual* citation from 1 Tim. 2:9-10 and 1 Pet. 3:3-4.[35] The use of makeup by women was widely condemned, and short hair, skirts, and sleeves, and the wearing of slacks were in some instances the objects of pulpit censure.

In August, 1942, the venerable H. H. Wise, pastor of Nashville First Church, wrote General Superintendent R. T. Williams concerning one of the leaders in the dissident group that withdrew from the church in 1955. He was a district superintendent whom the young people had called as their convention speaker. Not for many years, said Wise, had he heard such "tirading abuse and wildfireism." The visiting speaker had preached "for an hour on Friday night and mentioned Christ only once or twice. His theme was bobbed hair, short dresses and painted faces."[36]

Wise actually represented a polar position in respect to preaching on what were often described as "externals." At the time he wrote Williams, Wise had pastored Nashville First Church for 22 years and would continue there until his death in 1948 at age 68. He had developed a large urban congregation with some 700 members, and his church had mothered many of the 30 Nazarene congregations in Greater Nashville. He called widely, both within and outside his church family, reporting as many as 3,000 calls per year. He was a capable administrator.

Wise's preaching was described as "biblical, simple, and based on great and familiar texts." He was evangelistic in his pulpit ministry and regularly invited leading evangelists for revival services. He was a consistent supporter of Trevecca Nazarene College. He did, however, scorn preaching that dealt with issues of appearance and espoused the view that if the heart was right, externals would take care of themselves.

The first printed *Manual* of the seceding group illustrates the

---

35. Cf. supra, chap. 2, fn. 26.
36. Letter dated Aug. 11, 1942, H. H. Wise to R. T. Williams; Williams file, archives.

nature of the issues involved. There were no differences in doctrine evident. It is in the specifics named in the General Rules that the concerns of those leaving the church became evident. Women were required to "wear modest length dresses with not less than three-quarter length sleeves" and with modest neckline. "Slacks, shorts, jeans or any other clothing pertaining to men" were forbidden. Women were also "to abstain from patronizing the beauty parlor" and "to refrain from the use of make-up." They were not to cut their hair or that of their girls. "Public or mixed bathing" was taboo. Both men and women were required "to leave off wearing of all jewelry including the wedding ring or band," and "all adornment such as gaudy or decorative pins, tie clasps, beads, etc." were forbidden.[37]

Other specifics named as included in "evil of every kind" were the show, the dance, the racetrack, the rodeo, public competitive games, all forms of card playing, all forms of lottery, the circus, the carnival, worldly dramatic exercises, "and like places." "Attendance at skating rinks and bowling alleys are [sic] also forbidden. We consider the television equally as dangerous as the movie, therefore, all members are to abstain from its use. Our people are to refrain from any and all entertainments and socials which are not consistent with Christian principles."[38]

Special rules spoke to other issues. Divorce except for adultery and subsequent remarriage constitutes living in adultery and renders the persons "unworthy of membership" in the church.[39]

Prohibitions extended to all kinds "of church sponsored recreational programs such as ball clubs, gymnasiums, church kitchens, festivals, fairs, bazaars, scouts, caravans, etc." No "plays, skits or any other such programs" were to be permitted and "no motion pictures or slides of any kind shall be shown in the church."[40]

B. Seeking a Middle Course

During his later years, R. T. Williams had been keenly aware of the danger of extreme interpretations of the church's standards of conduct. The last general superintendents' quadrennial address for

---

37. *Manual* of the Bible Missionary church, 1956, pp. 6, 17.
38. Ibid., pp. 17-18.
39. Ibid., p. 20.
40. Ibid., p. 22.

which he was responsible was delivered in 1940 in Oklahoma City. Among a number of dangers Williams envisioned for the church was legalism. "This," he said, "is a very subtle force that works its devastation unsuspectingly in the hearts of men, resulting in the weakening of a whole institution where too many individuals are affected by it." He said:

> Legalism is the enemy to be feared. Legalism gives more attention to law than it does to human beings. It emphasizes the letter of the law. In other words, it is law without love. No church can survive unless it fulfills the law of love, both in experience and practice. The Church of the Nazarene operates under grace, backed by law. Legalism would draw us away from grace and put the entire emphasis of the ministry and of ethics upon the matter of law, without mercy and without love. This is a danger ever to be guarded against by the church.[41]

Among his friends, Williams used to say that if the church ever divided, it would be on the issue of legalism.[42] In the last January Superintendents' Conference he was to attend, Williams delivered the keynote address. He spoke specifically to the practice of a small minority of district superintendents in setting up extreme standards for membership in the churches on their districts.

When this is done, said Williams, the superintendent tends to rationalize that he has "a district of superior quality and higher standards and therefore more deeply spiritual than other districts in the denomination." Such an attitude leads to spiritual pride and undermines the spirit of "unity and New Testament humility." If one superintendent assumes the right to raise standards of membership, "other districts might with equal disregard of church law lower the standards. This would lead to confusion and the utter disintegration of all church laws and ethical standards."[43]

When the television issue began to simmer and the church approached the 1952 General Assembly, General Superintendent G. B. Williamson published a front-page editorial in the *Herald of Holiness* titled "The Errors of Eccentric Emphasis." When incidentals are made fundamental, the result is to "throw the conscience out of balance until it does not function as a reliable guide to conduct." Concern for marginal matters is to "go off on a tangent

---

41. GAJ, 1940, p. 217.
42. Personal interview, G. B. Williamson, July 17, 1976.
43. Mimeographed manuscript of address delivered Jan. 10, 1945; archives.

and miss the highway." Detours are not so bad; they eventually bring one back to the main road. But tangents always come to a dead end. They lead nowhere except into "a maze of darkness and chaos."

Giving too much attention to things on the surface results in superficial lives. When major concern is given to things external, the inner life is neglected and "opportunity is offered for anyone to exaggerate the significance of his pet notion." When people are "ready to die for the right," disunity, contention, and strife prevail. "Faith, love, and mercy are forgotten. God is grieved. The church is defeated. Many souls are lost forever."

The remedy for the confusion Williamson saw in eccentric emphasis is "the forthright, rugged preaching of the Word of God [with] a proper pressure on things central and fundamental." This will "keep all in balance. Everything will receive attention in proportion to its importance. The Word of God will mightily grow and prevail."[44]

While the message seems fairly oblique, it reached the audience for whom it was intended. Dr. Williamson's reelection vote in 1948 had been 96 percent of the ballots cast. In 1952, it dipped to 88 percent.[45]

The General Assembly committee on "State of the Church" took up the two memorials relating to television. Both asked that television viewing be banned and that the action be printed in the church *Manual*. The committee was sharply divided; the vote was 58 to 24 to reject the memorial from East Tennessee.[46]

In place of the rejected memorial and as a substitute for both, the committee prepared and presented a statement of its own. It acknowledged the "great moral confusion" which could result through "encroachment of the evils of the day into the sacred precincts of the home" through media such as current literature, radio, and television. Careful safeguards must be established to keep the home from becoming "secularized and worldly." While recognizing potential values in the media presentation of the gospel, "the low

---

44. HH, vol. 41, no. 5 (Apr. 9, 1952), p. 1.

45. GAJ, 1948, p. 72; 1952, p. 60. In 1952, Powers received 96 percent; Young, 95 percent; and Vanderpool, 94 percent of the votes on the first ballot.

46. The South Carolina memorial was unanimously rejected because when it came up for consideration the committee had already adopted the substitute motion.

moral tone" and "sensuous appeal" of much modern literature, "comic magazines," and radio and television programs were deplored. Viewing "programs of the Hollywood type of movies or shows of the vaudeville level" is certain to be detrimental.

Nazarene "leaders and pastors" in periodicals and pulpits were urged to emphasize "principles of discrimination between the evil and the good" in such a way as to enable their people to exercise proper judgment. A suggested basis for such discrimination could be Susanna Wesley's counsel to her son John, "Whatsoever weakens your reason, impairs the tenderness of your conscience, obscures your sense of God, or takes off the relish of spiritual things, whatever increases the authority of your body over mind, that thing for you is sin."

Special concern was expressed for proper "reading, listening, and viewing on the Sabbath day," and no television program should ever be permitted to become a substitute for church attendance.[47]

The substitute resolution passed the committee by a vote of 73 to 12. The action of the General Assembly itself was by voice vote both in rejecting the total ban against television and in adopting the committee substitute, so no record exists of opposition to these moves. That the opposition remained became clear as the quadrennium moved along.

Extremes generate their opposites. Some felt that the leadership of the church was too concerned with the opinions of the more radical segment. But every effort was made to maintain a midstream position while still combatting outright legalism. *Herald of Holiness* Editor White wrote on "The Middle of the Road" in September, 1953, in which, it is true, he saw even more danger on the liberal right than on the radical left.[48] Two months later, he wrote about those who are proud of their own plainness and the worldliness of those who "criticize others."[49]

Dr. Williamson returned to the theme on occasion in the period immediately following the 1952 assembly. He wrote of those "who cover spiritual poverty with the whitewash of Phariseeism." They are prone to thank God they are not as others are. "They

---

47. GAJ, 1952, pp. 139-41.
48. HH, vol. 42, no. 30 (Sept. 30, 1953), pp. 13-14.
49. HH, vol. 42, no. 35 (Nov. 4, 1953), p. 16.

make long prayers, fast often, pay tithes, and observe numberless rules of conduct." While giving attention to the letter "which killeth," they are "void of the Spirit which giveth life." They tend to forget that "the end of the commandment is love out of a pure heart, and of a good conscience, and of faith unfeigned: from which some having swerved have turned aside unto vain jangling."[50]

Williamson in a later article cited Richard Ellsworth Day's book *The Borrowed Glow* with its list of six signs common to Spirit-filled believers: inner life and disposition brought to Christlikeness; enjoyment of "faith's rest life"—freedom from all anxiety; separation, and holiness of character and conduct; glad and continuous enthronement of Jesus as Lord; quenchless passion to win lost men to Him; and unmistakable and incredible power in intercessory prayer.

"If we would but give attention to these things," he asked, "would not all the secondary considerations be harmonized through the Spirit of God within? 'The fruit of the Spirit is love, joy, peace, longsuffering, gentleness, goodness, faith, meekness, temperance.'"[51]

C. The Secession

It was not a coincidence that the break came when it did. The church had gone almost 50 years without a visible rupture. Individuals had left, some to the liberal left and some to the radical right. One factor in the unity of the church was the really remarkable continuity of leadership in the Board of General Superintendents. The ministry of Goodwin, Williams, and Chapman in the church all went back to Pilot Point in 1908 and before; the trio had served as general superintendents, 24, 30, and 19 years respectively. Then within less than 7 years, retirement and unexpected death had resulted in a complete change in the Board of General Superintendents. A second generation of leadership must always prove itself loyal to the ideals of the founders. Most people would be willing to give it time. But some would be wary and inclined to suspicion. The occasion for the defection was not really the cause. The coming of television posed some of the same issues

---

50. HH, vol. 41, no. 43 (Dec. 31, 1952), p. 1.
51. HH, vol. 43, no. 27 (Sept. 8, 1954), p. 1.

that had been encountered with the emergence of radio a generation earlier. It only served as a focal point to pull together a wide range of concerns in which degrees of emphasis became the real issue.

The first move to separate from the Church of the Nazarene was made by Evangelist Glenn Griffith in the fall of 1955. Griffith was then 61 years of age. He had served as both a pastor and an evangelist, and had been district superintendent for seven years in Idaho-Oregon and for six years in Colorado.

In September, Griffith held a five-week tent meeting near Nampa, Ida., and in early November organized the Bible Missionary Union with 126 charter members. (Within a year the name was changed to Bible Missionary Church.) Its rules are those quoted above. Louisiana District Superintendent Elbert Dodd joined the following year. Dodd was successful in taking several of his pastors with him, and the Louisiana District suffered the heaviest membership losses of any district.

Dodd soon took over the actual leadership of the BMC. He was the most radical on the wedding ring but took a more liberal stand on divorce. Griffith again withdrew to found a second group later known as The Wesleyan Holiness Association of Churches.[52]

The districts most affected by the secession were Louisiana, Colorado, Idaho-Oregon, Indianapolis, Southwest Indiana, Southwest Oklahoma, East Tennessee, and South Carolina. While other factors may have been involved, three of the affected districts registered membership losses during the crucial two years: Louisiana, 825; Southwest Oklahoma, 366; and East Tennessee, 193. Other districts reflected a slower rate of growth but did not actually lose in total membership. The church as a whole ended the crucial quadrennium with a net gain of 43,471 members, a percentage rate of 15.4 worldwide.

The action of the General Assembly in 1952 regarding television and the withdrawal of Griffith and Dodd did much to decide the direction of the church in the pattern of Bresee and Williams. Similar issues would come up again. But the conservative, rational stance was set. And the 1956 quadrennial address of the general superintendents recalled the words of J. B. Chapman

---

52. Dodd's more liberal stance on divorce was the main reason for Griffith's second secession.

uttered 20 years before: "When people divide over trivial matters, they testify to diminutive caliber. When they separate because of factional spirit, they proclaim their want of grace. When their separateness is traceable to the desire for pre-eminence on the part of leaders, it announces want of both sense and goodness."[53]

III. HEADQUARTERS
AND THE PUBLISHING HOUSE

The seminary building which was begun in 1952 was delayed by extended labor troubles in the Kansas City area and was not completed and occupied until the spring of 1954. In the meantime, work was begun in July, 1953, on a new headquarters building located just north of the seminary. The new address, 6401 The Paseo, was to become very familiar to Nazarenes as the location of their International Center.

The new headquarters building was designed to provide offices for the general superintendents, the general officers, and the executives of the General Board departments. It was a fireproof concrete block and brick structure 50 by 182 feet with three full floors and a partial fourth floor, the latter providing a studio and offices for the Radio League.

The structure was completed and occupied in December of 1954 and dedicated January 7, 1955, in connection with the 1955 General Board meeting. The project cost $325,000, but the amount was covered without the necessity of a special offering.[54]

As was noted earlier, the original relocation plans had included a move for the Nazarene Publishing House to the new International Center site, and the land had been divided with such in mind. However, when the headquarters staff moved from the publishing house facilities, it became clear to Manager M. Lunn and his son—and more slowly to the Board of General Superintendents—that adequate facilities for the printing and shipping functions of the house could be more economically obtained at the Troost Avenue location.

A compromise was finally worked out whereby the house built and paid for a spacious editorial building on the corner of

---

53. Personal interview, G. B. Williamson, July 17, 1976; GAJ, 1956, p. 196.
54. PGB, 1955, pp. 110-11; 1956, p. 107.

63rd and The Paseo and a new retail store on the corner of 63rd and Woodland, and expanded the manufacturing and shipping facilities on Troost Avenue.

By 1956, the annual gross income of the publishing house was nearing $2.5 million. A new hymnal titled *Praise and Worship* with 497 musical selections and 48 Scripture readings came off the press in 1953, and a quarter of a million copies were sold in the next three years. In 1955, the first of the Exploring series of college level introductory textbooks were published: *Exploring the Old Testament*, edited by W. T. Purkiser and written by him along with C. E. Demaray, Donald S. Metz, and Maude A. Stuneck as additional writers; and *Exploring the New Testament*, with Ralph Earle as editor-writer in conjunction with Harvey J. S. Blaney and Carl Hanson.

IV. EDUCATION IN THE MIDDLE FIFTIES

College enrollments made a 10 percent gain in the quadrennium ending in 1956, up from 3,455 in 1951-52 to 3,802 in 1955-56. The seminary enrollment peaked at 245 in 1953-54 before slipping to 190 in 1955-56.[55]

Two Nazarene schools gained new presidents: Hurlet Nazarene College, soon to relocate and become British Isles Nazarene College, saw Hugh Rae installed as its president in 1954. The Northwest Nazarene College Board of Regents elected college pastor John E. Riley as successor to Lewis Corlett when Corlett left to take the reins at the seminary in the summer of 1952.

A. Progress in the Colleges

In April, 1956, both Bethany and Olivet Nazarene colleges were accredited by the North Central Association, leaving only Trevecca still questing for full academic recognition. Olivet's total enrollment passed the 1,000 mark early in 1954. Bethany-Peniel College became Bethany Nazarene College by action of its Board of Trustees in February, 1955.

Most of the schools dedicated new buildings: King Memorial Chapel at Canadian; a student union and a dorm to house 225 men at Bethany; Klassen House, a dormitory for 118 men, at Pasadena;

---

55. GAJ, 1956, pp. 283-85.

and new library facilities at Eastern and Olivet—Floyd Nease Library at ENC and the $400,000 Memorial Library at ONC. The new seminary building was dedicated in September, 1954.

Trevecca finished and occupied its $150,000 fine arts building but suffered another fire when McKay Hall, a three-story brick dormitory for women with the college kitchen and dining hall attached, was gutted. Although insurance covered less than half the damage, a new kitchen and dining hall was soon constructed and the dormitory facilities repaired and remodelled.[56]

B. Samaritan Hospital School of Nursing

A major loss in the total educational program of the church was the closing of Samaritan Hospital and School of Nursing in 1954. The institution had existed as a stepchild of the general church, its status never clearly understood by most Nazarenes.

The hospital had its beginning with the arrival in Nampa, Ida., of Dr. and Mrs. T. E. Mangum. Dr. Mangum was a highly qualified physician and surgeon, and Mrs. Mangum was a registered nurse. They opened a small hospital in 1920 in a converted residence just across the corner from the Northwest Nazarene College campus. By 1926, a permanent, 50-bed hospital building was under construction adjoining the original buildings. In connection with it, in 1930, the school of nursing was formally organized and accredited by the state of Idaho for the training of nurses.

The Nazarene Missionary Sanitarium and Institute, as it was officially titled, was accepted as an institution of the Church of the Nazarene in 1923, but no consistent financial support from the church was ever provided. The governing board of the hospital and school was elected by the Idaho-Oregon district assembly, and the district provided some limited support.

Periodically, fund-raising campaigns were approved in wider church areas, none of which were particularly successful. Dr. and Mrs. Mangum poured thousands of dollars of their own money into the project, as did Dr. Mangum's two physician sons and Dr. W. C. Nolte, who joined Dr. Mangum in 1939.

By 1947, the daily patient average in the hospital peaked at slightly above 56, some 12 percent above capacity. The low bed

---

56. "Together," mimeographed newsletters from S. T. Ludwig dated from January, 1953, to April, 1955; cf. Wynkoop, *Trevecca Story,* pp. 202-5.

capacity of the hospital was creating problems for the graduates of the school of nursing in gaining registration outside the state of Idaho. It was decided, therefore, to enlarge the hospital to 125-bed capacity, and work was begun on an addition to cost $300,000, with $30,000 to be raised in the city of Nampa and $270,000 throughout the Nazarene denomination. Neither fund-raising campaign succeeded, and the addition remained unfinished.

At about the same time that the enlargement campaign was under way, other hospitals nearby expanded, and a large facility was constructed at nearby Caldwell. Doctors also began the practice of early ambulation for surgical patients, and that combined with the development of antibiotics further reduced the length of hospitalization.

The final blow came in the form of increased requirements made by nursing accreditation authorities for bed capacities in affiliated hospitals. By 1952, it became clear that the school of nursing could not possibly meet the new standards. A report to that effect was made to the Board of General Superintendents, and with sorrow the Samaritan board voted to place the school on inactive status after the graduation of the 1954 class.

Throughout the 24 years of its service to the church, the nursing school, hospital, and missionary sanitarium or rest home had filled a large place. The nursing school graduated 292 nurses, 43 of whom served as foreign missionaries in the Church of the Nazarene. At one time all of the directors of the schools of nursing in the four mission hospitals of the Church of the Nazarene—two in Africa, and one each in India and Papua New Guinea—were graduates of Samaritan Hospital School of Nursing.

The hospital continued to function as a community facility until 1967 when new fire codes went into effect and forced its closing. The grounds and buildings were turned over to Northwest Nazarene College and have been developed as part of its total campus.[57]

V. Foreign Mission Developments

A number of developments affecting the church abroad took place during the early and middle 1950s. Missions were opened in Israel

---

57. Personal letter, Mrs. Frances Mangum, dated Apr. 6, 1981; dittoed report of Samaritan Hospital School of Nursing to the Board of General

and Lebanon, both small in size but strategic in location. In the South Pacific, a beginning was made in Papua New Guinea in what was to become one of the most rapidly growing of the Nazarene mission fields. The church's endeavors in medical missions were reviewed, and the first of what would eventually be a number of non-English radio broadcasts was begun.

A. Israel

Until May, 1948, an Armenian Nazarene congregation occupied the strategically located, two-story stone building in what became that year the Israeli section of Jerusalem. When the state of Israel was created and Jerusalem became a divided city, the Armenians fled to the Old City and to Jordan. The property in Jerusalem-Israel was used as a residence until conditions stabilized sufficiently for the dispatch of Nazarene missionaries to reopen the church— really, to serve as the first Nazarene missionaries in the state of Israel.

Alexander and Hallie Wachtel were chosen for the task and arrived in Israel in 1952. Wachtel came from a Jewish family. He was converted at age 16 in a Nazarene tent meeting in Kingston, N.Y., called to preach, and subsequently was educated at Eastern Nazarene College, Nazarene Theological Seminary, and Central Baptist Seminary in Kansas City.

The work in Jerusalem was distressingly difficult, but a new, largely Arab church was started in Nazareth to the north with Missak Sarian as the national pastor. In 1958 the two congregations had only six full members and 30 enrolled in Sunday School.[58]

B. Lebanon

The Nazarene mission in Lebanon had its beginnings among Armenian Nazarene refugees from Palestine and Syria who had

Superintendents, Jan. 11, 1952; catalog, Samaritan Hospital School of Nursing (private printing, n.d.); Alline Swann, *Song in the Night: The Story of Dr. and Mrs. Thomas E. Mangum* (Kansas City: Beacon Hill Press, 1957), pp. 74-76; Minutes, Board of General Superintendents, meetings of Mar. 17 and July 27, 1949; Jan. 11, 1952; and Apr. 11, 1943; an excellent brief survey to that date, *Conquest,* vol. 2, no. 2 (November, 1947), pp. 19-24; and a description from a missionary's point of view by P. L. Beals, HH, vol. 27, no. 47 (Feb. 4, 1939), pp. 20-21.

58. Tracy, *Nations and Isles,* pp. 62-66; Gish, *Mediterranean Missions,* pp. 9-37.

made their way to Beirut in the troubled times resulting from organization of the new state of Israel. Some 35 of these refugees began meeting in the chapel of the Christian Medical Center near Beirut, headed by Dr. Pusant Krikorian, younger brother of the Nazarene missionary superintendent in Amman.

The strategic advantages of Beirut at the time made it a logical center for Bible school work. Even before resident missionaries were available, Donald de Pasquale, missionary in Syria, and Samuel Krikorian had laid the foundations for such a school, and building construction had actually begun.

Missionaries Donald and Elva Reed arrived in Beirut in July, 1954, and the Fitkin Memorial Nazarene Bible School opened in October. The building was a four-and-a-half-story stone and cement structure housing an auditorium seating 250 for both church and college chapel, kitchen, dining hall, classrooms, library, dormitory facilities, and three apartments for the director and teachers. Eleven students enrolled the first year.[59] By 1958, Nazarenes had six national workers in Lebanon, four churches with an aggregate of 35 members, five Sunday Schools enrolling 225, two day schools with 50 pupils, and the Bible school with 40 students.

C. Papua New Guinea

Halfway around the world, under conditions as different as night from day, the first Nazarene missionaries began to work in Papua New Guinea, the eastern portion of the island at that time being administered by the Australian government. Interest in Papua New Guinea came first from the young Nazarene church in Australia. The Nazarene Foreign Missionary Society took as its 40th anniversary project the raising of $50,000 for Papua New Guinea. The final count was approximately $100,000.

When General Superintendent Hardy Powers held the Australian district assembly in November, 1954, he and District Superintendent A. A. E. Berg made an exploratory visit to Papua New Guinea. Powers recommended an immediate entry, and at the 1955 meeting of the General Board, Sidney and Wanda Knox, pastoring the Nazarene church in Big Springs, Tex., were appointed to pioneer the work.

---

59. Tracy, *Nations and Isles,* pp. 133-37; Gish, *Mediterranean Missions,* pp. 108-10.

The Knoxes arrived in Port Moresby in October, 1955. Careful investigation led them to the choice of an area in the highlands surrounding a government outpost at Kudjip as the site for the new mission. It was 4 miles south of a small airstrip at Banz and 12 miles west of the larger landing strip at Minj, through which all personnel and supplies would have to be flown in. There were no other Protestant missions operating in the area.

A mission home and a chapel were soon constructed, and another preaching point five miles distant was established. By 1957, a Bible school had been started.

Tragically, early in 1958, Knox was found to have an abdominal cancer that developed rapidly. He was forced to return to the United States in June; and on October 14, three years to the day from his first arrival in Papua New Guinea, he died.

Six months before Knox had been forced to leave Papua New Guinea, Max and Mary Alice Conder arrived. The Conders were experienced missionaries, having served in Haiti for five years before being assigned to Papua New Guinea. Mrs. Conder was a registered nurse, and her work prepared the way for the hospital that was to be built in 1967. After her husband's death, Mrs. Knox returned to Papua New Guinea and served until 1975 when she became executive secretary of the Nazarene World Missionary Society.[60]

By the end of 1958, the infant work had enlisted two national workers, had three churches with 50 recognized as members, 600 enrolled in Sunday Schools, a day school with 50 students, and a dispensary that had treated 1,000 patients during the year.

D. Medical Missions

In 1949, the general superintendents appointed a Commission on Medical Missions to make a survey of the problems and policies of the medical missionary work of the church. The following year, the commission made a preliminary report to the General Board. It was reconstituted and directed to continue its study with a view to making specific suggestions. The reconstituted commission was composed of Hardy C. Powers, representing the Board of General

60. Ramquist, *No Respecter of Persons,* pp. 57-74; Earle, *Fields Afar,* pp. 110-17; Sidney C. Knox, *The Call of New Guinea* (Kansas City: Nazarene Publishing House, 1958).

Superintendents; Pasadena College President W. T. Purkiser, chairman; J. Robert Mangum, M.D., son of Dr. T. E. Mangum and General Board member, secretary; Louise R. Chapman, NFMS general president; and District Superintendents Oscar J. Finch and Harvey S. Galloway.

The commission's final report was handed to the General Board in January, 1953. It reviewed the development of Nazarene medical missions in China, Africa, and India, and clinics in British Honduras, Guatemala, and Nicaragua. The commission re-emphasized the ultimate evangelistic purpose of all missionary work in the Church of the Nazarene, but noted the value of medical services in opening doors otherwise closed to the preaching of the gospel.

As a matter of policy, the commission stated its view that the purposes of the church could best be realized by the development of small hospital and dispensary units rather than the concentration of resources in two or three larger units. The special circumstances in Swaziland in southern Africa were recognized as justifying the larger medical work which had been developed there.

The commission observed that government regulations made medical missions virtually impossible in Mexico, the Cape Verde Islands, and Korea. Seven other fields investigated appeared at the time to have no immediate need of medical work because of adequate government facilities. Seven fields were classified as needing dispensaries, while four fields were felt to need small hospitals.

Most of the perceived needs were covered in the following recommendations: (1) that a missionary doctor be appointed for British Honduras and the construction of needed hospital facilities be begun at the earliest possible moment, an appropriation for this project having already been made; (2) that dispensaries be provided as soon as possible for Barbados, Bolivia, Guatemala, Haiti, Nicaragua, Jordan, and Puerto Rico; (3) that nurses be appointed for dispensaries for the American Indian work at Goldtooth and Low Mountain; (4) that small hospitals and field clinics be provided as soon as possible for India at Shallod, for Peru at Choto, and for the Philippines; (5) that the use of mobile clinics be given careful study and consideration for Blouberg in South Africa, Guatemala, Haiti, India, and Nicaragua.

The report closed with a discussion of the spiritual and professional qualifications of medical workers in foreign missions. It suggested that while the church, as a church, should take no responsibility for financing medical education for prospective missionaries, it could well encourage persons of means to provide grants and loans for the purpose.

The report was received without argument and, as is often the case with such reports, for the most part went without implementation.[61] Even the hospital in British Honduras (now Belize) for which money had been provided failed to materialize. Dr. Quentin E. and Margie Howard were sent to that Central American country in 1954. They soon discovered that the planned facility would be far too expensive for the values offered. The government was rapidly expanding its public health facilities, and areas that had before been served only by a nurse now had resident doctors. The population of the country was concentrated in three widely separated centers, and no single facility could serve the entire field. After extended consideration, the Howards recommended and the mission council concurred that the plan be dropped. This was done and Dr. and Mrs. Howard returned to the United States in 1956.[62]

In India, a major medical move was made before the commission's report was heard. Dr. Ira Cox, Jr., and Mrs. Hilda Lee Cox were sent to the field to enlarge the Reynolds Memorial Hospital for women into a full-service facility with a men's ward as well. Dr. and Mrs. Cox served in the expanded hospital for a total of 21 years.[63] Also, on her return to India from furlough in 1953, Dr. Evelyn Witthoff took with her a jeep station wagon which she fashioned into a mobile clinic.[64]

In 1955, Dr. Howard Hamlin, who had played such a key role in reestablishing the church in Japan after World War II and who had served on the General Board for three years, met the Board of General Superintendents to volunteer for missionary service wherever the church might wish to send him. Nazarenes were thrilled when Dr. Hamlin left his flourishing practice in Chicago in 1964 and flew with his wife to South Africa for two terms of service in the Nazarene mission hospitals there.[65]

---

61. PGB, 1953, pp. 81-86.
62. PGB, 1956, pp. 56-57.
63. DeLong and Taylor, *Fifty Years of Nazarene Missions,* 2:42.
64. Ramquist, *No Respecter of Persons,* p. 99.
65. Minutes, Board of General Superintendents, meeting of Jan. 11, 1955.

E. "La Hora Nazarena"

Another step of significance for missions in Latin America was the beginning in June, 1953, of a Spanish counterpart to the "Showers of Blessing" radio broadcast. Called "La Hora Nazarena" with Spanish Department Director Honorato Reza as principal speaker, the program gained a wide hearing in Spanish-speaking countries. By 1958, "La Hora Nazarena" was being aired on 26 stations in 13 countries with 12 of the outlets carrying it as a sustaining feature without charge for broadcast time.[66]

VI. OVERSEAS HOME MISSIONS

All overseas and non-English work had at first been assigned to the Department of Foreign Missions for direction and support. However, in the rapid expansion that took place after World War II, it became apparent that overseas work in English-speaking areas and in more highly developed non-English countries where "foreign missionaries" would not readily be received would do better under "home mission" policies and procedures. So in 1948, such missions already begun (e.g., Hawaii) were transferred to the jurisdiction of the Department of Home Missions and became known as "Overseas Home Missions." The expansions into New Zealand and into the Panama Canal Zone are typical of such missions.

A. New Zealand

Nazarene beginnings in Australia naturally drew attention to the two major islands in the South Pacific lying 1,200 miles to the east and comprising the Commonwealth nation of New Zealand. Toward the end of 1950, General Superintendent and Mrs. G. B. Williamson spent three days in New Zealand. Williamson had a personal interest in the country. His great-uncle had labored there for 50 years as an Anglican missionary to the Maori tribes.

Dr. Williamson reported his findings in the *Herald of Holiness.* He spoke of "an open door of opportunity for preaching holiness and promoting revivals." His prayer, he said, was "that God will call some young man of daring faith and deathless passion to plant the Church of the Nazarene in this dominion."[67]

---

66. DeLong and Taylor, *Fifty Years of Nazarene Missions,* 2:118; PGB, 1959, p. 106.

There was no promise of support, but the call was heard by California Nazarene Evangelist Roland E. Griffith and his wife. With their six-year-old daughter, they set sail for Auckland, a city of 250,000 population on the North Island. Griffith quickly lined up a slate of some 26 revival meetings for several evangelical religious groups. The results were exceptional. More than 1,000 persons responded to his invitations to come forward for prayer.

By the end of the first year, Griffith was convinced that there must be a holiness church established to conserve the fruits of revival. He flew to the 1952 General Assembly in Kansas City and reported his work to the general superintendents and the General Board. The result was full authorization to represent the church officially and to proceed with the development of local congregations.

Property was purchased on a main thoroughfare in the city of Auckland. Within a year, Griffith was able to begin construction of a permanent church building. Forced to depend on donated labor and hampered by lack of adequate financing, the project took a little over two years to complete. The first congregation was organized as a church with 20 charter members in May, 1953.

A second church soon followed in Hamilton, 80 miles south of Auckland; and a third was organized early in 1957 in Dargaville, 125 miles distant. Another American minister, H. S. Palmquist, arrived in 1957, and by 1958, New Zealand had three churches with 60 members and 207 in Sunday School and an additional branch Sunday School with 60 enrolled.[68]

B. The Canal Zone

As was true in many Nazarene overseas home mission efforts, the church in the Canal Zone was the direct result of the concern of a layman, in this case E. W. Wilson and his wife. Wilson was chief radioman in the U.S. Navy radio station in Gatun. In response to his urging, the January, 1953, session of the General Board authorized a Canal Zone project as part of the overseas home mission program and set up a budget for it. Nashville Pastor Wayne A.

---

68. Taylor, *Fifty Years of Nazarene Missions*, 3:106-13; R. Taylor, *Our Pacific Outposts*, pp. 127-33; Earle, *Fields Afar*, pp. 126-27; HH, vol. 41, no. 51 (Feb. 25, 1953), p. 3; PGB, 1955, pp. 59-60.

Jordan with his wife and young son were picked for the task and arrived in the zone in August.

The Jordans began their work in Margarita, the Caribbean terminal of the canal, where they found a group of Nazarenes waiting. They organized a church with 15 charter members their second Sunday there.

In a little over a year, Jordan was able to purchase property in Ancon, on the Pacific end of the canal, where most of the American personnel in the zone had their homes.

Illness forced the Jordans to return to the United States in 1955, and they were replaced by Elmer and Dorothy Nelson who had pastored in Denhoff, N.D. Nelson made his headquarters in Ancon and became concerned about the Spanish-speaking population of the Republic of Panama on both sides of the zone.

The transient nature of the military and civilian population of the zone has worked against the development of large and stable congregations. In 1958, the two zone congregations reported an aggregate of 24 members with 125 enrolled in Sunday School and an average weekly attendance of 103.[69]

SUMMARY

As delegates and visitors gathered for the June, 1956, General Assembly in Kansas City, they could look back on a significant quadrennium. The church had held steady in the face of a minor defection and opted for a balanced interpretation of its historic ethical standards. The departure of those who wanted more extreme positions was hardly noticeable in terms of the growth of the church. The rate of gain in membership for the four years was 15.4 percent, within one-half of 1 percent of the postwar peak reached the quadrennium before. While the numbers involved were not large, the issues were significant and the answer of the church was clear. Lawfulness without legalism would characterize the Nazarene stance on behavioral issues. The church would thus remain true to its Wesleyan heritage where moral quality is seen to reside not only in the outer act but also in the light and motive behind it.

---

69. Taylor, *Fifty Years of Nazarene Missions,* 3:89-101; Prescott, *Light in Latin America,* pp. 112-17; minutes, Board of General Superintendents, meetings of Jan. 8 and 10, 1953; Sept. 6, 1954.

By its actions both in 1952 and 1956, the church came out strongly for morality without moralism and for genuine piety without an extreme "pietism."

Finances reflected the growing affluence of the United States in which American Nazarenes shared, but there was also the relentless march of inflation. Per capita giving rose from $111.76 in 1951 to $125.59 in 1955. While the 10 percent program tended to reach a plateau in acceptance during the quadrennium, the growing membership and increasing per capita giving provided well over one-half million dollars more for world evangelism in 1955-56 than in 1951-52—$10,276,929 for the quadrennium.[70]

Sunday School enrollment in the United States, Canada, and the British Commonwealth countries passed the half-million mark, from 499,698 in 1951 to 605,684 in 1955; while in foreign mission fields it grew from 38,112 to 62,498 in the same period. Youth membership rose by 9,514 to a total of 95,491 worldwide; while missionary society membership increased a phenomenal 44,000 to total 135,053—for which at least some credit may be given to the fact that four years earlier it had been changed from the Women's Foreign Missionary Society to the Nazarene Foreign Missionary Society, thus admitting men to membership.

It was quite appropriate that General Superintendent G. B. Williamson should begin the 1956 quadrennial address with an allusion to P. F. Bresee's whimsical practice of using the greeting "Good morning!" whatever the time of day, explaining, "It is morning in the Church of the Nazarene, and the sun never sets in the morning."

"It is *still* morning in the Church of the Nazarene," Williamson declared. "Our sun has not reached the zenith. God grant that it may continue to shine with increasing splendor for many generations to come."[71]

---

70. GAJ, 1952, p. 226.
71. GAJ, 1956, p. 193.

9
Back to Pilot Point

The General Conventions and Assembly in Kansas City in 1956 made few changes either in government or personnel. Each of the auxiliaries, the NFMS and the NYPS, met for their customary conventions the three days preceding the Sunday opening of the General Assembly itself. The church schools department convened its third quadrennial General Convention at the same time. The NFMS Convention again continued in office President Louise R. Chapman and General Secretary Mary Scott.[1] The NYPS moved its general president, Little Rock, Ark., First Church Pastor Ponder W. Gilliland, to the post of general secretary, replacing Lauriston DuBois, who joined the faculty of Nazarene Theological Seminary after 12 years in the youth office. The new NYPS general president was Gilliland's brother-in-law, Eugene Stowe, at the time pastor of Nampa, Ida., College Church.[2]

The Church Schools Convention was organized around the theme, "Pray more, Teach more, Win more," also the theme of Executive Secretary Albert Harper's keynote address. In addition to its Thursday afternoon, Friday, and Saturday sessions, the church schools workers met in a series of 16 different workshops Monday through Wednesday afternoons of General Assembly week.[3]

I. PLANNING AHEAD

In his quadrennial address for the Board of General Superintendents, G. B. Williamson noted with gratitude "the great upsurge of

---

1. *Proceedings,* Eighth Quadrennial Convention, NFMS, Kansas City, June 14-16, 1956.
2. *Proceedings* of the Ninth General Conference, NYPS, Kansas City, June 14-16, 1956.
3. HH, vol. 45, no. 20 (July 18, 1956), pp. 14-15.

interest in religion, especially *heartfelt* religion" and in a paraphrase of Shakespeare called on the assembly not "to miss the full tide which is now coming in, lest being tardy in launching our undertakings, we should lose our ventures."[4]

"The Church of the Nazarene was born amid revival fires," Williamson declared. "It is the product of a great evangelistic crusade to spread scriptural holiness throughout the world."[5]

Goals suggested for the four years ahead included the raising of $14 million for world evangelism, net gains in the NYPS of 25,000 in membership and in the NFMS of 50,000, a total of 1 million enrolled in Sunday School with 500,000 in average attendance, the organization of 1,000 new churches, and a net gain of 150,000 in church membership.

Special aims were announced for the 50th anniversary year of 1958 with an emphasis both numerical and qualitative. A net gain of 25,000 members was envisioned, with $4 million during the year for world evangelism.[6] "Let 1958 be the year of the mightiest Holy Ghost revival of Nazarene history. May it be a year of climax and of beginning again. Let us cry with Habakkuk, 'O Lord, revive thy work in the midst of the years, in the midst of the years make known; in wrath remember mercy.'"[7]

The five general superintendents were each elected with votes in excess of 96 percent of the ballots cast. General Secretary Ludwig, General Treasurer Stockton, and *Herald of Holiness* Editor White were also easily returned to office. The General Board reelected all its department executives and extended their tenures from the previous one year to four years. In addition, two new full-time secretaries were chosen: Dean Wessels to head the Department of Ministerial Benevolence, and Houston District Superintendent V. H. Lewis to lead a newly created Department of Evangelism.

The General Board itself was enlarged from 26 to 33 members and started the quadrennium with more than half of its members serving for the first time.

---

4. GAJ, 1956, p. 193.
5. Ibid., p. 196.
6. Ibid., pp. 208-10.
7. Ibid., p. 210.

A. Department of Evangelism

The new Department of Evangelism was created in part as a response to a ringing appeal made by Russell V. DeLong at the General Board meeting earlier in 1956. DeLong had left the seminary in January, 1954, to enter the field as a full-time evangelist. "Evangelism in all its types," he averred, "is too great and the need too imperative to be neglected, submerged, or forgotten, or relegated to a minor position under Home Missions. It should have a distinct place and positive care."[8]

The department, as DeLong envisioned it, would push programs for mass, personal, visitation, child, educational, industrial, and armed services evangelism. While DeLong had anticipated final action in 1960, his proposal caught fire and was put through within five months.

The 1956 General Assembly formulated the function of the Department of Evangelism to include promotion of "an aggressive evangelism throughout the Church of the Nazarene . . . [and] to inspire members of our local churches to zeal in soul winning through intercessory prayer, personal evangelism, and the distribution of gospel literature." It was also "to be responsible for the direction and promotion of the Crusade for Souls." A permanent seven-member Crusade for Souls Commission to include one evangelist and one pastor was authorized, the commission to report annually to the department.[9]

B. A Statement on Civil Rights

The General Assembly also responded to the sweeping civil rights movement of the 1950s with a statement on racial discrimination. Since the church must always place a due emphasis on the sacredness of human personality, it affirmed that "the almost world-wide discrimination against racial minorities [must] be recognized as being incompatible with the Scriptures' proclamation that God is no respecter of persons." Racial discrimination is also contrary to "the basic principle of the Christian faith that God is the Creator of all men, and that of one blood are all men created." More significant for holiness people is the fact that discrimination is "contrary to the experience and doctrine of perfect love." "Each member of the

---

8. PGB, 1956, p. 15.
9. *Manual,* 1956, pp. 188-99.

Church of the Nazarene" was called upon "humbly [to] examine his personal attitudes and actions toward other races as a first step in achieving the Christian goal of full participation by all in the life of the community."[10]

C. Holding Steady on Television

The question of an action on television was raised again in a proposal from the Louisiana District whose superintendent was leaving the church to join the dissident group headed by Glenn Griffith.

The committee on State of the Church voted 73 to 13 to reject the memorial but recorded a statement by its chairman, L. Guy Nees, expressing the consensus of those who voted against adopting the proposal. The committee did not wish to be misunderstood in its action to reject. Its majority shared the concern of those who proposed the action and were not in favor of throwing the door open for the careless and unguarded use of the medium. They rather wished to draw attention to the action of the assembly four years earlier in adopting the resolution that had been carried in the *Manual* urging discretion in the use of all media such as television, radio, and books and magazines.[11]

D. Ministerial Benevolence

Dean Wessels, as the first full-time executive of the Department of Ministerial Benevolence, was to push the enrollment of Nazarene ministers in the newly available Social Security coverage and to put on a sound fiscal basis the church's supplementary "basic pension" for its retired workers. By January, 1957, it appeared that 90 to 95 percent of the church's ministers would be covered by Social Security.[12] The percentage was to go even higher in the future.

II. Gospel Workers Church of Canada

Just prior to the Golden Anniversary celebration, another independent holiness group chose to cast its lot with the Church of the Nazarene. The Gospel Workers Church of Canada had its origin in

---

10. GAJ, 1956, p. 131.
11. Ibid., pp. 131-32.
12. PGB, 1957, p. 53.

the revival ministry of Frank D. Goff in the Georgian Bay area of Ontario in the first decade of the century. Several holiness churches were organized as a result and formed into the Gospel Workers Church. A campground at Clarksburg was developed.

The relationship of the Gospel Workers Church and the Church of the Nazarene had been close from the beginnings of Nazarene work in Ontario. Several Nazarene leaders had been converted through the Gospel Workers' influence.

A merger between the two groups had been under discussion for four years. It was consummated in June, 1958, at Clarksburg by General Superintendent Samuel Young representing the Nazarenes and Albert Mills and C. J. McNichol representing the Gospel Workers. The union brought five congregations with good church buildings and parsonages, the Clarksburg campground, and approximately 200 members into the Nazarene Canada Central District where H. Blair Ward was superintendent.[13]

III. THE CHURCH ABROAD

The middle to late 1950s saw Nazarene work extended to four additional world areas.

A. West Germany

A move into West Germany had been under discussion before General Superintendent Hardy Powers made an exploratory trip there after presiding over the British Isles district assemblies in the summer of 1957. His report to the other general superintendents and to the General Board resulted in a decision to move into West Germany as an overseas home mission project.

Eugene, Ore., Pastor Jerald D. Johnson and his wife were chosen as the first Nazarene representatives. The Johnsons arrived in Frankfurt in March, 1958. After intensive study, Johnson was preaching in German by fall.

A financial drive by the NYPS to provide a parsonage went over the goal set: $15,000 was asked, $27,000 was raised. A congregation had been gathered, buildings were under way, and the

---

13. HH, vol. 47, no. 36 (Nov. 5, 1958), pp. 3-4; cf. minutes, Board of General Superintendents, meetings of Jan. 8 and Sept. 1, 1957.

first Church of the Nazarene in West Germany reported 40 members before the end of the Golden Anniversary year.[14]

B. Okinawa

Okinawa, the island chain southwest of Japan, was recognized as part of Japan but was still under United States military control in 1958. It had been the concern of the missionaries in Japan since 1953 when Field Superintendent William Eckel visited Naha, the capital city. In 1956, the Japan Mission Council decided it was time to extend the work to Okinawa.

Doyle and Mattie Shepherd volunteered to make the move, accompanied by Rev. and Mrs. Shigeru Higuchi. The two couples arrived in Okinawa in July, 1958. Property was purchased on a hill overlooking the city of Naha and a substantial headquarters church erected.

By the end of the year, a church had been organized with 29 members, three other preaching points had been established, two Sunday Schools enrolled 200 members, and the mission was off to a good start.[15]

C. Taiwan

An early Nazarene contact on the island of Formosa or Taiwan came out of the independent work of Nazarene China Missionary Peter Kiehn who, when mainland China closed to missions, organized the Taiwan Gospel Mission near Taipei. In December of 1956, Raymond and Ruth Miller, veteran missionaries who had served in Trinidad since 1948, arrived in Taiwan, to be followed a month later by John and Natalie Holstead.

When it became evident that taking over the work of the Gospel Mission was inadvisable, the Millers and the Holsteads started from the beginning. Their efforts proved fruitful and within two years, joined by Leon C. and Emma Osborn, China missionaries since 1919, the six Nazarenes and five national workers were supervising eight churches with 200 members and 500 enrolled in Sunday Schools. They were also operating a Bible school with 38

---

14. Minutes, Board of General Superintendents, meetings of Sept. 1, 1957, and Jan. 2 and 14, 1958; PGB, 1958, pp. 11-12; 1959, pp. 79, 96. Cf. Jerry Johnson, *We Live in Germany* (Kansas City: Nazarene Publishing House, 1960).

15. Cf. Earle, *Fields Afar,* pp. 31 ff.; Merril Bennett, *Okinawa Lifeline* (Kansas City: Nazarene Publishing House, 1964); PGB, 1959, p. 76.

students enrolled. Growth from that point has continued at a rapid pace.[16]

D. Brazil

Although Brazil is the largest nation in South America, only slightly smaller in extent than the United States, and although Nazarene missions had flourished for years in neighboring nations, it was not until 1958 that the church entered "the awakened giant."[17]

The immediate point of contact was the urgent concern of Nazarene laypeople Mr. and Mrs. Ervin Stegemoeller. Stegemoeller worked for an American manufacturer in Campinas. In October, 1957, General Superintendent Williamson, Foreign Missions Executive Rehfeldt, and Spanish Department Director Reza made an exploratory trip to what Williamson called "the land of opportunity." They landed in São Paulo, then a city of 3 million population; and visited Campinas, 90 miles inland where the Stegemoellers were located; Belo Horizonte; and Londrina, cities where they found "tremendous opportunity for a great, soul-saving ministry."[18]

In July, 1958, Earl and Gladys Mosteller, missionaries in the Cape Verde Islands for 12 years, transferred to Campinas. The language of Brazil, like that of the Cape Verdes, is Portuguese. Charles and Roma Gates followed soon after. The remainder of 1958 was spent in canvassing the area with a view to finding the best location for a headquarters church and residence.[19]

IV. EDUCATION TO THE GOLDEN ANNIVERSARY

In keeping with the overall polity of the church, the General Assembly of 1956 adopted a provision to require the colleges of the Church of the Nazarene to structure their boards of control so that half of the members would be laypersons. Some of the colleges had boards composed chiefly of the district superintendents and

---

16. PGB, 1959, pp. 60-61, 76-77; Ramquist, *No Respecter of Persons*, pp. 9-32; Earle, *Fields Afar*, pp. 56-64.
17. Conrad, *South America in Perspective*, pp. 188-209.
18. HH, vol. 46, no. 40 (Dec. 4, 1957), p. 3.
19. OS, vol. 45, no. 3 (March, 1958), p. 3; no. 11 (November, 1958), pp. 3-4.

leading pastors on their respective zones without the balancing presence of respected laypeople.[20]

The General Assembly committee on education also considered four proposals that would have, in effect, repealed the somewhat ambiguous statement adopted in 1940 which some interpreted as a prohibition of any intercollegiate athletics in Nazarene colleges.[21] The committee at first adopted the memorials, but reversed itself when Dr. Hardy Powers, representing the Board of General Superintendents, urged caution in making any change. The matter was later resolved by referring it to the Department of Education of the General Board, which, with proper safeguards, opened the way for intercollegiate athletics in the colleges of the church.

Canadian Nazarene College and Pasadena each gained new presidents when Arnold Airhart resigned to take the pastorate of St. Clair Church in Toronto and W. T. Purkiser left Pasadena to join the faculty of Nazarene Theological Seminary. Willard H. Taylor assumed the presidency at CNC and Russell V. DeLong at Pasadena.

Three of the colleges materially enlarged their campus facilities: Canadian with Martin Memorial Tabernacle and Gymnasium; Bethany with Chapman Hall, a $383,000 men's dormitory, and a new library; and Olivet with Nesbitt Residence Hall, a women's dormitory costing $450,000. At Northwest Nazarene College, the regents approved a seven-year development program to provide facilities for a student body of 800.[22]

The colleges ended the Golden Anniversary Year with a total of 4,397 students, up 15.6 percent in two years. An additional 170 were enrolled in the seminary. Their total property holdings were appraised at $9,236,000 against which stood indebtedness of $1,243,241. Contributions from the church during the year for both capital and current expenditures stood at approximately $830,000.

20. GAJ, 1956, pp. 104-5.
21. The statement read, "We recommend that it be definitely provided that schools and colleges of the Church of the Nazarene engage only in intramural athletics" (*Manual,* 1956, p. 322, et al.).
22. Sutherland, "History of NNC," p. 84; Thomson, *Vine of His Planting,* p. 29; PGB, 1957, p. 126; HH, vol. 46, no. 1 (Mar. 6, 1957), p. 11; no. 11 (May 15, 1957), p. 19.

Theological faculties of the church's higher institutions observed the Golden Anniversary with a first—a theology workshop conducted at Bethany Nazarene College in July, 1958, sponsored by the Department of Education. Some 40 professors working in the field of theology and religion in all of the colleges and the seminary made up the gathering.

The workshop was organized around a consideration of three of the Articles of Faith of the Church of the Nazarene: those dealing with the Scriptures, with original sin, and with entire sanctification. Education Department Executive S. T. Ludwig reported that the results of the conference were highly rewarding. "For the first time in our educational work as a church," he said, "theology and Bible teachers were brought together for a conference concerning the cardinal doctrines of our faith. The fellowship of these men was wonderfully stimulating and encouraging. The splendid unity and clear vision of our task with which we left the conference greatly enriched us all."[23]

V. CHURCH SCHOOLS

Executive Editor Albert Harper reported a Golden Anniversary Year increase in Sunday Schools throughout the church of nearly 47,000, by far the largest ever made in one year. Particularly gratifying was the figure of 78,364 enrolled on foreign mission fields.

Harper was also pleased that branch Sunday Schools were being increasingly used as a means of reaching new communities and establishing new churches. He counted a total of 58 districts with one or more branches operating.

A major achievement of the year was the realization of a 10-year goal—the extension of graded Sunday School lessons up through junior high. This provided a graded curriculum from nursery through junior high school age. Other publication innovations included a manual for directors of Christian education, a new record and reporting system, and a series of Bible maps and charts to assist in classroom presentation.[24]

---

23. PGB, 1959, pp. 88-89.
24. Ibid., pp. 89-93.

VI. The Golden Anniversary

Much attention from Nazarene leadership during 1958 was given to observance of the 50th Anniversary of the merger of eastern, western, and southern groups that came together to make up the Church of the Nazarene in October, 1908. At their January meeting back in 1956, the Board of General Superintendents had appointed a 50th anniversary committee with G. B. Williamson as the representative of the board.[25]

The general superintendents published a "50th Anniversary Proclamation" in the *Herald of Holiness* early in December, 1957. "The official birthday of the Church of the Nazarene as a denomination has been decreed as October 13, 1908," they said.[26] The entire year 1958 was proclaimed the 50th Anniversary Year of the church. Calling attention to the goals set out in the 1956 quadrennial address of the board, the proclamation urged the church to "conscientiously and prayerfully seek to learn the lessons our history should teach us and to witness an unprecedented outpouring of the Holy Spirit, resulting in the salvation of the sinner and the sanctification of the believer." Only so could it be assured that, "if the Lord tarries, the church will continue to accomplish its divinely ordained mission as it moves forward into the next half century."[27]

Much, of course, would be said about the past. But the three-point program of the anniversary committee was: (1) Rejoice in our heritage, (2) Renew our commitment, and (3) Reach out to the task.[28] As Ohio Central District Superintendent Harvey Galloway put it, "The past is glorious, but the church does not propose to live in the yesterdays. The present and the immediate future are ours. *This is our day,* the day of advancement for the kingdom of Jesus Christ."[29]

---

25. Minutes, Board of General Superintendents, meeting of Jan. 13, 1956.

26. There is logic in this choice, since the church became a fully national organization at that time. Historians have a problem, however, in that the numbered series of General Assemblies begins not in 1908 but with the Chicago assembly of 1907 when the Association of Pentecostal Churches in the East united with the Church of the Nazarene in the West to become the Pentecostal Church of the Nazarene.

27. HH, vol. 46, no. 40 (Dec. 4, 1957), p. 1; cf. also the 52-page anniversary edition of the *Herald,* vol. 47, no. 1 (Mar. 5, 1958).

28. Minutes, Historical Film Strip Committee, J. Fred Parker, secretary, July 26, 1957; archives.

29. HH, vol. 47, no. 1 (Mar. 5, 1958), p. 17.

A full year of activities was planned, beginning with a watch-night service on New Year's Eve. The month of January featured a conference on evangelism and emphasis in the local churches on prayer groups, cottage prayer meetings, and special seasons of prayer and fasting for the ongoing work of the church.

The five months leading up to Pentecost Sunday would see special emphasis on revivals and holiness conventions, with a $1 million offering goal at Easter for world evangelism. Each local church was urged to hold a holiness convention during Pentecost week, May 18-25, or at least place specific emphasis on the church's "holiness heritage and doctrine."

July was to mark a youth observance of the anniversary with an international teenage institute. The first full week in October was to be a week of witnessing. Sunday, October 12, was "the time when all Nazarene churches should observe the union which took place at Pilot Point, Texas, October 13, 1908." November was the month for another $1 million Thanksgiving Offering for world missions.

General suggestions included the scheduling of local and zone missionary conventions, "Golden Anniversary Crusades" on a zone level through the church, Christian Service Training classes "training our people for better churchmanship and helping to deepen spiritual life and prepare for more effective service," and above all revivals, visitation evangelism, and holiness conventions "should help us reach out and gain others for Christ and the Church." Nazarene hymnist Haldor Lillenas wrote a special anniversary song, "The Sun Never Sets," to be used throughout the year.[30]

A. Conference on Evangelism

The first major event of anniversary year was the General Conference on Evangelism held in Kansas City, January 6-8, in the Music Hall of the Municipal Auditorium. As Evangelism Executive Secretary V. H. Lewis reported, "It set a record in attendance more than any conference in our church other than our General Assemblies,"[31] about 3,000 in all.

---

30. Mimeographed suggestion sheet prepared by the Department of Evangelism; archives.
31. PGB, 1959, p. 95.

Even a blinding snowstorm failed to cool the enthusiasm of the conferees. In addresses and papers, all aspects of the church's evangelistic mission were explored. As Norman R. Oke noted, "The Church of the Nazarene has declared herself for another half century. . . . The Church of the Nazarene faces its next fifty years with a sense of direction and a mood of unity."[32]

B. Servicemen's Retreat

The first of a series of overseas servicemen's retreats was sponsored by the Servicemen's Commission. It was held at the General Walker Hotel in Berchtesgaden, Germany, with Ponder Gilliland, youth executive, as director, assisted by Paul and Maxine Skiles, Northern California youth workers. Total registration added up to 203. "It was the hungriest crowd—for both fellowship and spiritual help—I have ever seen," Gilliland reported. "If you could have heard their testimonies, you would have felt, as we did, that the Retreat was of God."[33]

C. International Institute

Gilliland also directed another first, an International Youth Institute at the YMCA conference grounds in Estes Park, Colo., July 22-28. A total of 763 registered, almost 500 of them teenagers. All but three of the domestic districts were represented, and young people from Africa, Alaska, Canada, England, Hawaii, Mexico, and Scotland lent an international flavor to the gathering. Each district was allowed eight teens, four girls and four boys, along with the district NYPS president, the district institute director, and their spouses.

Conquest Editor J. Fred Parker summed up the impact of the gathering in a report written for the *Herald of Holiness:*

> None of the teen-agers or the two hundred fifty adult leaders who accompanied them, could ever forget the many mountaintop blessings of those days—times when the power of God fell upon the services and a regular camp meeting spirit prevailed; when at spontaneously called prayer meetings the Lord came very near; when around the campfire, as General President Eugene Stowe spoke, a holy hush seemed to settle down; and when at the climactic communion service the silent weep-

---

32. HH, vol. 46, no. 49 (Feb. 5, 1958), p. 11.
33. PGB, 1959, p. 101.

ing throughout the great congregation spoke of a deep spiritual experience. Times like these are unforgettable.[34]

D. Week of Witnessing

The week just prior to the day for observance of the 50th anniversary, October 5-12, was designed as a "week of witnessing." It was stressed as a major feature of the Golden Anniversary celebration. A special gospel leaflet was prepared, "You Are One in a Million," and Nazarenes were urged to witness to a total of 1 million unchurched people during the week. The final tally reported to the evangelism office was 1,126,477. Evangelism Secretary Lewis quoted a statement he found in a district paper:

> There were more than 15,000 witnessed to on our district and it is already paying off. A number have been converted as a direct result, and I am sure many more will be won if we follow through on this plan. I hope we know the thrill of telling others what Christ did for us. If we would keep up the same pace of witnessing, in a short time it would precipitate the greatest revival we have ever known, revolutionize our church, and double our membership.[35]

VII. PILGRIMAGE TO PILOT POINT

Anniversary day itself was Monday, October 13. The all-church observance was at Pilot Point, Tex., on the spot where the original General Assembly had been held that cemented the union between the east-west church formed in Chicago the year before and the southern Holiness Church of Christ. The small rural community is located about 55 miles north of Dallas-Fort Worth.

The memorable spot was on a corner of the property owned and occupied by Rest Cottage, the sole surviving social service institution in domestic territory owned by the church.

Rest Cottage had been founded in February of 1903 by Rev. and Mrs. J. P. Roberts as a home for unwed mothers and an adoption agency. Roberts served as superintendent for 34 years until his death in January, 1937, when he was succeeded by his brother John F. Roberts. At the time of the anniversary, ex-Chaplain Geren C. Roberts was supervising the operation of the home. By that time it was housed in a commodious main building with 22 rooms, a

---

34. HH, vol. 47, no. 26 (Aug. 27, 1958), p. 14; cf. PGB, 1959, pp. 96-97.
35. PGB, 1959, p. 95; cf. HH, vol. 47, no. 28 (Sept. 10, 1958), pp. 1-13.

chapel and office, a small but adequate hospital, and other buildings, all located on a 71-acre tract of farmland.[36]

The Rest Cottage Association Board of Directors, all Nazarenes from the seven districts in closest proximity to the home, deeded the one acre where the "canvas cathedral" had stood 50 years before to the General Board for $100 to be kept as a perpetual memorial of the union.[37] A substantial granite marker had been erected and some preliminary landscaping done.

The commemorative service was held at 2:30 p.m. Monday in a tent 60 feet wide by 180 feet long. It was seated with 2,200 chairs. Parking had been planned in a three-acre cornfield loaned by Rest Cottage for the occasion, and a catered lunch was to be served outdoors at noon. But the weather had been rainy and disagreeable, and the prospect of more rain, as S. T. Ludwig commented, "gave the Arrangements Committee butterflies in the stomach."[38] The fears were in vain. The day dawned bright and clear with a light, cool breeze, and fleecy clouds in the afternoon kept the temperature comfortable.

Maximum news coverage had been given the event by O. Joe Olson, a professional newsman and graduate of Nazarene Theological Seminary who had become the first full-time director of the Nazarene Information Service on March 1. A total of 3,357 persons actually registered, and the total gathering was estimated at between 4,500 and 5,000, filling the tent completely and ringing it some 5 to 10 persons deep.

Four of the general superintendents were present and took part in the service. Dr. Young was on an extended supervisory trip to South Africa at the time and could not be present. G. B. Williamson presided. Three ministers who had been part of the uniting groups represented their sections with brief addresses: C. P. Lanpher, the East; H. Orton Wiley, the West; and Emma Irick, the South. In all, 38 persons who had been present in 1908 were seated in reserved seats in front near the platform.

Senior General Superintendent Powers' address centered around four landmarks or "pilot points" guiding the church from

---

36. HH, vol. 25, no. 46 (Jan. 30, 1937), pp. 19-20; cf. *Rest Cottage Messenger* (Summer, 1956), pp. 2-5.
37. Minutes, Board of General Superintendents, meeting of Sept. 2, 1957.
38. Letter, S. T. Ludwig to Samuel Young, Oct. 16, 1958; archives.

its past into the future: the authority of the Scriptures, the adequacy of the Atonement, the reality of Christian experience, and the urgency of the church's mission.[39]

S. T. Ludwig characterized the spirit of the service as one of "liberty, freedom, and joyous enthusiasm." He wrote that "the presence of the Lord was unusually real in every part of the service." Two times, in particular, he said there had been "old fashioned shouting and praising the Lord all over the tent and outside. In the last instance I think it was about five minutes that a 'glory presence' was upon the people."[40]

With ceremonies concluded in the tent, the bronze marker installed on the granite monument was unveiled by the two lay executives of the General Board, M. Lunn and John Stockton. The marker reads:

> Phineas F. Bresee, in many respects the founder and moving spirit of the new organization, expressed the vision of them all in this confession: "We are debtors to every man to give him the gospel in the same measure as we have received it."

> Today some 350,000 people call themselves Nazarenes, and their missionary enterprise reaches into 40 world areas.[41]

VIII. EVALUATING RESULTS

There is no simple way to estimate the value of the concerted effort that went into the observance of the church's Golden Anniversary. As previously noted, final reports from the week of witnessing indicated that the million-person mark had been exceeded by 126,000. Each of the special offerings, at Easter and Thanksgiving, went above their million-dollar goals—the first time such goals had been set and met; General Budget and missions specials for the year aggregated $3.5 million.[42] The rate of growth in church membership increased from 12,359 or 4.3 percent for the two years 1956 and 1957 to 19,105 or 6.1 percent for the anniversary year and that immediately following it. Membership passed the

---

39. HH, vol. 47, no. 39 (Nov. 26, 1958), p. 5. Cf. pp. 4-7 for Olson's write-up of the event with accompanying pictures and pp. 12-14 for Editor White's personal reaction to Pilot Point.

40. Ibid., p. 3. Letter, Ludwig to Young, Oct. 16, 1958; archives.

41. Ibid., p. 6.

42. PGB, 1959, pp. 95, 104.

300,000 mark in 1958. There were 171 congregations added in 1956-57 and 199 in 1958-59.

On the other hand, V. H. Lewis, whose evangelism department had spearheaded the church growth aspect of the anniversary, lamented that "a large number of our churches are not operating a visitation evangelism program." Those that did, he observed, for the most part showed growth in receiving members by profession of faith.[43] Lewis noted:

> We must recognize that after more than two quadrenniums the Crusade for Souls has not become the dominant program of our local churches, since around 60 percent of them do not have any kind of visitation evangelism and in many of the 40 percent the program is operating very feebly; 1,322 or 28.8 percent of our churches this past year [1958] reported no one received by profession of faith.[44]

Roy F. Smee, Lewis' counterpart in Home Missions and Church Extension, found concern in what he saw as a lack of interest in home missions. He recognized the high cost of land and buildings and regretted the lack of long-range planning that would secure building sites in growing areas before the appreciation of land values put the cost beyond reach.

Smee was particularly burdened that the church was restricting its field by becoming too class-conscious, limiting its outreach to people within a certain economic bracket. Churches moving to the suburbs were leaving a vacuum in the inner city. "Are we being influenced by the materialistic attitudes of our suburban civilization?" he asked. "We are called to preach scriptural holiness and to cut across class and economic lines. The limitation of our field will dry up the sources of home mission growth."[45]

Of equal concern to Smee was the large number of new churches which were not growing. He noted that 35 percent of the congregations organized during his first quadrennium as Home Missions secretary, 1948-52, still had fewer than 25 members in 1958. "These churches were not born to remain small for twenty years or more," he growled. "They were organized to grow—to take their place among our churches and in their communities as a force for holiness." A large number of small, struggling churches

---

43. Ibid., p. 96.
44. Ibid., p. 50.
45. Ibid., pp. 80-81.

on any district made new home mission work virtually impossible.[46]

SUMMARY

Yet the long-range picture hardly gave cause for gloom. It would always be possible, in retrospect, to see how greater gains might have been made. The record of the Church of the Nazarene during its second 25 years of denominational history holds many high points.

The church began its second quarter-century with 111,905 members in 2,030 domestic congregations and 7,568 adherents overseas in 109 organized churches. It ended the quarter century with 301,675 members in 4,587 congregations and 46,493 members in foreign mission fields in 793 churches. Membership worldwide thus grew from 119,473 at the close of 1933 to 348,169 at the end of 1958—some 292.4 percent increase. The number of congregations worldwide more than doubled, from 2,139 to 5,380.

The geographical growth of the church (reflected in the number of congregations) had accelerated during the 25 years until Roy Smee, executive secretary of the Home Missions Department, could report in 1957 that 29 percent of all local congregations in the church had been organized during the eight-year period just preceding.[47]

The average size of the churches in the United States, Canada, and the British Isles grew from 55 in 1933 to 66 in 1958, a fact the more remarkable in view of the slow growth of many of the newer churches Roy Smee had reported.

Other statistics were equally significant. Sunday School enrollment, from which the church has always drawn many of its members, rose from 239,341 to 678,830 with average attendance each week moving from 141,111 to 403,549. Youth membership climbed from 48,533 to 93,069. The missionary society grew from 31,784 members to 155,778.

Even more striking is the record on foreign mission fields. In 1933, a total of 66 missionaries and 378 national workers served a total of 10,453 members in 399 churches, stations, and outstations

---

46. Ibid., p. 81.
47. PGB, 1947, p. 52.

in 14 countries or fields.[48] By 1958, the number of missionaries was 388 with 1,466 national workers serving 46,493 members in 1,609 churches and stations in 33 separate countries or fields. At the same time, Sunday School enrollments abroad went from 7,343 to 79,276.

Nine Bible schools on foreign mission fields in 1933 had become 30 by 1958, with the 252 enrollment growing to 680. Three hospitals were still operating after 25 years, with the loss of one in China and the gain of one in Africa; but 13 dispensaries had grown to 39, and the number of patients treated from 29,358 to 175,571.

In 1933, the eight Nazarene colleges in the United States and Canada (including Bresee College which was operating at the time) enrolled a total of 926 college-level students among them. In 1958, their enrollments totalled 4,397 with an additional 170 in the seminary. None of the institutions was regionally accredited in 1933. By 1958, five enjoyed full accreditation. Only Trevecca was still unaccredited, since Canada has no comparable system for accrediting colleges and Bresee had merged with Bethany. Nazarene Theological Seminary had been organized, equipped, and provided with adequate facilities for a student body that stabilized just short of 200.

In 25 years, the Nazarene Publishing House had become a major force in religious publication in America. While dollar values had inflated materially, the net worth of the business had risen from $347,998 with sales of approximately $218,000 for the year 1933 to $3,135,431 net worth in 1958 and annual sales of $2,880,607. Buildings and equipment had been immeasurably improved and the volume of publication increased manifold.[49] Manager M. Lunn and his assistant M. A. (Bud) Lunn had kept the equipment fully in step with the state of the art.

The headquarters departments and their officers had been provided with a commodious and up-to-date building to replace the cramped quarters in which they had worked in the early part of the period. While the polity of the church was unchanged, it had been fine tuned and was functioning smoothly, and all systems

---

48. For administrative purposes, Barbados and Trinidad were listed together as British West Indies; and Guatemala, British Honduras, and Nicaragua were listed as Central America. Statistics are from GAJ, 1936, pp. 291-92.

49. PGB, 1934, pp. 98-101; GAJ, 1936, p. 330; 1960, pp. 278-80.

were "go." The foundations of the first 25 years had received a worthy superstructure.

General Superintendent Powers closed his Golden Anniversary address at Pilot Point with an exhortation intended to point the way into the future:

> We must fast, pray, and believe God. The holiness message and witness must be maintained at all costs. For this the church was brought into existence. To allow the message to die by default would make us traitors. By pulpit, pen, and consistent lives we must be true to the faith.
>
> In a fever-ridden and frantic age ... we must tap new resources of divine power in the secret place of prayer and through Bible reading and meditation.
>
> We determine to pass on to future generations our glorious church with name unsullied and glory undimmed. Let us hold high the banner of holiness and join the battle. The gates of hell shall not prevail against us. With God leading us on, let us fully accept the responsibility and the challenge of the next fifty years if the Master shall tarry.[50]

---

50. HH, vol. 47, no. 39 (Nov. 26, 1958), p. 6.

Epilogue

"What's past," said William Shakespeare, "is prologue."[1] The story of the Nazarenes does not end with the Golden Jubilee of 1958. If it did, these lines would never have been written. Churches change; they rarely die. The Nazarenes would learn that loyalty to the fathers does not mean to stop where they fell but to follow the path they chose. True allegiance belongs not to the old but to the ageless.

No history of the years since 1958 could be written now. Only a brief epilogue can be given.

Placing the statistical chart for 1981 alongside that for 1958 yields some interesting results. The church that 23 years earlier had numbered 5,380 local congregations with 348,168 members reported in with 7,445 local churches and 686,984 members around the world. In 1958, a total of 19.8 percent of all Nazarenes lived outside the continental United States. In 1981 the figure was 28.3 percent.

Indeed, the cutting edge of Nazarene growth has moved from the United States to other world areas. The process of "internationalizing" the church began in 1964 with an eight-year study of the church's total missionary program. An interim step was taken in 1972 when the denomination was divided into three Intercontinental Zones outside the United States and Canada. In the four-year period ending in 1980, the church in the United States registered a percentage gain in membership of 6.27. The church in Canada gained 10.14 percent. In Intercontinental Zone I, Europe and Africa, the gain was 16.16 percent in membership. Intercontinental Zone II, the Orient and South Pacific, added 19.4 percent. Intercontinental Zone III, Central and South America, gained

---

1. *Tempest,* act 2, sc. i, line 261.

32.02 percent. But the "Pioneer/National Mission" districts, scattered through all the zones and consisting of districts that have not as yet gained full district status (at or near the point of self-support), racked up a 66.76 percent gain in membership during the quadrennium.

In 1980, the church was divided into 15 geographical regions. Eight of the regions are located in the United States and correspond roughly to the educational zones set up in 1964 as support areas for the eight liberal arts colleges now serving the 50 states. Canada constitutes a ninth region. The remaining six are the Africa Region; the Asian Region; Europe, Middle East Region; Mexico, Central America, and Caribbean Region; South America Region; and the South Pacific Region. The following table, reflecting church growth patterns from 1975 to 1979, illustrates the changing situation:[2]

Region	1975 Membership	1979 Membership	Percentage Rate of Growth
Central U.S.A. (ONC)	74,724	76,680	2.62
East Central U.S.A. (MVNC)	63,128	65,866	4.34
South Central U.S.A. (BNC)	54,316	57,128	5.18
Southwest U.S.A. (PLC)	55,878	59,018	5.62
Eastern U.S.A. (ENC)	42,971	46,185	7.48
North Central U.S.A. (MANC)	41,421	44,726	7.98
Southeast U.S.A. (TNC)	63,763	68,930	8.10
Northwest U.S.A. (NNC)	44,890	50,234	11.90
U.S.A. total	441,093	468,767	6.27
Europe, Middle East	5,083	5,553	9.25
Canada (CNC)	7,972	8,784	10.14
Africa	16,964	20,899	23.19
Asia	17,384	21,517	23.77
Mexico, Central America, and Caribbean	35,036	48,124	37.36
South America	9,412	13,436	42.75
South Pacific	1,818	2,652	45.87

2. Statistics abstracted from GAJ, 1980, pp. 312-36. Cf. Jerald D. Johnson, *The International Experience* (Kansas City: Nazarene Publishing House, 1982), pp. 9-71.

The church's institutions have made comparable progress. The number of schools and colleges in the United States has grown by three with the addition of Mount Vernon Nazarene College in Ohio; Mid-America Nazarene College in Olathe, Kans.; and the Nazarene Bible College in Colorado Springs. In 1979, the schools reported an aggregate enrollment of 11,763. All eight liberal arts colleges in the United States enjoy regional accreditation, and Nazarene Theological Seminary and Nazarene Bible College are accredited by their respective professional agencies.

The Nazarene Publishing House has grown into a $12 million business that during the quadrennium 1976-80 published 230 different books in the interest of getting the whole gospel to the whole world by the printed page, as well as millions of pages of periodicals and Sunday School materials.

The auxiliaries and the Church Schools department (now the Division of Christian Life and Sunday School) have kept step with 432,712 members in the Nazarene World Missionary Society, 205,100 in Nazarene Youth International, and 1,118,230 enrolled in Sunday School.

The General Board has reorganized its multiplying departments into divisions and now includes in its membership representatives from world areas outside the United States and the British Commonwealth. Fourteen out of its 51 members in 1980 made their homes outside the United States and Canada.

Inflation makes financial items almost meaningless. However, Nazarenes in 1981 gave $269,391,600 to support their worldwide work, a per capita total of $392.14. The sum of 11.25 percent of the total was given for general denominational interests.

Changes in society have not left the church untouched. Nazarenes are continuing to become increasingly middle class people. The growing affluence of its constituency has reflected itself in the church's levels of giving. But there is evidence that while Nazarenes are giving more, they are at the same time keeping more. The per capita giving has scarcely kept pace with either the cost of living or growth in average income.[3]

---

3. Nazarene per capita giving compared with per capita disposable personal income in the United States. Statistics from GAJ, 1980, pp. 307-8, and Bureau of

Superchurches are still rare among Nazarenes, but average sizes are growing, and a few large congregations are emerging. The average size of local Nazarene congregations worldwide in 1958 was 64 members; the comparable figure in 1981 was 92. The 1981 average size of local churches in the United States was exactly 100 members.

There are some evidences of changing evangelistic methods and concerns. The 10-day or two-week revival meeting is virtually a thing of the past. There seems to be some lessening of the "second blessing" emphasis in the preaching of entire sanctification. Holiness is more often conceived in terms of the work of the Holy Spirit than in Christological and perfectionist terms. Along with this is some slackening of denominational loyalty. The losses occasioned by the mobility of modern society tends to argue that a number of members are Nazarenes by convenience more than by conviction. The tendency reported by Harold W. Reed in his 1943 doctoral study for denominations to develop from the "sect type" (emphasizing their distinctives and their separateness) in the direc-

---

the Census, U.S. Department of the Interior, *Statistical Abstract of the United States,* 81st and 102nd editions, 1960 and 1981; data for selected years:

Year	Per Capita Disposable Personal Income	Nazarene Giving per Capita	Nazarene Giving as Percentage of National per Capita Personal Income
1929	$ 682	$ 43.96	6.45
1933	364	23.55	6.47
1940	576	38.24	6.64
1945	1,075	75.54	7.03
1950	1,369	104.56	7.64
1955	1,661	125.59	7.63
1957	1,798	133.77	7.44
1958	1,818	133.05	7.32
1959	1,891	135.51	7.17
1960	1,947	142.33	7.31
1965	2,448	168.33	6.88
1970	3,390	221.35	6.53
1973	4,313	273.75	6.35
1975	5,075	326.41	6.43
1976	5,477	309.78	5.66
1977	5,954	331.25	5.56
1978	6,571	355.52	5.41
1979	7,293	384.42	5.27
1980	8,002	373.24	4.66

tion of a "church type" (reflecting life-styles approximating those of other Christians) has not been reversed.[4]

Sociologists of religion tend to regard the pattern of church growth and development as proceeding through a series of definable stages. These may be stated in different ways, but all reflect more or less the same general sequence.

A denomination starts with minimum organization and a maximum of personal initiative, its units small and close-knit. It moves on to a stage of formal organization as its *Manual* or *Discipline* grows in size and complexity. It reaches the stage of its greatest efficiency. Then it passes into what may broadly be defined as a period of institutionalism. The final stage is one of stagnation and disarray, marked by "formalism, indifference, obsolescence, absolutism, red tape, patronage and corruption."[5]

We have noted in the Preface the thesis of Elmer Clark that all denominations originate as sects but begin to lose their distinctives in the second generation.[6] Nazarene sociologist Jon Johnston summarizes the stages through which social movements tend to pass as "an early stage of unrest to a later stage of settling down. In the final stage it is characterized by obligarchy, bureaucratization, and equilibration (focus on self-perpetuation)." This process is claimed to be "unilinear and determined."[7]

That such a scenario represents what has happened in many cases may be granted. That it represents a process that is in some way historically determined and therefore inevitable is by no means self-evident. In a sense, the story of the Nazarenes provides a critical testing of the thesis that all religious movements necessarily "run down" in power, zeal, and commitment to essential distinctives.

One of the still unresolved issues in church history is the extent to which spiritual dynamic with all its creative spontaneity can

---

4. "Growth of a Contemporary Sect-type Institution as Reflected in the Development of the Church of the Nazarene" (Th.D. diss., University of Southern California, Los Angeles, 1943). Many would argue that the Church of the Nazarene has always stressed "churchly" rather than "sectarian" attitudes.

5. Cf., e.g., Hollis Green, mimeographed lecture, "The Effects of Organization and Aging on Growth," Church Growth Colloquium, Emmanuel School of Religion, June 19, 1969.

6. Supra, p. 10.

7. Jon Johnston, *Will Evangelicalism Survive Its Own Popularity?* (Grand Rapids: Zondervan Publishing House, 1980), p. 212, n. 5.

survive the inescapable processes of organization and institutionalism that come with growth. Organization is inevitable. The survival of spirituality is not. The historic tension between prophet and priest finds an echo in the attempt to institutionalize the spontaneity of the Spirit.

The Church of the Nazarene is totally committed to the holiness message with its inherent potential for spiritual renewal. It is a message that is being purified from some of the more extreme interpretations that have at times been given. The tendency of folk theology to confuse ideals with standards, to ignore the human elements in the sanctified life, and to expect in the epoch of entire sanctification that measure of sanctity that comes only with Christian maturity is gradually being corrected.

In at least one significant respect, Nazarene commitment to entire sanctification is more pervasive than that of 19th-century Methodism. It is true that John Wesley included his "Standard Sermons" and *A Plain Account of Christian Perfection* in the doctrinal standards of the Methodist societies. But when Mr. Wesley condensed the 39 Articles of Faith of the Church of England into 24 articles for use in the American Methodist church, he omitted any reference to holiness or entire sanctification. In contrast, 2 of the 15 Articles of Faith in the Nazarene Constitution (the 5th on original sin, and the 10th on entire sanctification) unambiguously commit the Church of the Nazarene to "second blessing" holiness.

Wesley asked only that his ministers affirm their intention to "press on to perfection." All Nazarene ministers affirm a personal experience of entire sanctification, and all members of the church confess their adherence to the doctrine of holiness and either their present experience or their earnest desire for "the fullness of the blessing."

Obviously, doctrinal commitments can become verbal and empty. But where the truth is preserved and proclaimed, the Spirit can work. What Richard Lovelace has identified as "primary elements of continuous renewal" are pillars in the Nazarene temple of truth: justification, sanctification, the indwelling Spirit, and authority in spiritual conflict.[8]

---

8. *Dynamics of Spiritual Life*, pp. 93-144. See at this point, Timothy L. Smith, *Nazarenes and the Wesleyan Mission: Can We Learn from Our History?* (Kansas City: Beacon Hill Press of Kansas City, 1979), a perceptive analysis of the loss of effective holiness emphasis from the Methodist churches, and suggestions by which Nazarenes may safeguard their historic mission.

There is good evidence that the twin objectives of proclaiming holiness and world evangelization are Nazarene aims with high priority. Statistics do not tell the whole story, but neither are they meaningless. After a downturn in the rate of growth during the 1960s, the tide seems to have turned with a percentage increase of 35.9 in membership worldwide from 1972 to 1980.[9]

We come full circle to the truth that the church is unlike other human institutions. It has a divine dimension. Church history eventually passes into eschatology, and eschatology is a theological concern. The mystery of the church is the mystery of renewal, of revival. Such is the sovereignty of the Holy Spirit that none can tell when another Luther, or Wesley, or Finney, or Bresee, or Williams, or Chapman—and a thousand renewed and revitalized pastors and evangelists may be thrust forth by the Lord of the Church.

The church that successfully faces the challenge of the future must return again and again to the Fountainhead of its power and being. It must constantly find renewal of commitment, vision, and morale. Defeatist attitudes breed defeat. The future belongs to the church that can meet it with holy optimism.

This much of the future we know. The Lord our God is Lord of the new as well as Lord of the old. The future is His as well as the past. Nothing that happens can take Him by surprise. He is Alpha *and* Omega, the Beginning *and* the End.

The Christ whose title the Church of the Nazarene has taken into its name has trod the way before, and in the songwriter's words, "the glory lingers near." The greatest privilege given to people on earth is to be associated with the Church of the risen, living Lord. His purpose and His promise are true: "I will build my church; and the gates of hell shall not prevail against it" (Matt. 16:18).

---

9. Worldwide church growth statistics by decades from 1930 for the Church of the Nazarene:

Date	Membership	Percentage Rate of Growth for Preceding Decade
1930	90,309*	
1940	182,221*	107.3
1950	258,331	43.5
1960	372,178	44.1
1970	490,573	31.8
1980	674,329	37.5

*Adjusted by adding foreign missions members and probationers to make the figures comparable with the other statistics. Source, GAJ, 1980, pp. 302-3.

APPENDIX A
General Superintendents, 1933-58

John W. Goodwin, 1916-40
Roy T. Williams, 1916-46
James B. Chapman, 1928-47
J. G. Morrison, 1936-39
Orval J. Nease, 1940-44, 1948-50
H. V. Miller, 1940-48

Hardy C. Powers, 1944-68
G. B. Williamson, 1946-68
Samuel Young, 1948-72
D. I. Vanderpool, 1949-64
Hugh C. Benner, 1952-68

APPENDIX B
General Church Officers, 1933-58

General Church Secretary: E. J. Fleming, 1919-39
C. Warren Jones, 1939-44
Sylvester T. Ludwig, 1944-64
General Treasurer: M. Lunn, 1928-32, 1934-45
J. G. Morrison, 1932-34
John Stockton, 1945-70
Editor, "Herald of Holiness":   H. Orton Wiley, 1928-36
D. Shelby Corlett, 1936-48
Stephen S. White, 1948-60

APPENDIX C
General Board Members, 1933-58

Ministerial   *Lay*

Eastern Zone:

C. Warren Jones, 1928-37
Samuel Young, 1937-48
O. L. Benedum, 1948-52
E. E. Grosse, 1952-64
Kenneth Pearsall, 1956-59

E. S. Carman, 1932-48
L. M. Spangenberg, 1948-68
John S. Carlson, Sr., 1956-60

Southeast Zone:

C. E. Hardy, 1928-44

A. K. Bracken, 1944-56

John L. Knight, 1952-68

Lawrence B. Hicks, 1952-72

R. B. Mitchum, 1928-36

A. B. Mackey, 1936-56

J. F. Chilton, 1952-56

John T. Benson, Jr., 1956-68

Charles E. Oney, 1956-68

Central Zone:

Charles A. Gibson, 1933-36

E. O. Chalfant, 1928-32, 1936-44, 1946-48

Hardy C. Powers, 1940-44

R. V. DeLong, 1944-48

T. W. Willingham, 1944-46

Paul Updike, 1948-68

Harvey S. Galloway, 1948-68

E. D. Simpson, 1948-52

Don J. Gibson, 1956-59

John W. Felmlee, 1932-36

Grover Van Duyn, 1936-54

L. D. Mitchell, 1940-52, 1960-72

V. H. Carmichael, 1948-52

Howard H. Hamlin, 1952-64

Harlan R. Heinmiller, 1952-72

Morris W. Davis, 1955-60

Southern Zone:

A. K. Bracken, 1932-44

Hugh C. Benner, 1944-50

C. B. Strang, 1944-48

Ray Hance, 1948-56, 1960-68

Roy Cantrell, 1950-52

V. H. Lewis, 1952-56

E. S. Phillips, 1956-64

Orville W. Jenkins, 1956-64

C. A. McConnell, 1928-40

E. P. Robertson, 1940-48

J. W. Moore, 1944-52

A. E. Ramquist, 1948-55

Harry Craddock, 1952-56

Lawrence Crawford, 1955-64

E. W. Snowbarger, 1956-60, 1964-68

Southwest Zone:

J. T. Little, 1932-36

A. E. Sanner, 1936-56

George Coulter, 1956-60

Orval J. Nease, Jr., 1956-60

E. P. Robertson, 1932-36

Mrs. Paul Bresee, 1936-40

J. B. Deisenroth, 1940-56

Willis Brown, 1956-64

J. Wesley Mieras, 1956-73

Northwest Zone:

J. E. Bates, 1928-36

Thomas E. Mangum, 1936-40

R. V. DeLong, 1928-32, 1940-44

D. I. Vanderpool, 1944-49

Arthur C. Morgan, 1950-52

B. V. Seals, 1952-63

P. J. Bartram, 1956-60

S. W. True, 1928-37

T. S. Wiley, 1937-48

J. Robert Mangum, 1948-80

Gordon T. Olson, 1956-77

Canada-British Isles Zone:
> George Sharpe, 1932-36   Kenneth T. Olsen, 1956-72
> Robert Purvis, 1936-40
> George Frame, 1940-72
> A. E. Collins, 1944-48
> Edward Lawlor, 1948-64

Education:
> Orval J. Nease, Sr., 1932-36   A. B. Mackey, 1956-60
> T. W. Willingham, 1936-40
> H. Orton Wiley, 1940-48
> L. T. Corlett, 1948-52
> Roy H. Cantrell, 1952-64

Church Schools:
> C. B. Widmeyer, 1928-44
> Selden D. Kelley, 1944-49
> Harold W. Reed, 1950-56 (representation
>   of Church Schools ended in 1956)

WFMS/NFMS:
> Mrs. Susan N. Fitkin, 1924-48
> Mrs. Louise Robinson Chapman, 1948-64

NYPS:
> G. B. Williamson, 1932-40
> M. Kimber Moulton, 1940-48
> Mendell Taylor, 1948-52
> Ponder Gilliland, 1952-56
> Eugene Stowe, 1956-60

APPENDIX D

General Officers, Auxiliaries, 1933-58

WFMS/NFMS

President: Mrs. Susan N. Fitkin, 1915-48
                                      Louise Robinson Chapman,
                                         1948-64

Executive Secretary-Treasurer: Emma B. Word, 1940-50
                                         (Treasurer, 1932-40)

Executive Secretary: Mary L. Scott, 1950-75

NYPS

President:	G. B. Williamson, 1932-40
	M. Kimber Moulton, 1940-48
	Mendell Taylor, 1948-52
	Ponder Gilliland, 1952-56
	Eugene Stowe, 1956-60
Executive Secretary:	D. Shelby Corlett, 1923-36
	S. T. Ludwig, 1936-42, 1943-44
	John Peters, 1942-43
	Lauriston J. DuBois, 1944-56
	Ponder Gilliland, 1956-60

APPENDIX E

Executive Secretaries of the Departments of the General Board, 1933-58

Foreign Missions:	J. G. Morrison, 1927-37
	C. Warren Jones, 1937-48
	Remiss Rehfeldt, 1948-60
Home Missions, Evangelism, and Church Extension:	D. Shelby Corlett, 1933-34*
	J. G. Morrison, 1934-36*
	M. Lunn, 1936-37**
	C. Warren Jones, 1937-44*
	S. T. Ludwig, 1944-48*
	Roy F. Smee, 1948-64
Publication:	M. Lunn, 1923-60 (and manager of the Nazarene Publishing House)
Church Schools:	E. P. Ellyson, 1923-38
	Orval J. Nease, 1938-40
	J. Glenn Gould, 1940-45
	Albert F. Harper, 1945-75
Education:	H. Orton Wiley, 1928-40*
	M. Lunn, 1940-44*
	S. T. Ludwig, 1944-64*

Ministerial Benevolence:	E. J. Fleming, 1928-39*
	M. Lunn, 1939-56*
	Dean Wessels, 1956—
Evangelism:	V. H. Lewis, 1956-60

*Part-time.
**M. Lunn continued to serve as church extension secretary until 1948.

APPENDIX F

Presidents,
Institutions of Higher Education, 1933-58

Bethany Nazarene College:	A. K. Bracken, 1920-28, 1930-42
(Bethany-Peniel until 1955)	S. T. Ludwig, 1942-44
	O. J. Finch, 1944-47
	Roy Cantrell, 1947-72
Bresee College:	S. T. Ludwig, 1927-36
	Harold W. Reed, 1936-40
British Isles Nazarene College:	George Frame, 1945-54
(Hurlet until 1956)	Hugh Rae, 1954-66
Canadian Nazarene College:	C. E. Thomson, 1920-41
(Northern Bible College	Ernest Armstrong, 1941-42
until 1940)	William Allshouse, 1942-46
	A. E. Collins, 1946-47
	L. Guy Nees, 1947-49
	E. E. Martin, 1949-51
	Arnold E. Airhart, 1952-57,
	1961-74
	Willard H. Taylor, 1957-61
Eastern Nazarene College:	R. Wayne Gardner, 1930-36
	G. B. Williamson, 1936-45
	Samuel Young, 1945-48
	Edward S. Mann, 1948-70
Nazarene Theological Seminary:	Hugh C. Benner, 1945-52
	Lewis T. Corlett, 1952-66

Northwest Nazarene College: R. V. DeLong, 1927-3⁻ 1933-42
Reuben E. Gilmore, 1932-35
Lewis T. Corlett, 1942-52
John E. Riley, 1952-73

Olivet Nazarene College: T. W. Willingham, 1926-38
A. L. Parrott, 1938-45
Grover Van Duyn, 1945-48
Selden D. Kelley, 1948-49
Harold W. Reed, 1949-75

Pasadena College: H. Orton Wiley, 1933-49
W. T. Purkiser, 1949-57
R. V. DeLong, 1957-60

Trevecca Nazarene College: C. E. Hardy, 1928-37
A. B. Mackey, 1937-63

APPENDIX G

District Superintendents, 1933-58

Abilene: V. B. Atteberry, 1932-37
J. Walter Hall, 1937-40
John L. Knight, 1940-44
W. B. Walker, 1944-50
Orville W. Jenkins, 1950-60

Akron: O. L. Benedum, 1942-53
C. D. Taylor, 1953-69

Alabama: J. A. Manasco, 1931-34
H. H. Hooker, 1934-38
Paul Pitts, 1938-42
E. D. Simpson, 1942-47
Otto J. Stucki, 1947-53
C. E. Shumake, 1953-57
L. S. Oliver, 1957-64

Alaska: Bert Daniels, 1956-63

Albany: A. M. Babcock, 1938-46
Renard Smith, 1946-63

Alberta: *(See Canada West)*	E. S. Mathews, 1930-35 L. E. Channel, 1935-37 Dowie Swarth, 1937-42 A. Ernest Collins, 1942-46 Edward Lawlor, 1946-48
Arizona:	Oscar Hudson, 1933-35 L. W. Dodson, 1935-38 J. E. Bates, 1938-42 Dowie Swarth, 1942-44 M. L. Mann, 1944-77
Arkansas: *(See North Arkansas* *and South Arkansas)*	J. C. Henson, 1931-35 Holland London, 1935-44 J. W. Short, 1944-48 W. H. Johnson, 1948-53
Australia:	E. E. Zachary, 1948-50 A. A. E. Berg, 1950-79
British Isles:	Robert Purvis, 1931-40 George Frame, 1940-53
British Isles North:	George Frame, 1953-71
British Isles South:	James B. Maclagan, 1953-67
Canada Atlantic:	W. W. Tink, 1943-46 J. H. MacGregor, 1946-59
Canada Central:	T. E. Martin, 1952-55 H. B. Ward, 1955-61
Canada Pacific:	Edward Lawlor, 1956-57 Bert Daniels, 1957-64
Canada West:	Edward Lawlor, 1948-60
Carolina: *(See North Carolina* *and South Carolina)*	Raymond Browning, 1942-45 J. V. Frederick, 1945-47 C. E. Shumake, 1947-48
Central Northwest:	B. V. Seals, 1932-38 J. N. Tinsley, 1938-39
Central Ohio:	Harvey S. Galloway, 1944-73
Chicago Central:	E. O. Chalfant, 1923-52 Mark R. Moore, 1952-69
Colorado:	C. W. Davis, 1925-46 Glenn Griffith, 1946-51

C. B. Cox, 1951-55
O. J. Finch, 1955-60

Dallas: I. M. Ellis, 1927-36
I. C. Mathis, 1936-49
Paul H. Garrett, 1949-69

East Tennessee: Victor E. Gray, 1948-72

Eastern Kentucky: D. S. Somerville, 1952-72

Eastern Michigan: W. M. McGuire, 1950-62

Eastern Oklahoma: W. A. Carter, 1930-49
  (See Northeast Oklahoma Glenn Jones, 1949-51
  and Southeast Oklahoma)

Florida: J. E. Redmon, 1929-37
H. H. McAfee, 1937-38
Earle W. Vennum, 1938-43
Charles H. Strickland, 1943-46
John L. Knight, 1946-68

Georgia: P. P. Belew, 1931-42
W. H. Davis, 1942-47
Mack Anderson, 1947-69

Gulf Central: Leon Chambers, 1952-58

Hawaii: Leo Baldwin, 1946-51
Cecil Knippers, 1951-58

Houston: V. H. Lewis, 1947-56
W. Raymond McClung, 1957-77

Idaho-Oregon: Earl C. Pounds, 1930-37
Glenn Griffith, 1937-45
J. A. McNatt, 1945-52
I. F. Younger, 1952-69

Illinois: R. V. Starr, 1944-50
W. S. Purinton, 1950-58

Indianapolis: C. J. Quinn, 1928-33
Jesse Towns, 1933-44
Gene Phillips, 1944-48
J. W. Short, 1948-53
Luther Cantwell, 1953-64

Iowa: C. Preston Roberts, 1933-36
Hardy C. Powers, 1936-44
Remiss Rehfeldt, 1944-48
Gene E. Phillips, 1948-71

Kansas:	A. F. Balsmeier, 1927-39
	O. J. Finch, 1939-45
	E. E. Zachary, 1945-47
	Roy H. Cantrell, 1947-48
	Ray Hance, 1948-76
Kansas City:	N. B. Herrell, 1927-35
	E. E. Hale, 1935-40
	Glenn E. Miller, 1940-43
	Jarrette E. Aycock, 1943-61
Kentucky:	L. T. Wells, 1926-55
	D. D. Lewis, 1955-62
Los Angeles:	A. E. Sanner, 1950-52
	W. Shelburne Brown, 1952-63
Louisiana:	G. M. Akin, 1929-34
	B. F. Neely, 1934-36
	Ed. N. LeJeune, 1936-38
	Elbert Dodd, 1938-56
	V. Dan Perryman, 1956-60
Manitoba-Saskatchewan:	J. H. MacGregor, 1933-38
(See Canada West)	Walter W. Tink, 1938-40
	Norman R. Oke, 1940-43
	A. G. Blacklock, 1943-48
Maritime:	W. W. Tink, 1943-46
(See Canada Atlantic)	J. H. MacGregor, 1946-58
Michigan:	R. V. Starr, 1938-43
	C. A. Gibson, 1943-44
	W. M. McGuire, 1944-49
	Orville L. Marish, 1949-61
Minnesota:	J. N. Tinsley, 1939-42
	Roy H. Cantrell, 1942-46
	Arthur C. Morgan, 1946-53
	Roy F. Stevens, 1953-65
Mississippi:	R. H. M. Watson, 1933-38
	Cecil Knippers, 1938-49
	J. D. Saxon, 1949-54
	Otto Stucki, 1954-62
Missouri:	F. A. Welsh, 1933-40
	T. W. Willingham, 1940-45
	Holland B. London, 1945-47
	E. D. Simpson, 1947-68

Nebraska:

Horace N. Haas, 1932-34
Ira E. Hammer, 1934-37
T. P. Dunn, 1937-45
L. A. Ogden, 1945-51
Whitcomb B. Harding, 1951-71

Nevada-Utah:

H. H. Cochran, 1944-47
Raymond B. Sherwood, 1947-64

New England:

John Gould, 1930-35
Samuel Young, 1935-41
John Nielson, 1941-46
J. C. Albright, 1946-62

New Mexico:

B. F. Harris, 1932-38
R. C. Gunstream, 1938-66

New York:

J. Howard Sloan, 1933-37
A. M. Babcock, 1937-38
J. C. Albright, 1938-43
Lyle E. Eckley, 1943-49
O. J. Finch, 1949-53
Robert I. Goslaw, 1953-65

North Arkansas:

J. W. Hendrickson, 1953-62

North Carolina:

C. E. Shumake, 1948-53
Lloyd B. Byron, 1953-67

North Dakota:

Ira E. Hammer, 1931-34
S. C. Taylor, 1934-41
L. E. Grattan, 1941-43
A. G. Jeffries, 1943-45
G. W. Hendrickson, 1945-47
K. S. White, 1947-48
Harry F. Taplin, 1948-67

North Pacific:
(See Washington Pacific)

J. E. Bates, 1928-35
E. E. Martin, 1935-44

Northeastern Indiana:

J. W. Mongtomery, 1943-44
Paul Updike, 1944-68

Northeast Oklahoma:

I. C. Mathis, 1951-66

Northern California:

Roy F. Smee, 1931-48
George Coulter, 1948-60

Northwest:	J. N. Tinsley, 1932-38
	D. I. Vanderpool, 1938-49
	E. E. Zachary, 1949-61
Northwest Indiana:	R. V. DeLong, 1942-45
	George J. Franklin, 1945-53
	Arthur C. Morgan, 1953-64
Northwest Oklahoma:	Mark R. Moore, 1949-52
	J. T. Gassett, 1952-64
Northwestern Illinois:	Lyle E. Eckley, 1948-68
Ohio:	Charles A. Gibson, 1925-43
Ontario:	W. M. McGuire, 1936-38
(See Canada Central)	J. W. Towriss, 1938-40
	Roy H. Cantrell, 1940-42
	Robert F. Woods, 1942-47
	E. R. Ferguson, 1947-49
	A. E. Collins, 1949-51
	T. E. Martin, 1951-52
Oregon Pacific:	E. E. Martin, 1944-46
	Weaver W. Hess, 1946-51
	W. D. McGraw, 1951-70
Philadelphia:	William C. Allshouse, 1957-63
Pittsburgh:	C. Warren Jones, 1928-37
	O. L. Benedum, 1937-42
	R. F. Heinlein, 1942-57
	R. B. Acheson, 1957-64
Rocky Mountain:	Lewis E. Hall, 1931-38
	Harry W. Morrow, 1938-42
	William A. Eckel, 1942-47
	Alvin L. McQuay, 1947-71
San Antonio:	P. L. Pierce, 1932-35
	J. C. Henson, 1935-39
	W. L. French, 1939-45
	Hadley A. Hall, 1945-51
	Ponder W. Gilliland, 1951-54
	W. H. Davis, 1954-58
South African:	Charles H. Strickland, 1946-60
South Arkansas:	W. L. French, 1943-61

South Carolina:	J. G. Wells, 1943-44
	Arthur E. Kelly, 1944-47
	C. M. Kelly, 1947-51
	W. Ray Cloer, 1951-52
	D. W. Thaxton, 1952-58
South Dakota:	Earl C. Pounds, 1939-43
	Arthur C. Morgan, 1943-46
	William H. Deitz, 1946-52
	William H. Davis, 1952-54
	Crawford T. Vanderpool,
	1954-58
Southeast Atlantic:	J. H. Sloan, 1929-33
(See Carolina)	Theodore Ludwig, 1933-34
	R. E. Dobie, 1934-36
	W. H. Parker, 1936-38
	G. D. McDonald, 1938-39
	Raymond Browning, 1939-42
Southeast Oklahoma:	Glenn Jones, 1952-72
Southern California:	A. E. Sanner, 1933-50
	R. J. Plumb, 1950-56
	Nicholas A. Hull, 1956-76
Southwest Indiana:	Leo C. Davis, 1948-66
Southwest Oklahoma:	W. T. Johnson, 1948-77
Tennessee:	L. B. Matthews, 1933-37
(See East Tennessee)	J. D. Saxon, 1937-49
	D. K. Wachtell, 1949-57
	C. E. Shumake, 1957-70
Virginia:	A. D. Holt, 1943-45
	C. E. Keys, 1945-48
	James H. Garrison, 1948-50
	V. W. Littrell, 1950-68
Washington:	E. E. Grosse, 1957-69
Washington Pacific:	B. V. Seals, 1944-63
Washington-Philadelphia:	D. E. Higgs, 1928-44
	J. H. Parker, 1944-49
	E. E. Grosse, 1949-57
West Virginia:	Edward C. Oney, 1940-59
Western Ohio:	W. E. Albea, 1944-60

Western Oklahoma: J. W. Short, 1933-45
  (See Northwest Oklahoma   Ray Hance, 1945-48
   and Southwest Oklahoma)   W. T. Johnson, 1948-49
Wisconsin-Upper Michigan: C. T. Corbett, 1936-45
                               C. A. Gibson, 1945-57
                               Donald J. Gibson, 1957-62

APPENDIX H

Missionaries in Service, 1933-58

*(Listed by field of first appointment;
dates are total service dates and, as indicated in the footnotes,
may include service on other fields.)*

Africa

Grace Abla, R.N., 1952-55

Douglas and Ann Alexander, 1958—[1]

Kenneth and Mildred Babcock, 1948-50

Mary Bagley, R.N., 1952-68

Kenneth and Margaret, S.R.N., Bedwell, 1931-76*

Virginia Benedict, R.N., 1957—[2]

Henry and Lucy Best, 1919-55*

Dorothy Bevill (Eby), 1944-68

Cyril Blamey, 1938-68*

Della Boggs, 1944-79

Joan Bradshaw (Boesch), R.N., 1948-56*

Doris Brown, S.R.N., 1926-67*

Dora Carpenter, R.N., 1922-48

Morris and Margaret Chalfant, 1947-52

Fairy Chism, 1928-49

Clifford and Cassandra Church, 1947-61

Elizabeth Clark, R.N., 1946-53

Joseph and Lloree Clark, 1957-59

Manita Clegg, R.N., 1956-80

Fairy Cochlin, R.N., 1948-75

Elizabeth Cole, R.N., 1935-73[3]

Mary Cooper, 1928-70

Eric and Lilian Courtney-Smith, 1947-73*

Anna Lee Cox, R.N., 1928-49[4]

Maude Cretors, 1904-33

---

1. Also served in Germany.
2. Also served in Papua New Guinea.
3. Awarded M.B.E. by British government in 1960 for service to the Swazi people.
4. Also served North American Indian District.

Dorothy Davis (Cook), R.N.,
1940-72
Irvin and Fannie Dayhoff,
1919-60
Paul, M.D., and Margaret
Dayhoff, 1952—
Kathyren Dixon, R.N.,
1936-71
Armand and Pauline Doll,
1951-81[5]
Lois Drake, 1946-81
Rex and Betty Emslie,
1947-78*
William and Margaret, R.N.
(d. 1960), Esselstyn,
1928-70, Bessie Grose
Esselstyn, 1936-70
Miriam Evans, 1947-74*
Tabitha Evans, 1928-67*
Lawrence and Laura Ferree,
1925-43
Eileen Flitcroft, 1946-48
Evelyn Fox, R.N., 1932-47
Juanita Gardner, R.N.,
1950—[6]
James Graham, 1942-82;
Agnes Graham, 1944-82
Glenn Grose, 1936-41
Bessie (see Esselstyn)
Maurice and Geraldine Hall,
1956-75
George and Jeannette Hayse,
1947—
Paul Hetrick, Sr., 1945-79[7]
Abigail Hewson, R.N.,
1947-78*

Ivis Hopper (Powell), R.N.,
1945-62
David, M.D., and Agnes
Hynd, 1925-78[8]
Samuel, M.D., and Rosemary
(d. 1974) Hynd, 1950-78
Charles S. and Pearl Jenkins,
1920-64[9]
H. Irene Jester, 1938-70
David B. and Emily Jones,
1911-54*
Reginald E. and Ada Lilian
Jones, 1934-77*
T. Harold, M.D., and Aletta,
S.R.N., Jones, 1937-79*
Oliver and Louise Karker,
1952-81[10]
Irma Koffel, R.N., 1945—
Margaret Latta, 1931-54
Russell and Ruth Lewis,
1946-51, 1979—[11]
Frances Lively (Levens), R.N.,
1956-71
Edna Lochner, 1953—
Louise Long (Lesley),
1947-52
Ora Lovelace (West), 1917-44
Estella MacDonald, R.N.,
1934-54
Mary McKinlay, 1947-77
Avinell McNabb, R.N.,
1952—
Minnie Martin, R.N., 1919-45
Ruth Matchett, R.N., 1947—

---

5. Also served in Jamaica and the Caribbean.
6. Also served in Papua New Guinea.
7. Also served in Antigua.
8. Awarded O.B.E. in 1937, C.B.E. in 1947 by the British government.
9. Also served in Barbados.
10. Also served in Lebanon.
11. Also served in Barbados.

Wesley and Billie Ann Meek, 1946-51

Evelyn Mewes, 1958-74

Carl and Velma Mischke, 1932-63[12]

William and Juanita Moon, 1956—

Sylvia Oiness, R.N., 1946-77

Gladys Owen (Zahner), 1946-61

Bertha Parker, 1937-72

Hazel Pass, R.N., 1948—*

Lois Pass, R.N., 1943-77

Juanita Pate, R.N., 1955—

Marjorie Peel (Danner), 1956-76

Myrtle Pelley (Taylor), R.N., 1922-47

Joseph and Ellen Penn, Jr., 1945—

Joseph and Susan Penn, Sr., 1919-42

Floyd and Libbie Perkins, 1952-76

George and Gladys Pope, 1928-71*

Henry and Ruby Poteet, 1946-52

Evelyn Ramsey, M.D., 1957—[13]

Jessie Rennie, 1939-71

Eva Rixse, 1919-48

Louise Robinson (Chapman), 1920-42

Norman and Joan Salmons, 1949-72*

Arthur and Martha Savage, 1937-48

Elmer and Mary, R.N., Schmelzenbach, 1936-76

Lula Schmelzenbach, 1907-53

Paul and Mary Kate Schmelzenbach, 1944-51

Lorraine Schultz, R.N., 1943-77

Lauren, M.D., and Constance Seaman, 1944-49

H. A. and Etta Innis Shirley; H. A.,* 1911-45; Etta, 1907-46

Kenneth and Minnie Singleton, 1946—

Mabel Skinner, 1920-54[14]

Herman and Mary E. Spencer, 1951-80

Kenneth, M.D., and Anne Stark, 1949-73[15]

Philip and Mary Steigleder, 1941—

Oscar and Marjorie Stockwell, 1945—

Nellie Storey, S.R.N., 1949-72

Charles Hapgood and Irene Strickland, 1921-55*

John, M.D., and Eunice, R.N., Sutherland, 1955-68

Bessie Tallackson (Pointer), 1921-48

Mary Tanner, M.D., (Frame), 1930-41

Esther Thomas, R.N., 1947-72

Charles West, M.D., 1927-45;[16] see Ora Lovelace (West), 1917-44

---

12. Also served in the Virgin Islands.
13. Also served in Papua New Guinea.
14. Independent missionary to 1933; associate missionary, 1933-47.
15. Special Assignment in India, 1981.
16. Also served in China.

Lydia Wilke (Howard), R.N.,
1940-62[17]
John and Marjorie, R.N.,
Wise, 1946-79
Edwin and Phyllis
Wissbroecker, 1958-68[18]
Leona Youngblood (Myers),
1945-72

*International Holiness Mission before 1952.

Alaska

(transferred to Home Missions, 1948)
Lewis and Muriel, R.N.,
Hudgins, 1944-48[19]
Alfred and Bernice Morgan,
1940-47

Argentina

Dorothy Ahleman, 1944-81
Thomas and Ramona
Ainscough, 1956-76
John and Marie Cochran,
1936-73
Donald and Elizabeth Davis,
1958—
Spurgeon and Fae Hendrix,
1941-78[20]
Robert, R.N., and Lela, R.N.,
Jackson, 1943-51[21]

C. Lester and Veneta
Johnston, 1945-59,
1962-68[22]
Llewellyn and Florence
Lockwood, 1938-45
Guy C. and Ethel McHenry,
1921-34[23]
O. K. and Ruth Perkinson,
1952—[24]

Barbados

Mamie Bailey (Hendricks),
1936-52[25]
Robert and Grace Brown,
1956-80[26]
Robert and Susan Danielson,
1937-46
Lawrence and Betty Faul,
1952—[27]
Andrew Hendricks, 1948-52
(see Mamie Bailey
[Hendricks])
James I. and Nora Hill,
1926-39[28]
James and Helen Jones,
1944-72[29]

Bolivia

John and Janet Armstrong,
1950—[30]

---

17. Also served in the Cape Verde Islands.
18. Also served North American Indian District.
19. Alaska and Hawaii transferred to Home Missions in 1948.
20. Also served in Cuba, Uruguay, and Chile.
21. Also served in Africa.
22. Also served in Uruguay and as Latin American evangelist.
23. Also served in Peru.
24. Also served in Uruguay.
25. Also served in Trinidad.
26. Also served in Guyana; CHC missionaries in Pakistan, 1947-53.
27. Also served in Guyana, Trinidad, and Antigua.
28. Also served in Trinidad.
29. Also served in Panama.
30. Also served in Uruguay.

Ninevah and Eula Briles,
1945-52
Ronald and Sarah Denton,
1947-70[31]
Frank and Mary Van
Develder, 1955-57

Brazil
Charles and Roma Gates,
1958—

British Guiana (Guyana)
Donald and Elizabeth Ault,
1952-57
Everette Wayne and Elwanda
Knox, 1957-79
Herbert and Alyce Ratcliff,
1954—[32]

British Honduras (Belize)
Robert and Ina Ashley,
1954—[33]
Ronald and Ruth Bishop,
1944-61
Joyce Blair, R.N., 1943-76
David and Elizabeth
Browning, 1944—[34]
Lucille Broyles (Smith), R.N.,
1947-52
Edward and Margaret, R.N.,
Cairns, 1958-72
Ruth Dech, 1946—[35]
Mary Elverd, R.N., 1956-59

William and Gail Fowler,
1948—[36]
Quentin E., M.D., and Margie
Howard, 1954-56
Lois Santo (Labenski),
1953-57
Ina Smith, R.N., 1958-62
Leonard and Miriam York,
1952-60

Cape Verde Islands
John and Joana Diaz, 1900-38
Ernest and Jessie Eades,
1947-70
Clifford and Charlotte Gay,
1936-72
Roy and Gloria Henck,
1958—
Everette and Garnet Howard,
1935-75[37]
George and Mrs. Keeler,
1936-38
Earl and Gladys Mosteller,
1946—[38]
Elton and Margaret Wood,
1952—

Chile
Boyd and Neva Skinner,
1953—

China
Ruth Brickman (Williamson),
R.N., 1947-61[39]

---

31. Also served in Argentina, Uruguay, and Brazil.
32. Also served in Trinidad and Tobago, and Puerto Rico.
33. Also served in the Windward Islands.
34. Also served in Guyana and the Philippines.
35. Also served in Costa Rica.
36. Also served in Guyana, Trinidad, Nicaragua, and the Philippines.
37. Also served as superintendent of the Texas-Mexican District and Casa Robles.
38. Also served in Brazil and Portugal.
39. Also served in Africa.

Evelyn Eddy (Engstrom),
 R.N., 1938-41
Rudolph, M.D., and Lura
 Fitz, 1920-36, 1948-49
Catherine Flagler, 1903-38[40]
Hester Hayne, M.D., 1921-41
Bertie Karns (Ferguson),
 1919-41[41]
Arthur and Blanche, R.N.,
 Moses, 1939-44
Leon and Emma Osborn,
 1919-63[42]
Mary Pannell, R.N., 1925-41
John and Lillian Pattee,
 1936-72[43]
Geoffrey and Ann Royal,
 1936-41
Rhoda Schurman (Jones),
 1936-41
Mary Scott, 1940-49[44]
Francis and Ann Sutherland,
 1920-26, 1936-41
Myrl Thompson, R.N.,
 1930-35
Michael and Elizabeth Varro,
 1947-50
Ida Vieg, 1914-37
Henry, M.D., and Mabel
 Wesche, 1934-41

Harry and Katherine Wiese,
 1920-66[45]

Cuba
Howard and Modena
 Conrad, 1957—[46]
Ardee and Faith Coolidge,
 1952[47]
Frank and Lula (d. 1944)
 Ferguson, 1903-52[48]
Leona Gardner, 1902-38[49]
John and Patricia Hall,
 1947-67[50]
Lyle and Grace Prescott,
 1944-70[51]

Guatemala
Mayme Alexander, 1946-60
Richard and Annie
 Anderson, 1904-49
Russell (d. 1973) and
 Margaret, R.N., Birchard,
 1934-74[52]
William Coats, 1928-45, and
 Eugenia Phillips Coats,
 1917-45
Edward and Martha Davis,
 1921-45[53]
Elward and Cora Green,
 1955-67[54]

---

40. With other missions before 1929.
41. Also served in Japan.
42. Also served in Taiwan.
43. Also served in the Philippines.
44. Also served in Japan, 1976-78.
45. Also served in the Philippines and Taiwan.
46. Also served in Peru and Costa Rica.
47. Also served in Argentina, Chile, and Bolivia.
48. Also served in Ecuador, Peru, Bolivia, Argentina, and Mexico.
49. Also served in Guatemala and Belize.
50. Also served Miami Cuban work.
51. Also served in Puerto Rico and the Virgin Islands.
52. Also served in Nicaragua.
53. Also served Mexican-U.S. border.
54. Also served in Belize.

Harold and Gladys
    Hampton, 1941-80[55]
Harold and Ruth Hess,
    1942-56
Augie Holland, 1919-43[56]
Earl and Mabel Hunter,
    1946-58[57]
Robert and Pearl Ingram,
    1921-57
Neva Lane, 1921-55[58]
William (d. 1971) and
    Elizabeth Sedat, 1945—
Stanley and Norma Storey,
    1956—[59]
Ira and Valora True, 1921-25,
    1942-63[60]
William and Frances
    Vaughters, 1945-74[61]
Evelyn Ver Hoek (Guillermo),
    1951-73
Marilla Wales (Pope),
    1938-40
Allen and Elizabeth Wilson,
    1958—[62]

Haiti
Charles and Alberta, R.N.,
    Allstott, 1952-62
Max and Mary Alice, R.N.,
    Conder, 1953-61[63]

Paul and Mary Orjala,
    1950-64
Brian and Evelyn, R.N.,
    Vanciel, 1956-61[64]
Harry and Marion Rich,
    1957-71

Hawaii
*(transferred to Home Missions
    in 1948)*
Leo and Bernice Baldwin,
    1946-48

India
John and Mary Anderson,
    1936-70
Prescott and Bessie (d. 1958)
    Beals, 1920-63[65]
Ruby Blackman, 1920-54
Clarence and Marjorie, R.N.,
    Carter, 1950-62
Geraldine Chappell, R.N.,
    1941-78
Ralph[66] and Orpha (d. 1967)
    Cook, 1935-73
Ira, M.D., and Hilda Lee Cox,
    1952-73
Jean Darling, R.N., 1945—
Alberta Fletcher (Smith),
    R.N., 1951-60

---

55. Also served in Belize, Puerto Rico, U.S. Latin districts, and as Latin American evangelist.
56. Also served in Peru, Bolivia, and Belize.
57. Also served in Bolivia.
58. Also served in Peru.
59. Also served in El Salvador and Honduras.
60. Also served in Peru and as superintendent of the Western Latin American District.
61. Also served in the Spanish-American seminary, San Antonio.
62. Also served in El Salvador and Costa Rica.
63. Also served in Papua New Guinea.
64. Also served the North American Indian District.
65. Also served in Barbados, Trinidad, and Belize.
66. Also served in Trinidad and Tobago, and Jamaica.

Weldon and Ethel, R.N.,
Franklin, 1946-52
Leslie and Ellen Fritzlan,
1940-53
Agnes Gardner, R.N.,
1919-42
Bronell and Paula Greer,
1944—
Henrietta Hale
(Christianson), 1937-41
Mary Harper (Biddulph),
1952-59
Wallace and Phyllis Helm,
1956-67
Esther Howard, R.N., 1952—
Cleve and Juanita James,
1951-74[67]
Alvin and Naomi Kauffman,
1919-39[68]
Earl and Hazel Lee, 1946-60
John McKay, 1926-64; May
Tidwell McKay (d. 1935),
1920-35; Mary Hunter
McKay, 1937-64
Amanda Mellies, 1928-35
Hilda Moen, R.N., 1956—
William and Lenora Pease,
1954-80[69]
Ruth Rudolph, R.N., 1920-25,
1936-40
Bessie Seay, R.N., 1909-37[70]
Orpha Speicher, M.D.,
1936-77
Margaret Stewart, R.N.,
1932-40

Leighton and Gertrude Perry
Tracy, 1904-19, 1929-34
Agnes Willox, R.N., 1946-70[71]
Evelyn Witthoff, M.D.,
1941-73

Italy

Earl and Thelma (d. 1970)
Morgan, 1952-65,
1971—;[72] Norma Weis
Morgan, 1964-69,[73]
1971—

Japan

Merril and Myrtlebelle
Bennett, 1952—
Harrison and Doris Davis,
1950—
William and Florence (d.
1964) Eckel, 1916-64;
Catherine Perry Eckel
(Miller), 1952-64
Hubert and Virginia Helling,
1952-81
Bertie Karns (Ferguson),
1919-41[74]
Bartlett and Grace McKay,
1954-67
Maurice and Jeannette
Rhoden, 1956—
Doyle and Mattie Shepherd,
1948-67, 1979-81
Minnie Staples (Frazier),
1915-24, 1928-37
Pearl Wiley (Hanson),
1939-41[75]

---

67. Also served in Puerto Rico.
68. Also served in Palestine.
69. Also served one year in Jamaica.
70. Also served in Africa.
71. Also served in Belize.
72. Also served in Lebanon and Israel.
73. Also served in India.
74. Also served in China.
75. In Japan 1934-39 and after 1946 as an independent missionary.

Korea

Eldon and Marcella Cornett,
1957-72
Donald and Adeline Owens,
1954-66

Lebanon

Donald and Elva Reed,
1954-69

Mexico

Maurice and Arline (d. 1969)
Clinger, 1957-77;
Merilyn Manchester
Clinger (Nicaragua,
1966-69), Mexico,
1970-77[76]

Nicaragua

Esther Crain, 1945-59
Olvette Culley, R.N., 1952-61
Neva Flood, 1947—[77]
Dean and Gwendolyn
Galloway, 1953-71,
1974-77[78]
Lesper Heflin, R.N.,
1948-79[79]
James and Lucille Hudson,
1952-74[80]
Merilyn Manchester
(Clinger), 1966-77
Ruth Miller, 1956-71[81]

Louis and Evelyn Ragains,
1948-61, 1967—[82]
Cecil and Edna Rudeen,
1946-77[83]
Dale and Mildred Sievers,
1954-64
Harold and Evelyn Stanfield,
1943-77, 1976-80[84]
Cora Walker (McMillan),
1945-54
Mary Wallace, 1955—[85]

North American Indian

*(Only missionaries under
official appointment by
the department are listed.)*
G. H. and Olive Pearson,
1947—
Dowie and Theressa (d.
1952) Swarth, 1944-57

Palestine—Israel

Alexander and Hallie
Wachtel, 1952-76

Palestine—Jordan

Samuel and Hranoush
Krikorian, 1921-58[86]
William and Grace, R.N.,
Russell, 1947-57

Panama

Elmer and Dorothy Nelson,
1955—[87]

---

76. Also served in Mexico City language school.
77. Also served in Nicaragua.
78. Also served in Colombia.
79. Also served in Guatemala.
80. Also served in Mexico City language school.
81. Also served in Argentina.
82. Also served in Colombia.
83. Also served in the Spanish-American seminary, San Antonio.
84. Also served in Bolivia, Panama, Costa Rica, Guatemala, and Chile.
85. Also served in Chile.
86. Also served in Palestine-Israel.
87. Also served in Argentina.

Papua New Guinea

William Bromley, 1958-69, and Margaret Bromley, R.N., 1961—

Sidney (d. 1958) and Wanda Knox, 1955-75[88]

Peru

Clifford and Ruth Bicker, 1935-37

Oscar and Catherine Burchfield, 1940-54

Elvin and Margaret Douglass, 1947-80

Harry and Genevieve Flinner, 1954-65, 1970-77[89]

Clyde and Leona Golliher, 1952—

Howard Grantz, 1956-76, and Norine Roth Grantz, 1952-76

Robert and Maunette Gray, 1958—

Elsie Haselwood, 1928-34

Samuel and Gwladys Heap, 1935-75[90]

Darrel and Esther Larkin, 1944-45, 1949-51[91]

Marjorie Mayo, 1950-54

Mary Miller, 1954—

Harry and Jean Mingledorff, 1944-49

Ira and Lucille Taylor, 1934-67[92]

Phillip and Mary Torgrimson, Sr., 1947-77

David and Edith Walworth, 1928-38

Charles and Maud Wiman, 1920-22, 1935-41[93]

Roger Winans, 1914-49, and Mabel Park Winans, 1918-49

Edward and Ruth, R.N., Wyman, 1941-55, 1958-72[94]

Harry and Helen Zurcher, 1945-73[95]

Philippines

Roy and Erna Copelin, 1954—

Robert and Tillie McCroskey, Sr., 1956—

Joseph and Pearl Pitts, 1948-58

Adrian and Willene Rosa, 1952-55

Frances Vine, 1952-80

Stanley and Flora Wilson, 1958—

Puerto Rico

William and Juanita Porter, 1951—[96]

---

88. Wanda Knox also served in Palestine-Israel, 1980-81.

89. Also served in Chile and Uruguay.

90. Served in Colombia with the Calvary Holiness Church to 1955; also in Guatemala and Panama.

91. Also served in the Spanish-American seminary, San Antonio.

92. Also served in Bolivia.

93. Also served in Japan.

94. Also served in the Spanish-American seminary, San Antonio; and in Cuba, Belize, and as Latin American evangelist.

95. Also served in Puerto Rico.

96. Also served in the Spanish American seminary, San Antonio; and in New Zealand and Venezuela.

Syria

Donald and Frances
De Pasquale, 1945-69[97]
Laurice Thahabiyah, 1948-50
Mulhim and Emma
Thahabiyah, 1920-55

Taiwan

John and Natalie Holstead,
1956—[98]

Texas-Mexican

Fred and Lois Reedy, 1946-50

Trinidad and Tobago

Russell and Thelma Brunt,
1957—

Wesley and Modelle Harmon,
1952-74
Raymond and Ruth Miller,
1949-63[99]
Lelan and Wavy Rogers,
1944-52[100]
Ruth Saxon, D.Min., 1954—
Howard and Dorothy Sayes,
1953-65
Trueman and Ruthellen
Shelton, 1946-49

Uruguay

Robert and Retha Wellmon,
1945-65, 1976-77[101]

---

97. Also served in Lebanon.
98. Also served in Hong Kong.
99. Also served in Taiwan.
100. Also served in Guyana.
101. Also served in a special assignment in El Salvador.

Bibliography

Books

Ahlstrom, Sidney E. *A Religious History of the American People.* 2 vols. Garden City, N.Y.: Doubleday and Co., 1975.

Armstrong, Kenneth S. *Face to Face with the Church of the Nazarene.* Boulder, Colo.: Johnson Publishing Co., 1958.

Baird, William. *The Corinthian Church: A Biblical Approach to Urban Culture.* New York: Abingdon Press, 1964.

Baker, Robert A. *A Summary of Church History.* Nashville: Broadman Press, 1959.

Bangs, Carl. *Our Roots of Belief: Biblical Faith and Faithful Theology.* Kansas City: Beacon Hill Press of Kansas City, 1981.

Beals, Prescott L. *India Reborn: The Story of Evangelism in India.* Kansas City: Beacon Hill Press, 1954.

Bedwell, Kenneth. *Black Gold: The Story of the IHM in Africa.* Kansas City: Beacon Hill Press, 1953.

Bennett, Merril. *Okinawa Lifeline.* Kansas City: Nazarene Publishing House, 1964.

Birchard, Russell and Margaret Anderson. *Richard Simpson Anderson: Pioneer Missionary to Central America.* Kansas City: Beacon Hill Press, 1951.

Bowes, Alpin P., ed. *He That Winneth Souls: Illustrations of Personal Evangelism in the Mid-Century Crusade for Souls.* Kansas City: Nazarene Publishing House, 1950.

Brauer, Jerald C. *Protestantism in America.* Rev. ed. Philadelphia: Westminster Press, 1974.

Bustle, Louie and Ellen. *Miracles Are Happening in the Dominican Republic.* Kansas City: Nazarene Publishing House, 1978.

Cameron, James B. *Eastern Nazarene College: The First Fifty Years, 1900-1950.* Kansas City: Nazarene Publishing House, 1968.

Carlson, Russell L. *A Documentary Sourcebook for the History of the Church of the Nazarene.* Unpublished B.D. thesis. Kansas City, Mo.: Nazarene Theological Seminary, 1955.

Chalfant, E. O. *Forty Years on the Firing Line.* Kansas City: Beacon Hill Press, 1951.

Chapman, James Blaine. *A History of the Church of the Nazarene.* Kansas City: Nazarene Publishing House, 1926.

―――. *30,000 Miles of Missionary Travel.* Kansas City: Nazarene Publishing House, 1931.

―――. *My Wife.* Kansas City: Nazarene Publishing House, 1940.

―――. *Bud Robinson: A Brother Beloved.* Kansas City: Beacon Hill Press, 1943.

Chapman, Louise Robinson. *The Problem of Africa.* Kansas City: Beacon Hill Press, 1952.

Clark, Elmer T. *The Small Sects in America.* Rev. ed. Nashville: Abingdon-Cokesbury Press, 1949. First published in 1937.

Cole, Elizabeth. *Give Me This Mountain.* Kansas City: Nazarene Publishing House, 1959.

Conrad, W. Howard. *South America in Perspective.* Kansas City: Nazarene Publishing House, 1974.

Cook, Franklin. *Water from Deep Wells.* Kansas City: Nazarene Publishing House, 1977.

Corbett, C. T. *Soldier of the Cross: The Life of J. G. Morrison.* Kansas City: Beacon Hill Press, 1956.

———. *Our Nazarene Pioneers.* Kansas City: Nazarene Publishing House, 1958.

———. *Pioneer Builders: Men Who Helped Shape the Church of the Nazarene in Its Formative Years.* Kansas City: Beacon Hill Press of Kansas City, 1979.

Corlett, D. Shelby. *Spirit-filled: The Life of the Rev. James Blaine Chapman, D.D.* Kansas City: Nazarene Publishing House, 1948.

———. *Soul Winning Through Visitation Evangelism.* Kansas City: Nazarene Publishing House, 1948.

Dayton, Donald W. *Discovering an Evangelical Heritage.* New York: Harper and Row, 1976.

DeLong, Russell V., and Taylor, Mendell L. *Fifty Years of Nazarene Missions.* Vol. 2 of 3 vols. Kansas City: Beacon Hill Press, 1955.

Dieter, Melvin E. *The Holiness Revival of the Nineteenth Century.* Metuchen, N.J.: Scarecrow Press, 1980.

Dooley, Bertha. *Northwest Nazarene College.* Nampa, Ida.: Northwest Nazarene College, 1938.

DuBois, Lauriston J., ed. and comp. *The Chaplains See World Missions.* Kansas City: Nazarene Publishing House, 1946.

———. *The Pastor and Visitation Evangelism.* Kansas City: Nazarene Publishing House, 1948.

Dunn, Samuel L.; Reglin, G. Ray; Nielson, Joseph; and Deasley, Alex R. G. *Opportunity Unlimited: The Church of the Nazarene in the Year 2000.* Kansas City: Beacon Hill Press of Kansas City, 1981.

Earle, Ralph. *Fields Afar: Nazarene Missions in the Far East, India, and the South Pacific.* Kansas City: Nazarene Publishing House, 1969.

Eckel, William A. *Japan Now.* Kansas City: Nazarene Publishing House, 1949.

———. *The Pendulum Swings.* Kansas City: Beacon Hill Press, 1957.

Esperilla, Moises. *South of the Border.* Kansas City: Nazarene Publishing House, 1981.

Esselstyn, William C. *Nazarene Missions in South Africa.* Kansas City: Nazarene Publishing House, 1952.

Fisher, C. William. *The Time Is Now.* Kansas City: Nazarene Publishing House, 1950.

Ford, Jack. *In the Steps of John Wesley: The Church of the Nazarene in Britain.* Kansas City: Nazarene Publishing House, 1968.

Frame, George. *Blood Brother of the Swazis: The Life Story of David Hynd.* Kansas City: Nazarene Publishing House, 1952.

Fritz, Maxine Fitz. *But God Gives a Song: The Story of Dr. and Mrs. R. G. Fitz.* Kansas City: Nazarene Publishing House, 1973.

Garraty, John A. *The American Nation: A History of the United States.* 4th ed. New York: Harper and Row, Publishers, 1979.

Gaustad, Edwin Scott. *A Religious History of America.* New York: Harper and Row, 1974.

Gish, Carol. *Touched by the Divine: The Story of Fairy Chism.* Kansas City: Beacon Hill Press, 1952.

————. *The Magic Circle of the Caribbean.* Kansas City: Nazarene Publishing House, 1953.

————. *Missionary Frontiers at Home.* Kansas City: Nazarene Publishing House, 1960.

————. *Mediterranean Missions.* Kansas City: Nazarene Publishing House, 1965.

Goodnow, Edith P., ed. *New Missionary Frontiers.* Kansas City: Nazarene Publishing House, n.d.

Hamlin, Howard H. *The Challenge of the Orient.* Kansas City: Beacon Hill Press, 1949.

Handy, Robert T. *A History of the Churches in the United States and Canada.* New York: Oxford University Press, 1977.

Harper, Albert F., and Kauffman, Elmer H. *First Steps in Visitation Evangelism.* Kansas City: Nazarene Publishing House, 1948.

————, ed. *Northwest Nazarene College: Twenty-five Years of Progress: Silver Anniversary, 1913-1938.* Nampa, Ida.: Northwest Nazarene College, 1938.

Henry, Carl F. H. *The Uneasy Conscience of Modern Fundamentalism.* Grand Rapids: William B. Eerdmans Publishing Co., 1947.

Herberg, Will. *Protestant, Catholic, Jew: An Essay in American Religious Sociology.* New ed., rev. Garden City, N.Y.: Anchor Books, Doubleday and Co., 1960.

Hinshaw, Amy N. *In Labors Abundant: A Biography of H. F. Reynolds, D.D.* Kansas City: Nazarene Publishing House, n.d.

Hudson, James. *Guatemala: 60 Years.* Kansas City: Nazarene Publishing House, 1976.

Hudson, Winthrop S. *American Protestantism.* Chicago History of American Civilization, edited by Daniel Boorstein. Chicago: University of Chicago Press, 1961.

————. *Religion in America.* 2nd ed. New York: Charles Scribner's Sons, 1973.

Hynd, David. *Africa Emerging.* Kansas City: Nazarene Publishing House, 1959.

Isayama, Nobumi. *Consider Nippon: Incidents from My Life.* Kansas City: Beacon Hill Press, 1957.

Johnson, Jerald D. (Jerry). *We Live in Germany.* Kansas City: Nazarene Publishing House, 1960.

―――. *The International Experience.* Kansas City: Nazarene Publishing House, 1982.

Johnson, Paul. *A History of Christianity.* London: Weidenfeld and Nicholson, 1976.

Johnson, Jon. *Will Evangelicalism Survive Its Own Popularity?* Grand Rapids: Zondervan Publishing House, 1980.

Jones, Charles Edwin. *Perfectionist Persuasion: The Holiness Movement and American Methodism, 1867-1936.* ATLA Monograph Series, no. 5. Metuchen, N.J.: Scarecrow Press, 1974.

Kida, Ross. *The Many Faces of Japan.* Kansas City: Nazarene Publishing House, 1964.

Knott, James Proctor. *History of Pasadena College.* Pasadena, Calif.: Pasadena College, 1960.

Knox, John. *Life in Christ Jesus.* Greenwich, Conn.: Seabury Press, 1961.

Knox, Sidney C. *The Call of New Guinea.* Kansas City: Nazarene Publishing House, 1958.

Latourette, Kenneth Scott. *A History of Christianity.* 2 vols. Rev. ed. New York: Harper and Row, 1975.

Lillenas, Haldor. *Down Melody Lane.* Kansas City: Nazarene Publishing House, 1953.

Link, Arthur S., and Catton, William B. *American Epoch: A History of the United States Since 1900.* 3 vols. 4th ed. New York: Albert A. Knopf, 1973.

Lovelace, Richard E. *Dynamics of Spiritual Life: An Evangelical Theology of Renewal.* Downers Grove, Ill.: InterVarsity Press, 1980.

Lunn, M. *Hiram F. Reynolds: Mr. World Missionary.* Kansas City: Nazarene Publishing House, 1968.

McConnell, C. A. *The Potter's Vessel.* Kansas City: Beacon Hill Press, 1946.

Marsden, George M. *Fundamentalism and American Culture: The Shaping of Twentieth-Century Evangelicalism, 1870-1925.* New York: Oxford University Press, 1980.

Miller, Basil. *Susan N. Fitkin: For God and Missions.* Kansas City: Nazarene Publishing House, n.d.

―――. *Out Under the Stars.* Kansas City: Nazarene Publishing House, 1941.

―――. *Missionaries in Action.* 2 vols. Kansas City: Nazarene Publishing House, 1941, 1942.

―――. *Bud Robinson: Miracle of Grace.* Kansas City: Beacon Hill Press, 1947.

―――. *Miracle in Cape Verde: The Story of Everette and Garnet Howard.* Kansas City: Beacon Hill Press, 1950.

Miller, Ruth A. *The Darkest Side of the Road.* Kansas City: Nazarene Publishing House, 1962.

Mitchell, T. Crichton. *To Serve the Present Age: The Church of the Nazarene in the British Isles.* Kansas City: Nazarene Publishing House, 1980.

Moberg, David. *The Great Reversal: Evangelism Versus Social Concern.* Philadelphia: J. B. Lippincott, 1972.

Mulder, John M., and Wilson, John F., eds. *Religion in American History.* Englewood Cliffs, N.J.: Prentice-Hall, 1978.

Mund, Fred A. *Keep the Music Ringing: A Short History of the Hymnody of the Church of the Nazarene.* n.p., n.d.

Nazarene Foreign Missionary Society. *Ten Years of Alabaster.* Kansas City: Nazarene Publishing House, 1958.

Norwood, Frederick A. *The Story of American Methodism.* Nashville: Abingdon Press, 1974.

Orjala, Paul R. *This Is Haiti.* Kansas City: Nazarene Publishing House, 1961.

————. *Christ in the Caribbean.* Kansas City: Nazarene Publishing House, 1970.

Owens, Donald. *Sing, Ye Islands.* Kansas City: Nazarene Publishing House, 1979.

Parker, J. Fred. *From East to Western Sea: A Brief History of the Church of the Nazarene in Canada.* Kansas City: Nazarene Publishing House, 1971.

————. *God's Little Giant: Prescott L. Beals.* Kansas City: Nazarene Publishing House, 1980.

Parrott, Leslie. *Sons of Africa: Stories from the Life of Elmer Schmelzenbach.* Kansas City: Beacon Hill Press of Kansas City, 1979.

Pattee, John W. *Hazardous Days in China.* Pasadena, Calif.:N.p., n.d.

Patterson, James T. *America in the Twentieth Century: A History.* New York: Harcourt Brace Jovanovich, 1976.

Pearson, G. H. *The Transformed Red Man.* Kansas City: Beacon Hill Press, 1956.

Peters, John L. *Christian Perfection and American Methodism.* New York: Abingdon Press, 1956.

Pitts, Joseph S. *Mission to the Philippines.* Kansas City: Beacon Hill Press, 1956.

Powers, Hardy C. *And Now New Guinea.* Kansas City: Nazarene Publishing House, 1955.

Prescott, Lyle. *Light in Latin America.* Kansas City: Nazarene Publishing House, 1961.

————. *Our 25 Years in the Caribbean.* Kansas City: Nazarene Publishing House, 1970.

Price, Ross E. *H. Orton Wiley: Servant and Savant.* Nampa, Ida.: Northwest Nazarene College, 1963.

Ramquist, Grace. *And Many Believed.* Kansas City: Nazarene Publishing House, 1951.

————. *No Respecter of Persons.* Kansas City: Nazarene Publishing House, 1962.

————. *H. Orton Wiley: The Boy Who Loved School.* Kansas City: Beacon Hill Press, 1963.

Rauhut, Dorothy DeBoard. *My Papá: W. I. DeBoard, a Nazarene Pioneer.* Kansas City: Pedestal Press, 1980.

Redford, M. E. *The Rise of the Church of the Nazarene.* Kansas City: Nazarene Publishing House, 1948.

Robinson, Reuben. *My Life's Story.* Kansas City: Nazarene Publishing House, 1928.

Rogers, Warren A., with Vogt, Kenneth. *From Sharecropper to Goodwill Ambassador.* Kansas City: Beacon Hill Press of Kansas City, 1979.

Sanner, A. E. *John W. Goodwin: A Biography.* Kansas City: Nazarene Publishing House, 1945.

Scott, Mary L. *Kept in Safeguard.* Kansas City: Nazarene Publishing House, 1977.

Shelley, Bruce L. *Evangelicalism in America.* Grand Rapids: William B. Eerdmans Publishing Co., 1967.

Shoemaker, Helen Smith. *I Stand by the Door: The Life of Sam Shoemaker.* New York: Harper and Row, Publishers, 1967.

Smee, John M. *The Rising Caribbean Tide.* Kansas City: Nazarene Publishing House, 1978.

Smith, H. Shelton; Handy, Robert T.; Loetscher, Lefferts A. *American Christianity: An Historical Interpretation with Representative Documents.* 2 vols. New York: Chas. Scribner's Sons, 1963.

Smith, Timothy L. *Called unto Holiness: The Story of the Nazarenes: The Formative Years.* Kansas City: Nazarene Publishing House, 1962.

———. *Revivalism and Social Reform: American Protestantism on the Eve of the Civil War.* Baltimore: Johns Hopkins University Press, 1980.

———. *Nazarenes and the Wesleyan Mission.* Can We Learn from Our History? Kansas City: Beacon Hill Press of Kansas City, 1979.

Spangenberg, Alice. *Jerusalem and Beyond.* Kansas City: Nazarene Publishing House, 1950.

———. *South America: Eucalyptus Country.* Kansas City: Nazarene Publishing House, 1967.

Spell, Kathleen. *Haiti Diary: Compiled from the Letters of Paul Orjala.* Kansas City: Beacon Hill Press, 1953.

Spruce, Fletcher Clark. *Revive Us Again.* Kansas City: Beacon Hill Press, n.d.

Strickland, Charles H. *African Adventure.* Kansas City: Nazarene Publishing House, 1958.

Swain, R. Alfred. *Ecuador: Open Door on the Equator.* Kansas City: Nazarene Publishing House, 1974.

Swann, Alline. *Song in the Night: The Story of Dr. and Mrs. Thomas E. Mangum.* Kansas City: Beacon Hill Press, 1957.

Swarth, Dowie, with Oster, John C. *Ever the Pioneer: The Romance of Home Missions.* Kansas City: Nazarene Publishing House, 1978.

Swim, Roy E. *A History of Nazarene Missions.* 3rd ed. Kansas City: Nazarene Publishing House, 1936.

Synan, Vinson. *The Holiness-Pentecostal Movement in the United States.* Grand Rapids: William B. Eerdmans Publishing Co., 1971.

Tashjian, Jirair. *Taiwan in Transition.* Kansas City: Nazarene Publishing House, 1977.

Taylor, Lucile. *Tribes and Nations from the South.* Kansas City: Nazarene Publishing House, 1960.

Taylor, Mendell. *Nazarene Youth in Conquest for Christ.* Kansas City: Nazarene Publishing House, 1948.

———. *Fifty Years of Nazarene Missions.* 3 vols. Vol. 2 with R. V. DeLong. Kansas City: Beacon Hill Press, 1952, 1955, 1958.

Taylor, Myrtle A. Pelley. *'Neath the Warm Southern Cross.* Kansas City: Nazarene Publishing House, 1959.

Taylor, Richard S. *Our Pacific Outposts.* Kansas City: Beacon Hill Press, 1956.

Temple, Helen. *Of Whom the World Was Not Worthy: The Story of Samuel Krikorian.* Kansas City: Nazarene Publishing House, 1972.

———. *Like a Tree by the River: The Story of C. E. Morales.* Kansas City: Nazarene Publishing House, 1973.

Thomson, Dorothy J. *Vine of His Planting: History of Canadian Nazarene College.* Edmonton, Alberta: Commercial Printers, 1961.

Tracy, Olive G. *Tracy Sahib of India.* Kansas City: Beacon Hill Press, 1954.

———. *The Nations and the Isles.* Kansas City: Nazarene Publishing House, 1958.

Tyner, Juliaette, and Eckel, Catherine. *God's Samurai: The Life and Work of Dr. William A. Eckel.* Kansas City: Nazarene Publishing House, 1979.

Vanderpool, Ramon P. *The Life and Ministry of J. G. Morrison.* Unpublished B. D. thesis. Kansas City, Mo.: Nazarene Theological Seminary, 1955.

Vaughn, Ruth. *Proclaiming Christ in Central America.* Kansas City: Nazarene Publishing House, 1976.

Vaughters, William C. *Fruits of Progress: The Church of the Nazarene in Mexico and Central America.* Kansas City: Nazarene Publishing House, 1968.

Wells, David F., and Woodbridge, John D. *The Evangelicals.* Nashville: Abingdon Press, 1975.

Whitsett, Eleanor. *A History of the Lillenas Publishing Company and Its Relationship to the Music of the Church of the Nazarene.* Abstract of a Master of Music thesis presented to the University of Missouri, 1972. Kansas City: Nazarene Publishing House, n.d.

Wiley, H. Orton. *Christian Theology.* 3 vols. Kansas City: Nazarene Publishing House, 1940-43.

Wiley, H. Orton, and Culbertson, Paul T. *Introduction to Christian Theology.* Kansas City: Nazarene Publishing House, 1946.

Williamson, G. B. *Sent Forth by the Holy Ghost: The Life of R. C. Ingram.* Kansas City: Nazarene Publishing House, 1960.

———. *Missionary Safari.* Kansas City: Nazarene Publishing House, 1962.

———. *Roy T. Williams: Servant of God.* Rev. ed. Kansas City: Nazarene Publishing House, 1970.

Wise, George C. *Reverend Bud Robinson.* Louisville, Ky.: Pentecostal Publishing Co., 1946.

Witthoff, Evelyn M., M.D., and Chappell, Geraldine V., R.N. *Three Years Internment in Santo Tomas.* Kansas City: Beacon Hill Press, n.d.

Woodbridge, John D.; Noll, Mark A.; and Hatch, Nathan O. *The Gospel in America*. Grand Rapids: Zondervan Publishing House, 1979.

Worcester, Paul W. *The Master Key*. Tabor, Ia., 1966.

Wynkoop, Mildred Bangs. *The Trevecca Story: 75 Years of Christian Service*. Nashville: Trevecca College Press, 1976.

Yearbook of American Churches, published variously by the Association Press, The Yearbook of American Churches Press, and the National Council of Churches; volumes as cited.

Young, Samuel. *God's Unfailing Faithfulness: The Life of Charles S. Jenkins*. Kansas City: Nazarene Publishing House, 1961.

Articles or Chapters

Handy, Robert T. "The American Religious Depression." In *Religion in American History*, edited by John M. Mulder and John F. Wilson. Englewood Cliffs, N.J.: Prentice-Hall, 1978.

Linder, Robert B. "The Resurgence of Evangelical Social Concern." In Wells, David F., and Woodbridge, John D., *The Evangelicals*, Nashville: Abingdon Press, 1974. pp. 204-5.

Moberg, David O. "Fundamentalists and Evangelicals in Society." In Wells and Woodbridge, *The Evangelicals*, pp. 156-74.

Rees, Paul S. "The Positive Power of Negative Thinking." *World Vision Magazine*, vol. 14, no. 2, p. 32.

Unpublished Materials

Barney, Willis Dell. "The Church of the Nazarene and the North American Indian." B.D. thesis, Nazarene Theological Seminary, Kansas City, 1949.

Cantrell, Roy H. "The History of Bethany Nazarene College." D.R.E. diss., Southwestern Baptist Theological Seminary, Fort Worth, 1955.

Cubie, Alexander P. "The History of the International Holiness Mission." B.D. thesis, Nazarene Theological Seminary, Kansas City, 1954.

Galloway, Chester O. "The Development and Growth of the Lay Training Program of the Church of the Nazarene." B.D. thesis, Nazarene Theological Seminary, Kansas City, 1955.

Harding, Robert E. "A History of the General Board of the Church of the Nazarene." B.D. thesis, Nazarene Theological Seminary, Kansas City, 1948.

Harper, Albert F. "The Administration of President Gilmore." Paper, Northwest Nazarene College, Nampa, Ida., 1976.

Hubbard, Walter M. "History of the First Seven Years of Nazarene Theological Seminary." B.D. thesis, Nazarene Theological Seminary, Kansas City, 1953.

Ingle, Robert Lewis. "The Changing Spatial Distribution of the Church of the Nazarene." M.S. thesis, Oklahoma State University, Norman, Okla., 1973.

Jordan, Orbus E. "A History of the Official Publications of the Church of the Nazarene." B.D. thesis, Nazarene Theological Seminary, Kansas City, 1949.

Ketner, Francis D., Jr. "The History of the Church of the Nazarene in Great Britain." B.D. thesis, Nazarene Theological Seminary, Kansas City, 1956.

Keys, Clifford E., Jr. "Some Values of the Chaplaincy for the Nazarene Minister." B.D. thesis, Nazarene Theological Seminary, Kansas City, 1953.

Lakey, Billy J. "The Contribution of the Nazarene Publishing House to the Church of the Nazarene." B.D. thesis, Nazarene Theological Seminary, Kansas City, 1954.

McNeely, Robert William. "The Work and Message of Armed Service Chaplains from the Church of the Nazarene." B.D. thesis, Nazarene Theological Seminary, Kansas City, 1953.

Mewes, Evelyn. "Foreign Mission Fields Entered by the Church of the Nazarene Between 1946 and 1956." Nazarene Theological Seminary, Kansas City, 1946.

Philo, L. C. "The Historical Development and Present Status of the Educational Institutions of the Church of the Nazarene." Ph.D. diss., University of Oklahoma, Norman, Okla., 1958.

Prince, Bill J. "Comparative Study of the Lives and Homiletical Style of Charles G. Finney and Howard V. Miller." B.D. thesis, Nazarene Theological Seminary, Kansas City, 1955.

Rawlings, Elden Everette. "A History of the Nazarene Publishing House." M.A. thesis, University of Oklahoma, Norman, Okla., 1960.

Ray, Roy Fremont. "The Church of the Nazarene and Its Colleges." Th.D. diss., Central Baptist Theological Seminary, Kansas City, Kans., 1958.

Reed, Harold W. "Growth of a Contemporary Sec-type Institution as Reflected in the Development of the Church of the Nazarene." Th.D. diss., University of Southern California, Los Angeles, 1943.

Rice, Kenneth S. "The History and Significance of Leadership Training and Christian Service Training in the Church of the Nazarene." D.R.E. diss., Southwestern Baptist Theological Seminary, Fort Worth, 1956.

Robinson, Kenneth. "Educational Development in the Church of the Nazarene." B.D. thesis, Nazarene Theological Seminary, Kansas City, 1948.

Rogers, Homer. "A History of the Crusade for Souls and Its Effect upon the Church of the Nazarene." B.D. thesis, Nazarene Theological Seminary, Kansas City, 1956.

Sanner, A. E. "The History of Casa Robles." Paper, Mar. 31, 1979.

Scott, Earl Prentice. "The Historical Development of Polity in the Church of the Nazarene." B.D. thesis, Nazarene Theological Seminary, Kansas City, 1950.

Sutherland, Francis C. "The Ten Years of President Lewis T. Corlett, D.D." Amendments by Dr. L. T. Corlett, edited by L. Alline Swann. Manuscript, Northwest Nazarene College, Nampa. Ida., 1975.

———. "History of Northwest Nazarene College." Manuscript, Northwest Nazarene College, Nampa, Ida., 1962.

Swartley, Charles William. "A History of Evangelism in the Church of the Nazarene." B.D. thesis, Nazarene Theological Seminary, Kansas City, 1955.

Taylor, Mendell L. "Handbook of Historical Documents of the Church of the Nazarene." Mimeographed, Nazarene Theological Seminary, Kansas City, n.d.

Watkin, Frank W. "A History of the General Superintendency of the Church of the Nazarene." B.D. thesis, Nazarene Theological Seminary, Kansas City, 1949.

Representative Personal Interviews

Lewis T. Corlett, Nov. 12, 1981
Oscar J. Finch, May 16, 1981
Howard H. Hamlin, Dec. 11, 1981
Albert Lown, July 11, 1979
M. A. "Bud" Lunn, Nov. 11, 1980
Percy H. Lunn, Nov. 6, 1980
Mark R. Moore, Dec. 10, 1981
Honorato T. Reza, Dec. 8, 1981
A. E. Sanner, Apr. 3, 1981
John Stockton, Apr. 29, 1981
C. H. Strickland, Dec. 9, 1981
G. B. Williamson, July 17, 1976
T. W. Willingham, Dec. 9, 1981
Samuel Young, Feb. 16, 1977, and Dec. 10, 1981

Minutes and Proceedings

"Minutes of the Board of General Superintendents, Church of the Nazarene," 1930-60. Unpublished.

Proceedings of the General Conventions of the Nazarene Young People's Society. Published in connection with each General Convention, 1932-60.

Minutes of the General Conventions of the Women's Foreign Missionary Society/Nazarene Foreign Missionary Society. Published in connection with each General Convention, 1932-60.

Manual of the Church of the Nazarene. Published in connection with each General Assembly. Kansas City: Nazarene Publishing House, 1932-60.

Journal of the General Assembly of the Church of the Nazarene. Published in connection with each General Assembly. Kansas City: Nazarene Publishing House, 1932-60.

Proceedings of the General Board of the Church of the Nazarene and Its Departments. Published in connection with each annual meeting of the General Board. Kansas City: Nazarene Publishing House, 1932-60.

Index

Advent Christian Church 47
Accreditation (colleges) 128, 149, 275
Africa 27, 28, 39, 117
Africa Evangelistic Band 247
Ahlstrom, Sydney 18, 23
Airhart, Arnold E. 238, 294
Alabaster Fund 236-37
Alaska 145, 175-77
Alberta School of Evangelism 45
"All Out for Souls" 160-61, 229
Allshouse, William C. 148, 212
Alstott, Charles and Alberta 253
American Association of
    Theological Schools 207
Anderson, T. M. 61
La Antorcha Dominical 196
Apostolic Holiness Church 44
Argentina 39, 116, 118
Arkansas Holiness College 43
Armstrong, Ernest 148
Armstrong, Jack and Janet 193
Armstrong, William T. 140
Articles of Faith 59-60
Asbury College 27
Association of Pentecostal Churches
    of America 24-26, 28, 38, 58
Atkinson, Elbert L. 139-40
Atteberry, V. B. 51
Aughey, Mrs. T. D. 50
Ault, Donald and Elizabeth 194
Australia 180-85
Aycock, Jarrette and Dell 50, 69, 147
Baldwin, Leo 177-78
Barbados 40
Bates, J. E. 49
Beacon Hill Press of Kansas City 148
Beals, Prescott 93, 95, 209
Beech Lawn College 204, 263, 265
Belew, P. P. 51, 77, 105
Belize 38
Benedum, O. L. 123, 226
Benner, Hugh C. 207-9, 214, 222, 242, 259
Bennett, Merril and Myrtlebelle 189
Benson, Erwin G. 102, 173
Benson, Mrs. John T. 36
Berg, Albert A. E. 181, 184, 279
Bethany Nazarene College 275, 294

Bethany-Peniel College 42, 124, 212, 238, 275
BeVier, Charles 24
Bhujbal, Samuel J. 115
Bible Missionary Church 273
Bicker, Rev. and Mrs. Clifford 94, 97
Birchard, Russell and Margaret 94, 97
Blacks, Among the 197-200
Board of General
    Superintendents 162, 168-70
Bolivia 192-93
Bowes, Alpin P. 225, 230
Bowman, Clarence 199
Bracken, A. K. 43, 49, 77, 120, 124, 148
Brazil 293
Bresee College 44, 102, 110, 148, 212
Bresee Memorial Hospital
    (China) 93, 96
Bresee, P. F. 11, 25, 27, 28, 32, 47, 167
Bresee, Mrs. Paul (Ada) 36, 50, 110, 133, 202
Brickman, Ruth 190
Briles, Ninevah and Eula 192
British Guiana (now Guyana) 194
British Honduras (now Belize) 38
British Isles 260-66
British Isles Nazarene College 204, 266, 275
British West Indies 40, 116
Brotherhood of Saint Stephen 37
Brown, Robert and Grace 265
Browning, David and Elizabeth 194
Browning, Raymond 69, 123, 147
"By My Spirit" 257
Byron, Lloyd B. 147
Cairns, Edward and Margaret 265
Calgary Bible Institute 45
Calvary Holiness Church 106, 204, 261-66
Canadian Nazarene College 45, 125, 148, 213, 240, 294
Canal Zone 284-85
Cantrell, Roy H. 123, 212, 226
Cape Verde Islands 25, 28, 38, 97
Caravan program 173
Carman, E. S. 49
Carmichael, Vernal 226

Carpenter, Dora 94
Casa Robles 53, 201-2
Central Evangelical Holiness
    Association 24
Central Nazarene University 43
Chalfant, E. O. 51-52, 105, 206, 242
Chambers, Leon 199-200
Chapman, J. Wilbur 19
Chapman, James B. 27, 47, 56, 68, 70,
    74, 83, 96, 99, 111, 114-15,
    133-34, 147, 154, 159, 164,
    166-68, 205, 211, 220, 222, 233
Chapman, Louise Robinson 123, 219,
    226, 237, 256, 281, 287
Chappell, Geraldine 141
Chesson, A. C. 182, 183, 184
China 27-28, 39, 93, 95-96, 106,
    116, 140-41, 190-91, 219
Christian Service Training 149-50
Christian Theology, Vols. 1, 2, 3 145-47
Chung, Robert 249-51
Church Extension 35
Church of God (Anderson, Ind.) 23
Church School Builder 173
Church Schools 37
Civil Rights 289
Clarke, Arthur A. 182, 183, 184
Codding, Rev. and Mrs. Roy G. 50
Cole, Elizabeth 97
Collins, A. E. 212
Come Ye Apart 147
Commission on Education 239-41
Commission on Location of
    General Interests 242-43
Commission on Medical
    Missions 280-82
Communism 75-76
Company E 37
Conder, Max and Mary Alice 253, 280
Conference on Evangelism 211, 297
Congregationalism 32
Conquest 175
Conrad, Howard and Modena 194
Conscientious objectors 136
Conscription Law 132
Cook, Ralph and Orpha 97
Coolidge, Ardee and Faith 194
Corlett, D. Shelby 9, 37, 49, 50, 70,
    74, 84, 98, 100, 105, 110,
    112, 135, 137, 139, 167, 223-24
Corlett, Lewis T. 148, 226, 259
Cornett, Eldon and Marcella 251
"Correlated Board" 35
Cove, Mary E. 50

Cox, Dr. Ira Cox, Jr., and
    Hilda Lee 282
Cretors, Maude 92
Crusade for Souls 105, 232, 258, 289
Cuba 29, 193-94
Culbertson, Paul T. 146
Cunningham, R. W. 198-99
Davis, C. W. 51
Davis, C. Howard 19
Davis, Mrs. Florence 50
Davis, Harrison and Doris 189
Deets Pacific Bible College 26, 44
Deisenroth, J. Bruce 149, 242
DeJernett, E. C. 27
Del Rosso, Alfredo 191
DeLong, Russell V. 104, 148, 206, 208,
    210, 215, 289, 294
DeLong, Mrs. R. V. 158
Denton, Ronald and Sarah 193, 253
Department of Church Schools 35, 50
Department of Education 35, 46, 50,
    101, 158
Department of Evangelism 289
Department of Foreign Missions 35,
    245
Department of Home Missions and
    Church Extension 35, 98, 100, 158
Department of Home Missions and
    Evangelism 35, 98, 225
Department of Ministerial
    Benevolence 122, 290
Department of Ministerial Relief 35,
    100, 136
Department of Publication 35
De Pasquale, Donald 279
Depression 73, 79
Diaz, John J. 25, 97
Diffee, Agnes 214
Divorce 63-64, 75
Doctrine 58-61
Dodd, Elbert 123, 273
Donnelly, John T. 140
Drake, V. P. 202
DuBois, Lauriston J. 158, 209, 219,
    230, 231-32, 256, 287
Earle, A. B. 18
Earle, Ralph 208
Easter Offering, 1949 235
Easter Recovery Offering 93
Eastern Illinois Holiness
    Association 44
Eastern Nazarene College 25, 43,
    102-3, 149, 212, 213, 238
Eckel, Baldwin 187

Eckel, Rev. and Mrs. William A. 94, 116, 142, 188, 189
Education, Philosophy of 240
Educational conferences 239
Egen, Carlos Louis 251-53
Ellyson, Edgar P. 19, 28, 37, 48, 119-20
Emerson, Eugene 45
Encarnacion, Marciano 185
Esselstyn, W. C. 262
Ethel Lucas Memorial Hospital 261
Ethical Standards 266-72
Evangelism 67
Evangelists 67, 98
"Exploring" Series 275
"Externals" 267
Fascism 75
Federal Council of Churches 71-72
Felmlee, John W. 49
Ferguson, Rev. and Mrs. Frank 39, 92, 94
Ferguson, T. P. and Manie Payne 26
Ferree, Lawrence and Laura 97
50th Anniversary Year 288, 296
Filer, Clifford 261
Finance Committee 114
Finch, Oscar J. 110, 123, 212, 281
Finley, Harvey E. 209
First Steps in Visitation Evangelism 230
Fisher, Rev. and Mrs. C. William 179, 231
Fitkin, Susan N. 36, 50, 109-10, 133, 147, 158, 195, 202, 218-19
Fitkin Memorial Nazarene Bible School 279
Fitz, Dr. and Mrs. R. G. 145, 177, 190
Flame, The 264-65
Fleming, E. J. 48, 86, 98-99, 107, 112, 117, 122, 135
Ford, Jack 106, 261, 263-64
Foreign Missions (see Department of) 31, 35, 37, 48, 89, 119
Fox, Evelyn 97
Frame, George 203, 261-62, 264-65
Franklin, George J. 106
Free Literature 100, 138
Free Methodists 22
Fritzlan, A. D. 92
Fundamentalism 70
Galloway, Harvey 226, 281, 296
Gamble, Albert 251
Gardner, Leona 193
Gardner, R. Wayne 43, 77, 103, 140
Garratt, C. A. 184

Gates, Charles and Roma 293
Gazaland 90-91
General Assembly 12, 29, 32-34, 46, 56, 86, 109-10, 219
General Board 11, 32, 34, 49, 51, 288
General Board of Church Extension 34-35
General Board of Education 34-35
General Board of Foreign Missions 35
General Board of Ministerial Relief 34-35
General Board of Mutual Benefit 34-35
General Board of Publication 34-35
General Board of Rescue Work 34
General Board of Social Welfare 35
General Budget 36
General Church Loan Fund 225
General Church Schools Convention 257
General Church Secretary 113
General Colportage Board 34-35
General Headquarters 53-54, 274-75
General Holiness Assembly 22
General Missionary Board 34, 48
General Orphanage Board 34
General Rules 32, 61-62, 257
General Stewardship Committee 113
General Superintendents (see Board of) 34, 162, 168-70, 222
Geographical districts 32
Geographical regions 308
Gibson, C. A. 49, 51-52
Gilliland, Ponder W. 231, 256, 287, 298
Gilmore, Reuben E. 45, 104
Gish, Delbert R. 209
Golden Anniversary 296-97, 299, 301
Goodwin, John W. 19, 47, 56, 61, 112, 114, 133, 159, 164, 195, 220
Gould, J. Glenn 119, 135, 139, 172
Gospel Workers Church of Canada 290-91
Gould, John 51
Gould, Mrs. Olive M. 50
Graham, Carlotta 40
Great Depression 79-82
Grider, J. Kenneth 203, 209
Griffith, Glenn 123, 273
Griffith, Roland E. 284
Grimm, Alden D. 140
Grose, Glenn 144
Guatemala 29, 38, 89
Gulf General District 199-200

Gunstream, R. C. 123
Haiti 251-53
Hale, E. E. 135, 199
Hall, Bruce 163
Hall, John and Patricia 194
Hamlin, Dr. Howard 188, 282
Hance, Ray 226
Hardy, C. E. 44, 49
Hardy, Ed. K. 147
Harper, Albert F. 172, 209, 230, 257, 287, 295
Harris, Robert Lee 27
Hawaii 177-80
Hayne, Dr. Hester 94
He That Winneth Souls 230
Headquarters 53, 274
    (Stone Mansion) 174
    (Relocation) 174, 241
Headquarters Building 243
Heap, Samuel and Gwladys 265
Heinmiller, Harlan 206
Helling, Hubert and Virginia 189
Henson, J. C. 51
Hephzibah Faith Missionary
    Association 239
Herald of Holiness 41, 47, 48, 49, 74, 99-100, 166
El Heraldo de Santidad 196-97
Herrell, N. B. 51, 68, 147
Hess, Weaver W. 50, 183
Higuchi, Rev. and Mrs. Shigeru 292
Hill, J. I. 116
Hillery, Fred A. 24
Hills, Aaron M. 19, 27, 42, 44, 61
Hodges, R. R. 150
Hoke, Mattie 44
Holiness Association of Texas 27
Holiness Christian Association 29
Holiness Church of Christ 27-28, 39, 47
Holiness Church of Korea 249
Hollingsworth, Meredith T.
    (Ted) 180-81
Holstead, John and Natalie 292
Honolulu Christian College 180
Hoople, William 19, 24
Howard, Everette and Garnet 97
Howard, Dr. Quentin E. and
    Margie 282
Hudgins, Lewis and Muriel 176
Hudson, Oscar 51
Hudson, Winthrop 17, 21
Humble, Mrs. Bertha 110
Hunter, Earl and Mabel 193

Hurlet Nazarene College 203-4, 265
Hynd, Dr. and Mrs. David 39, 93
Idaho-Oregon Holiness College 45
Illinois Holiness University 10, 44
Independent Holiness Church 27, 39, 47
India 25, 27-29, 38, 89, 95, 115
Inner City 302
Institutionalism 311-12
Intercollegiate athletics 128-30, 294
Intercontinental zones 307
International Center 274
International Holiness Mission 260-62
International Youth Institute 298
Internationalizing 307
Irick, Emma 300
"Irregulars" 91-92, 96
Isayama, Nobumi 142, 187, 189
Israel 278
Italy 191-92
Jacobs, Clarence 198
James, Maynard 106, 261, 263-64
Japan 95-96, 117, 142-43, 187-90
Jenkins, Rev. and Mrs. C. S. 92
Jernigan, C. B. 27, 61, 200
Jerrett, Howard W. 147
Jerusalem 40, 278
Johnson, Jerald D. 291
Jones, C. Warren 49, 51, 81, 113, 118, 135, 139, 224, 233, 250-51
Jones, Mrs. C. Warren 110
Jones, David B. 260
Jones, Dr. T. Harold 261
Jordan 247-49
Jordan, Wayne A. 285
Kansas Holiness College 44
Karns, Bertie 94, 142
Kauffman, Elmer H. 230
Kauffman, Alvin and Naomi 94
Kelley, Selden Dee 226, 238
Kida, Aishin 190
Kiehn, Peter and Anna 39, 292
Kilvert, Mr. and Mrs. Hubert 181
Kinne, C. J. 37, 41
Kitagawa, Hiroshi 142, 190
Kletzing College 212
Knight, John L. 123
Knippers, Cecil C. 123, 179
Knox, Sidney and Wanda 279
Knox, Wayne and Elwanda 194
Korea 249-51
Kramer, George 87
Krikorian, Dr. Pusant 279
Krikorian, Samuel 279

Kring, J. A. 61
"La Hora Nazarena" 283
Lamplighters' League, The 231
Lanpher, C. P. 300
Lawlor, Edward 226
Laymen's Holiness Association 30, 118
Lebanon 278-79
Lee, Chaplain Byron 139, 250
Legalism 266, 269
Lewis, V. H. 242, 288, 297, 299, 302
Life-style 61-66
Lillenas, Haldor 214, 244
Little, J. T. 49, 102
London, A. S., and family 69
Lovelace, Ora 92
Ludwig, S. T. 44, 110, 133, 138, 148,
158, 209, 212, 214, 216,
255, 259, 288, 295, 301
Lunn, M. 9, 42, 48, 87, 101,
112, 135, 139, 171, 206, 207,
214, 242, 244, 300-301, 304
Lunn, M. A. (Bud) 13, 244
MacDonald, Estella 94, 97
McClintock, J. C. 22
McClurkan, J. O. 19, 29, 43
McConnell, Charles A. 49
McGraw, James 209
McHenry, Rev. and Mrs. Guy 92
McKay, Bartlett and Grace 189
McKay, John and May 94-95
McKay, John T. (Buddy) 95
McNichol, C. J. 291
McReynolds, May 39
Mackey, A. B. 103, 123-24
Maclagan, J. B. 261, 262, 264-65
Madder, Harold R. 184
Mangum, Dr. J. Robert 226, 281
Mangum, Dr. and Mrs. T. E. 276, 281
Mann, Edward S. 238
Manual 30, 55, 58-59, 61, 63-64
Martin, E. E. 238
Martin, Paul 231
Martin, Ted 14
Mathews, E. S. 45, 51
Mathis, I. C. 123
Matthews, L. B. 51
Mattson, Edward J. 139
Medical Missions (see Commission on)
Mellies, Amanda 98
Meredith, Archel R. 139
Methodist Church, The 10, 19
Mexico 27-28, 39
Mid-America Nazarene College 309

Mid-Century Crusade for Souls 218,
228-32
Milby, L. G. 69
Military Chaplains 139-40
Miller, Basil 61
Miller, H. V. 106, 112, 135, 154, 181,
192, 215, 220, 222, 226, 252
Miller, Raymond and Ruth 292
Mills, Albert 291
Ministerial Benevolence (see
Department of)
Ministerial Pension plan 135
Ministerial Relief 35, 98
Minyard, Alfred 139
Mischke, Carl and Velma 97
Mitchum, R. B. 49
Montgomery, J. W. 51
Moore, Eleanor L. 209
Moore, Josiah E. (Jr.) 185
Moore, Mark R. 139
Moore, Rev. and Mrs. Norman 178
Moore, Ray H. 214
Morgan, Albert and Bernice 145
Morgan, Arthur C. 69, 226, 242
Morgan, Earl and Thelma 192
Morrison, Henry Clay 111
Morrison, J. G. 30, 40, 48, 61, 81,
88-89, 90-93, 100,
112, 116-17, 128-29
Morse, Deacon George 18
Moses, Arthur 141
Mosteller, Earl and Gladys 293
Mott, John R. 79
Moulton, M. Kimber 110, 133, 158,
202, 206, 219
Mount Vernon Nazarene College 309
National Association of
Evangelicals 71
National Holiness Association 19, 71
Nazarene Bible College 309
Nazarene Bible Institute 199
Nazarene Foreign Missionary
Society 256, 279
Nazarene Information Service 300
Nazarene Korean Theological
Institute 251
"Nazarene Manifesto" 205
Nazarene Messenger 26
Nazarene Ministers' Benevolent
Fund 135
Nazarene Missionary Sanitarium
and Institute 276
Nazarene (Christian) Mutual Benev-
olent Association 48, 120, 122

Nazarene Publishing House   41, 48,
            51, 100, 147-48,
    173-75, 244-45, 274-75, 304
Nazarene Radio League   214
Nazarene Theological Seminary   158,
            204-11
Nazarene Young People's Society   35,
            37, 50, 110, 133
Nease, Orval J. (Sr.)   50, 100, 119, 134,
            152-55, 222, 228, 250
Neely, B. F.   105
Nees, L. Guy   212, 238
Nelson, Elmer and Dorothy   285
New Guinea (see Papua New Guinea)
New Testament Church of Christ   27
New Zealand   283-84
Nicaragua   144-45
Nippon Kirisuto Kyodan—Christian
    Church of Japan   143
Nippon Nazarene Seminary   189
North American Indian
    District   200-201
Northern Bible College   45, 103, 125
Northwest Nazarene College   45, 102,
            104, 118, 128, 149,
            212, 238, 275, 294
Oathbound secret orders   64
Ogburn, D. G.   200
Oke, Norman R.   298
Okinawa   292
Oklahoma Holiness College   10, 42
Olivet Nazarene College   44-45,
        125-27, 149, 212, 238, 294
Orjala, Paul and Mary   252
Osborn, Rev. and Mrs. L. C.   141, 292
Other Sheep   41
Owens, Donald and Adeline   251
Pacific Bible College   26, 44
Palmquist, H. S.   284
Papua New Guinea   279-80
Park Kee Suh   251
Parker, J. Fred   298
Parrott, A. L.   125, 212
Pasadena College   44, 102, 125,
            149, 238, 294
Pastor and Visitation Evangelism   230
Pattee, Rev. and Mrs. J. W.   141,
            186, 190
Pelley, Myrtle   92, 94
Pearson, G. H.   201
Peña, Hilario   214
Peniel College   27-28, 42
Peniel Mission (Los Angeles)   25
Penrod, Everett D.   140

Pentecostal Alliance   29
Pentecostal Church of Scotland   30
Pentecostal Church of the
    Nazarene   27-28
Pentecostal Collegiate
    Institute   10, 25, 43
Pentecostal Literary and Bible
    Training School   43
Pentecostal Mission   29, 38, 193
People's Evangelical Church   24
Per capita giving   86, 99
Perkins, Floyd and Libby   247
Peru   40, 89
Peters, John L.   138-39
The Philippines   185-87
Pilot Point, Tex.   28, 299
Pinch, Douglas and Maysie   182, 184
Pitts, Joseph S.   140, 186
Pitts, Paul   123
Point Loma College (see Pasadena
    College)   26
Powers, Hardy C.   118, 123, 154-55,
            161-62, 189, 222, 252,
        257-59, 279-80, 300, 305
Preacher's Magazine   66
Prescott, Lyle and Grace   193
Prohibition   63, 76-77
Puerto Rico   144
Purkiser, W. T.   209, 239, 281, 294
Purvis, Robert   51
Quadrennial Address (1932)   56
Quadrennial Address (1936)   111
Quadrennial Address (1940)   134
Quadrennial Address (1948)   220
Quadrennial Address (1952)   257
Quadrennial Project—NYPS   180
Radio Commission   158
Rae, Hugh   204, 266, 275
Raleigh Fitkin Memorial Hospital
    (Africa)   39
Ratcliff, Herbert and Alyce   194
Ravenhill, Leonard   261
Red Men's Hall   26
Reed, Donald and Elva   279
Reed, Harold W.   123-24, 226, 238
Reed, L. A.   50, 70, 135,
            207-8, 215, 260
Rees, Seth C.   19
Rehfeldt, Remiss   224, 293
Rescue Commission   34
"Reserve Army"   87-88, 91, 114
Rest Cottage   299
Retired Missionaries   92, 98
Revivalism   67

Reynolds, Hiram F.   25, 27-28, 37,
                          48, 105, 117, 164
Reynolds Memorial Hospital
     (India)   95, 115, 282
Reza, Honorato   195-96, 282, 293
Rhoden, Maurice and Jeannette   189
Rich, Harry and Marion   253
Riley, John E.   275
Roberts, Geren   251, 299
Roberts, Rev. and Mrs. J. P.   299
Roberts, John F.   299
Robertson, E. P.   49
Robinson, Uncle Bud 111, 147, 150-51
Rogers, Rev. Lelan   194
Rogers, Warren A.   198, 200
Ruskin Cave College   43
Russell, William and Grace   249
Ruth, C. W.   29, 98, 150
Sabbath observance   65
Samaritan Hospital School of
     Nursing   276-77
Sanner, A. E.   51, 53, 105,
                          201, 202, 204
Sarian, Missak   278
Schmelzenbach, Harmon   39
Schmelzenbach, Mrs. Lula   92
Scott, Mary   13, 141, 190,
                          226, 256, 287
Seals, B. V.   51
Secret orders   62
Seminary Board of Trustees   207
Seminary Commission   206
Seminary Sunday   209
El Sendero de la Verdad   196
Servicemen's Commission 138-39, 298
Sharpe, George   19, 30, 49
Shaw, Lt. Col. and
     Mrs. Robert H.   188, 251
Shelhamer, E. E.   61, 180
Shepherd, Lt. Doyle   188-89, 292
Shirley Press (Africa)   195
Shoemaker, Melvin   251
Short, J. W.   49, 51, 200
"Showers of Blessing"   214-16
Silver Anniversary Observance 82-86
Simmons, Stanley   183
Simpson, E. D.   226
Sims, Glennie   39
Skiles, Paul and Maxine   298
Smee, Roy F.   51, 225, 302
Smith, Donnell J.   37, 50
Smith, Milton   50, 110
Smith, Timothy L.   14, 31, 72
Social Awareness   71, 72

Sol, David   197
Soul Winning Through Visitation
     Evangelism   230
South Africa European   246-47
Southeastern Nazarene College   43
Spangenberg, Leonard M.   226, 236
Spanish Department   195-97
Spanish Nazarene Bible and Mis-
     sionary Training Institute 213-14
Special Rules   63-65, 257
Speicher, Dr. Orpha   115
Spencer, Gilbert J.   139
Spratt, Erlee   183
Spruce, Fletcher   231
Stanfield, Harold and Evelyn   144
Starr, R. V.   51, 204
Stegemoeller, Mr. and Mrs. Ervin 293
Steininger, Leo   178
Stewart, Margaret   92, 97, 158
Stillion, Earl   69
Stockton, John   149, 172, 189, 214,
                     233, 242, 259, 288, 301
"Storehouse tithing"   63
Stowe, Eugene   287
Strang, C. B.   147
Strickland, Charles   14, 246, 247
Stroman, Henry   251
Sunday Schools   37
Superintendents' Conference 51, 160
Swarth, Dowie   123, 200
Sweeten, Howard W.   61, 69
Swim, Roy E.   209
Syria   40
Taiwan   292-93
Taylor, Rev. and Mrs. Ira B.   94, 97
Taylor, Jeremy   20
Taylor, Mendell L.   208, 219, 226
Taylor, Richard S.   184
Taylor, Willard H.   232, 294
Taylorson, J. George   110, 147
Television   257, 269-70, 290
Temperance   63
Ten Percent program   235-36
Texas Holiness University   10, 27,
                               42, 47
Theater   62
Theology Workshop   295
Thomas, David   260
Thomson, Charles E.   45, 49, 148
Time Is Now, The   231
Tink, Mrs. W. W.   158
Tinsley, J. N.   105
Tithing   63
Tobacco   62, 64

Tongues speaking 263-64
Tracy, Leighton S. and Gertrude 94,
98, 150
Trevecca Nazarene College 29, 43,
102-3, 213, 238
Trinidad 40
True, S. W. 49
Trumbauer, W. G. 29
Twenty-fifth Anniversary (WFMS) 133
Unified budget 36
Updike, Paul 147, 226
Uruguay 253
Vanciel, Brian and Evelyn 253-54
Van Duyn, Grover 238
Vanderpool, D. I. 53, 123, 227,
242, 252, 259
Vanderpool, Wilford N. 140
Varro, Michael and Elizabeth 190
Wachtel, Alexander and
Hallie 248, 278
Walker, E. F. 119
Ward, H. Blair 291
Week of Witnessing 297, 299
Wells, L. T. 51
Welch, Reuben and Mary Jo 178
Wesche, Dr. and Mrs. H. C. 94, 141
Wesleyan Church 22-23
Wesleyan Holiness Association of
Churches, The 273
Wessels, Dean 288
West Germany 291-92
Whitcanack, Stanley N. 214
White, John N. 185
White, Stephen S. 208, 224, 259, 288

Widmeyer, C. B. 50
Widney, J. P. 26
Wiese, Harry A. 106, 116, 140, 190
Wiley, H. Orton 9, 37, 44-45, 48,
57-58, 67, 75, 82, 99, 101, 105,
112, 145, 201, 204, 209, 239, 300
Wiley, Pearl 142
Williams, J. E. 214
Williams, Roy T. 47, 51, 61, 68, 84-85,
87, 105, 111, 128, 133-35, 152-57,
160, 162-65, 167, 205-6, 220, 222
Williams, R. T. (Jr.) 163
Williamson, G. B. 50, 53, 103, 110,
123, 147, 154, 165-66, 212,
222, 259, 270, 272, 287, 293, 300
Willingham, T. W. 45, 125,
135, 214, 242
Wilson, E. W. 284
Wilson, W. C. 47
Wiman, Rev. and
Mrs. Charles H. 94, 97
Winans, Roger and Mary Hunt 40
Witthoff, Dr. Evelyn 141, 282
Women's Foreign Missionary
Society 31, 36, 50, 132, 256
Woodruff, Bond 186
Word, Emma B. 49, 50, 110, 226
World War II 79, 109, 131-32
Wyman, Edward 214
Young Women's Organizations
(WFMS) 133
Young, Samuel 12, 105, 113, 204,
212, 222-23, 236, 238, 259
Zachary, E. E. 183